REMAKING THE AMERICAN DREAM

Urban and Industrial Environments

Series editor: Robert Gottlieb, Henry R. Luce Professor of Urban and Environmental Policy, Occidental College

For a complete list of books published in this series, please see the back of the book.

REMAKING THE AMERICAN DREAM

THE INFORMAL AND FORMAL TRANSFORMATION OF SINGLE-FAMILY HOUSING CITIES

VINIT MUKHIJA

The MIT Press
Cambridge, Massachusetts
London, England

© 2022 Massachusetts Institute of Technology

This work is subject to a Creative Commons CC-BY-NC-ND license.
Subject to such license, all rights are reserved.

The MIT Press would like to thank the anonymous peer reviewers who provided comments on drafts of this book. The generous work of academic experts is essential for establishing the authority and quality of our publications. We acknowledge with gratitude the contributions of these otherwise uncredited readers.

This book was set in Stone Serif and Stone Sans by Westchester Publishing Services. Printed and bound in the United States of America.

Library of Congress Cataloging-in-Publication Data

Names: Mukhija, Vinit, 1967– author.
Title: Remaking the American dream : the informal and formal transformation of single-family housing cities / Vinit Mukhija.
Description: Cambridge, Massachusetts : The MIT Press, [2022] | Series: Urban and industrial environments | Includes bibliographical references and index.
Identifiers: LCCN 2022000715 (print) | LCCN 2022000716 (ebook) | ISBN 9780262544764 (paperback) | ISBN 9780262372404 (epub) | ISBN 9780262372411 (pdf)
Subjects: LCSH: Urbanization—United States. | Housing, Single family—United States. | American Dream.
Classification: LCC HT123 .M74 2022 (print) | LCC HT123 (ebook) | DDC 307.760973—dc23/eng/20220307
LC record available at https://lccn.loc.gov/2022000715
LC ebook record available at https://lccn.loc.gov/2022000716

10 9 8 7 6 5 4 3 2 1

To Patricia

CONTENTS

ACKNOWLEDGMENTS   ix

I   SINGLE-FAMILY HOUSING CITIES

1   THE CHANGING NORMS AND REGULATIONS OF SINGLE-FAMILY HOUSING   3

2   THE IDEOLOGY OF SINGLE-FAMILY LIVING   37

II   INFORMAL SECOND UNITS IN LOS ANGELES

3   CITY OF DREAMS: SINGLE-FAMILY HOUSING AND SECOND UNITS IN LOS ANGELES   61

4   THE EVERYDAY PREVALENCE OF INFORMAL SECOND UNITS   93

III   FORMAL SECOND UNITS AND INSTITUTIONAL CHANGES IN SINGLE-FAMILY HOUSING

5   ENFORCEMENT AND FORMALIZATION OF UNPERMITTED SECOND UNITS IN LOS ANGELES   141

6   THE FORMALIZATION OF SECOND UNITS: THE ROLE OF LOCAL GOVERNMENTS   179

IV THE NEW AMERICAN DREAM

7 REMAKING THE SUBURBAN CITY 235

NOTES 257
REFERENCES 277
INDEX 333

ACKNOWLEDGMENTS

I have accumulated several debts in journeying through this project. Many strangers, acquaintances, students, colleagues, friends, and family members have generously shared their time to talk about their homes and work. I am grateful to all of them.

At the University of California, Los Angeles (UCLA), I am grateful to several colleagues for joint research projects contributing to this book. My collaboration with Anastasia Loukaitou-Sideris bookends the research. We partnered to examine *the prevalence of informal economic activities in US cities,* and along with Kian Goh, we explored the challenges of justice in urban design. Both these projects led to edited books with MIT Press: *The Informal American City* and *Just Urban Design*. My chapters in the edited books draw from my research on this project, and the collective ideas developed in the edited volumes contributed to the intellectual arguments in this book. I thank Anastasia and Kian for their deliberations, support, and encouragement.

I also want to thank Dana Cuff. Dana, scholars and researchers at cityLAB, and I examined the regulatory hurdles to building second units before the California state government intervened in accessory dwelling unit (ADU) regulations statewide in the mid to late 2010s. With Anne Brown and Donald Shoup, I researched how homeowners can convert their garages to affordable second units. In addition, I thank Jonathan Zasloff for discussing strategies to estimate unpermitted housing in the Los Angeles region; Lois Takahashi for exploring the social interactions of single-family housing and ADU occupants; and Silvia González for a partnership to examine the significance of unpermitted second units in Pacoima, a Latinx neighborhood in the city of Los Angeles, and public policies for improving their living conditions.

I am grateful to the John Randolph Haynes Foundation for funding my research with Dana on regulatory hurdles to second units; the Lincoln Institute of Land Policy and the UCLA Ziman Center for Real Estate for supporting my work on regulatory changes in US cities to make it easier for homeowners to receive permits for adding second units; and the UCLA Academic Senate for grants to study unpermitted second units. I also benefited from an opportunity to evaluate a JP Morgan Chase PRO Neighborhoods grant to Genesis LA and Housing Trust Silicon Valley for expanding access to construction finance for moderate-income homeowners interested in adding second units for low- and moderate-income renters. In addition, I am grateful to UCLA's Department of Urban Planning for supporting the Informal American City and Just Urban Design speaker series with the Harvey Perloff Lecture series funds.

This research would not have been the same without the enthusiastic support of staff and board members at LA Más. I am incredibly grateful to the co–executive directors, Helen Leung and Elizabeth Timme, for their generosity with their ideas, reflections, and time. I also want to thank Pacoima Beautiful's staff and community members for their generosity with their time, willingness to share experiences, and teaching me about their housing challenges and solutions. I am particularly grateful to Veronica Padilla, the executive director, and Dora Frietze-Armenta, the lead project planner. Thanks are also due to State Senator Bob Wieckowski and his outstanding staff, particularly Jeff Barbosa and Francisco Montes, for their collaboration and support.

This scholarship would not have been possible without the excellent research assistance and help I was fortunate to receive from many UCLA urban planning students. My sincere thanks to Clarrissa Cabansagan, Katie Gladstein, Kate Mayerson, Erin Coleman, Emily Gable, Daniela Simunovic, Mark Simpson, Carlos Hernandez, Alyssa Kohen, Cate Carlson, Shine Ling, Samantha Meyer, Taylor Holland, Kaitlyn Quackenbush, Jeffrey Ross, Alejandro Gonzalez, and Trong Kim. I am also grateful to the students in my Informal American City seminars and Pacoima Comprehensive Capstone Projects. And my thanks to Bradley Cleveland, Gustavo De Haro, Meg Healy, Nate Holmes, Susan Hernandez, Erik Johnson, Ben Palmquist, Emmanuel

Soriano, and Casey Stern for sharing their experiences and research about informal or unpermitted second units and legalization of ADUs.

Max Dubler, Jae-Hyeon Park, and Jessica Bremner were instrumental in producing this book. Max's editing significantly improved the text, Jay's graphics added to its legibility, and Jessica's organization of the material, including the permissions, enhanced the flow of the book.

Over the years, I have benefited from exchanging ideas with several friends and colleagues. I am grateful to all of them, particularly Victoria Basolo, Karen Chapple, Margaret Crawford, Nicole Gurran, Annette Kim, Becky Nicolaides, Deirdre Pfeiffer, Brent Ryan, Bish Sanyal, David Sloane, Larry Vale, Peter Ward, and Jake Wegmann. I am also grateful for the opportunities to present parts of the research shared in this book at various venues, including at multiple sessions of the Association of Collegiate Schools of Planning, University of California, Berkeley, University of California, Irvine, and the University of California Center Sacramento. The feedback I received from colleagues was invaluable.

I am indebted to numerous planners and housing advocates in Los Angeles for sharing their experiences, ideas, and information, including Eric Agar, Lauren Ahkiam, Ashley Atkinson, Jonathan Pacheco Bell, Ken Bernstein, Jane Blumenfeld, Marcia Choo, Connie Chung, Tom De Simone, Matthew Glesne, Gabriela Juarez, John Kamp, Kevin Keller, Nick Maricich, Jason Neville, Sally Richman, Elsa Rodriguez, James Rojas, Liseth Romero-Martinez, Todd Tipton, and Mark Vallianatos. Additionally, I am grateful to Mark Primack, David Foster, and Carol Berg in Santa Cruz; Alan Durning, Greg Nickels, Jim Holmes, Mike Podowski, and Bruce Parker in Seattle; Kol Peterson, Eli Spevak, Martin Brown, and C. J. Gabbe in Portland; Nell Kamp and Paul Mogush in Minneapolis; and Neal LaMontagne, Andy Yan, Tom Durning, Ann McAfee, and Patrick Condon in Vancouver.

Finally, I owe an intellectual debt to several of my urban planning colleagues at UCLA. They will see their research, particularly on housing and informal economic activities, reflected in this book. I am grateful to the highly supportive editorial team at MIT Press. Beth Clevenger, Anthony Zannino, and Bob Gottlieb could not have been more encouraging and helpful. Most of all, I am thankful to Patricia Diefenderfer for her love, suggestions, insights, support, and patience throughout this journey. Thank you!

1 Single-Family Housing Cities

1 THE CHANGING NORMS AND REGULATIONS OF SINGLE-FAMILY HOUSING

As a symbol of wholesome American values, the detached single-family home ranks up there with baseball, mothers, apple pie, and Fourth of July fireworks. Thanks to explicit public policy and deft marketing, homeownership of single-family housing is seen as an expression of fundamental American ideals like freedom, individuality, and prosperity and is synonymous with the American Dream. Americans love their single-family houses. They actively use planning policies, land use regulations (particularly single-family zoning, which limits land use to single-family houses), and neighborhood activism to protect their single-family neighborhoods from the perceived threat of multifamily housing. The reverence for single-family living is so strong that single-family dwellings are called single-family *homes* in everyday language. Multifamily houses, on the other hand, are merely multifamily housing or buildings.

Politicians in the US understand the symbolic power of the single-family home. During the 2020 presidential election, Republican president Donald Trump attempted to scare and win over "the suburban housewives of America" by pointing out that his Democratic opponent, former vice president Joe Biden, supported the Affirmatively Furthering Fair Housing (AFFH) rule, an obscure federal regulation instituted by President Barack Obama in 2015 that required local governments to document patterns of housing discrimination and develop plans to address them (Megeriain, Dillon, and Stokols 2020). In doing so, President Trump aimed to tap into and leverage the racial and economic anxieties of single-family housing homeowners and their preference for homogeneity and stability. On Twitter, Trump claimed that Biden's embrace of the AFFH rule would "ABOLISH Suburban Communities as they currently exist" and expose "people living their Suburban Lifestyle Dream" to urban crime and violence bad enough to "destroy your neighborhood and your American Dream" (Finnegan 2020; Megeriain, Dillon, and Stokols 2020). In a telephone town hall with Wisconsin voters, Trump warned that Democrats could "eliminate single-family zoning, bringing who knows [who] into your suburbs, so your communities will be unsafe and your housing values will go down" (Weigel 2020).

As is the case with many other issues, President Trump's tweets about AFFH were an unusually vulgar expression of a view that has some resonance with populist positions in the country, where efforts to reform single-family zoning run into paranoia and political pushback. With the COVID-19 pandemic emerging in 2020, many Americans like Alex Azar, secretary of health and human services, incorrectly associated multifamily living with a greater chance of getting infected (Cancryn and Barrón-López 2020).[1] In the run-up to the 2020 election, conservative commentators like Stanley Kurtz (2020) cautioned that the Democrats were "set to abolish the suburbs" through federal fair housing regulations. President Trump raised the stakes by repealing the AFFH rule in July 2020. In a *Wall Street Journal* op-ed coauthored with Housing and Urban Development (HUD) secretary Ben Carson (Trump and Carson 2020), the president claimed, "We'll protect America's suburbs." They added, "We stopped the last administration's radical social-engineering project that would have transformed an Obama-Biden regulation that would have empowered the Department of Housing and Urban Development to abolish single-family zoning."

President Trump and Secretary Carson expected their message to resonate with the majority of Americans, including owners of single-family housing, who consider themselves suburban, even if they live in cities. According to the 2010 Census, about 83 percent of US households lived in cities and urban areas, but over 60 percent of all households lived in detached single-family housing. Most federal definitions of urban and rural in the US Census do not distinguish suburbs as separate categories. In 2015, a survey by Trulia, an online real estate marketplace company, asked respondents if they described their neighborhoods as suburban, urban, or rural. The majority of the respondents, 53 percent, described their communities as suburban. Correspondingly, only 26 percent described their neighborhoods as urban, and 21 percent identified as rural. According to the survey, almost half of the people classified as urban residents by the Census perceived themselves as suburban residents (Kolko 2015).[2] The nation and the American Dream are suburban (Duany, Plater-Zyberk, and Speck 2000).

Though single-family housing is generally associated with the suburbs, the debate over single-family zoning has significant implications for US cities because single-family neighborhoods are America's dominant urban form. To illustrate, in the city of Los Angeles, almost 40 percent of the housing units are detached single-family houses (US Census Bureau 2013a). In the more expansive Los Angeles County, which consists of eighty-seven additional cities, over half of the housing units are detached single-family dwellings. Single-family zoning accounted for about three-quarters of the city of Los Angeles's residentially zoned land (Badger and Bui 2019; Cuff, Higgins, and Dahl 2010; Los Angeles Department of City Planning 2016a; Morrow 2013). In fast-growing southwestern cities like Phoenix and San Antonio, which primarily developed after World War II, or postwar, over 60 percent of the housing stock was in detached single-family houses (US Census Bureau 2013a).

However, the detached single-family house is an increasingly poor economic, social, and cultural fit. Many scholars argue that single-family living, associated suburban low density, and separated land uses were never a good idea. From John Keats's (1956) scathing social criticism in *The Crack in the Picture Window*, to Peter Blake's (1964) ecological indictment of the wastes of suburbia in *God's Own Junkyard*, to Dolores Hayden's ([1984] 2002) gender-conscious calls for remaking housing choices in *Redesigning the American Dream* through physical and social transformations of single-family housing and its neighborhoods, to Lars Lerup's (1987, 14) architecturally motivated design interventions to address "the tyranny of the single-family house" in *Planned Assaults*, to Robert Beauregard's (2006) condemnation of single-family housing-based suburbanization as parasitic urbanization that hollowed out US cities in *When America Became Suburban*, this popular but controversial housing arrangement, and its corresponding urban form, has been the focus of numerous investigations and calls for reform and change. Scholars argue that the land requirements and regulations for single-family living contribute to and exacerbate the country's affordable housing challenges. They call for ending single-family zoning (Manville, Monkkonen, and Lens 2020; Wegmann 2020). Despite all this criticism, single-family living stubbornly remains the American ideal.

As housing prices continued to rise through the 2010s and housing affordability became a more openly discussed challenge, critics on both the left and the right sides of the political spectrum began to argue in favor of increasing the housing supply by allowing greater density on single-family-zoned lots (Dougherty 2017; A. Durning 2015; Marohn 2020; Primack 2019). Observers on the left argued that single-family zoning is illiberal, has a racist legacy, and exacerbates racial and class segregation (Schneider 2019; Vallianatos 2018). Critics on the right condemned it for constraining freedom and choice in the housing market (Greenhut 2020). Several of the Democratic candidates for the 2020 presidential primary, particularly Senator Cory Booker, former HUD secretary Julian Castro, and Senator Elizabeth Warren, called for the federal government to use its influence to encourage a greater diversity of housing stock and affordable housing (Schuetz 2019).[3] Unlike the Republicans, they called for strengthening the AFFH rule within the 1968 Fair Housing Act. They agreed with housing scholars who argue that the rule was well meaning but substantively weak. The AFFH rule advocated for fair housing but did not restrict federal money for housing and urban development projects to local governments that removed their barriers to fair housing (Zasloff 2020).

While the political debates continue, the character of existing single-family housing is slowly changing. Although scholars and policy makers rarely discuss these adaptations, the single-family house is quietly transforming through unapproved or informal modifications, conversions, and workarounds by homeowners. Owners across the country are adding unpermitted units by building backyard cottages, converting their garages, basements, and recreation rooms, and carving out independent dwellings from their homes to increase and diversify the housing supply.

Although some observers refer to these unpermitted units as illegal units, I favor calling them informal housing.[4] I find the term "informal housing" less pejorative, more precise, and constructive as it removes the misplaced focus on criminality and legality to emphasize how necessary housing units can be improved, formalized, and legitimized.

Single-family housing is also changing through gradual institutional changes in rigid land use regulations. Many jurisdictions are changing their zoning requirements to allow homeowners to formally add Accessory Dwelling Units (ADUs) on their single-family-zoned lots. ADUs are also colloquially known as granny flats, in-law apartments, backyard cottages, and secondary units. I prefer to call them second units to emphasize their potential for being independent and nonaccessory. In some cities and states, policy makers follow initial policy changes to allow ADUs with more ambitious land use reforms to allow duplexes, triplexes, and fourplexes. This book focuses on these incremental but transformative changes and their implications for American urbanism. While there is very little academic research and literature on these changes, they will likely remake US cities' landscape, nature, and culture. Therefore, this book's premise is that the nascent transformation of single-family housing can significantly redefine American urbanism and the American Dream.

I document and explain how homeowners challenge single-family living norms by informally adapting their homes to their needs and, correspondingly, how formal rules of single-family zoning are evolving in several US cities and states. I examine why the idea of single-family living is changing and the parallel reordering of contemporary cities in the US. I explore how planners and policy makers respond to the informal changes to single-family housing and discuss how they should address these unexpected makeovers. To analyze and understand the ongoing transformation of single-family housing, I center and highlight these everyday informal changes as a deliberate counterpart to their invisibility in conventional accounts of US cities.

THE IDEA OF SINGLE-FAMILY HOUSING AND THE SIGNIFICANCE OF ITS REDEFINITION

What is the American Dream, the ethos of the US? Is it "Life, Liberty, and the pursuit of Happiness," the well-known phrase from the Declaration of Independence attributed to Thomas Jefferson (1776)? Is it, in writer and historian James Truslow Adams's (1931, 404) words, "that dream of a land in which life should be better and richer and fuller for everyone, with opportunity for each according to ability or achievement?" Is it the more socially just ideal of freedom and equality embodied in Martin Luther King's evocative "Letter from Birmingham Jail" (1963) and "I Have a Dream" (1965) speech in Washington, DC? Or is it the material goal of prosperity through homeownership, ideally of a detached single-family house?

While the American Dream is a broad cultural concept that defies narrow definition, buying a detached single-family house is widely understood as a key step toward achieving it on an individual level, and helping people purchase this kind of home is a central goal of US housing policy.[5] The implications and consequences of this narrow definition of the American Dream extend far beyond the private single-family house's threshold.

Throughout the twentieth century, private interests and public efforts have helped manufacture the country's single-family living ethos while investing a higher moral purpose and cultural value in the detached single-family house. In these narratives, ownership of a single-family home symbolizes the Anglo-Protestant ideals of self-reliance, individualism, thrift, and hard work. This single-family living ideology was carefully crafted and promoted with adept messaging and marketing. As Clifford Edward Clark Jr. noted in *The American Family Home: 1800–1960*, "In magazine after magazine, plan book after plan book, the same theme was repeated over and over again. A properly designed single-family house would protect and strengthen the family, shoring up the foundations of society and instituting the proper virtues needed to preserve the republic" (1986, 238).

Single-family living gained more momentum as a populist dream in the postwar period when American affluence and cold war rhetoric were at their peak. For its champions, single-family homeowners epitomized the necessary Cold War–era qualities of nuclear families, property ownership, and anticommunism while showcasing American prosperity.

Although the desire to own your home is not a uniquely US attribute, ownership of a detached single-family house has strong claims to American exceptionalism (Hirt 2014). Affluent people in other countries aspire to own single-family houses too. But no other nation has had the resources or national policies to support single-family living as an ideal and goal. The US, however, has had remarkable success in this endeavor. As Kenneth Jackson (1985, 72) noted in *Crabgrass Frontier*, ". . . the significant fact is that in the United States the average family was more able to realize its dream of a private home." Jackson's often-cited history of American suburbanization explains how the federal government's policies providing subsidies, tax benefits, insurance options, and affordable transportation access actively encouraged widespread single-family living.

These public policies changed the pattern of urban living in the US. Table 1.1 lists the most populous cities in the country, shows how they have changed, and illustrates the widespread popularity and significance of detached single-family housing. Traditionally, cities are defined by urban density, mixed land uses, and public spaces. However, contemporary US cities—particularly

Table 1.1

The ten most populous cities in the US, their populations, densities, and share of detached single-family housing

Rank	City	Population in 1950	Population in 2010	Population change between 1950 and 2010 (%)	Density in 2010 (people/ sq. mi.)	Detached single-family units as percentage of housing stock (2013)
1.	New York*	7,891,957	8,175,133	3.56	26,821	9.2
2.	Los Angeles*	1,970,358	3,792,621	92.49	8,092	39.0
3.	Chicago*	3,620,962	2,695,598	−25.56	11,842	26.6
4.	Houston	596,163	2,099,451	252.16	3,502	46.7
5.	Philadelphia*	2,071,605	1,526,006	−26.34	11,380	8.4
6.	Phoenix	106,818	1,445,632	1,253.36	2,798	63.0
7.	San Antonio	408,442	1,327,407	225.10	2,880	64.2
8.	San Diego	333,865	1,307,402	291.61	4,020	46.9
9.	Dallas	434,469	1,197,816	175.71	3,517	46.4
10.	San Jose	95,280	945,942	892.80	5,359	54.0

Sources: Population and density data are from the decennial US Census 1950, 2010 (US Census 1950, 2010); and housing stock data are from the 2013 American Community Survey 1-Year Estimates (US Census Bureau 2013a).
*These cities were among the ten most populous cities in the US in 1950.
Note: Philadelphia is known for its row houses. The American Community Survey classifies them as attached single-family housing. According to data from the US Census Bureau (2013a), attached single-family houses contributed 58.6 percent of the city's housing stock.

those that have grown predominantly in the automobile-oriented, postwar era—are characterized by single-family housing, low-density living patterns, and separated land uses. In Los Angeles, Houston, Phoenix, San Antonio, San Diego, Dallas, and San Jose, detached single-family houses constitute 39–64 percent of the housing stock and dominate land use. In San Jose, for example, detached single-family dwellings account for 54 percent of the housing stock, and 94 percent of the city's residentially zoned land is restricted to detached single-family houses (Badger and Bui 2019).

Seemingly successful US public policies to make single-family housing accessible to its citizens notably excluded people of color, for whom achieving the dream of homeownership was unrealistic and unaffordable (G. Wright [1981] 1983). Black Americans were systematically denied opportunities to purchase single-family houses by discriminatory government policies and institutional practices of restrictive covenants, predatory lending, redlining, and blockbusting (Rothstein 2017). Where restrictive covenants and lending discrimination were ineffective at maintaining residential segregation, white residents turned to violence against minorities (Jeannine Bell 2013; Freund 2007; Loewen 2006). Racial and ethnic minorities found their chances for safe housing, education, and jobs severely restricted (Briggs 2005; Massey and Denton 1998). Blacks in particular found the "white spaces" of single-family living off-limits and unwelcoming (E. Anderson 2015).

In addition to racial justice criticisms, several observers found the homogeneity and sterility of postwar suburban neighborhoods monotonous and called for their transformation (Huxtable 1964; Mumford 1961). Contemporary New Urbanist urban designers echoed this criticism in their calls for changing conventional suburbia (Duany, Plater-Zyberk, and Speck 2000). Although extensive public subsidies made the private price of suburbanization cheap, the dream came at a high environmental cost of land and resources needed to sustain its low-density urban form. Scholars criticized it for "the costs of sprawl" (National Research Council 2002; Real Estate Research Corporation 1974). Furthermore, while envisioned as ideal for the stereotypical American nuclear family, the single-family house became a poor fit for an infinitely more complex country with a diverse population and a wide range of household sizes and family forms. Dolores Hayden ([1984] 2002) perceptively argued that the single-family house and its neighborhoods failed to fulfill the ambitions and hopes of women and minorities. As she insightfully observed, "We have not merely a housing shortage, but a broader set of unmet needs caused by the efforts of the entire society to fit itself into a housing pattern that reflects the dreams of the mid-nineteenth century better than the realities of the twenty-first century" (30).

HOUSING, AFFORDABLE HOUSING, AND INFORMAL HOUSING

While gender-equity concerns did not lead to a broader questioning of single-family living, the housing shortage, record-setting home prices, and increase in homelessness refocused attention on its shortcomings and costs. Single-family housing consumes more residential land per unit, making it more expensive than similarly located multifamily housing. Its land use and zoning requirements limit housing production, and scholars describe them as a zoning tax on supply that bids home prices up (Gyourko and Krimmel

2021). Moreover, single-family housing residents routinely oppose housing developments adjacent to their homes and neighborhoods for causing congestion, limiting parking, and blocking views (Dougherty 2020; Einstein, Glick, and Palmer 2019; Shaw 2018). Their opposition further restricts the housing supply and increases prices. Ironically, neighborhood opponents of housing development projects—derisively referred to as the "not in my back yard" (NIMBY) proponents—often use environmental laws to stop housing projects, pushing them to outlying areas. For example, in California, most California Environmental Quality Act lawsuits in 2018 were against housing development (J. Hernandez 2019).

The supply limitations contributed to higher housing costs and new-home price highs in California (Buhayar and Cannon 2019; Kamin 2021) and the US (N. Friedman 2021). The housing cost burden, or the share of income spent on housing, also significantly increased. In 1960, less than a quarter of US renter households paid more than 30 percent of their income on rent and were considered cost-burdened (Ellen, Lubell, and Willis 2021). Almost sixty years later, in 2019, close to half of US renters were cost-burdened, and around a quarter of them were severely cost-burdened because they paid more than 50 percent of their income for housing (Joint Center for Housing Studies of Harvard University 2021). Although there were regional differences, housing costs increased nationwide. California renters were among the most adversely impacted. Around a third of them spent more than half their income on housing (*Los Angeles Times* 2019).

Academic research strongly suggests that lack of supply leads to housing price increases, and that new housing moderates price increase and helps make housing more affordable (Been, Ellen, and O'Regan 2018). While there is consensus on the need to increase housing production, there are sharp differences about how to do so.

Some market-based housing supply advocates argue for urban expansion, more sprawl, and new single-family housing on the periphery (Kotkin 2021; Berger and Kotkin 2017). Between 2000 and 2019, urban growth through sprawl continued to be the defining feature of the fastest-growing US metropolitan regions, including Houston, Phoenix, Las Vegas, and Atlanta (Levitt and Eng 2021). But the climate crisis and the costs of sprawl (National Research Council 2002; Peterson, Peterson, and Liu 2013) make it increasingly necessary to focus growth inward and expand housing opportunities within cities. Moreover, planning scholars note that young adults aged twenty-five to thirty-four are more interested in urban amenities and living in cities (Lee, Lee, and Shubho 2019).

To advocate for land use regulation reforms and more centrally located housing opportunities, millennial-led "yes in my back yard" (YIMBY) groups emerged across US cities as a countervailing power to NIMBY groups more associated with home-owning boomers (Holleran 2021). YIMBY advocates highlighted the racial legacy of single-family zoning (Kahlenberg 2021; Vallianatos 2018) and the growth in visible homelessness during the 2010s in the US (Colburn and Aldern 2022; Resnikoff 2021) to argue for ending single-family zoning and for more housing construction through infill development.

Some scholars and housing advocates criticize the YIMBY supporters for their market-based approach to addressing the affordable housing challenges of less affluent Americans and call for constructing more nonmarket housing (Tapp 2021). They are also concerned that zoning changes allowing denser development would lead to redevelopment and the displacement of existing vulnerable residents, particularly communities of color (Moskowitz 2017). Even scholars advocating for increasing the housing supply agree that it is unlikely that the housing market can supply adequate, decent housing for low- or moderate-income households and call for preserving existing low-rent housing and expanding public spending on affordable housing (Been, Ellen, and O'Regan 2018; Ellen, Lubell, and Willis 2021).

Direct government support for increasing housing affordability is necessary owing to stagnating incomes in the country. While inflation-adjusted median US household income increased by 49 percent between 1970 and 2018, most income gains were in the earlier decades (Horowitz, Igielnik, and Kochhar 2020). Between 1970 and 2000, the median household income increased by 41 percent at an annual rate of 1.2 percent. In contrast, between 2000 and 2018, the median household income was relatively flat, growing at an anemic yearly rate of 0.3 percent.

Public spending on housing can help bridge the gap between increasing housing prices and stagnating incomes. Governments can expand the supply of nonmarket housing by building public housing, subsidizing housing developers that agree to rent their units below market rate, and providing rental subsidies to households so they can afford to pay market rent. However, in the US, the federal government sharply cut its funding for affordable housing in the 1980s and 1990s (Basolo 1999). Despite stagnating median income, federal spending on housing barely increased in the 2000s. In inflation-adjusted dollars, federal spending on affordable housing, including public housing, homeless assistance grants, and rental subsidies, was almost flat between 1995 and 2018 (McCarty, Perl, and Jones 2019).

While homelessness, particularly the growth in unsheltered households, is the most visible manifestation of the national housing crisis, many housing challenges are less visible. As in the Global South, households address the limitations on the housing supply, the rising cost of housing, inadequate household capacity to pay for housing, and the lack of public support for affordable housing through informal housing. Most of the informal housing supply is market based. Some of it is unsafe and dangerous. Although only a few scholars in the US have examined informal second units on lots with single-family housing (Baer 1986; Gellen 1985; Mukhija 2014; Wegmann 2015), collectively, their research suggests the commonness of this practice. Given the dominance of single-family housing in the US built environment, the ease of carving out secondary units from single-family houses, the potential to discreetly add unpermitted units on single-family lots, and the need for housing, the prevalence of informal housing on single-family-zoned lots is not surprising. As planners and policy makers look to expand the housing supply while preserving and minimizing the loss of existing low-rent housing, they need to be particularly careful about existing informal housing units. Many of them likely house especially vulnerable residents who may become homeless if they lose their precarious foothold in the housing market.

A PREVIEW OF THE ARGUMENTS

INFORMAL HOUSING AND THE REMAKING OF SINGLE-FAMILY LIVING

My early scholarship focused on informal settlements, which are sometimes dismissively referred to as slums, in the Global South, specifically Mumbai, India (Mukhija 2001, [2003] 2017). Homeowners in informal settlements usually expand and upgrade such housing through incremental development (Abrams 1964; Holston 1991; Peattie 1968; Turner 1967, 1977; UN-Habitat 2003). Families may use discarded construction waste to start with a single wall and gradually expand and improve their homes wall by wall, room by room, and floor by floor. Most housing regulations do not allow for housing conditions to begin with low initial standards and improve gradually. But when interested households cannot access affordable loans or mortgages to pay for fully built houses, or when tenants cannot afford anything more conventional, incremental development is the only viable pathway. Economists argue that incremental housing development shows how residents unbundle various shelter attributes and consume them gradually (Malpezzi 1994; Mohan 1994). However, urban development scholars suggest that in addition to economic unbundling, the incremental development process is institutionally bounded and enabled through public policies that tolerate or encourage incremental housing construction and support it through gradual infrastructure provision and legal recognition (Doebele 1987; Peattie 1994; Sanyal 1996).

Paul Baross (1990) was the first to emphasize the symmetrical contrast between conventional housing development and informal processes. The formal process in both the Global North and the Global South typically starts with land use planning and approval (table 1.2, second column), which rezones agricultural land at the urban periphery as residential. Subsequently, public agencies install infrastructure and provide services to the urbanized land. Later, developers and home builders build new housing units to the required standards and norms. Finally, through savings, loans, and mortgage finance, home buyers pay builders the total cost of the developed housing and occupy the new houses. Informal housing (table 1.2, third column) ingeniously inverts the conventional process. In some cases, families squat on public land, but typically, informal brokers locate and subdivide land that is not zoned for residential development and lacks adequate infrastructure.[6] The brokers sell the subdivided lots to low- and moderate-income households, who occupy the land while gradually building and improving their homes through self-help or self-managed help (i.e., subcontracted labor) (Turner 1982). Often, they add secondary units for tenants (Kumar 1996). As neighborhoods and communities grow in size, homeowners and tenants organize and demand local governments to provide infrastructure and services such as electricity, water, sanitation, and roads. Usually, the final step in a settlement's consolidation is getting official recognition or planning approval and inclusion in a jurisdiction's formal documents, maps, and plans.

Most scholars and policy makers in the Global North associate informal housing with the Global South. The mainstream academic literature on housing policies does not typically discuss informal housing. One notable exception in the US is the scholarship on informal subdivisions—called *colonias* in federal and state policy—in the US-Mexico border region (Ward

Table 1.2
Comparison of conventional and informal housing processes

Sequence of steps	Conventional housing process	Informal incremental development process in the Global South	Informal trailer parks and subdivisions in the Global North	Informal second units in the Global North
1.	Planning and legal recognition	Occupancy	Housing construction	Infrastructure and services
2.	Infrastructure and services	Housing construction	Occupancy	Housing construction
3.	Housing construction	Infrastructure and services	Infrastructure and services	Occupancy
4.	Occupancy	Planning and legal recognition	Planning and legal recognition	Planning and legal recognition

Source: Adapted from Baross 1990.

1999). In the same vein, with my interest in how households with limited resources meet their housing needs, I turned to rural California's border region with Mexico (Mukhija 2012; Mukhija and Mason 2015; Mukhija and Monkkonen 2006). There, informal subdivisions, or *colonias*, and unregulated trailer parks, often called *polancos* in the state, usually house poorly paid migrant farmworkers. Stylistically, their development sequence (table 1.2, fourth column) falls between the conventional process and the informal housing sequence in the Global South. Residents start living in their trailers, usually without adequate infrastructure and permits. Although these *colonias* and *polancos* are only around two hundred miles from the city of Los Angeles and are relatively common, they are usually ignored in public policy and academic research and can seem a world away. They are referred to with a Spanish name and mistakenly dismissed as marginal and a foreign issue (Mukhija and Monkkonen 2007).

Through my students, colleagues, friends, and the local newspaper, I gradually became aware of a more common form of informal housing in the Los Angeles region: unpermitted second units on single-family-zoned lots. Many of my current and former students have lived or currently live in such unpermitted dwellings. Some of the homes are unpermitted garage conversions, others are unapproved detached structures built in the backyard, and still others are carve-outs from the main house without permits. One charming but unregulated garage conversion has passed from graduating students to incoming students (figure 1.1). This studio-like home close to the University of California, Los Angeles (UCLA) campus is a prized property for graduate students keen on a quiet place close to campus. The owners, who live on the property, prefer quiet graduate students too.

Similarly, one of my friends and a UCLA colleague at the Luskin School of Public Affairs has an informal backyard cottage. He bought his single-family house with the unapproved unit with his parents in mind. Sadly, his

FIGURE 1.1
An informal second unit close to the UCLA campus. Photo credit: Student #2 and Student #3.

father passed away after being seriously ill. Nonetheless, he considers himself very fortunate that his parents could live with him when they needed help and that he has a place where his mother can continue to live independently but close to him.

Housing conditions in Los Angeles's informal second units are not comparable to the living conditions in Mumbai's informal settlements or even some of the *colonias* and *polancos* in rural California. Still, unregulated housing can be dangerous, and low-income tenants in particular are vulnerable to hazards. While students at prestigious universities are typically more fortunate, many students with high student debt and an acute need for affordable housing are also vulnerable. A detailed three-part investigative series called "Shadow Campus" in the *Boston Globe* documented students' crowded and unsafe off-campus housing (Abelson 2014; Farragher and Ross 2014; Saltzman 2014). The newspaper reported the tragic death of a Boston University student in an unpermitted attic conversion in Boston's western neighborhood of Allston. Oakland's disastrous Ghost Ship fire in a converted warehouse with illegal construction and shoddy electric work in 2016 was more horrifying. Thirty-six residents of the warehouse's arts collective and their friends died from smoke inhalation (Queally 2019). In September 2021, the remnants of Hurricane Ida hit New York with a deluge of rain. The flooding killed twelve people in the city. Eleven of them died in their basement apartments, most of which were unpermitted cellar conversions (Zaveri and Haag 2021). Informal basement apartments with precarious living conditions are an "open secret" in the city but are accepted for their contributions to affordable housing (Stewart et al. 2019).

Middle-class and upper-middle-class people like my friend usually expect their unpermitted second units to be safe. However, family and kin of less affluent households, many of whom are immigrants, have fewer protections from dangerous unregulated housing. Unfortunately, news reports describing garage fires and fatalities in unpermitted conversions during the winter months are common in Los Angeles because of poor insulation, faulty wiring, unsafe heaters, and the lack of smoke alarms (NBC Los Angeles 2020; Serna 2016). The worst fires have multiple victims. For example, twenty-one members of an extended family in Pacoima, a neighborhood northeast of the city of Los Angeles with mostly single-family zoning, were "illegally using some detached structures as a living area" through "unpermitted construction at the rear of the house" and a fire displaced all of them (Reyes 2015).

My interviews with building inspectors, legal aid attorneys, community organizers, and residents highlight the potentially dangerous housing conditions in unregulated second units (J. P. Bell interview 2016b; Bell and Rodriguez interview 2014; Participant #7 interview 2013; Romero-Martínez interview 2017; Sayeed interview 2014). In the light of such everyday tragedies, planners and policy makers cannot ignore the possibility of poor housing conditions in informally produced housing. They need strategies, policies, and new institutional approaches to address and improve them.

Informal second units in single-family houses in the US follow a development process that shares some attributes of the Global South's incremental development process (figure 1.2; table 1.2, last column). Single-family neighborhoods typically have excellent infrastructure, and occupants usually move in after the addition of second units. However, both infrastructure and housing conditions can be substandard. While housing and infrastructure might improve over time, the development sequence stops at this stage in the US. There is limited public policy support for upgrading informal units and incorporating them into the formal planning process. In most jurisdictions, the policy emphasis is on prevention, enforcement, and clearance of unpermitted units. Or they are ignored.

Contrastingly, Global South countries are more familiar with informal housing and recognize the difficulties in stopping its development. Some countries' policies focus on affordable formal alternatives to informal housing to reduce its need (Monkkonen 2011). Global South countries also offer lessons on improving and upgrading informally developed housing, mainly through infrastructure provision, grants and loans for upgrading informal housing, and various formal and informal recognition strategies, including titles, guarantees, and moratoriums on clearance (Ward 1999). Their experiences illustrate the value of public policies that improve infrastructure, provide financial assistance, and offer pathways to formal recognition. Such policies can positively increase private investments in unpermitted housing, making it safer and more livable. They provide rich lessons for US policy makers and planners.

One of my key objectives in this book is to highlight the everyday prevalence of urban informality in Los Angeles and the affluent Global North. I use the empirical case of unpermitted second units on single-family-zoned lots to elaborate on the nature of informal activities. I build on my coedited volume—*The Informal American City*—with Anastasia Loukaitou-Sideris

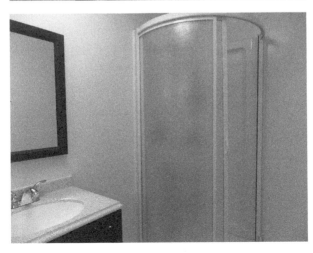

FIGURE 1.2
A new detached and unapproved backyard unit in the San Francisco Bay Area. Photo credit: Author.

(2014), which includes a chapter I authored on unpermitted second units in the city of Los Angeles (Mukhija 2014). Although informality is typically associated with the Global South, I argue that the scope of informality in the Global North is broader than conventionally assumed. I show that informal economic activities, specifically unpermitted second units, are common in the city of Los Angeles and are distributed widely throughout the region. They are not confined to immigrant or low-income neighborhoods.

According to my research, there are likely fifty thousand unpermitted second units on single-family lots in the city of Los Angeles and over two hundred thousand in the county. Ten to 15 percent of the single-family lots have an additional dwelling. Los Angeles is not an exceptional case. San Francisco has about four hundred thousand housing units (San Francisco Planning Department 2021) and an estimated thirty thousand to fifty thousand unpermitted secondary units (Bhatia and Komlos 2015; Wildermuth 2014). According to the Asian Law Caucus (2013), one in three single-family houses in the Excelsior District, an ethnically diverse neighborhood with a majority of Asian American residents, has an unpermitted unit. In response, San Francisco started a bold legalization program for owners willing to meet planning requirements in 2014 (City and County of San Francisco 2014). Informal housing is also common in New York. Scholars estimate that home owners added over one hundred thousand unpermitted units between 1990 and 2000 (Pratt Center for Community Development and Chhaya Community Development Corporation 2008). According to field research by Chhaya, a local nonprofit organization that works with South Asian immigrants in the city, more than a third of the houses it surveyed in Jackson Heights, Briarwood, and Jamaica Hills in Queens had an unpermitted unit (Chhaya Community Development Corporation & Citizens Housing and Planning Council 2008).

Apart from the everyday presence of informal housing, I am interested in examining how informal housing develops and persists despite regulations and enforcement. In the academic literature, there is an emphasis on scrutinizing how urban informality is intertwined with global financial networks, economic exploitation, and arbitrary governments and laws (Portes, Castells, and Benton 1989; Portes and Sassen-Koob 1987; Roy 2005; Sassen 1991; Yiftachel 2009). There is less emphasis on examining the day-to-day workarounds and practices that sustain informal economic activities, which can be an arena for policy intervention. In a more policy-oriented approach,

I show how informal housing is embedded in the economic, institutional, social, and spatial context of markets, and creates varied and uneven living conditions. Informal housing reflects what is needed in the housing market and how households have adapted to its limitations. It often reproduces the advantages of the wealthy and the disadvantages of the less affluent. Unpermitted housing also underscores the risks and dangers of unsafe housing with few protections and rights for vulnerable tenants. In this context, low-income and disadvantaged residents, including immigrants, are more at risk because they typically rely more on housing regulations and enforcement for safe and decent housing than do affluent households.

Policy makers and planners should address the need to upgrade informal housing and learn policy lessons about what households can afford, where they want to live, and what designs or housing typologies meet their needs. Experiences worldwide show that informal activities can be transformed (made safer and less precarious) and transformative (lead to broader cultural and institutional changes). I focus on the formalization and legalization of second units, particularly through institutional changes in single-family housing regulations, and their transformative potential in the following subsection.

SECOND UNITS AND INSTITUTIONAL CHANGE IN SINGLE-FAMILY ZONING

One strategy for increasing private investments in unpermitted units in single-family housing is to change the regulations for single-family living and make it easier for homeowners to obtain permits for second units.

Urban studies scholars see many benefits of second units. Some argue that second units increase the housing supply, add diversity, and help make housing affordable (Chang 2011; Downs 1991; Levine 2006; Liebmann 1990). Karen Chapple (2014) found that backyard cottages in the San Francisco Bay Area rented for less than comparable units and were more affordable than infill multifamily housing developments. Patrick Hare (1981), an early champion of ADUs, dismissed critics who saw the transformation of single-family houses as "carving up the American Dream" by noting that second units expanded access to the dream by providing a more diverse and affordable housing stock. Moreover, the possibility of creating and renting out a second unit can make the objective of homeownership more accessible for many middle-income households willing to share their single-family lots (Maass 1996; Weber 1999). Second units allow extended families to live together, provide options for families with adult children, and enable older adults to live independently with family members and caregivers nearby (Calthorpe 1993; Chapman and Howe 2001; Cuff, Higgins, and Dahl 2010; Hayden [1984] 2002; Myers and Gearin 2001; Newman 2012). Surveys indicate that owners were using or intended to use most second units as long-term residences for themselves, family members, tenants, or caregivers (Brown 2014; Crane 2020; Wegmann and Chapple 2012).

Because of such advantages, scholars have predicted the return of second units for decades, with a sharp rise in optimism in the 1980s. Gwendolyn Wright ([1981] 1983, 272) hopefully noted, "The day of two-family or three-family houses . . . is returning." Several scholars believed that the suburban form of single-family housing and its exclusive neighborhoods failed to meet simple social needs and was likely to evolve (Hayden [1984] 2002; Jackson 1985; Liebmann 1990). Others saw the likelihood of change from surplus space transformation within single-family houses, mainly due to the decline in household size (Gellen 1985; Hare, Conner, and Merrian 1981; Moudon and Sprague 1982). Yet others expected the aging population to drive policy changes (Hare 1981, 1982; Varady 1988). Their predictions appeared to be on the right track when, in 1992, the US Congress authorized a federal initiative called the Elder Cottage Housing Opportunity demonstration program to use backyard cottages for housing in five states (Koebel, Beamish, and Danielsen 2003; Pollak 1994). The AARP (2000), formerly known as the American Association of Retired Persons, and the American Planning Association (AARP and APA 2000) followed up with the Model State Act and Local Ordinance on second units. These initiatives, however, gained little traction.

There was limited progress in changing the single-family living culture and its underlying zoning rules. In places where zoning allows accessory units, minimum lot size requirements, minimum setbacks, owner-occupancy mandates, and off-street parking requirements are usually difficult to overcome (Brown, Mukhija, and Shoup 2018; Chapple et al. 2011; Mukhija, Cuff, and Serrano 2014). Most cities, often supported by homeowners who fear second units and their tenants' potential adverse effects on the character of their neighborhood's single-family housing, require that second units meet demanding standards that can be virtually impossible to comply with.

Although the existing literature is pessimistic about the prospect of significant reforms, I document several examples of institutional changes to allow second units formally on single-family-zoned lots. I focus on the city of Los Angeles, which has about four million residents and is one of the eighty-eight incorporated cities in Los Angeles County. The county has over ten million inhabitants, including over a million who live in its unincorporated areas. As in the rest of the country, land use planning is decentralized. The cities have responsibility for decision-making in their jurisdictions, and the county has the authority for the unincorporated areas. The California state government can intervene in cities' land use regulations and zoning for the public interest. However, until the mid to late 2010s, it had refrained from significant state preemption of local zoning (Camacho and Marantz 2020).

In the mid-2010s, policy makers and housing advocates in the city of Los Angeles pushed for reforms to single-family zoning through a second unit pilot project. The associated land use reforms ran into neighborhood-based opposition. The city's efforts received a boost with aggressive state government intervention in 2016 to deregulate single-family zoning regulations to allow ADUs statewide. Subsequently, formally approved ADUs became an essential part of the local housing market. They accounted for a fifth of the city's housing permits in 2018 (Los Angeles Department of City Planning 2019). Furthermore, the state made it feasible for homeowners to add a third unit by carving out a junior ADU from existing dwellings. California's active preemption for secondary units helped support the growing conventional wisdom favoring state government interventions to reform single-family zoning (Glaeser 2017; Infranca 2019; Lemar 2019). In 2021, state policy makers followed with more legislation to allow single-family houses to be converted to duplexes and single-family-zoned lots to be split into two parcels under certain conditions (Healey and Ballinger 2021).

While I focus on the city of Los Angeles in this book, I compare its second unit experience with other jurisdictions. Contrary to the emerging conventional wisdom in support of state preemption, several cities in the US, particularly Santa Cruz, California, Seattle, Portland, Oregon, and Minneapolis, and Vancouver, Canada, made significant progress in allowing second units by relaxing planning standards for lot sizes, off-street parking, building setbacks, height limits, and unit sizes. These secondary cases show that there are multiple pathways to institutional change for second units. They help highlight the importance of local initiatives in the city of Los Angeles, like the second unit pilot project, in the city's exceptional success with ADUs. Indeed, state policy makers pointed to the city's success in making a case for their subsequent efforts to change single-family zoning by allowing duplexing and lot splitting statewide. There may be synergies between local and state interventions. One of my contributions is to highlight the relevance of local governments in reforming single-family zoning. I show that even though local communities strongly support single-family living, they may accept second units. This is significant for policy making because top-down changes to single-family zoning are controversial, difficult to implement, and not likely in many US states.

As successful examples of municipal zoning reform become more common and well known, other cities are likely to follow suit. To illustrate, in December 2014, the Minneapolis City Council amended its zoning code to allow accessory units on single- and two-family lots citywide (City of Minneapolis 2014a). Planners in Minneapolis cited the public acceptance of ADUs in Santa Cruz (figure 1.3), Seattle, and Portland as precedents for their proposal (City of Minneapolis 2014b). Other cities across the country, including Boston, Chicago, Denver, Raleigh, Washington, DC, and Tucson, followed their example and changed their zoning regulations to allow secondary units citywide or

FIGURE 1.3
A formally approved second unit in Santa Cruz. Photo credit: Author.

created pilot programs for permitting them (Freishtat 2021; A. Johnson 2020; Kutz 2021; Rosen 2021). The *Wall Street Journal* provided homeowners advice on adding second units and converting their garages (R. Friedman 2021).

Locally led second unit reforms can be a gateway to more radical deregulation in single-family neighborhoods. Minneapolis, for example, approved a new comprehensive plan in December 2018 to allow triplexes on all single-family-zoned lots (City of Minneapolis 2018d). In March 2019, the Seattle City Council upzoned single-family properties near high-frequency transit to allow low- and medium-density housing (Bicknell 2019). In July, it agreed to allow two ADUs—one attached and one detached—on every single-family-zoned lot (Fester 2019). The Portland City Council (City of Portland 2020) ended single-family zoning in August 2020 by allowing fourplexes on all residential lots. More ambitiously, the city council voted to allow six units if at least half of them were price-restricted as affordable. Vancouver's planners initially changed single-family zoning requirements in neighborhoods expressing openness to second units. Later, the city administration expanded the secondary suites policy to all single-family neighborhoods without significant community opposition (City of Vancouver 2004). In 2013, the city's planning department again changed its land use regulations citywide to allow three units per lot, including alley-facing "laneways," in most of Vancouver (figure 1.4) (City of Vancouver 2013; Montgomery 2014). In September 2018, the Vancouver City Council agreed to allow two duplexes with separate secondary suites, or four units per lot, on almost all single-family-zoned properties (City of Vancouver 2019a).

As in Los Angeles, informal housing is prevalent in most of my secondary cases. Vancouver's example is particularly illustrative. It is Canada's most expensive city for housing. The informal market has become an important avenue for the supply of affordable housing. Vancouver's single-family houses have a lower-level or semibasement floor that is often underused and easily converted into unpermitted secondary suites (figure 1.5). City data suggested that there were around twenty-five thousand unpermitted secondary suites on Vancouver's almost seventy thousand single-family-zoned lots (Vancouver City Council 2017). A Global North city, Vancouver has been at the forefront of recognizing the importance of informal housing in meeting its affordable housing needs. It did not emphasize enforcement and clearance of unpermitted units and is transparent about their

FIGURE 1.4
New laneway apartments on single-family-zoned lots in Vancouver. Photo credit: Author.

FIGURE 1.5
A lower-level secondary suite in Vancouver. Photo credit: Author.

presence. However, like other Global North cities, it did not do enough to directly help owners upgrade and improve their units either.

My research suggests many reasons to privilege local action over direct zoning changes by state governments. There are more opportunities to increase public participation at the local level and foster civic life. There is also better knowledge at the local level about spatial conditions, social circumstances, and existing informal housing. State governments, nonetheless, have an important role to play too. They should create and enforce a framework for regional collaboration and action, push for locally led land use reforms, and provide financial support for upgrading informal housing and physical and social infrastructure in densifying neighborhoods. They can also take a more proactive role in supporting home buyers, housing developers, and nonprofit organizations from communities of color to ensure that the benefits of housing development are shared broadly, particularly by groups traditionally disadvantaged in the property market.

While the ideology of single-family living has created immense obstacles for new housing development, its single-family pattern of urban development and ownership may offer a feasible path forward. Many single-family homeowners oppose second units because they fear that their property values will decline. However, in cities and inner suburbs with the most demand for second units and duplexes, homeowners likely find that their property values increase because of the potential rent from additional units. Homeowners collecting rent from their informal housing units and disclosing them on their real estate listings already know this. The new supply should dampen housing price increases, but single-family housing homeowners should see their land and property values benefit from the zoning change. Property value gains for homeowners are likely why many cities are having success in reforming single-family zoning. The economic interests of single-family homeowners in cities are likely to drive the remaking of American urbanism. Without the active involvement of federal, state, and local governments in creating housing opportunities for disadvantaged households, this market-supported transformation is unlikely to be inclusive.

RESEARCH DESIGN

While scholars are critical of single-family housing and neighborhoods, this book's underlying premise is that the ideology of single-family living is slowly losing some of its orthodoxies and transforming. However, for the most part, scholars have not discussed under what conditions homeowners might change their single-family houses informally or support formal changes to single-family zoning regulations to allow second units. On the one hand, property owners are taking the lead in adapting their single-family houses and the social norms of single-family living through informal means without permits. On the other, some governments follow them with formal changes to single-family zoning. These are significant transformations in culture, institutions, and urbanism. Understanding them is my primary motivation in this book. I have one guiding question: How and why are the norms and regulations of single-family living changing? I am interested in examining the underlying motivations, challenges, strategies, processes, and what replaces single-family housing.

My research follows a case study approach. I focus on the city of Los Angeles as my in-depth case to understand how and why homeowners are informally adding unpermitted second units. I place these informal changes in the context of local and statewide institutional attempts to make it easier for homeowners to add formal second units on their single-family lots. Additionally, I examine a series of secondary cases—Santa Cruz, Seattle, Portland, Minneapolis, and Vancouver—in less depth (figure 1.6). These cities are known for their regulatory changes to allow second units on single-family-zoned lots. I focus on them to clarify how and why some local governments successfully overcome conventional resistance to changing single-family living rules and regulations. Researching the secondary cases has also helped me think about the issues to expect and data to look for in my primary case.[7]

RESEARCH METHODS

I used multiple methods to collect and analyze primary and secondary data. These methods include participant observation, review of publicly available documents, open-ended interviews, a web-based survey, analysis of sales listings of homes with informal second units, and analysis of complaints about unpermitted second units. While I lived in Los Angeles, I conducted fieldwork of about two weeks in each of the secondary case cities, including two Vancouver visits, between the fall of 2013 and the winter of 2019. The case studies build on my review of the academic literature, planning reports, publicly available government documents (including city council meeting minutes), and reporting in newspapers and news magazines.

FIGURE 1.6
My research sites. Graphic: Jae-Hyeon Park.

I actively participated in the ongoing policy debate about second units in the city of Los Angeles and California. Over a decade ago, I was introduced to the policy challenges of second units as a participant observer. I led a delegation of fifteen students from UCLA's Luskin School of Public Affairs (then known as the School of Public Policy and Social Research) to Los Angeles City Hall for meetings with elected and appointed city leaders. Our "City Hall Day" topic was the formalization of informal second units in the city. Although there were no reliable estimates of the number of unpermitted second units, there was consensus among officials that informal ADUs were common in the city. City officials recognized the vital contribution of unpermitted units to affordable housing, the likelihood of dangerous living conditions within several of them, and the need to increase the housing supply. Nonetheless, they were unanimous in their opinion that legalizing second units was an intractable planning challenge and a politically contentious subject.

Subsequently, I researched the regulatory and neighborhood-based hurdles to legalizing second units with Dana Cuff, my UCLA colleague who founded and directs cityLAB, an award-winning urban design research center at the university (Mukhija, Cuff, and Serrano 2014). From 2015 to 2022, I served as a member of the board of directors of LA Más, a community-based organization with a history of innovation in planning and urban design. LA Más and cityLAB were at the forefront of advocacy for second units in the city of Los Angeles. In 2016, the mayor of Los Angeles invited both organizations to develop ADU pilot projects, and they became fully involved in the city's regulatory reforms. I have also had the opportunity to see and understand second unit policy making in the California state legislature through my collaboration with State Senator Robert (Bob) Wieckowski (Wieckowski and Mukhija 2019).

My own firsthand experiences have informed my research. Living in a single-family house in the city of Los Angeles, and thinking about the challenges and possibilities of adding a second unit for parents, has helped me understand the topic from a homeowner's perspective. During my fieldwork, I stayed in second units in Santa Cruz, Seattle, Portland, and Vancouver to have more opportunities for observations and interviews with homeowners. While I deliberately searched for second units for my visits, by chance, my lodgings included both formally permitted and unpermitted second units.

Interviews were an essential source of data. I draw from over one hundred semistructured, open-ended interviews with a range of stakeholders, including homeowners, second unit residents, planners, architects, building inspectors, attorneys, housing developers, real estate brokers, mortgage brokers, bankers, neighborhood activists, and elected officials. I conducted the majority of the interviews, and my graduate student researchers conducted the rest. Most of our interviews were in person, and they were typically an hour long. We did not record the conversations, but we took extensive notes during the interviews. It is easier to get respondents to talk candidly about informality without recording them. We followed up with the interviewees by telephone or email for clarification or additional information in several cases. To protect the confidentiality of interview participants, including former students, who discussed their personal experiences with informal housing as tenants or owners, I have concealed their identities and report their data anonymously. I list them as participants or students and number them chronologically.

Additionally, I talked informally with extended family members, friends, colleagues, students, acquaintances, and even strangers about unpermitted housing units for the last few years. Almost everyone I spoke with was familiar with the topic. Many had lived in or knew someone who had lived in an unpermitted unit. Some of my most insightful conversations were with generous bartenders, baristas, servers, taxi drivers, and Uber and Lyft drivers in cities across the US and Canada. None of them were surprised by my research topic or the widespread prevalence of informal housing. They were also deeply sophisticated about the challenges involved in improving housing conditions in unpermitted units while keeping the rents affordable.

In addition to these broader approaches, I have used three other distinct research methods to understand the nature and context of second units in the city of Los Angeles:

1. My cityLAB colleagues and I organized a web-based survey of the city of Los Angeles's Neighborhood Councils (elected neighborhood-level groups). We aimed to better understand community-level positions on second units, including neighbors' perception of the prevalence of unpermitted second units, and how frequently Neighborhood Councils faced complaints about such housing.
2. I reviewed publicly available real estate listings of single-family houses for sale in the city and county of Los Angeles and public property records from the county assessor's office to determine the prevalence, distribution, and typology of unpermitted second units.
3. I examined complaints to the Los Angeles Department of Building and Safety to get data on the public's concerns about and acceptance of unpermitted second units and how these vary spatially in the city. I also compared the sales listings in the city with the complaints data for similarities and differences in pervasiveness, spatial distribution, and social acceptance of informal second units.

As I share the book's evidence, I describe more details of the research methods, including their limitations.

A GUIDE TO THE CHAPTERS THAT FOLLOW

My central claim is that the ideal of single-family living is transforming in unexpected ways through informal and formal changes and is likely to remake the form and nature of US cities. I have organized the book into four parts.

Part I, including this chapter, introduces the research, discusses its significance, frames the study's context and contributions, and shares some relevant existing literature. Chapter 2 reviews the scholarship on single-family housing, its growth, criticism, and the evolving context in more detail. I discuss how the idea of single-family housing polarized the housing supply between single-family homes and multifamily buildings, and how single-family housing neighborhoods became the defining feature of American urbanism. Within the stratified housing market, single-family housing ownership became increasingly and narrowly associated with the American Dream, with its attendant economic and social success. Policy makers deliberately supported the ideology of single-family living. The federal government, in particular, played a central role in promoting homogenous and segregated communities and single-family living through its mortgage insurance support. Planners, architects, artists, and market-based developers played a pivotal role in creating single-family living culture as an urban ideal. Racial and class prejudice and a deep-seated desire of many white Americans for homogenous communities also motivated the rise of detached single-family houses. In the chapter, I review the scholarship that is critical of the single-family housing model too. I discuss the vast gap between the dream and its reality for people of color. And I examine more recent literature that discusses socioeconomic imperatives, particularly economic and demographic changes, that may be increasing the market demand for other types of housing and weakening the cultural and political hold of the single-family housing ideal.

Parts II and III are based on my original research and form the empirical core of the book. In part II, I discuss the city of Los Angeles and informal adaptations to its single-family housing. In chapter 3, I introduce the context of Los Angeles as a dream city-region of single-family living. Institutional planning efforts—often pushed by well-organized homeowners' associations and interests—have emphasized strategies for protecting single-family neighborhoods from significant change. I discuss how the dream is unraveling with the rise of cost-burdened and severely cost-burdened households relying on overcrowding and informal housing for living. I describe early legislative attempts in the 1980s, 1990s, and 2000s by the state government of California to create a new property right for owners of single-family housing and to convince and compel local governments to more readily allow formal second units on lots zoned for single-family housing. I share findings from a survey on neighborhood-level attitudes to easing the city's land use regulations to make such housing viable. Interestingly, I found that neighborhood opposition to second units was neither unanimous nor absolute. Additionally, I share neighborhood-level perceptions of informal second units, which indicate that residents are aware and somewhat accepting of their neighbors' unpermitted units.

In chapter 4, I elaborate on the nature of Los Angeles's unpermitted second units. First, I analyze advertising data from real estate listings of single-family houses to tease out the presence of informal second units and estimate their prevalence, typology, and distribution in the city of Los Angeles. In an appendix to the chapter, I approximate the number of unpermitted second units and their distribution in the county and compare my estimates with US census data on likely informal housing across the country, including the Los Angeles metropolitan area. Second, I use data on complaints against informal second units to the city of Los Angeles's Department of Building and Safety to assess the level of social acceptance of unapproved housing. I compare the pattern of complaints against informal second units' spatial distribution from the city's sales listings. Third, I draw on interviews with homeowners, tenants, and other stakeholders involved with informal second units. I explain how owners creatively use the spatial possibilities on single-family lots; social networks, including direct and indirect relationships with neighbors; and formal institutions, such as partial permits, rental contracts, and purchase contracts, to help make informal housing viable. Finally, I elaborate on housing conditions in unpermitted second units and the socially embedded and socially constructed nature of informal housing. I discuss the disparate implications of unregulated housing for the rich and privileged in contrast to the drawbacks for low-income and disadvantaged residents.

In the two chapters of part III, I examine institutional planning responses to informal second units and attempts to allow second units formally in Los Angeles and beyond. In chapter 5, I focus on the city of Los Angeles. I discuss the opportunities to formalize the city's informal second units. I consider formalization a broader category that includes legalization through zoning reforms and regularization through public and private upgrading efforts to improve living conditions within substandard housing units. I review previous debates and experiences with the formalization of informal housing in the city and discuss ongoing deliberations to enable homeowners to add legally approved second units in the light of more aggressive State of California interventions in local land use regulations in the mid to late 2010s. The state's preemption of local zoning helped liberalize single-family zoning and opened up the market for second units, particularly in the city of Los Angeles. I briefly discuss the private sector's involvement, including innovations by small entrepreneurs and strategies of large national homebuilders—Lennar, Toll Brothers, Pardee Homes, KB Homes, PulteGroup, and Ryland Homes. I note and criticize the lack of significant policy support for informal housing tenants and low-resourced owners interested in upgrading their unpermitted second units.

In chapter 6, I present case studies of Santa Cruz, Seattle, Portland, Minneapolis, and Vancouver and discuss them through a similar framework. Informal housing is common in most of these cities, particularly Vancouver. In the case studies, I compare the political approaches and relative success in changing single-family zoning regulations to allow second units. I describe how policy makers have focused on formalizing second units through zoning changes and legalization. Their experiences show potential local pathways for remaking single-family housing. Although the pace of change is typically slow and incremental, the cases show more ambitious zoning reforms through local initiatives. Several case study cities are engaged in pushing single-family zoning boundaries with ideas for third and fourth units. I also examine the progress in upgrading the existing unapproved second units in the cities, including the disappointing limited direct public policy support for improving housing conditions. Nonetheless, the case of Vancouver stands out for the city's acknowledgment of its unpermitted housing stock and attempts by policy makers to guide private investment into improving them.

Chapter 7, which constitutes part IV, concludes this book. In the chapter, I expand on the book's main contributions by elaborating on the rationality of informal and formal second units. I discuss the nature of informal housing and unapproved second units, including the potential of upgrading and improving the informal units; the possibility of successful zoning reforms to allow second units in single-family neighborhoods; and the prospect of more just cities with changes in the orthodoxy of single-family living, more spatial and institutional diversity in housing options, and more supportive policy attention to informal housing.

After almost a century of public policy and cultural support for an ideology of single-family housing homeownership, there is a growing recognition that the social, economic, and environmental cost of single-family living may outweigh its benefits. Informal and formal second units have played an essential role in this emerging acceptance. Ultimately, this book calls for more extensive land use regulation changes, public policy support to make it easy and financially feasible for owners to build additional units on single-family lots and even across property lines, and public investments in the social and physical infrastructure of changing neighborhoods. It asks for recognizing the widespread informal or unregulated housing in US cities and detailed and deliberate planning strategies to upgrade and improve living conditions in informal units. Planners and policy makers need to better understand how informal and formal institutions change and how they interact with, overlap with, and affect each other, particularly in local built environments. Planners, urban designers, and local and state elected officials have an opportunity to learn policy lessons from places that have successfully addressed similar issues, including areas beyond US borders. They need to consider how new spatial forms of housing and novel institutional arrangements of property ownership can constructively change the landscape of housing options for disadvantaged groups. More inclusive development will require governments to go beyond land use deregulation and become more actively engaged in the housing market and affordable housing production. Governments will need to be directly involved to ensure that households without property ownership and homeowners without financial resources or access to conventional loan products, particularly in communities of color, benefit from the housing opportunities and development of possibilities arising from market-oriented zoning changes. In gradually changing norms, regulations, and practices, learning from other places, and new ownership forms and spatial housing arrangements, I see the potential for a more open, diverse, just, and sustainable American city.

2 THE IDEOLOGY OF SINGLE-FAMILY LIVING

In the early 1980s, the *New York Times* (Geist 1981) detailed the strong opposition to modest changes in single-family housing neighborhoods by quoting a Springdale, Connecticut,[1] resident named Mrs. Green. She criticized her neighbors for adding tenants and rental apartments by subdividing their houses without permits and noted, "They are trying to carve up the American Dream itself—the family home—and I'm going to fight it." Mrs. Green's opposition to second units must be understood in the context of the rise of single-family housing as a defining feature of contemporary American urbanism.

Neighborhoods exclusively made up of detached single-family houses, now seemingly ubiquitous in US cities and suburbs, are a relatively new spatial and cultural form. While detached housing had emerged as the preferred suburban ideal in the late nineteenth century, neighborhoods of single-family houses were uncommon and affordable only to affluent families in the early twentieth century (Warner and Whittemore 2012). Studies of land use in prewar US cities show very few neighborhoods of exclusively single-family houses (Bartholomew 1932). Barbara Flint (1977), for example, examined zoning maps from 1910 to 1940 of Los Angeles, Chicago, and St. Louis and found that land use districts allowing only single-family housing were rare in all three jurisdictions. Nonetheless, in the span of a few decades after World War II, single-family dwellings and their neighborhoods became the ideal for successful middle-class living in the US.

The prevalence of detached single-family houses for urban living is unique to US, Australian, and Canadian cities (Hirt 2014). In other parts of the world, detached single-family dwellings with private yards are typically located in small towns or villages. To the extent that their cities have single-family housing, it is mostly in the form of attached houses with shared side walls that are often called town houses, row houses, or terrace houses. The US, Australia, and Canada are exceptional in having achieved both high urbanization levels and an extraordinary commonness of detached single-family housing—over 63 percent of the housing units in the US, "nearly twice the EU average; almost 76 percent in Australia; and over 55 percent in Canada" (Hirt 2014, 21).

Scholars have described the detached single-family dwellings as "houses for a new world" (B. Lane 2015) that are emblematic of the contemporary American Dream in the US. They suggest that the homes resonate with Americans' long-standing pastoral ideals and have helped create a unique, anti-urban culture of urbanism (Marx 1964; Rowe 1991). Single-family living is both a goal to aspire to and a symbol of its inhabitants' social and economic success (Jackson 1985). In the US, land for other uses "may sell for more per acre and the buildings on them may cost more per square foot to occupy, but none is valued socially as highly as the single-family house on its own lot" (Perin 1977, 45).

Gradually, a comprehensive ideology of single-family living has developed in the US. Its subscribers associate values of spatial individualism, egalitarian democracy, and the family with the urban and social form of single-family housing and its communities. Many homeowners believe that their property values are associated with single-family living. They view changes to single-family housing as detrimental to their neighborhoods' social and physical character and dogmatically oppose even modest reforms like second units. Nonetheless, single-family living's limitations can push homeowners to modify their houses informally.

THE RISE OF HOMEOWNERSHIP AND SINGLE-FAMILY HOUSING AS THE AMERICAN DREAM

The first explicit reference to the American Dream, as invoked by James Truslow Adams in his 1931 book, *The Epic of America*, is an abstract call for a society that recognizes an individual's capabilities over their stature as the guiding principle for a country with few shared traditions and conventions:

> That dream of a land in which life should be better and richer and fuller for everyone, with opportunity for each according to ability or achievement. It is a difficult dream for the European upper classes to interpret adequately, and too many of us ourselves have grown weary and mistrustful of it. It is not a dream of motor cars and high wages merely, but a dream of social order in which each man and each woman shall be able to attain to the fullest stature of which they are innately capable, and be recognized by others for what they are, regardless of the fortuitous circumstances of birth or position. (404)

For Adams, material prosperity was not central to the American Dream. His more open call for a national aspiration and moral standard built on Thomas Jefferson's enshrining of the "pursuit of Happiness" as a basic right in the Declaration of Independence.

Jefferson and others of the founding generation, however, saw property ownership as a pathway to autonomy, security, and national expansion. Jefferson in particular envisioned land ownership as a means of settling and belonging. His agrarian preferences and advocacy for democratic participation in property ownership inspired architects and planners to imagine new forms of urbanization. For example, the modern master architect Frank Lloyd Wright (1932) acknowledged Jefferson's influence in his proposal for Broadacre City, which he designed with homes on one-acre lots. More pragmatically, the idea of owning a detached single-family house on a modest-sized lot with a private garden emerged as a plausible alternative. It brought together the spatial individualism and economic security that Jefferson advocated with the potential of egalitarian accessibility, becoming entrenched as key to the American Dream.

The federal government took the lead in expanding homeownership, particularly of single-family housing. In 1919, the federal government took over the National Association of Realtors' (then known as the National Association of Real Estate Boards) homeownership campaign, Own Your Own Home (Kiviat 2010). The promotional campaign emphasized owning single-family dwellings as a patriotic duty (Rothstein 2017). Republican Herbert Hoover, first as secretary of commerce (1921–1928) and subsequently as president (1929–1933), actively promoted single-family living and homeownership as part of good citizenship (Hise 1999).[2]

The public policy push for homeownership showed significant success in the early decades after World War II. The homeownership rate climbed from about 40 percent in 1940 to nearly 63 percent by 1965 (James Jacobs

2015). The apparent success in democratizing homeownership led the US to push the policy globally as both an economic development plan and a strategy to resist the spread of communism (Kwak 2015). Subsequent progress in increasing the homeownership rate in the US was more limited. By 1980, the homeownership rate had inched to almost 65 percent and may have peaked at about 69 percent in 2004 (Nelson 2013). Data from 2019 indicated a homeownership rate of slightly over 64 percent and suggested that it may be plateauing at around the two-thirds mark (Joint Center for Housing Studies of Harvard University 2020).

In 1985 CBS News and the *New York Times* conducted one of the first national surveys to directly examine the relationship between homeownership and the American Dream (Hanson and White 2011). Seventy-six percent of the survey respondents agreed that homeownership was an essential part of the American Dream. Subsequent surveys and studies showed similar results, and the overwhelming majority of Americans continue to see homeownership as central to the American Dream (Gallagher 2013).[3]

In the US public's imagination, successful homeownership is usually equated with owning a single-family house.[4] Although this stylized assumption is not entirely correct, there is some truth to the public perception.[5] As figure 2.1 shows, in 2013, homeowners lived in around 88 percent of the single-family houses in the US, while renters occupied nearly two-thirds of the multifamily housing stock. Since single-family houses account for about two-thirds of the country's housing stock, the overwhelming majority of homeowners in the US do live in single-family dwellings.

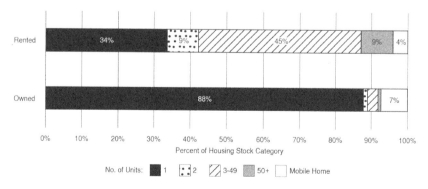

FIGURE 2.1

Relationship between building tenure and type. *Source*: 2013 American Housing Survey (US Census Bureau 2013b). Graphic: Jae-Hyeon Park.

PUBLIC AND PRIVATE EFFORTS IN SUPPORT OF SINGLE-FAMILY LIVING

Single-family dwellings dominate new housing construction in the US. According to Arthur Nelson's (2013) analysis of American Housing Survey data from 1989 to 2009, more than twenty-four million new dwelling units were built in the country, and 85 percent were single-family houses.[6] Below, I discuss the key contributions of both policy makers and private market actors in manufacturing the supply and demand for single-family living.

Federal Support for Homeownership and Suburban Expansion: The federal government has played a leading role in making homeownership, particularly of single-family houses, affordable through insurance support for mortgage lenders. Its policies helped boost the demand for detached single-family housing in exclusively single-family neighborhoods by explicitly endorsing and supporting these homes as ideal investments for home buyers and the lenders who extend mortgages to them.

The federal government began its large-scale direct intervention in housing markets at the height of the Great Depression, when millions of homeowners were losing their homes to foreclosure. After attempting to stem the tide of foreclosure with ineffective small-scale programs, President Franklin D. Roosevelt created the Homeowners Loan Corporation (HOLC), which was empowered to directly refinance mortgages that were in danger of default or foreclosure, in 1933. The HOLC was empowered to directly refinance mortgages that were in danger of default or foreclosure. The need was enormous, and the scale of the HOLC's loan program was unprecedented. It produced two significant innovations that have shaped US housing through the present day.

First, the HOLC revolutionized mortgage finance. Kenneth Jackson (1985, 196) sums it up well: "The HOLC is important to history because it introduced, perfected, and proved in practice the feasibility of the long-term, self-amortizing mortgage with uniform payments spread over the whole life of the debt." In the 1920s, most mortgages required high down payments and were extended for only five or ten years, after which the buyer was expected to refinance or lose their home to foreclosure. The HOLC's low interest rates, long repayment periods—typically twenty years—and stable payments made buying a home more affordable and more secure than it had been. Second, the HOLC created the first large-scale, standardized methods for appraising mortgages (Jackson 1985).

The Roosevelt administration followed up with the National Housing Act in 1934, which led to the creation of the Federal Housing Administration

(FHA), a successor to the HOLC. The FHA adopted the HOLC's system for appraising lending risk, and it had a tremendous impact on the character and location of postwar American housing. Whereas the HOLC directly extended credit to distressed homeowners facing foreclosure, the FHA provided mortgage insurance to private lenders (Jackson 1985). Roosevelt's administration also adopted the Servicemen's Readjustment Act of 1944 (popularly known as the GI Bill), which led to the establishment of the Veterans Administration (VA) and guaranteed loans to help returning World War II veterans buy homes. Both the FHA and the VA were pivotal in the development of the modern mortgage industry. Providing government insurance for mortgage lenders helped to make lending less risky and mortgages more readily available.

The FHA's ability to pick and choose which mortgages would receive federal backing gave it incredible power over housing and development. To receive FHA backing, a property had to meet the FHA's housing standards. Those standards, which the agency published in its underwriting manuals, reflected the attitudes and values of the white, male middle class to the wealthy real estate professionals and bankers who wrote them. They favored detached single-family houses over multifamily buildings, new construction instead of rehabilitating existing buildings, suburban development rather than urban, and single-use zoning to create homogenous environments, which the agency considered economically stable. For example, the agency "insisted that any single-family residence it insured could not have facilities that allowed the dwelling to be used as a store, an office, or rental unit" (Jackson 1985, 207–208).

Fiscally, the federal government's support for mortgage interest deduction (MID) allows taxpayers in the US to reduce their taxable income by the amount of interest paid on loans for owner-occupied homes. The deduction subsidizes homeownership and helps make single-family houses more affordable, particularly in cities with expensive housing. Homeowners can deduct interest on mortgage debt up to $750,000 for a principal home and a secondary home.[7] Although MID's stated objective is to promote homeownership, it is more likely to help homebuyers borrow more to buy bigger and more expensive houses (Gruber, Jensen, and Kleven 2017; Hilber and Turner 2013).

At the cost of unprecedented sprawl, the federal government used transportation and urbanization policy to encourage single-family living and homeownership through its ambitious road construction program. The

Federal Highway Act of 1956, formally known as the Interstate and Defense Highways Act, significantly increased the supply of land serviced by highways. The act authorized the construction of forty-one thousand miles of freeways, which exponentially opened up inexpensive agricultural land for urbanization, housing construction, and affordable single-family houses (Moudon 1995). State governments decided the location and alignment of new highways (Taylor 2000), and scholars hold them responsible for displacing urban communities of color across the country for their construction (Avila 2014).

Market Actors and the Push for Single-Family Housing: Large-scale builders responded splendidly to the federal financial incentives for building single-family housing communities, particularly after World War II as the highways network expanded (Jackson 1985). The advent of balloon-frame construction allowed them to build housing quickly and at large scale while lowering costs. Builders realized cost savings from assembly-line construction techniques, economies of scale, and mass production methods (Warner and Whittemore 2012). US policy makers regarded such construction best practices as transferable and promoted them in other urbanizing countries struggling to increase their housing supply (Abrams 1964). Builders such as Levitt & Sons in Levittown, New York, and Louis Boyar, Mark Taper, and Ben Weingart in Lakewood, California,[8] kept their construction costs down through spatial innovations. These changes included building modest-sized single-family houses with simple layouts on small lots, often with unfinished attics, allowing for lower initial costs and opportunities for subsequent additions and expansions, much like incremental development in the Global South (Hayden [1984] 2002; Kelly 1993; Waldie 1996).

Federal agencies and market-based private actors made a significant marketing push to build a culture of homeownership, particularly around single-family housing and its associated lifestyle. The FHA and the VA supported promotional campaigns with posters, booklets, and advertising to encourage single-family living and homeownership (Hise 1999). The National Association of Homebuilders, a federation of state and local associations, coordinated immensely popular homeownership and new housing festivals, including National Home Week (NHW). The association celebrated the first NHW in 1948, with seventy-five participating cities. By its tenth year, 1957, the NHW included ten thousand houses in 185 communities and attracted over ten million visitors (James Jacobs 2015).

Along with regular features on suburban communities in well-known publications like *Time, Newsweek, Life, Business Week,* and *Fortune,* so-called homemaking magazines like *Better Homes & Gardens, American Home, Ladies' Home Journal, Women's Home Companion,* and *Good Housekeeping* played a pivotal role in influencing domestic life and building a constituency for middle-class living based on single-family housing (D. Harris 2012; James Jacobs 2015). As technology improved, it became easier to publish photographs and graphics in periodicals and for homebuyers to visualize the comforts of single-family life. The circulation of homemaking magazines exploded, and their influence on consumer demand skyrocketed. *Better Homes & Gardens,* for example, had a circulation of almost eight million by the early 1970s (James Jacobs 2015).[9]

Race and Prejudice: The history of federal efforts to support homeownership and the construction of single-family housing in US cities is, in large part, the history of spatial segregation and systemic racism. Both public and private sector actors brought their racial prejudices to the endeavor of remaking the country's housing market.

Notoriously, the FHA's lending standards openly promoted and reinforced racial housing segregation by appraising all-white neighborhoods as "low-risk" areas for investment while labeling mixed-race or Black communities "high-risk" (Rothstein 2017). Irrespective of potential borrowers' income, wealth, and creditworthiness, the FHA refused to provide lenders with mortgage insurance for housing loans within neighborhoods it classified as high risk, which it outlined in red on agency maps (Rothstein 2017). This countrywide practice became known as redlining. It systemically starved Black communities of investment and shifted resources to exclusionary, all-white enclaves. This top-down push for white communities institutionalized federal support for segregation in American cities and suburbs, perpetuated and strengthened existing spatial patterns, and continues to be a defining feature of the national landscape (Massey and Denton 1993; Rugh and Massey 2014).

Local zoning regulations, including explicitly racial ordinances, played a crucial role in institutionalizing such social and spatial discrimination patterns. Racial prejudice often drove interest in zoning regulations (Whittemore 2018). The city of Los Angeles passed "the country's first zoning law in 1908" (M. Weiss 1987, 13). Several other cities followed with zoning regulations. Particularly noteworthy are New York City, which legislated the country's first comprehensive citywide zoning in 1916 to regulate land use and design (Fischler 1998), and Berkeley, California, which, also in 1916, pioneered the use of exclusive zones for single-family houses as separate and distinct land use districts (M. Weiss 1986).

In 1910, Baltimore, Maryland, introduced the country's first explicit racial segregation-based land use law to prevent people of one race from living in neighborhoods with people of another race (Silver 1997). While Baltimore was the first to introduce racial zoning, it was a widespread practice in the region within a few years.[10] In 1914, Louisville, Kentucky, was zoned to prevent Black owners from buying property in white-majority neighborhoods and vice versa (Toll 1969). Local governments' efforts to implement explicit racial zoning were stalled in 1917 when the business-friendly US Supreme Court—which ruled against minimum wage and labor safety laws in other cases—struck down Louisville's explicit racial zoning for its interference in property rights and the freedom of contract in *Buchanan v. Warley* (Rothstein 2017).

The judicial impediment did not immediately end the practice of race-based zoning. In 1922, for example, local policy makers divided Atlanta, Georgia, into three race-based districts: R-1, white district; R-2, colored district; and undetermined district. When the zoning ordinance was challenged in the courts, the city's attorneys unsuccessfully argued that the law only prohibited living in specific neighborhoods and was not an infringement on the right to buy property (Rothstein 2017). In 1924, Richmond, Virginia, which had antimiscegenation laws prohibiting interracial marriage, unsuccessfully tried to work around the courts and institute racial zoning by banning people from living in neighborhoods where they could not marry a majority of the residents. Although the city's attorneys argued that Richmond's law, unlike Louisville's, was not about limiting property rights, the Supreme Court rejected their reasoning in 1930 (Rothstein 2017).

After losing the ability to enshrine explicit housing discrimination into public ordinances, private developers and homeowners attempted to preserve their all-white neighborhoods through private contracts. They embraced racially restrictive covenants, clauses in a property's deed forbidding its sale or rental to people of color. Racially restrictive covenants had been introduced in the mid-nineteenth century but gained widespread use in the 1920s and proliferated through the 1940s (Jones-Correa 2000). They helped developers meet their white homebuyers' perceived market demand for segregated neighborhoods and made it easier for white households to access mortgage insurance from the FHA. In 1948, in *Shelly v. Kramer*, the US Supreme Court ruled racially restrictive covenants were unenforceable. However, the use of discriminatory contracts continued for two more decades until the federal Fair Housing Act of 1968 outlawed them (Brooks and Rose 2013).

The restrictions on governments to institute racial zoning, and the limitations on private developers to impose and enforce racially restrictive covenants, contributed to the rise in popularity of single-family zoning.[11] Single-family zoning became the legally acceptable and socially sanctioned approach for sorting and segregating households based on class. It was a convenient proxy for race-based discrimination too (Connerly 2005; Freund 2007).

REDEFINITION OF AMERICAN URBANISM

Several observers note that the lack of medium-density housing—or the missing middle—is a characteristic of contemporary American urbanism (Leinberger 2007; Parolek 2012, 2020). Previously, two-family houses were a regular feature of the late nineteenth-century streetcar suburbs and urban neighborhoods across the country (Warner 1969). They were common in cities and widely known as the duplex in Los Angeles, the double in Indianapolis, and the two-flat in Chicago, but they started becoming rare in new construction after the mid-1930s (Gellen 1985). The FHA discouraged them through its mortgage underwriting requirements by arguing that rental income was unpredictable, and demanded higher insurance rates from homebuyers of two-family houses. Similarly, the once-typical construction of triple-deckers in New England and three-flats in Chicago became uncommon.

Jurisdictions throughout the country also pushed for the end of second units as accessory dwellings. In Washington, DC, for example, Congress approved the District of Columbia Alley Dwelling Act of 1934 to establish a housing authority for removing coach houses built on alleyways by equating them with slums and prohibiting alley habitation (Borchert 1980). Scholars such as James Borchert (1980) and Amy Lavine (2010) argued that these housing policy reforms were primarily motivated by the desire to remove Black residents from Washington, DC's central areas.

The postwar housing construction boom of 1945–1970 dramatically transformed US cities and suburbs. Single-family housing became the dominant urban form. According to James Jacobs (2015), the author of the aptly named *Detached America*, between 1945 and 1970, private builders constructed over thirty-five million housing units, and the overwhelming majority were detached single-family houses. In contrast, in what scholars have described as the "anti-apartment movement in the US" (Baar 1996), "multifamily construction declined to 7 percent of construction between 1946 and 1956 as the private sector adjusted to the booming FHA-driven market for single-family homes" (Whittemore 2012a, 627). This transformation was not limited to the suburbs or the periphery of US cities. Rather, it was a defining feature of most US cities, many of which grew and developed significantly in the postwar era.

Federal home financing policies, local zoning practices, and racial prejudices prepared Americans to think that their home values depend on neighborhood homogeneity, segregation by race and class, and the absence of other land uses and housing types (Badger 2018). As housing has grown in importance as an asset for most homeowners, mainly through the 1970s, homeowners have become more active and politically organized against changes to their neighborhoods (Fischel 2001). Their interests and concerns about residential property values have expanded beyond the limits of their private lots or property lines (Fennell 2009). While some homeowners claim that they are heroically fighting against elite development interests to protect their communities and the environment (Gendron and Domhoff 2008; Logan and Molotch 1987), others see them as driven by their racial and class prejudices and an antiurban sentiment of "freedom from unwanted social contact and the possibility of social conflict" (Perin 1977, 90).

THE REALITY OF THE AMERICAN DREAM

Critics of the American Dream (i.e., single-family housing and its neighborhoods) disapprove of the high environmental and social costs associated with its dominance in the country's urbanization pattern. They criticize public policy support for sprawl and the ownership of single-family housing in exclusively single-family housing neighborhoods for crowding out other housing options and adversely affecting those who cannot afford it or want alternatives. Single-family living has four key challenges: environmental costs, spatial and social exclusion, affordability, and demographic mismatch. Some of these challenges may motivate and enable policy makers, planners, and residents to reform single-family zoning. Others, particularly the last two, are likely to cause homeowners to consider adding informal second units.

Environmental Costs: Critics of single-family housing find the sprawl associated with these neighborhoods wasteful and indefensible in an era of climate crisis. Their fundamental criticism is that single-family houses are inherently inefficient because of their high consumption of land, building materials, infrastructure, amenities, and other resources (Owen 2009; Peterson, Peterson, and Liu 2013). This contrasts with the claim by cultural historians that the detached single-family house represents a "middle landscape" between the city or urban living and the village or rural living (Marx 1964; Rowe 1991). They suggest that the private gardens of single-family dwellings allowed for living with the natural environment amid the dramatic changes of urbanization. As I elaborate in the next chapter, homeowners in the city of Los Angeles strongly believe that their single-family dwellings and neighborhoods are ecologically and environmentally friendly.

The environmental cost of single-family living keeps growing and will increase exponentially with more sprawl. The average size of a detached single-family house more than doubled during the second half of the twentieth century.[12] Scholars see an environmentally vicious cycle of consumption driven by bigger homes, more sprawl, and more dependence on driving and private transportation (Peterson, Peterson, and Liu 2013). Worse, this ecologically destructive urbanization pattern is enabled by public policies through hidden and perverse subsidies for homeowners and land developers (Blais 2010).

Exclusion: Single-family neighborhoods exacerbate spatial and social exclusion, particularly along the lines of race, class, and gender. First, scholars argue that discrimination and racial exclusion are at the core of single-family living (Hunt and Ramón 2010; Freund 2007; Rothstein 2017). They describe the resulting geography of housing and neighborhoods and the different opportunity structures they created as "American apartheid" (Massey and Denton 1993). In her well-known essay "Whiteness as Property," Cheryl Harris (1997) argued that the centrality of property ownership in the US is instrumental in producing racial identity and perpetuating racial inequality. Ownership of single-family housing, critics argue, is similar (Schneider 2019; Vallianatos 2018).

Even though the American Dream is theoretically egalitarian and open to everyone, discrimination in mortgage lending ensures that homeownership—and the generational wealth that can come with it—is less accessible to people of color. Once white home buyers found their dream communities, they worked to maintain neighborhood racial homogeneity directly through outright hostility and violence (Jeannine Bell 2013; Freund 2007; James Jacobs 2015; Loewen 2006). The adverse effects of redlining, mortgage discrimination, violence, and segregation persist in Black neighborhoods across the US. The inequities in private investment have been worsened by disparities in public investment in the same communities. For example, scholars have identified fewer trees and more paved areas in previously redlined Black communities. Consequently, the neighborhoods are hotter than their white counterparts, and residents have more heat-related illnesses (Hoffman, Shandas, and Pendelton 2020). In this context, Ta-Nehisi Coates (2014, 2015) denounced the American Dream and its enduring and exacerbating impacts and made a case for reparations.

In *Ghetto*, Mitchell Duneier (2016) reminded readers that Black neighborhoods were formed and persist because of forced confinement. He detailed the role of planning institutions like zoning, racially restrictive covenants, and discrimination in mortgage access in constructing the geography of segregation and confinement. He described racially restrictive covenants as the "invisible wire-fence" of off-limit neighborhoods. Duneier's scholarship built on Kenneth Clark's (1965) criticism of "white control" and the "institutionalization of powerlessness" and their roles in the segregation of Black Americans in the classic *Dark Ghetto*.

Second, single-family neighborhoods are designed to exclude tenants, and class-based exclusion drives the differences in residential zoning at different densities. The 1926 US Supreme Court case of *Village of Euclid v. Ambler Realty Company* established the constitutional validity of zoning regulations as the legitimate expansion of the police power of local government to separate housing from potentially polluting industries. Its detailed opinion made the class basis and bias of the institution clear. In the dispute between Euclid, Ohio, a suburb to the east of Cleveland, and Ambler Realty, which was interested in developing its land for industry, the Supreme Court dismissed the company's claim that the town's zoning was arbitrary and deprived it of its property rights without due process (Boudreaux 2011). In the ruling, the justices accepted the need for policy makers to distinguish between different housing types in zoning ordinances, such as single-family and multifamily housing. They established as legal doctrine the idea that denser forms of housing, particularly for renters, are inferior to single-family houses, with which they have a parasitical relationship:

> With particular reference to apartment houses, it is pointed out that the development of detached house sections is greatly retarded by the coming of apartment houses, which has sometimes resulted in destroying the entire section for private house purposes; that in such sections very often the apartment house is a mere parasite, constructed in order to take advantage of the open spaces and attractive surroundings created by the residential character of the district. (Quoted in Haar 1959, 163)

In the process, the justices reversed on appeal the opinion of the conservative trial judge in the Euclid case, Judge David Westenhaver. In his criticism of zoning's elitism and discriminatory outcomes, Judge Westenhaver noted that "the result to be accomplished is to classify the population and segregate them according to their income and situation in life" (Liebmann 1990, 2).

In a market economy, land prices play a role in segregating households based on their income and wealth. Instead of challenging or mitigating such socially adverse effects, conventional zoning deepens and strengthens market outcomes and social prejudices by mandating maximum density limits, minimum lot sizes, and other subjective housing standards that increase the cost of housing under the rubric of neighborhood character and general welfare. Zoning regulations, particularly single-family zoning, discriminate and "zone out" people in a socially acceptable manner based on their economic class and income (Levine 2006).

Collectively, the empirical evidence examining the relationship between zoning and segregation indicates that spatial separation between households with different incomes is exacerbated by land use regulations, particularly through zoning for low-density, single-family housing (Davidoff 2005; Jargowsky 2015; Pendall 2000; Rothwell and Massey 2010). For example, my colleagues Michael Lens and Paavo Monkkonen (2016) found clear evidence of the association between low-density regulations and the segregation of higher-income groups. As they noted, "The relationship between urban form and income segregation is complex, but certain types of urban form, in particular low-density development patterns, can contribute to income segregation. Higher population densities, in contrast, could lead to greater integration if neighborhoods include more multifamily and smaller housing units" (7).

Third, single-family housing and neighborhoods pose a challenge for gender equity. Dolores Hayden, in *Redesigning the American Dream: The Future of Housing, Work, and Family* ([1984] 2002), comprehensively critiqued the harmful gender assumptions underlying the design of single-family life. She criticized built environments centered on single-family housing for perpetuating and strengthening gender categories and stereotypes, particularly the expectation that women would forgo paid employment outside the house and instead perform domestic labor as stay-at-home moms taking care of their gender-specific chores. As Hayden noted, "These houses encode Victorian stereotypes about a 'woman's place,' while single-family neighborhoods sustain the separation of the household from the world of jobs and public life. Together, houses and neighborhoods form an architecture of gender unsuited to twenty-first-century life" (29). She argued that the anachronistic housing patterns of single-family living failed to reflect the aspirations of contemporary women or the reality of women-headed households.

Unaffordability: Modest-sized single-family housing, particularly with subsidized land development and postwar construction innovations, was one of the least expensive housing options to build. Contemporary single-family housing, however, is costly and unaffordable to a growing proportion of US households. Progressive legal scholars have optimistically speculated for decades that the US judiciary will eventually agree with Judge Westenhaver's concerns for fairness and find single-family zoning unconstitutional for its explicit economic discrimination (Babcock 1969; Hagman 1971, 1983; Ziegler 1983). There has been little progress in this regard. However, owing to changes in the economic ability of middle-class Americans to afford single-family houses, as well as demographic shifts in the country, the demand for different forms and configurations of housing is increasing.

First, the US has a "vanishing middle class" with a declining share of national earnings (Temin 2017). Peter Temin defined the middle class as households earning between two-thirds of the median income and twice the median income. Its share of US earnings dropped from 60 percent in 1971 to 40 percent in 2014. Temin discussed many reasons for this change, including new technologies, globalization, the decline in unionization, and harmful public policies, such as low tax rates, racially motivated incarceration policies, and housing markets constrained by single-family zoning.

Second, scholars argue that high housing costs have resulted in declining economic mobility opportunities in the US. They claim that housing costs affect access to labor markets, making it difficult for less skilled workers to move to places where better employment opportunities are inviting but housing costs are exorbitant (Ganong and Shoag 2017; Hsieh and Moretti

2015). Peter Ganong and Daniel Shoag (2017) used state appeals court records to estimate strictness in land use regulations, including single-family zoning, and model their effects on income inequality. They found that income convergence across states and population flows to wealthy places declined sharply between 1980 and 2010. They concluded that "rising housing prices in wealthy areas deter unskilled migration and slow income convergence" (1).

In a similar vein, Chang-Tai Hsieh and Enrico Moretti (2015) used metropolitan-level data from 1964 to 2009 to examine how cities contribute to national growth. They argued that housing supply restrictions in the highly productive cities constrain the mobility of workers and limit their access to the top US cities with higher-paying jobs. They also estimated the adverse effects of the lack of mobility in the labor market on the national economy. They argued that easing regulatory constraints in the housing markets of highly productive cities like New York, San Francisco, and San Jose to the level of the median city would encourage mobility, expand their workforces, and increase US gross domestic product by 9.5 percent or over $1.5 trillion a year.[13]

Additionally, there is increasing empirical evidence that neighborhoods— their location, services, amenities, and safety—affect residents' long-term economic mobility (Chetty and Hendren 2015; Chetty, Hendren and Katz 2016; Sampson 2012). Neighborhoods help determine access to schools, one of the main attributes considered by Richard Reeves (2017) in his criticism of "opportunity hoarding" by the US upper-middle class. Reeves identified zoning and its role in limiting access to housing and neighborhoods as one of the primary reasons for constrained opportunities for economic mobility for the vast majority of US households.[14]

Demographic Complexity: The originally imagined consumer for detached single-family housing was a nuclear family of two parents (with the mother staying at home) and their two or three children. However, the US's demographic reality is more complex and changing. The housing market dominated by single-family housing does a poor job of meeting the needs of a growing number of families.

First, the average household size in the US fell from 3.33 in 1960 to 2.62 in 1990 to 2.58 in 2010 before climbing back to 2.62 in 2018 (Pendall et al. 2012; Fry 2019). While the average US household size declined, the average and median sizes of new single-family houses increased. Figure 2.2 illustrates these divergent changes. A key reason behind the fall in household size is

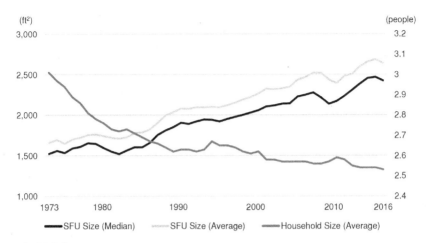

FIGURE 2.2
Relationship between US single-family unit (SFU) size and household size. *Sources*: US Census Bureau 2021a, 2021c. Graphic: Jae-Hyeon Park.

the declining share of nuclear families of two parents with children. In 1950, families of two parents living with their children composed over half of all US households (Lombard 2015). In 2010, only 30 percent of US households lived with their children, and scholars estimated that their share would decline to 27 percent by 2030 due to baby boomers becoming empty nesters (Nelson 2013).

Second, the fall in average household size is partly due to the sharp rise in single-person households, the fastest-growing family form in the US. Demographers estimated that there would be thirty-nine million single-person households by 2025 (Nelson 2006). Sociologist Eric Klinenberg (2012b) discussed this demographic shift extensively in his book *Going Solo: The Extraordinary Rise and Surprising Appeal of Living Alone*. He pointed out that the proportion of US solo households steadily increased from 5 percent of households in 1900 to 9 percent in 1950, to 25 percent in 1990, and 28 percent in 2010. Klinenberg noted the need for appropriately sized and designed housing, as well as neighborhoods with more shared and social infrastructure for solo households, particularly elderly residents. The proportion of single-person households is even higher in cities, where the need for suitable housing is most acute. For example, within the city boundaries of San Francisco, Seattle, Atlanta, and Denver, more than 40 percent of all households are single-person, and almost half of the households in New York City and

Washington, DC, are formed by people living alone. Single-person households are also a significant constituency of metropolitan regions. Figure 2.3 shows the leading urban areas with single-person households in the US.[15]

The third significant demographic change is the rise of multigenerational households. According to the US Census Bureau's American Community Survey data from 2009–2011, approximately 4.3 million households, or 5.6 percent, were multigenerational (i.e., consisted of three or more generations living together) (Lofquist 2012). In contrast, only 3.7 percent of US households were multigenerational in 2000. Demographers at the Pew Research Center define multigenerational households more liberally. In addition to families with three generations, they consider families with skipped generations (grandparents and grandchildren) or two generations of adults (parents

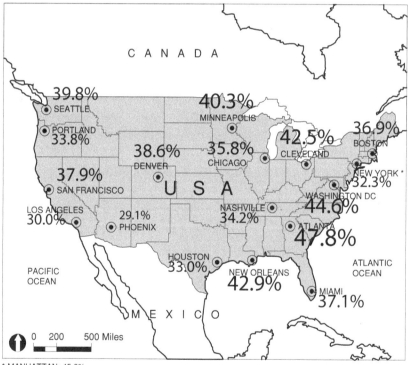

* MANHATTAN: 45.6%

FIGURE 2.3
Leading urban areas with one-person households. *Source*: 2014 American Community Survey data (US Census Bureau 2014); based on an illustration by Klinenberg 2012a. Graphic: Jae-Hyeon Park.

or in-laws with adult children twenty-five years old or older) as multigenerational.[16] According to their estimates, fifty-seven million Americans lived in multigenerational households in 2012, sharply doubling from twenty-eight million in 1980 (Fry and Passel 2014). They estimated that multigenerational living is more common among households headed by foreign-born Americans. While 10 percent of households with US-born household heads are multigenerational, 16 percent of households with foreign-born household heads are multigenerational (Fry and Passel 2014).

Finally, Americans are aging and living longer, and single-family houses and neighborhoods poorly address their needs. The share of households headed by someone aged sixty-five years or older is increasing at an accelerated rate. The Joint Center for Housing Studies of Harvard University (2016) estimated that the US population aged sixty-five years and over would rise from forty-eight million in 2015 to seventy-nine million by 2035. As a result, "while today older households represent one-quarter of all households, by 2035 they will account for one-third" (6). Correspondingly, in the US, "the population aged 85 and over [is] projected to grow more than five-fold between 2000 and 2050, from 4 million to 21 million" (Smith, Rayer, and Smith 2008, 290). This growth suggests that the number of households, including persons with disabilities, will increase significantly. Their homes will likely need to transform for aging-in-place, long-term care, and accommodation of caregivers.

As I noted in chapter 1, second units can play a central part in addressing the country's demographic evolution. They can help accommodate two smaller households on single-family-zoned properties, single-person households, and multigenerational households across two dwellings on the same lot. Scholars from a diverse field of disciplines, including architecture, public policy, urban planning, and gerontology, see the possibility of aging-in-place through second units and caregivers living close by (Chapman and Howe 2001; Cuff, Higgins, and Dahl 2010; Dahl 2010; Folts and Muir 2002; Howe 1990; Liebig, Koenig, and Pynoos 2006; Spevak and Stanton 2019). Research conducted by the AARP suggests that second units are valued in the housing market. Its "consumer preference surveys of seniors indicate that 80 percent or more of older households would like to remain in their current homes," and "over one-third would consider modifying their home to include an ADU if they needed assistance" (AARP and APA 2000, 9). Even though second units represent a relatively modest change to single-family zoning and there is a growing market for them, the allure of single-family living is so strong that many homeowners strongly oppose them. And local governments, until recently, rarely permitted them. As a result, most homeowners interested in second units had to forgo them or add them informally.

CONCLUSION

Mrs. Green, the Springdale resident who shared her displeasure about her neighbors' unpermitted second units with the *New York Times* (Geist 1981) and complained about their potential to destroy her American Dream, also noted,

> We will fight to maintain the character of the neighborhood.... Now we have parking problems, our driveway is frequently blocked, and there are noisy parties at all hours of the night.... Apartments bring in a different class of people. They have no stake in the community.... This is down zoning, which lessens property values. Once they allow this, they can move on to high rises and, who knows, I could wake up with a factory next door. Apartments are a sign of deterioration. It takes the sparkle out of the American Dream, just knowing there are apartments on the block.

She added, "Now they want to undermine the foundation of the dream itself, the home, by subdividing it. We will fight them to the finish" (Geist 1981).

Like Mrs. Green, many owners of single-family housing oppose second units and other changes to their neighborhoods' social and physical characteristics. They regard any change from single-family zoning a downzoning to less desirable uses. Although zoning reforms to allow second units are likely to increase their property values because of the potential to earn additional rent, many homeowners worry about renters eroding the quality of life in their communities and their property values declining.

For about a century, public policies and private actors have assured homeowners that single-family housing is the cornerstone of their economic success and social order and is nationally significant as a symbol of a unifying American Dream. In particular, the federal government's financial and institutional support played a central role in its material development. Other levels of government and market-based actors actively supported and contributed to the idea of single-family living too. Architects, planners, journalists, and other cultural tastemakers also played a vital role in influencing the demand for single-family living and gradually constructing the ideology of single-family living.

Racial and class prejudice and exclusion have been central to the growth of single-family living. Single-family neighborhoods developed inequitably along the lines of race, class, and gender. While homeowners resist physical and social changes to their single-family houses and communities, the reality of the American Dream is markedly different for those left out. Single-family living also imposes a steep environmental cost. Carbon pricing policies, which remove hidden public subsidies and shift actual environmental costs to consumers, particularly for transportation and infrastructure, will likely make single-family living less affordable and accessible.

As demand for single-family living diminishes and changes, single-family housing neighborhoods are likely to transform. The addition of second units might be a modest change to single-family houses that becomes increasingly acceptable to economically motivated homeowners, neighbors, and local governments. Meanwhile, as this chapter suggests, the need and market demand for second units persist, and as a result, owners—like Mrs. Green's neighbors—typically build them without planning permits. An earlier *New York Times* story from the late 1970s on suburbs in the city's metropolitan region also discussed unpermitted second units: "Legal or Not, Single-Family Homes Adding Apartments" (A. Brooks 1979). It noted how strong demand for housing made it likely that homeowners would continue to add second units on their single-family-zoned lots. The story quoted Paul Davidoff, a pioneer in US planning history (Davidoff, Davidoff, and Gold 1970), admired for his opposition to restrictive zoning in the suburbs. He advocated for more liberal zoning that allowed smaller, affordable homes. Davidoff welcomed the informal supply of housing units and the ingenuity of owners and tenants. He noted, "It's beautiful. These apartments are a magnificent answer to the tremendous shortage of less expensive housing in the region. They are to everybody's advantage" (A. Brooks 1979).

II Informal Second Units in Los Angeles

3 CITY OF DREAMS: SINGLE-FAMILY HOUSING AND SECOND UNITS IN LOS ANGELES

The opening of US transcontinental railway lines in the 1880s, including the Santa Fe railroad line from Chicago to Los Angeles, launched Southern California's real estate boom of the late nineteenth century and transformed the former pueblo of Los Angeles. In a nod to its Mediterranean climate, boosters and developers successfully advertised the Los Angeles region as "The New Greece" and "The American Italy" (McWilliams 1946, 97). The city of Los Angeles's population increased spectacularly from about five thousand people in 1870 to around one hundred thousand residents in 1900, and subsequently to an iconic global city of four million in 2020. Correspondingly, its metropolitan area—the Los Angeles–Long Beach–Anaheim Metropolitan Statistical Area, consisting of Los Angeles and Orange Counties—grew from about 190,000 residents in 1900 to around 13.2 million in 2020.[1] Some of the most significant and rapid population increases in the city of Los Angeles were in the almost two decades between the two world wars and the two decades immediately after World War II. The city added about a million new residents in each of the two periods. Many of them, particularly during the postwar period, moved into single-family houses. To spatially accommodate this growth in single-family living, city administrators made nearly eighty political annexations to expand the city from roughly 28 sq. mi. (73 sq. km) in 1895 to about 442 sq. mi. (1,145 sq. km) in 1930 (Gish 2007). Around ninety years later, the city was relatively similar at 469 sq. mi. (1,215 sq. km). The single-family housing-based growth of the city-region helped Los Angeles replace Chicago as the City of American Dreams (Davis 1990).

While David Brodsly (1981, 51) noted the importance of the highway system in Los Angeles's growth, calling it "the city's great synecdoche, one of the few parts capable of standing for the whole," the single-family house may be an even more appropriate metaphor for the city-region. Owners of single-family houses tend to wield political power in their neighborhoods and jurisdictions (Fischel 2001; Jun 2013; Musso et al. 2006). While they hold a formal property right to their single-family-zoned lots, they have become accustomed to exercising an informal property claim to preserve their single-family neighborhoods' physical and social character (Fennell 2009). They routinely and successfully oppose development projects in and near their communities that might adversely affect their views, add traffic congestion, or change the demographic composition of their neighborhoods. Many single-family homeowners vehemently oppose even modest changes, like allowing second units.

CITY OF DREAM HOMES

The use of public authority has been crucial to the city of Los Angeles's development. Planning institutions and regulations were central to its growth (Fogelson 1967a). In particular, the city's zoning, influenced by real estate developers and privileged residents, grew increasingly complex and sophisticated over time. In 1855, the city government instituted fire districts (Whittemore 2010). Following San Francisco, the city's laundry ordinances established exclusionary districts in 1904 to prohibit laundries due to potential fire risks from their hot stoves (Whittemore 2010). Like the state's other laundry ordinances, these districts were racially motivated and driven by a desire to exclude the city's Chinese American residents, who depended on their laundry businesses for making a living, from elite neighborhoods.[2]

In 1908, policy makers created six residential districts and six industrial districts to regulate land use (M. Weiss 1987). The following year, the city government divided the entire municipality into residential and industrial zones (Kolnick 2007; Whittemore 2010). As noted in chapter 2, Berkeley, California, was the first city to institute districts exclusively for single-family housing and to proscribe the construction of multifamily housing within them (M. Weiss 1986). Charles Cheney, who was instrumental in writing Berkeley's 1916 zoning law, was invited by the Los Angeles Realty Board to develop the city's zoning revisions (M. Weiss 1987). Acting on his advice, the city planning commission split Los Angeles's residential district into two types in 1921, making one exclusively for single-family houses (M. Weiss 1987; Whittemore 2012c).[3] In 1930, planners revised the city's zoning again, and the two residential districts were replaced by four: R-1, R-2, R-3, and R-4, with R-4 the densest (Whittemore 2012b).

The popularity and prestige of single-family housing, as discussed in the previous chapter, were boosted by the creation of the Federal Housing Authority (FHA) in 1934. The FHA provided insurance to lenders for mortgages covering up to 80 percent of the cost of housing with twenty-year loans. The agency imposed its preference for single-family houses in exclusively single-family housing districts through its underwriting practices, which dramatically reshaped the Los Angeles region's housing market. For example, it was difficult for potential borrowers to get FHA-insured financing for single-family housing with duplex neighbors (Whittemore 2012a). As a consequence, in the two decades after the creation of the FHA, the majority of the city of Los Angeles's residentially zoned land was gradually recategorized as R-1 by the city council (M. Weiss 1987).[4]

In the postwar years, there was a significant increase in the construction of single-family housing for middle-income home buyers. Contrary to popular perception, this construction boom was not confined to the suburbs. In Los Angeles, as Robert Fishman noted (1987, 155), "the single family detached suburban house escaped from the periphery to become, paradoxically, the central element in the structure of the whole city." The Los Angeles county assessor's data show that in the city of Los Angeles, builders and developers built over 225,000 single-family houses on single-family lots between 1946 and 1966, the peak of American Dream home construction in the city (Mukhija, Cuff, and Serrano 2014).

NEW URBAN CULTURE

The architectural historian Reynar Banham loved Los Angeles's urban form and culture. In contrast to traditional cities, he saw Los Angeles as an affordable city-region, which in its sprawl, dispersion, and departure "from all the rules for civilized living" (Banham 1971, 42) created a city of immense potential. As he argued,

> There is also still a strong sense of having room to manoeuvre.... Unlike older cities back east—New York, Boston, London, Paris—where warring pressure groups cannot get out of one another's hair because they are pressed together in a sacred

labyrinth of cultural monuments and real estate values, Los Angeles has room to swing the proverbial cat, flatten a few card-houses in the process, and clear the ground for improvements that conventional types of metropolis can no longer contemplate. (224–225)

More than anything else, the region's single-family housing symbolized this new urban culture of freedom and endless possibilities. Los Angeles's famous case study houses, which in part attracted Banham to the city, showcased the desirability of single-family living. The now-defunct Los Angeles–based *Arts and Architecture* magazine (1929–1967) sponsored the Case Study House Program, which was introduced in its January 1945 issue and ended in 1965. These experimental homes were built as inexpensive and efficient model homes by many of the leading architects of the era, including Charles and Ray Eames, Craig Elwood, Pierre Koenig, Richard Neutra, Eero Saarinen, and Raphael Soriano. *Arts and Architecture* published alluring images of several of the houses taken by the iconic photographer Julias Shulman. The magazine shared a total of thirty-five designs, of which roughly two dozen were built, almost all in the Los Angeles region. The overwhelming majority of the projects were single-family houses. Only two of the projects, one built and one unbuilt, were for multifamily housing.

According to Robert Fogelson (1967a), the suburban ethic led by single-family housing drove the Los Angeles region's municipal fragmentation and the rise of so-called contract cities. His thesis might be most evident in Lakewood, Southern California's Levittown. The residents of Lakewood resisted a hostile annexation by the city of Long Beach. Instead, they incorporated as an independent city in 1954 and took the then-unprecedented step of contracting with Los Angeles County to provide public services, including police and public safety. Lakewood became the country's first contract city. Subsequently, many other suburban communities in the Los Angeles region adopted the "Lakewood Plan" to incorporate autonomously and contract with the county or adjoining municipalities for services (Fulton 2001).

Single-family urbanism afforded an unprecedented opportunity for urban living seemingly in union with nature. The Los Angeles region, bordered by the Pacific Ocean and bisected by the Santa Monica and San Gabriel Mountain ranges, was fertile terrain for a growing environmental ethic in the US. Residents like Richard G. Lillard, a former chair of the English Department at California State University, Los Angeles, and the first president of the Residents of Beverly Glen, in 1952 cofounded the Federation of Hillside and

Canyon Associations, or Hillside Federation—an association of organized residents, mostly homeowners, in the Santa Monica Mountains. The Hillside Federation led the fight against mountain cropping and the expansion of new freeways through the Santa Monica Mountains. Lillard wrote the acclaimed and polemical *Eden in Jeopardy* (1966). Like Rachel Carson's *Silent Spring* (1962), *Eden in Jeopardy* highlighted the dangers of unrestrained urban development. Homeowners like Lillard and respected environmentalist nonprofit organizations like the Sierra Club and the Friends of Santa Monica Mountains successfully fought public and private real estate and infrastructure development projects to establish the Santa Monica Mountains National Recreation Area in 1978, which is considered one of the most significant examples of ecosystem preservation in an urban area (Davis 1990).

Like many of the Los Angeles region's environmental advocates in the 1960s, Lillard (1966, 314) was passionate about "single-dwelling home life," which he saw as "love for unspoiled nature and adjustment to it." Through the 1950s and 1960s, the number of homeowners' groups, particularly from the west side of the city of Los Angeles and the San Fernando Valley, associated with the Hillside Federation continued to grow. Preserving the Los Angeles region's single-family living pattern became one of the Hillside Federation's central objectives. In the mid-1960s, the federation pushed for several policies that would now be associated with the NIMBY movement, including an increase in residential parking requirements, height limits to protect vistas and views, opposition to infill development, and advocacy against zoning changes to increase density (Whittemore 2012c). One of the federation's key representatives, Marvin Braude, was elected to the Los Angeles City Council in 1967.

Contrary to Banham's optimism of a provisional metropolis with endless imagination and immense possibilities of infill and redevelopment, many Los Angeles region residents, with the support of their influential homeowners' associations, reflexively opposed changes to their neighborhoods. The disdain for density was so extreme that in the late 1960s, residents of areas designated as Residential Estates (RE) with an extra-large minimum lot size requirement, fought against potential designation as single-family neighborhoods (R-1) with standard lot size requirements, which they condemned as "slums" (*Los Angeles Times* 1969).[5]

In addition to fears of congestion and traffic, as well as changes in views and vistas, racial prejudice likely played a significant role in neighborhood-level resistance to higher density and more diverse neighbors. The demographic composition of the city of Los Angeles, an overwhelmingly white community in the 1930s and 1940s, changed significantly after World War II. By the 1970 census, almost two-fifths of the city was people of color. Moreover, in 1948, the US Supreme Court in *Shelley v. Kramer* ruled that the courts could not enforce racially restrictive covenants. While the 1948 ruling did not abolish race-based contracts entirely—covenants allowing private parties to adhere to racial restrictions persisted—the 1968 Fair Housing Act explicitly prohibited them. The act made integration of white neighborhoods more likely.[6] Scholars (Allen and Turner 1997) estimate that between 1960 and 1970, the Latinx population of the city of Los Angeles increased from less than 10 percent to over 17 percent. In the absence of covenants or other explicit mechanisms of racial exclusion, some homeowners found that opposing changes to their single-family neighborhoods was a convenient strategy for ensuring that the demographic composition and social character of their communities did not change.

MAKING LOS ANGELES POLYCENTRIC

The Los Angeles region's low-density, single-family lifestyle was made possible by the state and federal highway system and the widespread use of private cars for transportation. Driving came with costs, specifically congestion and pollution. In a vicious cycle, as the private automobile became the primary mode of transportation, traffic and congestion increased, residents pushed for lower-density developments, public transit became less viable, and the use of cars increased. By the 1960s, the city of Los Angeles had become the country's third most populous city, and the high environmental cost of the region's horizontal, land-consuming development pattern, including smog and degraded hillsides, had become more visible (Temko 1968). As the freeway system grew and driving expanded, the region's air quality sharply declined. Crisis-level pollution led to the federal Clean Air Act of 1963 (Elkind 2014). Critics blamed many of the problems on the lack of adequate planning in the city (Mumford 1961). Criticism of Southern California's development pattern and automobile-centric transportation system gained particular urgency in the wake of the 1965 Watts Uprising, when the McCone Commission (1965) highlighted the region's inadequate public transportation as an important cause of the unrest (*Industrial Design* 1971).[7]

THE CENTERS PLAN

To help make Los Angeles's urban form more viable for public transportation, planners in the city of Los Angeles made a significant effort to change its dispersed and horizontal pattern to an organized polycentric metropolis through a region-wide approach (Los Angeles Department of City Planning 1970). This landmark plan, released in 1970, became known as the Centers Concept or Centers Plan (Hamilton 1986). In 1974, it led to the first comprehensive citywide plan—called the General Plan in California—in the modern city's history. Calvin Hamilton, who was the city's planning director and led the planning department for almost twenty years, initiated an ambitious program of conceptual studies and development goals to inform the plan (Temko 1968). Hamilton (1986) claimed that over twenty thousand residents participated in background studies and surveys. However, critics argue that most of the active participants in the public outreach process were members of homeowners' associations (Fulton 2001).[8] With the aid of its research and analysis, the planning department developed four distinct alternatives varying in housing density, spatial form, transportation, and population growth (Los Angeles Department of City Planning 1967).

The Centers Concept, one of the alternatives, proposed intensely developed nodes connected by a rapid transit system and preserved most existing single-family housing neighborhoods (figure 3.1). In January 1970, it became the basis for the planning department's final proposal for restructuring the city's urban form (Los Angeles Department of City Planning 1970). Hamilton recommended that the Los Angeles City Council approve the Centers Plan and adopt it as the framework for the city's new General Plan. The plan underscored the privileged position of single-family housing in Los Angeles. It would maintain most of the city's single-family neighborhoods while directing future growth to a network of twenty-nine centers of high- and medium-density housing. Planners expected the centers to form a framework for regional rail rapid transit and proposed that each center have a high-density core with rail transit stations (figure 3.2).

Significantly, the planners adopted a regional perspective and suggested a total of forty-eight centers throughout the county of Los Angeles to capture a majority of the region's future growth. While planners have envisioned Los Angeles as a polycentric urban region since the early twentieth century (Hise 1993), the city's planning department innovatively shifted the focus from dispersion to centralization in the Centers Plan. In 1974, the Los Angeles City Council approved it as its General Plan (Hamilton 1986).

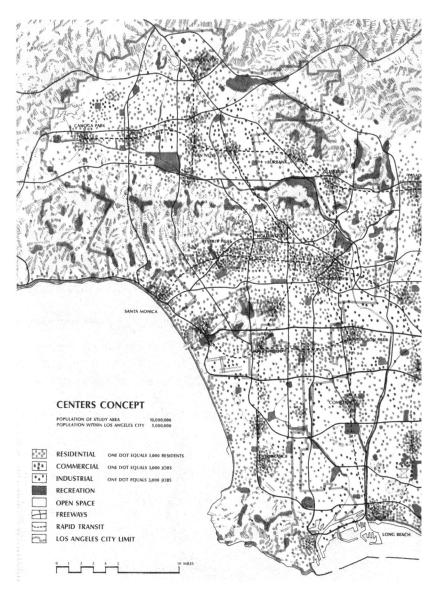

FIGURE 3.1
Proposed population distributions in Los Angeles's Centers Concept. *Source*: Los Angeles Department of City Planning 1967, 33.

FIGURE 3.2
A sectional perspective showing details of a proposed center, including a transit station, in Los Angeles's Centers Concept. *Source*: Los Angeles Department of City Planning 1970, 32.

IMPLEMENTATION

There were, perhaps predictably, significant hurdles in implementing the Centers Plan. Some of the potential problems started becoming apparent during the plan development phase. There was no institutional framework to support the plan's regional implementation. There were challenges in the city too. While the physical vision of the plan depended mainly on the duality of centers and single-family housing, single-family homeowners in neighborhoods near proposed centers opposed the centers for their potential adverse effects on traffic, congestion, and sightlines. Figure 3.3, for example, shows how planners changed their illustrations of the same vista in a single-family neighborhood during the plan's development to remove the centers' visual cues. Presumably, they were appeasing residents of single-family houses critical of neighboring towers—even though the new developments would have been some distance from their communities. To make things worse, funding for the proposed rail transit network, which was the plan's proverbial spine, did not materialize,[9] and community opposition to density, rooted in now-familiar concerns about traffic congestion and parking, increased.

Many homeowners' associations were displeased that the city was not revising its underlying zoning per the adopted General Plan. While the General Plan stipulated a land use capacity for housing 4.5 million residents, the prevailing zoning ordinance, adopted in 1946, could accommodate 10 million residents (Fulton 2001; Hamilton 1986). In 1984, the Hillside Federation asked Carlyle Hall, the cofounder of the Center for Law in the Public Interest in 1971 and a veteran of many successful environmental litigation cases, to file a lawsuit against the city for failing to adhere to state legislation requiring it to bring its zoning ordinance in conformity with the plan (Alperin 1987).[10] Before the litigation, the city had "barely completed a quarter of the downzoning" (Davis 1990, 190). In 1985, the city lost the lawsuit, which forced planners to launch a consistency program to follow the General Plan and rezone within three years (Fulton 2001). The loss of the lawsuit hastened the end of Hamilton's tenure in the planning department. As Sam Kaplan (1986), the *Los Angeles Times* architecture critic, noted, "Public planning in Los Angeles [was] at its nadir."[11]

According to Greg Morrow's (2013) analysis, even with zoning changes, the city's land designated for different land use categories remained relatively stable through the 1970s, 1980s, and 1990s, with about half of the zoned land classified for residential use. Planners designated almost three-quarters of the residentially zoned land for single-family housing. By and large, planners preserved the city's existing single-family zoning while increasing allowable density on multifamily-zoned parcels.

While accepting the political power of single-family homeowners, the city of Los Angeles's planners developed a new comprehensive plan in the mid-1990s: the Framework Element of the General Plan (Curtiss 1995; Los Angeles Department of City Planning 1995). The plan, released in 1995 and adopted in 1996 by the city council, proposed preserving single-family neighborhoods and accommodating 75 percent of future growth on 5 percent of the

FIGURE 3.3
Vignettes of single-family residential areas in the "Concepts for Los Angeles" and the "Centers Concept." *Sources*: Los Angeles Department of City Planning 1967, 61; 1970, 21.

city's land, particularly the city's underused commercial corridors as mixed-use streets (Morrow 2013).

Though the plan received praise for its dual approach, many residents of the city's single-family neighborhoods were once again unhappy with the proposal for new developments near their communities, particularly on adjacent corridors. Many of the city's more politically active single-family homeowners were accustomed to exercising a say on development beyond their tranquil lots and neighborhoods. They were ready to fight any development that even marginally changed the character of their communities. As Barbara Fine of the Hillside Federation stated in opposition to the Framework Plan, "Why are we all so upset about this? We see this as an attack on the single-family residence" (Curtiss 1995).[12]

While Los Angeles's single-family neighborhoods do not house most of the city's residents, the Hillside Federation's representative was correct in assuming that single-family homeowners' voices carry disproportionate weight in city politics.

UNRAVELING OF THE DREAM

For many years, Southern California's appetite for affordable single-family living was satisfied by expanding across its seemingly endless supply of land, enabled first by the region's excellent streetcar network and later by the highway system. Before World War II, the expanse of the Los Angeles city-region and the ease of converting land from agricultural to urban uses helped keep housing affordable. The FHA's 1939 *Annual Report*, for example, noted that "31 percent of the new homes accepted for mortgage insurance in Los Angeles were valued below $4,000. In contrast, of the largest twenty metropolitan areas in the country, only St. Louis had more than 10 percent of its FHA homes within that range" (Hise 1993, 103). In the postwar period, the region continued to urbanize through sprawl, particularly in Riverside and San Bernardino Counties to the east of Los Angeles.[13]

However, the housing supply failed to keep up with the demand owing to zoning constraints, residents' opposition to denser developments in their vicinity, environmental concerns against sprawl, and the physical limits of daily commutes and regional expansion. As existing single-family neighborhoods became mostly closed off to new development in Los Angeles County, housing production shifted to multifamily housing (figure 3.4).

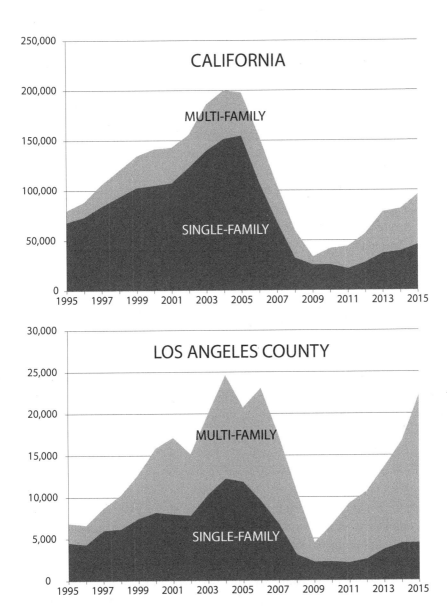

FIGURE 3.4
New construction permits by housing type, California and Los Angeles County, 1995–2015. *Source*: US Census Bureau 2021b. Graphic: Jae-Hyeon Park.

Nonetheless, developers still built single-family housing in outlying areas. In most of the state, single-family houses continued to dominate the market. As economists predict (Glaeser 2011; Glaeser and Gyourko 2003; Saiz 2010), supply constraints contributed to the high cost of housing. The city of Los Angeles and its region became one of the most expensive and unaffordable housing markets in the US. According to monthly housing price data from the Standard & Poor / Case-Shiller index, "Los Angeles's housing prices have shot up more than any other city since 2000" (Kudler 2015). The median sales price for a house in the six-county Los Angeles region crossed $680,000 in July 2021 and approached $800,000 in Los Angeles County (Khouri 2021). In comparison, the median US home price in mid-2021 was slightly over $360,000 (N. Friedman 2021).

While housing prices climbed up, average incomes in the Los Angeles region stagnated (Storper et al. 2015).[14] According to a 2015 study by the Institute for Research on Labor and Employment at the University of California, Berkeley, 567,000 residents of Los Angeles County earned the minimum wage (L. Fung 2015), and about half of these workers had children. The Los Angeles–based Economic Roundtable, a nonprofit public policy research organization, estimated that 700,000 people worked in Los Angeles County's informal economy and earned an annual wage of $12,000 in 2004 (Huerta 2021). Consequently, the proportion of household income spent on housing increased significantly. Urban planners assume that spending 30 percent of household income on housing is reasonable. According to the city of Los Angeles's 2020 data (Los Angeles Department of City Planning and Los Angeles Housing Department 2020), over half of all the households in the city were rent burdened and spent more than 30 percent of their income on housing, and almost a third were severely rent burdened and spent more than half their income on housing. Similarly, in Los Angeles County, 58.3 percent of households spent more than 30 percent on housing, and almost a third (32.8 percent) spent over half their income on housing (Joint Center for Housing Studies of Harvard University 2013). A report by the California Housing Partnership Corporation (2014) indicated that Los Angeles County was the least affordable housing market for extremely low-income renters. On average, homeowners in the Los Angeles metropolitan region spent 40 percent of their income on housing, and renters spent close to half their income (Grabar 2015).

These dire affordability conditions were typical throughout the Golden State. The situation was especially grim for renters and low-income families. A third of renters statewide spent more than half their income on rent (*Los Angeles Times* 2019). The poorest 25 percent of households were particularly precarious and spent, on average, more than two-thirds of their income on rent. In contrast, the top quartile, the majority of which consists of homeowners, were comfortable and spent only about 16 percent of their income on housing (California Legislative Analyst's Office 2015). Figure 3.5 shows household spending across the income quartiles and comparisons between California and the rest of the country.

The housing market became a source of great wealth and inequality. For homeowners, the appreciation in housing prices increased their wealth and exacerbated the disparity between owners and renters (Desmond 2016, 2017). Homeownership and the legacy of historical racist policies in housing and zoning substantially contributed to the racial wealth gap. In the US, the average Black family had only 5.04 percent of the wealth of an average white family (Kraus, Rucker, and Richeson 2017). The racial wealth gap in the

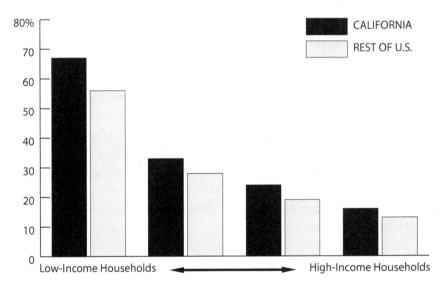

FIGURE 3.5

Median share of household income spent by income quartile on housing in California. *Source*: 2013 American Community Survey data in California Legislative Analyst's Office 2015. Graphic: Jae-Hyeon Park.

Los Angeles metropolitan area was even more extreme. Melany De La Cruz-Viesca and her colleagues (2016, 5) found that "White households in Los Angeles have a median net worth of $355,000. In comparison, Mexicans and US Blacks have a median wealth of only $3,500 and $4,000, respectively."[15]

State-level public policy played a key role in creating and maintaining the wealth inequality between owners and renters. California homeowners benefit from low property taxes owing to Proposition 13, a 1978 ballot initiative that lowered property taxes and limits how they increase. It reset the state's property taxes to 1 percent of sale value and caps annual inflation to 2 percent per year. Renters, on the other hand, have no such protection from rising housing costs. The Costa-Hawkins Rental Housing Act of 1995—the state legislation most relevant for renters—significantly restricted the ability of local governments to impose rent stabilization requirements.

The high cost of housing causes the official poverty rate to understate the real extent of poverty in California. According to the US Census Bureau's traditional measure of poverty, California's poverty rate in 2018 was 12.8 percent. However, the federal government's supplemental poverty measure, which considers local costs such as housing, sets the state's poverty rate at 18.1 percent (Fox 2019). Similarly, according to the California Poverty Measure, which was developed by the Stanford Center for Poverty and Inequality and the Public Policy Institute of California to factor in the local cost of living and safety net benefits, the state's poverty rate was 17.6 percent in 2018, and in 2019 more than a third of Californians (34.0 percent) were poor or near poor (up to one and a half times above the poverty line) (Bohn, Danielson, and Malagon 2021). Additionally, poverty disproportionately affects Californian people of color. About half the state's Latinx population and about 40 percent of its Black residents experienced or were close to experiencing poverty in 2017 per the California Poverty Measure (Mattingly et al. 2019). It is likely that the COVID-19-induced recession of 2020 pushed even more households into poverty and near poverty.

Although the residents of Los Angeles and California spent a disproportionate amount of their income on housing, it did not ensure that they got to live in their dream homes. On the contrary, many paid more and got much less. Compared with residents of other states, Californians commuted farther to work, were four times more likely to live in overcrowded housing, and had a higher incidence of homelessness (California Legislative Analyst's Office

2015). Los Angeles and Orange Counties were described as the "epicenter of overcrowded housing," with half of the top 1 percent of census tracts with the worst household overcrowding in the country (Reyes and Menezes 2014). Similarly, seven of the ten zip codes with the most overcrowding in the US were in Los Angeles County (*Los Angeles Times* 2015).

STATE GOVERNMENT INTERVENTION AND A NEW PROPERTY RIGHT FOR OWNERS

In recognition of the increasing cost of housing in California, the high share of residentially zoned land for single-family houses, and the seemingly intractable opposition to land use changes at the local level, the state government intervened in local land use regulations to increase the supply of housing, mainly through second units. In the early 1980s, it took the lead in creating and strengthening a new property right for owners of single-family-zoned lots to add extra units.

The state government's interventions in single-family zoning have been gradual and incremental. The state legislature's first intervention, Senate Bill 1160, was approved in 1981 and enacted in January 1982. Known as the "Granny Bill," it allows cities and counties to permit second units for adults aged sixty and over (Birkinshaw 1982; Kyle 2000). The following year, the state legislature approved State Senator Henry Mello's Companion Unit Act, Senate Bill 1534, to allow second units for people of all ages (Whittemore 2012c).[16] The Companion Unit Act was enacted in January 1983 and noted that "second units provide housing for family members, students, the elderly, in-home health care providers, the disabled and others, at below-market prices within existing neighborhoods. Homeowners who create second units benefit from added income, and an increased sense of security" (quoted in Goldin 2003). The state legislature subsequently approved minor amendments in 1986, 1990, and 1994 (for example, increasing the allowed size of second units to 1,200 sq. ft. or up to 30 percent of the size of the primary unit in 1990), but the law remained mostly similar to the original Companion Unit Act (Bobrowsky 2007).

Following the state's initiatives, many local governments, including the city of Los Angeles, made it possible for homeowners to receive approval for second units in single-family neighborhoods through discretionary reviews.

Most cities, however, discouraged second units in practice and granted permits for them only if homeowners met unrealistic minimum lot sizes and covered-parking requirements. Moreover, the discretionary review process for getting the necessary permits was time-consuming and daunting. Cities approved few units.

The next significant intervention from the state government was in 2002–2003. Responding to local governments' reluctance to issue permits for second units, the State of California approved Assembly Bill 1866 in 2002. The bill, which streamlined permitting processes by directing cities to create "by right" approval systems, was proposed by South Los Angeles–area assemblymember Roderick Wright. A wide range of cosponsors, including the California Association of Realtors and the California Rural Legal Assistance Foundation, supported AB 1866 (*Santa Barbara News Press* 2002). It also had ideologically diverse opponents, such as the League of California Cities, the Planning and Conservation League, and the Natural Resources Defense Council. They were critical of state intervention in local land use matters and concerned about the risk that the bill "could spur unwanted development (and blight)" (Wasserman 2002a, 2002b). Nonetheless, the bill was approved by the state legislature and took effect in July 2003. It mandated against the discretionary process and directed cities to allow second units by right, recommended lower standards for permits, and noted the following:

> It is the intent of the Legislature that any second-unit ordinances adopted by local agencies have the effect of providing for the creation of second units and that provisions in these ordinances relating to matters including unit size, parking, fees and other requirements, are not so arbitrary, excessive, or burdensome so as to unreasonably restrict the ability of homeowners to create second units in zones in which they are authorized by local ordinance. (quoted in Creswell 2003, 3)

In effect, AB 1866 mandated that cities allow all owners of single-family-zoned lots the property right to build second units by right, provided they meet their local jurisdictions' rules for ADUs.

While many, though not all, local governments started allowing second units without discretionary reviews, they maintained their effective bans by creating permitting standards that were extremely demanding and difficult to meet. (The city of Santa Cruz, discussed in chapter 6, stands out as a notable exception.) Take the example of Pasadena, a city northeast of downtown Los Angeles. In August 2004, its city council approved an ordinance allowing owners of single-family-zoned lots to build second units by right but required a minimum lot size of 15,000 sq. ft., mandated two covered parking spaces for the second unit, demanded a minimum distance of 500 ft. between houses with second units, and instituted a cap of twenty new second units per year (Bobrowsky 2007). Policy makers in the city of Los Angeles reluctantly agreed to allow second units by right but only on lots that were one and a half times the size of regular lots. They stipulated a minimum lot size of 7,500 sq. ft. and mandated that eligible lots must be "at least 50 percent larger than the minimum area required for a lot in the zone in which it is located" (City of Los Angeles 2003).

In response to local governments' attempts to comply with the letter of the law while violating its spirit, Assemblymember Darrell Steinberg (subsequently president pro tempore of the California State Senate and later mayor of Sacramento) proposed Assembly Bill 2702, which would impose maximum standards for second units, including the prohibition of covered parking requirements. Both legislative houses approved the bill in 2004. It was, however, opposed by the state chapter of the American Planning Association, California State Association of Counties, and League of California Cities for interference in local land use issues. Subsequently, Governor Arnold Schwarzenegger vetoed the bill, arguing that AB 2702 ignored infrastructure inadequacies in cities and restricted local governments and communities from making informed, place-based decisions (Antoninetti 2008; Liebig, Koenig, and Pynoos 2006).

In 2005, city of Los Angeles voters elected Antonio Villaraigosa as mayor—the first Mexican American to hold this office in 130 years. With the ongoing challenges of unaffordable housing and inadequate public transit in the city, Mayor Villaraigosa started his two-term tenure discussing the need for higher density and transportation investments (Gottlieb and Ng 2017). He suggested that the city's cherished model of living in single-family houses with big front and back yards was anachronistic in the twenty-first century. Joel Kotkin, an advocate of traditional suburban living and coeditor of *Infinite Suburbia* (Berger and Kotkin 2017), was one of the first to criticize Villaraigosa for his audacity to challenge single-family living. In a *Los Angeles Times* op-ed, "Hands Off My Yard, Mr. Mayor," Kotkin responded to Villaraigosa with a tired trope of equating density with Global South chaos:

> But what sets L.A. apart from other great cities—and what makes it so attractive—has traditionally been exactly the opposite: its pattern of dispersion and its strong attachment to the single-family home. Assault that basic form and you will turn

L.A. not into Paris but something more like an unruly, congested, dense Third World city. A Tehran, if you will, or a Mexico City. (Kotkin 2005)

Although the mayor continued to advocate for "elegant density" and was condemned as a density hawk (S. Morris 2009), he avoided openly opining on the need to reexamine the single-family house.

Spurred by a 2009 lawsuit, the city of Los Angeles's planning department initiated a public hearing process to develop a new second unit or ADU ordinance in compliance with AB 1866. It scheduled three public hearings between October and November 2009 in the neighborhoods of Hollywood, Van Nuys, and Pacoima (figure 3.6). According to the planner in charge of the hearings, they were "uneventful; neither heavily attended nor contentious" (Juarez interview 2019). The outreach attempts, however, were dismissed as misguided and inadequate and triggered a wave of overreaction and angry criticism by people like Ron Kaye, the former editor of the *Los Angeles Daily News*. Kaye claimed, "Can there be any doubt that the city is at war with the middle class, with homeowners, with ordinary people who pay most of the city's bills?" (quoted in Boudreaux 2011, 175). Kaye (2009) disapprovingly added, "For many single-family owners . . . the proposed ordinance represents an attack on the quality of life they cherish."

Similarly, in the article "Invasion of the Granny Flat" in *LA Weekly*, Los Angeles's alternative—and ostensibly progressive—newspaper, its theater critic fiercely criticized the city for considering zoning revisions to make it easier to obtain permits for second units (S. Morris 2009). He argued that instead of making it easier to obtain permits for second units, the city should follow the example of its neighboring jurisdictions like Pasadena, "resist the effort to increase granny flats," and consider banning them altogether to protect the character and openness of the city's single-family communities (S. Morris 2009) (figure 3.7). Comments from readers on the newspaper's website are not a reliable indicator of public sentiment. Still, a strong majority agreed with the newspaper's criticism and denounced the addition of second units as a decline in the quality of their single-family neighborhoods. Many commentators cautioned that liberal second unit policies would lead to an explosion of slum-like housing.

In response to the criticism, which included rebukes from Carmen Trutanich, the city attorney, and some city councilmembers, the planning department retreated and "put the development of a City ADU ordinance on hold indefinitely" (Goldberg 2009; Juarez interview 2019). In the wake of the

Accessory Dwelling Units (ADUs) **Workshops**

City of Los Angeles Department of City Planning

The City is responding to the provisions of AB 1866, Government Code §65852.150 et seq., which mandates ministerial processes for Accessory Dwelling Units (ADUs) in single family zones. An Accessory Dwelling Unit, also called a granny flat, secondary dwelling unit, elder cottage housing opportunity (ECHO), or mother-daughter residence, is an apartment that can be located within the walls of a single-family home, an addition to an existing home, or a free-standing structure on the same lot.

You are invited to attend and give us your input at one of our upcoming workshops, at the time and location that is most convenient for you.
(Note: the same information will be discussed at each.)

For more information, please contact Gabriela Juárez at (213) 978-1337 or by email at gabriela.juarez@lacity.org

Saturday, October 3, 2009
11 am – 3 pm
Yucca Community Center
6671 Yucca Street
Los Angeles, CA 90028
Please note there is only on-street parking. Carpooling and public transit are highly encouraged.

Saturday, October 17, 2009
10 am – 2 pm
Marvin Braude Constituent Service Center
6262 Van Nuys Boulevard,
Room 1B, 1st Floor
Van Nuys, CA 91401

Saturday, November 7, 2009
10 am – 2 pm
David M. Gonzales/ Pacoima Recreation Center
10943 Herrick Avenue
Arleta, CA 91331

Talleres Comunitarios para Unidades Accesorios (ADUs)

Ciudad de Los Angeles Departmento de Planificación

La Cuidad esta respondiendo a las provisiones de la ley de AB 1866, Codigo del Gobierno §65852.150 et seq., cual dicta un proceso sin consideración sujetivo para Unidades Accesorios (ADUs) en lotes zonados para familas sencillas. Una unidad accesorio, o unidad secundario o casita, es un apartamento cual puede ser localizado dentro de las paredes de una casa de familia sencilla, puede ser una agregación a la casa, o puede ser una estructura adicional en el lote.

Le invitamos que atiende y nos de su opinión en uno de nuestros próximos talleres comunitarios en la fecha y local cual es más conveniente para usted.
(Nota: la misma información será presentada en cada taller)

Para más información, póngase en contacto con Gabriela Juárez al (213) 978-1337 o por correo electrónico: gabriela.juarez@lacity.org

Sábado, 3 de octubre, 2009
11 am – 3 pm
Yucca Community Center
6671 Yucca Street
Los Angeles, CA 90028
Favor de notar que solamente hay estacionamiento en la calle. Se le sugiere usar transito público o compartir uso de vehículos.

Sábado, 17 de octubre, 2009
10 am – 2 pm
Marvin Braude Constituent Service Center
6262 Van Nuys Boulevard,
Cuarto 1B, 1o piso
Van Nuys, CA 91401

Sábado, 7 de noviembre, 2009
10 am – 2 pm
David M. Gonzales/ Pacoima Recreation Center
10943 Herrick Avenue
Arleta, CA 91331

FIGURE 3.6
Notices announcing the city of Los Angeles's ADU workshops in 2009. *Source*: Los Angeles Department of City Planning 2009.

FIGURE 3.7
LA Weekly's negative reaction to the city's ADU Workshops in an article titled "Invasion of the Granny Flat." *Source*: S. Morris 2009.

Great Recession and the accompanying budget cuts, the director of the planning department argued that her department lacked the resources to launch a time-consuming program to adequately understand the opinions of the residents of the city's single-family neighborhoods.

THE NEIGHBORHOOD PERSPECTIVE: OPPOSITION
AS WELL AS POTENTIAL SUPPORT

Although the city of Los Angeles's planning department abruptly stopped its public outreach for developing a new ADU policy, it is unclear whether community opposition to second units is consistent and uniform across all neighborhoods in this vast city. To develop a more grounded understanding of the neighborhood-level perspective, I collaborated on a research project with my colleagues at UCLA's cityLAB, which is headed by Dana Cuff (Mukhija, Cuff, and Serrano 2014). We focused on examining the different neighborhood-level concerns of ADUs, the conditions under which some residents would consider supporting second units in their neighborhoods, and the potential for changing land use policies for second units.

As a component of the research project, my students and I surveyed the Neighborhood Councils in the city of Los Angeles. In the City Charter reform of June 1999, voters approved the establishment of certified neighborhood-level local groups, or Neighborhood Councils, as elected advocates of decentralized interests to increase public participation in citywide decision-making. Scholars, however, caution that the city's Neighborhood Council system is undemocratic. It is dominated by elite homeowners who are unrepresentative of their neighborhoods (Musso et al. 2006). According to Kyu-Nahm Jun (2013), in the early 2010s, 41 percent of Neighborhood Councils' board members had a household income of over $100,000, while only 14 percent of the city's households had a similar income.

With caveats about the elite perspective of Neighborhood Councils' leaders, our survey results indicated opposition to second units in the city. Many of the survey's respondents made their hostility to transforming single-family zoning and prejudice against the occupants of second units clear. The responses, however, indicated some surprising support for second units too. The unexpected support suggests that there may have been opportunities for policy reform through public participation.

To conduct the survey, we used Survey Monkey, a web-based survey platform, and emailed the board members representing all the Neighborhood Councils in the city in July 2012.[17] At that time, there were ninety-five Neighborhood Councils. We received responses from thirty-four Neighborhood Councils for a response rate of almost 36 percent.

NEIGHBORHOOD-LEVEL CONCERNS ABOUT SECOND UNITS AND THE POTENTIAL FOR SUPPORT

The survey probed the leaders of Neighborhood Councils about their apprehensions and positive impressions of second units in an open-ended manner, and we coded their responses into common and overlapping categories. We allowed our respondents to list up to five concerns and five positive attributes of second units. Overall, they listed twice the number of concerns than positive qualities. While only three of the survey respondents did not name a single apprehension, nine of them, or over a quarter of the group, were unwilling to list any positive attributes of second units.[18] In contrast, thirteen respondents used the opportunity to note the maximum allowed five concerns or criticisms, but only two of the respondents listed five positive characteristics.

Table 3.1 shows the respondents' top and most common concerns. Unsurprisingly, the primary concern in the survey is the potential adverse effect of second units on the availability of street parking. Almost a third of

Table 3.1
Concerns about permitting second units in neighborhoods

	Top concerns		Most common concerns	
Concern (N=34)	Number of times listed	% of total	Number of respondents	% of respondents
Parking	11	32	19	56
Density and overcrowding	8	24	14	41
Infrastructure capacity	3	9	13	38
Disorder and crime	3	9	9	26
Safety of housing	2	6	11	32
Renters, low-income residents	2	6	4	12
A decline in property values	1	3	4	12
Changes to single-family character and form	1	3	4	12
None or unanswered/blank	3	9	NA	NA
Enforcement of rules	—	—	6	18
Noise	—	—	5	15
Other	—	—	2	6
Existing unpermitted units	—	—	1	3
Total	34	100		

Source: Author's Neighborhood Council survey.
Note: Some respondents listed the same concern multiple times (or they were so similar that they fall into the same coding category), but they are listed only once in the table.
NA = Not applicable

the respondents listed street parking as their top concern, and over half the respondents mentioned the availability of street parking as a concern. The city of Los Angeles's single-family homeowners, like their counterparts in other cities, can be highly parochial when it comes to street parking issues. Not only do they want convenient access to parking spaces, but they assume that they have an inherent property claim to park on the street right in front of their homes (Shoup 2005). Second units are often unwelcome because they threaten this expectation. Interestingly, only one respondent listed a decline in property values as their top concern, and only four respondents mentioned it as a concern.

The overwhelming majority of the survey respondents, nonetheless, recognized that second units have positive qualities. Table 3.2 shows the top positive attributes listed in the survey. In recognition of the changing household composition of families in the city's single-family neighborhoods, nine respondents listed housing for extended family as the most attractive quality of second units, and three respondents listed housing for elderly parents as the most attractive quality. Almost half the respondents (sixteen of thirty-four respondents) recorded this quality in their list of positive attributes. While five Neighborhood Council leaders listed rental income or higher property values as the top attribute of second units, twelve of the respondents, or over a third of the group, noted these potential benefits as an attractive attribute of second units. Almost a third of all respondents agreed that second units would expand the housing supply, and this could help address the city's affordable housing crisis. (As table 3.2

Table 3.2
Top positive attributes of allowing second units in neighborhoods

Top attribute	Number of times listed	% of total
Housing for extended family	9	26
Higher property value or rental income	5	15
Housing supply and affordability	5	15
Housing for elderly parents	3	9
A more dense and efficient way to use land	2	6
Other/unclear	1	3
None or unanswered/blank	9	26
Total	**34**	**100**

Source: Author's Neighborhood Council survey.

shows, five respondents listed this characteristic of second units as their top positive attribute.) These potentially positive qualities of second units may provide the basis for productive discussions at the neighborhood level. Illustratively, more than half of our respondents indicated a willingness to work with a team of UCLA architects, urban designers, and urban planners to explore innovative policies and designs to address the need and demand for second units in context-specific ways.

Even more encouragingly, when we asked respondents under what conditions they would support second units, a majority of them were willing to consider them if they met strict design standards or received community consent. As table 3.3 shows, over 60 percent of the respondents would consider allowing second units with strict design standards. And, almost 60

Table 3.3
Under what conditions should it be easier to build second units in single-family neighborhoods?

Condition	% Yes	Yes	No	Blank
SUs that meet strict design standards to help preserve the visual character of single-family neighborhoods	62	21	11	2
SUs on very large single-family lots	59	20	11	3
SUs on streets in which all property owners agree to allow such units	59	20	11	3
SUs that are attached to the main house	53	18	13	3
SUs on properties with large driveways for parking cars	53	18	12	4
SUs that receive a sign-off from adjacent neighbors	53	18	13	3
SUs on single-family properties adjacent to multifamily properties or commercial properties	50	17	14	3
SUs within a quarter mile of a light rail or subway stop, where residents might use public transit more frequently	44	15	14	5
SUs that are spaced far away from one another to limit their total number in the neighborhood	41	14	17	3
SUs on lots with back alleys that buffer the impact of the SUs on neighbors behind them	38	13	17	4
SUs on corner lots that provide an opportunity for parking on two streets	35	12	17	5

Source: Author's Neighborhood Council survey.
SUs = second units.

percent of them would consider supporting them if the majority of residents on the street favored the approach. Similarly, over half of them were willing to consider policies permitting second units if adjacent neighbors did not have an objection. Thus, overall there may be some potential for crafting more permissive second unit policies and changes to single-family zoning by focusing on design requirements and democratic decision-making.

While many of the responses in the survey are more encouraging than what I expected, planning departments are not always prepared to continue engaging with communities and homeowners on the question of second units. In part, this is because many homeowners are vehemently opposed to second units and determined to thwart any progress on the subject. For example, in response to the survey question about whether respondents would be willing to work with a team of UCLA planners and architects to craft a better policy for second units, one of them noted, "No No No No No No No" (Respondent #6). Another wrote, "No. UCLA needs to stop social engineering. Stick to academics" (Respondent #22). Respondent #34 similarly noted, "No; we'll work with you to find these units and have them demolished, however."

Even though the survey responses were not anonymous, many respondents were unrestrained in sharing their disapproval. In table 3.4, I share

Table 3.4
Selected comments from the Neighborhood Council survey

Respondent	Comment
#2	There is nothing inherently wrong with single-family neighborhoods. Los Angeles is not New York City, nor should it try to be.
#3	It is obvious where this is going . . . Ruining the character of neighborhoods.
#14	The more crowded with tenants, the more crime in our neighborhood. The tendency to overcrowd units is prevalent in our neighborhood and cannot be acceptable.
#20	Second Dwelling Units are slums in the making; they should never be allowed in single-family residential neighborhoods.
#21	The reason I moved here was no rentals. There are enough apartments. If someone wants to add to their property, that's cool but not to rent out.
#34	TEAR THEM [second units] DOWN

Source: Author's Neighborhood Council survey.

some of the more negative comments on the survey. These comments indicate the prejudices held against tenants and denser housing by the most extreme homeowners, who unfortunately may be the most likely to participate in planning workshops.

PERCEPTION OF THE PREVALENCE OF UNPERMITTED SECOND UNITS

In the absence of realistic land use regulations that make it viable for homeowners to receive permits for adding second units, many owners resort to building them without permits. We designed a question in the survey to find out how our respondents perceived the prevalence of unpermitted second units in their neighborhoods. Table 3.5 shows the responses and indicates that most often—nine times out of thirty-four—respondents thought that unpermitted second units were "somewhat common," or 11–15 percent of the single-family houses in their neighborhoods had an informal second unit. Additionally, nearly 45 percent of them (fifteen of thirty-four) estimated that 11 percent or more of the single-family houses in their neighborhoods had second units lacking permits ("somewhat common" and "common"). In other words, the presence of informal second units is an open secret in Los Angeles's neighborhoods.

In table 3.5, I also break down our respondents' perceptions of the prevalence of informal second units according to their positions on enforcement against unpermitted units. We asked them what should be done about existing unpermitted second units in their neighborhoods and coded their responses as supportive or not of enforcement and removal. Though the number of respondents is too small to use statistical tests, the results indicate that they are split on enforcement. Some suggested that the units needed to be demolished, others suggested that they be allowed, and still others were ambivalent about the appropriate policy response. Overall, there does not seem to be a clear and strong relationship between perceptions of how common informal second units are and interest in their enforcement and removal by the city.

CONCLUSION

The Los Angeles region was at the forefront of the dramatic reinvention of American cities and neighborhoods through single-family housing. Though single-family zoning did not start in the city of Los Angeles, it was one of the

Table 3.5
Perception of the prevalence of informal second units in neighborhoods

Perception of prevalence of informal second units

Rare (<1%)	Somewhat rare (1%–5%)	Not uncommon (5.1%–10%)	Somewhat common (10.1%–15%)	Common (>15%)	Unsure	Count	% of total	Position on enforcement
1	5	1	3	3	1	14	41	Support enforcement
1	1	3	4	2	1	12	35	Ambivalent
1	1	3	2	1	—	8	24	Against enforcement
3	7	7	9	6	2	34	100	**TOTAL**

Source: Author's Neighborhood Council survey.

first major cities to separate single-family houses from other types of housing. These single-family housing developments drove the city and region's spectacular growth in the twentieth century, particularly during the postwar boom. In the two decades after World War II, large parts of the city of Los Angeles urbanized, and over 225,000 single-family houses replaced agricultural land uses. By the early 1980s, the city overtook Chicago as the nation's second-largest city.

Local, regional, and federal policies played their part in supporting single-family living. At the national level, federal home-financing policies helped families afford the single-family houses of their dreams. Regionally, an excellent highway system enabled urbanization and dispersion. At the city level, local governments like the city of Los Angeles zoned most of their residential land for single-family housing. Scholars and residents admired the Los Angeles region for turning the conventional urban model of centralization on its head through its dispersed growth and for offering an unprecedented sense of possibility.

However, the sense of openness to new ideas disappeared as the interests of single-family housing neighborhoods coalesced and became entrenched against change and further development. Although single-family homeowners do not constitute the majority of voters, they occupy most of the residentially zoned land, their preferences and lifestyles dominate the urban culture of Southern California, and they hold disproportionate power in determining how the city of Los Angeles and its region grow. Like the FHA, which demanded homogenous neighborhoods of single-family houses to safeguard its investments, privileged single-family housing residents routinely assert their property claims to maintain the character of their communities by opposing zoning changes in and around their neighborhoods. They are driven by opposition to traffic congestion, a desire to protect views, and suspicion of changes to the social character of their neighborhoods. Some worry about a potential decline in their homes' property values. They are open about their bias against low-income renters. Though they are less explicit about their fears of neighbors from different racial and ethnic groups, it is difficult to imagine racial and ethnic prejudice playing no role in their NIMBYism.

While single-family living helped generate a particular kind of suburban aesthetic environmentalism, it is premised on sprawl and reliance on privately owned cars for transportation that has caused severe environmental problems, including greenhouse gas emissions, smog, pollution, and congestion. With sprawl and congestion becoming increasingly untenable, planners in the city of Los Angeles tried to change the region's urban development trajectory. However, they ran into both regional and local challenges. There was no meaningful institutional framework for regional collaboration and planning. At the local level, planners aimed to meet the concerns and preferences of residents by maintaining the current zoning in single-family neighborhoods while concentrating new developments in a network of centers and corridors. Many residents of single-family neighborhoods found even this deferential approach highly objectionable and opposed it for bringing new development adjacent to their homes. Their hostility helped turn a region once known for its affordable housing into one of the least affordable in the US.

Such housing challenges are not limited to the city of Los Angeles or Southern California. Single-family housing and the interests of its owners dominate statewide. In response, policy makers at the state level proposed and implemented changes to single-family zoning to accommodate more development. During the 1980s, 1990s, and 2000s, they focused on modest changes to allow second units on single-family-zoned lots. Their efforts, however, encountered strong local opposition. In the city of Los Angeles, in the early 2000s, Mayor Villaraigosa became one of the first prominent politicians to suggest a need to reinvent single-family houses. The idea ran into reflexive criticism from supporters of single-family living, and they accused the mayor of turning Los Angeles into an unruly and congested Third World city.

While the state and local governments have been reluctant to engage in deliberation and debate with homeowners, my research suggests that opposition to second units in single-family neighborhoods is neither unanimous nor absolute. The Los Angeles Neighborhood Council survey showed that some residents are likely to be more open to second units, and there may be opportunities for decentralized policies for accommodating housing density. Many single-family housing residents are concerned about parking challenges in their neighborhoods. Still, many also recognize that homeowners can benefit from extra rent and property values increases from additional units. Indeed, some homeowners have added unpermitted second units to their single-family-zoned lots.

There are significant opportunities for policy action. Planners in single-family housing cities like Los Angeles can creatively seize potential openings in public opinion for land use reform. Such institutional changes, however, will be time-consuming. There will be conflicts and disagreements. While some homeowners are open to change, many—including some of the most vocal—strongly oppose losing their single-family neighborhoods. State governments can support local governments interested in land use reforms by fostering strong institutions and frameworks of regional planning. Additionally, some of the profound affordability challenges in the state, such as households in the poorest quartile spending more than two-thirds of their income on housing, require a more direct government role in producing and subsidizing affordable housing. But without transformations, the housing supply will lag demand and homeowners are likely to address housing shortages by building informal housing.

4 THE EVERYDAY PREVALENCE OF INFORMAL SECOND UNITS

A 1987 *Los Angeles Times* story—"Substandard Housing: Garages: Immigrants in, Cars Out" (Chavez and Quinn 1987)—offered a groundbreaking but misleading perspective on how Angelenos were meeting their housing needs by converting garages of single-family houses into second units without permits. Reporters obtained the addresses of all single-family houses in the county, selected a simple random sample of five hundred single-family houses, surveyed those addresses for the presence of unpermitted garage conversions, and concluded that there were over forty-two thousand illegal garage units in the county. They estimated that more than 210,000 people were living in these garage units. The newspaper article helped focus attention on housing shortages and informal coping strategies in the region.

I build on the newspaper's reporting to examine the characteristics of unpermitted second units and the nature of informal housing in the Los Angeles region. Although the newspaper's data showed that the garage units were distributed all across the county, its narrative, as the story's title suggests, focused on the substandard and slum-like housing conditions in low-income immigrant communities. I question the criminality and stigma the newspaper's reporters associated with unpermitted housing. My research suggests that informal housing in the city of Los Angeles is more prevalent and diverse than what the reporters found.

While the 1990 census indicated that the average household size in Los Angeles County at that time was 2.96, the reporters assumed that most residents of the informal units were immigrants with large families. They used a family size of five to estimate the total number of people living in garage housing. In many ways, their biased perspective reflects the conventional wisdom on informal economic activities, particularly informal housing, and its inaccurate association with the Global South and its immigrants in the Global North. The story fed into many white Southern California residents' racial prejudices and anxieties about the growing number of Latinx and Asian immigrants in the region. It came in the wake of President Ronald Reagan's Immigration Reform and Control Act of 1986, which made it illegal to knowingly hire undocumented immigrants but provided a pathway to amnesty and legalization for some based on payment of fines, back taxes due, and the admission of guilt.[1] The practice of associating informality with disadvantaged and immigrant groups is common in academic literature too. But the popular association of informal housing only with immigrants and low-income and disadvantaged households is flawed since unpermitted second units are common throughout the Los Angeles city and region.

The *Los Angeles Times* story and its title reflect the car-centric culture in single-family housing communities and the heightened fears of street parking congestion in the region. As I discussed in the previous chapter, converted garages are particularly frowned upon as they may both remove off-street parking and add additional residents with cars that require on-street parking (Brown, Mukhija, and Shoup 2020). The news story implied that most unpermitted housing in the region's single-family neighborhoods is through garage conversions. These underlying assumptions about the typology or form and nature of informal housing are incorrect too.

I find that unpermitted second units are common in both wealthy and poor neighborhoods throughout Los Angeles. Their widespread prevalence suggests that homeowners find them both necessary and viable. Informal housing is embedded in the economic context as well as the local spatial, social, and institutional conditions. Owing to its market-driven character and embedded nature, its conditions are varied and uneven. Informal housing has disparate impacts on households with different economic resources. It is easy to admire the ingenuity and resourcefulness of disadvantaged families using informal housing to survive and, at times, prosper. Consequently, many activists and scholars suggest a hands-off approach to unregulated economic activities. Nonetheless, unpermitted housing often reproduces the advantages and privileges of the wealthy and adds to the disadvantages and plight of the poor. This housing requires recognition and acknowledgment, along with deliberate and thoughtful policy responses.

INFORMAL ECONOMIC ACTIVITIES: A BRIEF LITERATURE REVIEW

Academic literature explaining informal economic activities has grown richer and more sophisticated over time. It has advanced from a narrow dual perspective of the formal and informal sectors as separate economic realms to a more integrated view based on linkages and overlaps between formal and informal economic activities. While popular opinion typically associates informality with the Global South, there is growing scholarship on informal economic activities in the US and the Global North. Although the Global North literature still focuses mostly on immigrants from the Global South, it is slowly changing.

FROM THE INFORMAL SECTOR TO THE INFORMAL ECONOMY

The idea of the informal sector, as introduced by British economic development anthropologist Keith Hart (1973; International Labour Organization 1972), is built on the dual-sector model of the economy explained by Nobel Prize winner W. Arthur Lewis (1954). In the dual-sector model, scholars saw the economy divided between modern and traditional sectors. The modern or advanced sector consisted of industries where workers were paid wages. The traditional or nonwage sector represented subsistence employment in agricultural work. The pathway to economic progress, according to conventional wisdom, involved transitioning employment from the traditional agriculture sector to the modern capitalist manufacturing sector (Averitt 1968; W. Lewis 1954; Rostow 1960). To encourage economic progress and growth in manufacturing, many countries adopted import substitution policies with high tariffs to protect and develop local industries. This protectionist approach became accepted industrial policy, particularly in countries regarded as "underdeveloped" (i.e., where more than half the male labor force worked in agriculture) (Bairoch 1973; Moser 1978).

Through his fieldwork in Ghana during the 1960s, Hart found extensive urban self-employment in the informal sector, which he distinguished from regular wage earning in the formal sector. As in the dualist model of traditional and modern sectors, he contrasted the informal sector with the firm-centered formal sector, which he described as rational, planned, organized, and regulated. Unlike most dual-sector scholars, Hart was optimistic about the creativity, enterprise, and potential for efficiency in the informal sector's unregulated economic activities. He saw the possibility of higher productivity in the informal sector, noting that it provided the economically disadvantaged with essential opportunities for earning a livelihood necessary for their survival, and observed that many workers in the formal sector supplemented their wage employment with additional informal sector work. Pragmatically, Hart questioned the feasibility of shifting all employment from the informal to the formal sector. He recognized that countries in the Global South lacked the institutional capacity to monitor informal economic activities adequately and that the sector was too big to be easily formalized.

As scholars found more evidence of extensive small-scale manufacturing work in the urban informal sector (Moser 1978; Peattie 1982), informal employment opportunities helped explain the puzzle of an ongoing migration to cities in the apparent absence of growth in industrial employment. Their work built on the Todaro model (Todaro 1969) and related scholarship by John Harris and Michael Todaro (1970). Harris and Todaro argued that rural to urban migration in the context of inadequate and declining opportunities in villages was more likely dependent on the expectation of finding better jobs in cities rather than the existence of enough jobs. The growing understanding of the scope of the informal sector suggested that urban areas in the Global South had more jobs and opportunities than the official records indicated, and that they played a significant role in sustaining and encouraging rural-urban migration. Subsequently, the concept of the informal sector moved beyond labor markets and economic development to explain urban development, particularly land and housing markets, in the Global South (Peattie 1987). While the Global South did not have enough affordable housing, it was likely that migrants expected that they would find better living conditions in cities and were sustained by informal housing.

Contemporaneously, Patricia Ferman and Louis Ferman (1973) found similar unmeasured and unmonitored economic activities in inner-city neighborhoods in the US, which they called the "irregular economy." While international development scholars identified economic explanations for the informal sector, the Fermans focused on racial discrimination. They argued that in addition to economic conditions, racism was the structural reason for the irregular economy in US cities. They pointed out that inner-city residents were routinely denied access to typical services provided by electricians, plumbers, taxi drivers, and others, as well as professional licenses to offer such services because of their race. Consequently, residents of inner cities had to participate in the irregular economy as consumers and suppliers. Furthermore, they noted that while the disadvantaged participated in the irregular economy because of the lack of choices available to them, the irregular economy provided additional options to the affluent. While the International Labour Organization focused on unions and labor organizing as an avenue for increasing formal economic activities and wage-based employment, the Fermans saw unions and their institutional interest in limiting the number of licensed professionals, as well as their often racist views, as part of the problem.[2]

As the scope of scholarship expanded and the informal sector concept became more widely used, scholars questioned the underlying dualistic model (Bromley 1978; Rakowski 1994). The extensive scale of economic activities suggested that the informal sector and the formal sector were linked (Moser 1978). It became widely accepted that informal economic activities have complex linkages with formal economic activities, are integrated into the larger economy, and represent a continuum of economic activities, which are often overlapping (Portes, Castells, and Benton 1989; Portes and Sassen-Koob 1987; Sanyal 1988).

Most informal economic activities are market-based exchanges (Angel et al. 1983; Belk, Sherry, and Wallendorf 1988; Gilbert and Ward 1985) that overlap with formal economic activities. In the case of informal housing development, some transactions are informal, while others might be formal. Informal activities frequently use the institutional arrangements of the formal economy. For example, research from the Global South shows how developers of informal settlements, as well as home buyers, employ and rely on formal legal systems, including land registries and property records, to manage informality (Razzaz 1992; 1993; Santos 1977; Tian 2008).

Social relations and networks are crucial in sustaining informality. Hart (1973) noted the importance of ethnic networks in Ghana's informal economy. Other scholars described the significance of cultural ties (Lomnitz 1988). In the absence of formal arrangements and institutions of enforcement, social and interpersonal relations become crucial for sustaining trust in informal exchanges (Granovetter 1985; Powell 1990).

As a consequence of the overlaps and linkages, it is difficult to clearly distinguish and demarcate the informal economy from the formal economy. Scholars have highlighted the fuzziness of informality and the difficulty in defining it narrowly and robustly (Peattie 1987). Some argue that the use of the word "informal" continues to risk the perpetuation of dualist or binary interpretations and their associated stereotypes (Varley 2013). Nonetheless, informality as a concept provides significance and standing to a range of economic activities that are often ignored in conventional accounts but are deeply embedded and entangled in the larger economy. Consequently, the broader term "informal economy" has become more common (Peattie 1987; Portes, Castells, and Benton 1989). As I noted in chapter 1, scholars have, for the most part, settled on a working definition of informal activities as unregulated but licit activities (Feige 1990; Portes, Castells, and Benton 1989).[3]

BEYOND THE GLOBAL SOUTH: INFORMAL HOUSING IN THE US

Most scholarship and research on the informal economy focuses on the Global South, where informality is increasingly regarded as the norm (OECD 2009; Roy 2009b).[4] Attention on informality in the Global North has been growing, though, and informality is seen as an outcome of increased globalization, trade, and economic linkages between the North and the South, as well as increased immigration from developing countries to rich nations. Scholars, for example, document the role of informal workers in the Global South linked to the Global North through international supply chains (Carr, Chen, and Tate 2000; Mies 1982). Saskia Sassen (1991, 1997) argued that deregulation and other market-oriented neoliberal changes in the political economy of Western economies, including massive cuts in traditional social safety nets, are driving the growth of the informal economy in the Global North. Other researchers in the Global North documented the impact of globalization and immigration on labor markets in the US (Bernhardt et al. 2008; Burnham and Theodore 2012; Valenzuela 2003; Valenzuela et al. 2006). The literature has grown from the increased scholarly emphasis on the presence and relevance of informal economic activities in the lives of immigrant and marginalized groups (Gowan 2009; Hondagneu-Sotelo 2001; A. Morales 2010; Mukhija and Mason 2015; Mukhija and Monkkonen 2007; Venkatesh 2006; Ward 1999).

The conventional wisdom in the US is to consider informal housing as something that happened in the past or something that is limited to immigrants from the Global South.[5] Becky Nicolaides (2002), for example, discussed the commonness of self-managed and self-built housing in the Los Angeles region's working-class suburbs before World War II. Similarly, Richard Harris (1994) noted that a substantial part of Chicago was built informally before the Great Depression (1929–1939). Harris (1996) also pointed out that a significant portion of Toronto's prewar suburbs were unregulated settlements with self-help housing, which he argued was typical of North American suburban history. Marilynn Johnson (1993, 95) focused on the informal housing in communities of color in prewar Oakland, noting that "without credit and without building permits, people did the best they could."

Other scholars have written about prewar immigrants, including Mexican laborers in self-built housing courts in Los Angeles (Cuff 2000) and Polish workers in incrementally built and rented housing in Milwaukee at the turn of the century (Hubka and Kenny 2000). More contemporary accounts of informal housing in the US focus on immigrants too. Sarah Mahler (1995), for example, in *American Dreaming: Immigrant Life on the Margins*, described the renting and subletting of unpermitted apartments, owned mostly by white homeowners, to Salvadorian and Latin American immigrants in a Long Island suburb of Manhattan as the *encargado* industry. Wendy Cheng (2013), in *The Changs Next Door to the Díazes: Remapping Race in Suburban California*, focused on Latinx and Asian Americans in the San Gabriel Valley, east of the city of Los Angeles. She noted how they actively shaped their everyday environment through their unpermitted garage apartments and use of home spaces as workspaces. Similarly, Stephen Fan (2014), in *SubUrbanisms: Casino Urbanization, Chinatowns, and the Contested American Landscape*, carefully documented how immigrant Chinese workers who work at the Mohegan Sun Casino informally adapt their single-family houses in Montville, Connecticut, as multifamily and shared housing.

Peter Ward's (1999) seminal scholarship on unserviced or poorly serviced subdivisions in Texas showed that developers legally built these settlements in the absence of regulations. His research demonstrated that such communities were not limited to Mexican American residents or the border areas of the state (Ward and Carew 2001). Nonetheless, the official name of such settlements as *colonias* in US public policy wrongly suggests that they have an association with Mexico and Mexican immigrants (Mukhija and Monkkonen 2007). With the adoption of new infrastructure regulations in Texas in 1995, its *colonias* were replaced by "model subdivisions," which had basic services but also included unregulated housing built over time through self-help (Durst and Ward 2016). Thus, as Noah Durst and Peter Ward (2016) noted, informal housing in the model subdivisions is interwoven with formal housing. Similarly, Jake Wegmann (2015) found that informal units in

Los Angeles County's immigrant communities sometimes had partial permits and were spatially entwined with formal housing.

The growth of new urban design scholarship in the US suggests informality is relevant beyond immigrants and disadvantaged groups. Proponents of do-it-yourself and tactical urbanism see the possibility of richer designs, greater flexibility, autonomy, and civic-mindedness through citizen urban designers (Bishop and Williams 2012; Campo 2013; Franck and Paxson 2007; Franck and Stevens 2007). Their work builds on the insights and advocacy of "everyday urbanism" scholars who focus on the possible transformative role of immigrants and other traditionally marginalized groups in reinventing US cities through bottom-up placemaking practices (Chase, Crawford, and Kaliski 2008; Crawford 2008). The predominant focus of the Global North informality literature, nonetheless, is on the employment and housing activities of poor and near-poor immigrant groups. Progressive scholars interested in drawing attention to urban poverty in the Global North continue to emphasize the association between informality and disadvantaged immigrants from the Global South (Devlin 2011, 2018; Lemon 2019).

Scholars argue that a key characteristic of informal housing in the US is that it is hidden, and consequently the lack of public awareness and robust data on its magnitude is responsible for the lack of policy attention (Durst and Wegmann 2017; Wegmann and Mawhorter 2017). However, as the Neighborhood Council survey in chapter 3 and numerous reports in newspapers, including the *New York Times* (A. Brooks 1979; Geist 1981) and the *Los Angeles Times* (Chavez and Quinn 1987), indicate, while informal housing *is* hidden and less visible in the US, the lack of policy attention is not because policy makers are unaware of informal housing. Public awareness of informal housing seems to be well ahead of the academic literature. To illustrate, a year after the *Los Angeles Times*'s reporting of garage conversions, the city of Los Angeles's Blue Ribbon Committee for Affordable Housing noted the following:

> For the most part, residents at the lower-tier of the housing market have been making life-style adjustments that have kept the housing problem more or less hidden from view.... These life-style adjustments or coping mechanisms include doubling up, living in illegal units, families occupying SRO (single residence occupancy) hotels, endurance of substandard conditions, and payment of large proportion of income for housing. (quoted in Mathews 1988)

UNPERMITTED SECOND UNITS IN LOS ANGELES: PREVALENCE, DISTRIBUTION, AND TYPOLOGY

The *Los Angeles Times's* reporters visited each of the five hundred addresses in their sample to visually inspect the houses and, if possible, interview the residents (Chavez and Quinn 1987). They found sixteen houses, or 3.2 percent of the addresses in their sample, had an occupied garage, which extrapolates to over forty-two thousand garage conversions in the county.[6] Even though the reporters found evidence of converted garages across the county, they concluded that "garage people" were mostly low-income immigrants. They noted that several of the converted garages did not have proper electrical connections or plumbing, but it is unclear how many of the sixteen conversions were accessible to them. Nonetheless, the reporters decided they were dealing with "slums" and warned of severe public health concerns owing to outbreaks of "intestinal ailments such as salmonella and shigella." Their emphasis on converted garages is questionable too. It assumes that the dominant strategy for supplying informal housing is through garage conversions. The malleability of single-family houses and the several options they offer for expansion and subdivision (Moudon and Sprague 1982) make it likely that there are many other forms of informal second units on single-family lots.

While the newspaper's reporting provides a useful point of departure, it does not adequately explain how prevalent informal housing is, who lives in it, or what form it takes in the Los Angeles region. I add more complexity to the news report's portrait of informal housing, particularly its prevalence, distribution, and typology in the city of Los Angeles, by examining publicly available real estate sales listings for clues. I analyzed data from the spring of 2012, which precedes the significant local and state efforts to reform second unit regulations in the mid to late 2010s. Because it became easier to build permitted second units, the geography of informal housing in the city of Los Angeles has likely changed since then.

INFORMAL SECOND UNITS IN PUBLIC REAL ESTATE LISTINGS

With the help of my research team, I analyzed publicly available real estate sales listings from Redfin, one of the leading web-based real estate brokerages. I assumed that many sellers with unpermitted second units are likely to acknowledge them in their listings because they expect to sell their homes at a higher price.[7]

My research team developed a sample of single-family houses for sale in the city of Los Angeles in May 2012 from Redfin's public data.[8] The data included sales descriptions or listings from the Multiple Listings Service and public property records from the county assessor's office. We found 5,609 single-family houses for sale in the city. From the initial sample we excluded all the homes on multifamily-zoned lots, as well as properties under foreclosure or in short sale because their listings often did not include descriptions or photographs. These exclusions reduced the sample size to 3,113 single-family houses on single-family-zoned lots. We searched the listings for clues indicating the presence of informal second units in the property descriptions and combed for corroborating evidence in the photographs. We scrutinized discrepancies between the advertised size of the house and its recorded size in the assessor's database. We looked for potentially revelatory keywords in the listings, including rental, income, accessory, granny, mother-in-law, second unit, guest home, quarters, kitchenette, back house, studio, converted, private entrance, permit, verify, and detached. Figure 4.1 presents a word

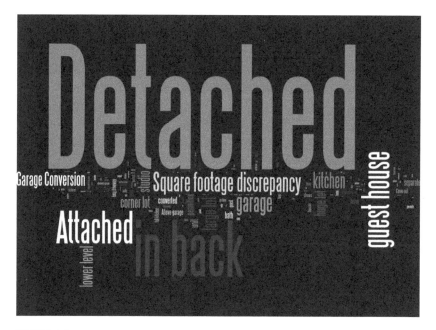

FIGURE 4.1
Word cloud of clues of informal second units in real estate listings. Graphic: Erin Coleman.

cloud of the second unit clues and their frequency in the listings from the sample.

Listings often merely hinted at the presence of second units by mentioning the possibility of additional rental income. Sometimes, listings explicitly noted the presence of a converted garage or an unpermitted unit and even included photographs of the units. Some real estate brokers recommend against explicit photographs or references to informal second units and suggest using euphemisms in the listings (Campbell interview 2013). Frequently, sellers acknowledged that they had a second unit but noted that buyers needed to verify whether they were permitted. Subsequently, I learned that sellers in California are required to disclose second units without permits or other unpermitted construction to prospective buyers in their transfer disclosure statement before any sale can be finalized (Agar interview 2014a).

It is unclear what proportion of sellers with informal units will disclose them in their listings. Some sellers might worry about being caught. Others may be concerned that second units can reduce their potential sales prices.[9] We took a conservative approach to identify informal second units in the sample. We did not include unpermitted workspaces, playrooms, or guesthouses (which, according to the city's planning regulations, are formally known as "Accessory Living Quarters" and could have toilets but not kitchens). Many of them, however, can easily convert to second units and may have served as such. Besides, there are ad hoc garage conversions and other temporary second units that are unlikely to be mentioned in real estate listings.

It is challenging to address this inherent methodological weakness of some sellers not disclosing their unpermitted second units. Previous estimates of unapproved units in San Francisco suggest a crude strategy. In the 1980s and 1990s, planners in San Francisco's planning department tried to estimate the scale of informal housing in the city both by analyzing real estate sales records and by conducting partial field surveys. They found about twice the number of informal units through their fieldwork than from the sales data (SPUR 2001).[10] Citywide fieldwork is likely more accurate in revealing informal housing as not all owners will disclose their unpermitted units in listings. As in San Francisco, it may be that any estimate of informal housing from the real estate listings in Los Angeles reveals only about half the total informal units.

PREVALENCE, SPATIAL DISTRIBUTION, AND TYPOLOGY

Prevalence and Distribution: As table 4.1 shows, we identified 168 cases in the sample of 3,113 single-family houses on single-family-zoned lots that appeared to include an informal second unit. One hundred sixty-eight cases translates to about 5.4 percent of homes. According to our analysis of data from the Los Angeles county assessor's records, there were over 462,000 single-family houses on lots zoned for single-family housing in the city of Los Angeles. My estimate of 5.4 percent extrapolates to almost 25,000 single-family houses in the city where owners have made significant investments in permanent construction to add unpermitted second units. Following San Francisco's experience, if I double the estimate from 5.4 percent to 10.8 percent, there were probably close to 50,000 informal second units with single-family houses on lots zoned for single-family use.[11]

Table 4.1 shows our analysis of the distribution of informal housing in the city too. To analyze the spatial distribution, we used the city's seven area planning commissions (APCs) as our unit of analysis (figure 4.2). Owing to the city's size, its planning department divided Los Angeles into seven geographical divisions for easier management. While the coastal access of West Los Angeles makes it the most expensive APC in the city, South Los Angeles (previously South Central Los Angeles) has some of the least resourced

Table 4.1
Informal second units and their distribution in the city of Los Angeles

Area Planning Commission (APC)	Number of single-family houses	Number for sale	Median house list price	Unpermitted and likely unpermitted second units in listings	Proportion for sale with unpermitted second units (%)
Central	31,941	434	$1,117,000	32	7.4
East Los Angeles	42,465	258	$420,000	18	7.0
Harbor	22,973	82	$345,200	3	3.7
North Valley	117,012	450	$424,450	15	3.3
South Los Angeles	64,675	551	$202,250	21	3.8
South Valley	119,955	726	$627,250	47	6.5
West Los Angeles	63,623	612	$1,722,500	32	5.2
Totals	462,644	3,113	$879,000	168	5.4

Sources: Author's research of for-sale listings in the spring of 2012 and Los Angeles county assessor's records, 2012.

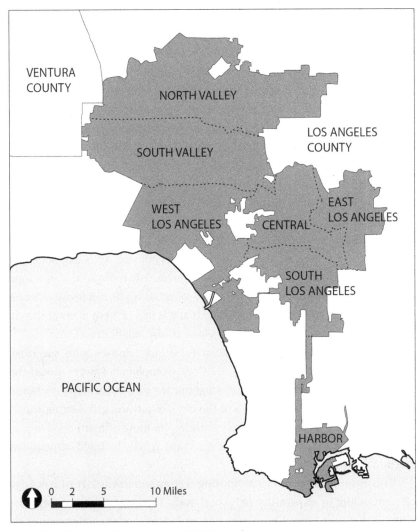

FIGURE 4.2
The seven APCs of the city of Los Angeles. Graphic: Erin Coleman.

neighborhoods of the city. We used the median home list price from our sample as a proxy of each APC's wealth and affluence or lack thereof. (Since we only looked at single-family houses and deleted properties under foreclosure as well as in short sale, the median list prices in our sample for the city and each of its APCs are higher than typical). As table 4.1 shows, there is significant variation in wealth across the seven areas. According to the median list price, the West Los Angeles APC is the wealthiest area, with almost twice the city's median list price, and the South Los Angeles APC, with less than a quarter of the city's median list price, is the least affluent. While informal second units are prevalent all over the city, there does not appear to be a correlation between their distribution and wealth or poverty at the APC level. The data suggest that unpermitted second units are most prevalent in the Central, East Los Angeles, and South Valley APCs, but there is no association with their home prices. It is possible that less affluent APCs like South Los Angeles, Harbor, and North Valley have significantly more ad hoc or temporary informal housing that the real estate sales listings do not reveal. There is, nonetheless, no evidence in these data that the less affluent areas of the city have more informal housing than their wealthier neighbors.

Andrew Baker (interview 2013), a real estate attorney who specializes in second units and is known as the Code Compliance Lawyer, noted that unpermitted units are pervasive throughout the city, particularly on houses with bigger lots. While residents of the city's disadvantaged neighborhoods may have more need for informal housing, its more affluent residents are likely to have the means—and the backyard space—to build unpermitted second units.

The upshot is that informal housing is common in the city of Los Angeles, including in its wealthy neighborhoods. The city is not an exceptional case. When I broadened my analysis to include real estate listings across the whole county of Los Angeles, I found informal housing even more prevalent. As in the city of Los Angeles, there was no spatial association between the presence of informal housing and household incomes. I share the results in the appendix. I also estimated the likely scale of informality in the country's top metropolitan areas from US Census data with colleagues (Brown, Mukhija, and Shoup 2018, 2020). Again, informal housing is significantly pervasive throughout the US. I summarize the results in the appendix as well.

Typology: Although the *Los Angeles Times* reporters focused on converted garages, my team's analysis of the data from the real estate listings suggests a very different picture. By examining the descriptions and photographs of the second units in the listings, as well as satellite photographs of the addresses from Google Maps, we identified five common spatial strategies for adding second units (figure 4.3; table 4.2). As table 4.2 shows, garage conversions account for less than a tenth of the informal second units. Additions to garages, including construction above garages, account for a little more than a tenth of the units. Detached backyard units, in contrast, are the most common typology, accounting for more than half of the unpermitted second units.[12]

Backyard units might be more prevalent because homeowners can conceal them easily from the street views of neighbors and passersby. Besides, backyards likely provide convenient space for adding a unit. Older one-car garages are too small for conversion, and many homeowners want to maintain their garages for parking cars or storage.[13] In addition to searching for unpermitted second units, we looked for permitted and legal nonconforming second units in the real estate listings. (Legal nonconforming uses are land uses that predate existing zoning requirements and are accorded legal status even though they do not conform to prevailing zoning requirements.) We identified forty-six formal units in the data (table 4.2). As with informal second units, detached construction accounts for half of the total units, further highlighting the dominance of this typology of second unit. Garage conversions and additions to garages account for about one-fifth of the formal second units.

We also examined the typology of the lots that have single-family houses with second units to see if any physical characteristics make it easier and more likely for homeowners to build second units (table 4.3). The results for both formal and informal second units are strikingly similar. Most of the houses in the sample that had second units have long driveways, which makes it easier for residents to park their cars and serves as a good proxy for the size of the lot. The median lot size of houses with second units was 7,200 sq. ft., much larger than the city's standard lot size of 5,000 sq. ft. Thus, homeowners with larger lots, who are probably more affluent, are more likely to have second units.

The commonness of second units without permits raises the question of code enforcement by public agencies.

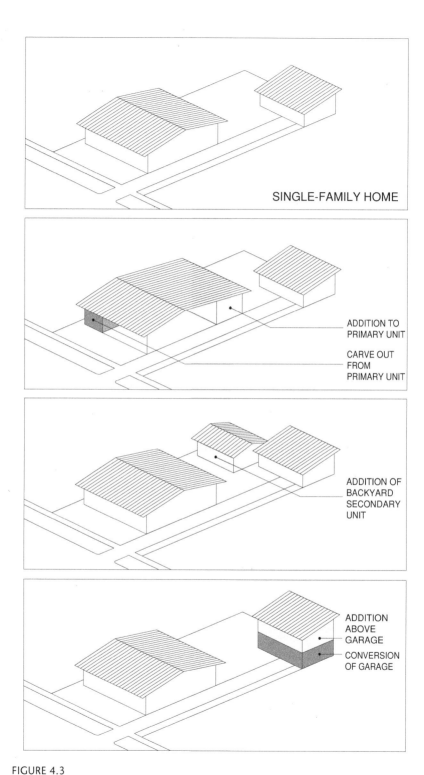

FIGURE 4.3

Schematic drawings of the most typical configurations of second units on single-family lots. Graphic: Jae-Hyeon Park.

Table 4.2
Typology of unpermitted and permitted second units in the city of Los Angeles

Category	Garage conversions	Garage additions	Main unit additions	Main unit carve-out	Detached construction	Other	Total
Informal second units (1)	15	18	23	7	97	8	168
Percentage of informal	**8.9%**	**10.7%**	**13.7%**	**4.2%**	**57.7%**	**4.8%**	**100%**
Formal second units (2)	3	6	12	2	23	0	46
Percentage of formal	**6.5%**	**13.0%**	**26.1%**	**4.4%**	**50.0%**	**0%**	**100%**
Total second units (1+2)	18	24	35	9	120	8	214
Percentage of total	**8.4%**	**11.2%**	**16.4%**	**4.2%**	**56.0%**	**3.7%**	**100%**

Source: Author's research of for-sale listings in the spring of 2012.

Table 4.3
Typology of single-family-zoned lots with second units in the city of Los Angeles

Type	Total	Corner lot Yes	Corner lot No	Back or side alley Yes	Back or side alley No	Long driveway Yes	Long driveway No	Unclear
Informal second units (1)	168	27	141	22	146	103	60	5
Percentage of informal	100%	16%	84%	13%	87%	61%	36%	3%
Formal second units (2)	46	7	39	11	35	32	13	1
Percentage of formal	100%	15%	85%	24%	76%	70%	28%	2%
Total second units (1+2)	214	34	180	33	181	135	73	6
Percentage of total	100%	16%	84%	15%	85%	63%	34%	3%

Source: Author's research of for-sale listings in the spring of 2012.
Note: I characterize driveways longer than the parking length of three vehicles, or approximately 50 ft., as long.

THE SOCIAL ENFORCEMENT OF REGULATIONS: LADBS COMPLAINTS DATA

To examine how neighbors and the city respond to informal second units, I analyze complaint data from the Los Angeles Department of Building and Safety (LADBS). Instead of actively looking for unpermitted second units, LADBS relies on complaints from neighbors. Complaints can be filed online or by phone. Complainants choose from forty codes to indicate their concerns. LADBS's Customer Service Request (CSR) classification includes codes for maintenance, outdoor storage, graffiti, unpermitted businesses, parking, garage conversions, and illegal land uses in single-family zones. The LADBS's complaint data sets, which we accessed through a public records request, exclude the identity of the complainant but provide information about the complaint and the city's follow-up action at the address level. For our research on informal second units, the most relevant CSR codes are GARCV, "garage converted to dwelling or use other than parking," and ILUSE, "building or property converted to other use," which covers the conversion of a single-family residence to two-family use. To allow for comparison with the real estate listings data from 2012, I obtained complaints data for the entire city for 2011, and my research team analyzed complaints coded as GARCV and ILUSE across the seven APCs.[14]

GARAGE CONVERSION AND ILLEGAL USE COMPLAINTS

According to the *Los Angeles Times*'s reporting, the city receives 2,500–3,000 complaints annually about unpermitted conversions of garages and commercial buildings to housing (Reyes and Logan 2014), almost half of which are for garage conversions (Brandt and Gittelsohn 2014). In 2011, there were around 1,300 GARCV and 900 ILUSE complaints, and for twenty-six addresses, there were both GARCV and ILUSE complaints. In total, there were 2,175 single-family addresses with complaints (table 4.4). Given the high number of informal housing units in the city, these numbers suggest that for an individual homeowner, the likelihood of a complaint against their unpermitted housing is low. Under certain conditions, neighbors accept informal housing. Table 4.4 shows that building inspectors found informal housing units in about a third of the addresses with complaints (753 of 2,175) and recorded them as violations. It is likely that in some cases, homeowners abated or removed their informal second units after receiving a complaint notice and before the building inspectors visited them.

While the real estate listings data did not reveal a relationship between less affluent parts of the city and the prevalence of more informal housing, the complaints data suggest a different geography of informality. West Los Angeles and Central APCs, the two most affluent areas, each account for about a fifth of the informal second units in the sales data for the city—32 of 168 (table 4.1), or 19 percent (last column of table 4.4)—but they have significantly fewer complaints and violations (columns 6 and 7 in table 4.4). In contrast, in the South Los Angeles APC (where housing prices are the lowest), which has fewer informal second units as per the real estate listings—21 of 168 (table 4.1), or 12.5 percent (last column of table 4.4)—there are more complaints as well as violations (columns 6 and 7 in table 4.4). This may be because the less affluent owners in South Los Angeles have fewer resources to invest in informal second units, and the poor quality of housing draws more complaints. Moreover, homeowners in neighborhoods with more complaints are likely wary about investing in their informal units, which results in their poor quality and further increases the likelihood of complaints.

It is possible that less affluent owners are more likely to convert their garages instead of building backyard units, and converted garages draw more ire and complaints. As the Neighborhood Council survey reported in chapter 3 showed (table 3.1), most neighbors are concerned about second units' adverse effect on the availability of street parking. Tables 4.5 and 4.6

Table 4.4

Complaints and likely informal second units in 2011 GARCV and ILUSE complaints to LADBS, and comparison with informal units in sales listings

APC	Number of single-family houses	Number of single-family houses with complaints	Violations and likely informal second units in complaints	Percentage of city's single-family houses	Percentage of city's single-family houses with complaints	Percentage of city's likely informal units in complaints (violations)	Percentage of city's likely informal units in sales listings
Central	31,941	220	42	6.9%	10.1%	5.6%	19.0%
East Los Angeles	42,465	247	55	9.2%	11.4%	7.3%	10.7%
Harbor	22,973	93	35	5.0%	4.3%	4.7%	1.8%
North Valley	117,012	564	271	25.3%	25.9%	36.0%	8.9%
South Los Angeles	64,675	569	220	14.0%	26.2%	29.2%	12.5%
South Valley	119,955	346	105	25.9%	15.9%	13.9%	28.0%
West Los Angeles	63,623	136	25	13.8%	6.3%	3.3%	19.0%
Total	**462,644**	**2,175**	**753**	**100%**	**100%**	**100%**	**100%**

Sources: LADBS data on ILUSE and GARCV complaints in 2011; author's research of for-sale listings in the spring of 2012.
Note: When the addresses in the GARCV and ILUSE data sets overlapped, we removed the duplicates.

Table 4.5
Typology of second units in GARCV and ILUSE complaints to LADBS in 2011

APC	Garage conversions	Garage additions	Main unit additions	Main unit carve-outs	Detached construction	Trailer	Other or unclear	Total
Central	22	0	1	2	0	0	17	**42**
East Los Angeles	42	0	1	6	1	0	5	**55**
Harbor	31	0	0	0	0	0	4	**35**
North Valley	239	0	4	5	1	3	19	**271**
South Los Angeles	196	0	3	4	1	1	15	**220**
South Valley	93	0	3	1	0	0	8	**105**
West Los Angeles	20	0	2	0	0	0	3	**25**
Total 2011	**643**	**0**	**14**	**18**	**3**	**4**	**71**	**753**

Source: LADBS data on ILUSE and GARCV complaints in 2011.
Note: When the addresses in the ILUSE and GARCV data sets overlapped, we removed the duplicates. We coded all the unpermitted units identified in the GARCV data as garage conversions, which may inflate the number of conversions in these results.

Table 4.6
Typology of second units in ILUSE complaints to LADBS in 2011

APC	Garage conversions	Garage additions	Main unit additions	Main unit carve-outs	Detached construction	Trailer	Other or unclear	Total
Central	2	0	1	2	0	0	17	22
East Los Angeles	7	0	1	6	1	0	5	20
Harbor	2	0	0	0	0	0	4	6
North Valley	18	0	4	5	1	3	19	50
South Los Angeles	11	0	3	4	1	1	15	35
South Valley	9	0	3	1	0	0	8	21
West Los Angeles	3	0	2	0	0	0	3	8
Total 2011	**52**	**0**	**14**	**18**	**3**	**4**	**71**	**162**

Source: LADBS data on ILUSE complaints in 2011.

show the results of our analysis of the typology of informal second units in the complaints. The analysis suggests that Angelenos are more likely to complain about converted garages than any other typology of informal second units. This may be due to the visibility of garages as well as the region's car-centric culture: residents prize convenient street parking and disapprove of neighbors converting garages, losing off-street parking, and parking multiple cars on the street.

Table 4.5 includes addresses with either GARCV or ILUSE complaints in 2011. In contrast to the findings from the real estate listings, the LADBS data suggest that garage conversions are more common and are more likely to trigger complaints. Table 4.6 shows only ILUSE complaints. The results are stark. Even though LADBS offers a separate code for complaints about converted garages, the most common complaints about second units in the ILUSE category are about garage conversions. We were unable to categorize the typology of second units in seventy-one complaints. But in the ninety-one cases where we could identify the typology (including four trailers—figure 4.4), garage conversions accounted for fifty-two of ninety-one grievances, or more than half of the informal second unit complaints.

These numbers correspond with the experience of Jonathan Pacheco Bell (communication 2016a), a former student and zoning inspector for the county of Los Angeles, who noted at a salon on second units that the vast majority of the informal housing complaints he attended to were for converted garages. I accompanied zoning inspectors in Los Angeles County on their field inspections in 2014 and 2016 and had similar observations: three-fourths of the complaints they responded to were for single-family housing violations, and the majority of them were related to garage conversions.

MANAGING AND NEGOTIATING INFORMALITY

How do homeowners minimize attention to their informal second units, avoid complaints from neighbors, and evade enforcement action from local governments? As the previous section suggests, homeowners with economic resources are likely to face fewer complaints. In this section, I draw on data from interviews to describe some of the common spatial, social, and institutional strategies of avoiding complaints and making informality work.

FIGURE 4.4
A trailer parked in the front lawn of a house screened from the street by hedges. Photo credit: Author.

SPATIAL EMBEDDEDNESS

One of the likely explanations for the dominance of detached backyard construction as the main typology of informal second units in the real estate listings is its lack of visibility from the street. My former students, who are familiar with informal second units owned by their friends or family members or have lived in them, have emphasized the importance of keeping them discreet (Student #9 interview 2014; Student #7 interview 2013a). Large lots are particularly helpful in achieving this. The zoning requirements of most cities, like the city of Los Angeles, mandate shorter fences for the front yard but allow taller barriers in the backyard, which makes it easier to conceal backyard units. Second units carved out from the main house offer a similar advantage of being hidden in plain sight (Participant #8 interview 2013). In many cases of converted garages, homeowners maintain the original garage door, so it continues to look like a garage from the street, but build an insulated wall behind it (Participant #12 interview 2013). In one case, the owner kept the front garage door as a facade and retained about 2 ft. of depth to use as a workbench (figure 4.5). From the street, the facade made it look like the garage was being used actively (Participant #4 interview 2013).

The incremental development or gradual construction of informal housing, as I discussed in the first chapter, is not only an economically defined decision but also a spatially determined one. As a former student of mine who used to live with his roommate in an informal second unit carved out from the

FIGURE 4.5
A converted garage in Los Angeles with the garage door intact and used to access a shallow storage space. The unit behind the storage has jerry-rigged electric wiring. Photo credit: Daniela Simunovic.

main unit on the second floor wrote to me, "First six months we were there, we walked through her front door and her living room to get upstairs . . . but she put in a kitchen upstairs and eventually a separate entrance" (Student #4 communication 2013). Similarly, another former student (Student #1 communication 2011; interview 2014) eloquently described how her family's second unit in its split-level house in the Bay Area came together gradually:

> The lowest floor of our home shared the same footprint as the rest of the house and consisted of a one-car garage and an empty, cement-floored basement. I recall the basement's transformation from a dusty, empty expanse to a makeshift carpeted playroom with a full bathroom. Over a few years, my parents added walls for rooms, a kitchenette, and subsequently closed off the informal granny flat from the rest of the house.

As in the Global South, the incremental process of building informal housing can be based on self-help or self-management by homeowners, in which owners work with family members and friends or hire workers to complete the construction (Rojas interview 2015).

The possibility of accessing the main house's kitchen and toilet can help in facilitating the incremental development of informal second units. Former students of mine, who have lived in converted garages without kitchens, routinely accessed the main house to use the kitchen (Student #6 interview 2013; Student #7 interview 2013a). One homeowner offered to add a kitchen to the informal second unit in which my student was living if he committed to staying there for a year, which would allow her to recoup the cost of adding the kitchen (Student #7 interview 2013a). Another student's family in Los Angeles's northeast San Fernando Valley converted their garage and upgraded it incrementally, gradually adding sliding glass doors, smoke alarms, and, last of all, an external toilet, which could be used by occupants of both the second unit and the main house (Student #8 interview 2014). Participant #11 (interview 2013), a friend of one of my former students, lived in an informal cottage in the backyard of his parents' single-family house in the suburban city of Lakewood. His father, a carpenter, built the cottage himself. The unit was still in its early stages of consolidation. Not only did my informant use the kitchen and bathroom in his parents' house, but his unit's electricity was provided by an extension cord from the main unit.

James Rojas (1993, 2014), who is known for his insights on Latinx urbanism, has noted how families adapt their homes and neighborhoods to meet their cultural needs. He has shown how Latinx homeowners add fences to use the front yards of their single-family houses as street-facing, semipublic

THE EVERYDAY PREVALENCE OF INFORMAL SECOND UNITS 119

plazas. Rojas (interview 2015) and I discussed how the spatial configuration of single-family dwellings with their private backyards allows larger extended Latinx families to share amenities—including kitchens, toilets, laundry rooms, and external washing machines and dryers—between the main house and the second unit. This arrangement allows family members to treat the backyard as a shared private space along the lines of a residential courtyard. Figure 4.6 shows a stylized interpretation of a single-family house and a converted and expanded garage as a second unit with fences and landscaping used to create the public plaza in the front, and a private, family courtyard in the back.

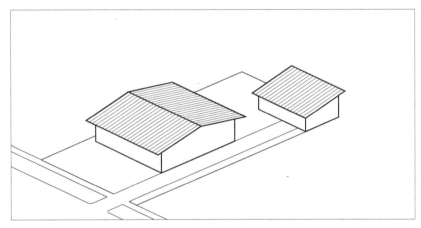

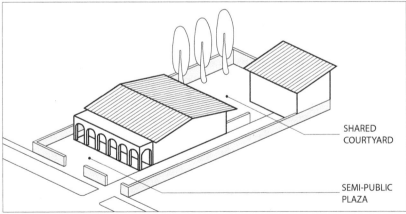

FIGURE 4.6
Schematic drawing showing modifications to a single-family house to create a front plaza and a back courtyard between the main home and the second unit. Graphic: Jae-Hyeon Park.

SOCIAL EMBEDDEDNESS

According to zoning inspectors (J. P. Bell interview 2016b; Bell and Rodriguez interview 2014; Rodriguez interview 2014), many complaints about informal housing originate from tenants who are unhappy with their housing conditions. To minimize the likelihood of complaints, many owners prefer to rent only to friends or family members or through their extended social networks, including their church congregations (Participant #15 interview 2014; Student #1 interview 2014). For example, Participant #8 (interview 2013), who owned a house with an informally carved-out second unit in San Fernando Valley and lived with his mother, had around ten different tenants in the unit over the last fifteen years, all of whom were family members or friends. In addition to reducing the possibility of complaints from tenants to the city, some homeowners prefer to rent to someone they know because they will be sharing the same lot and backyard with them.

Many homeowners are willing to charge less for a tenant they can trust. Participant #8, for example, rented his second unit to his friends, Participants #9 and #10 (interview 2013), for less than the market rate. Homeowners often forgo future rent increases to develop better relationships with their tenants. For example, Participant #5 (interview 2013), who lived in the backyard cottage converted from a garage in figure 4.7, thought her 500 sq. ft. unit was below market rate. Her aging landlord had skipped potential rent increases and even reduced her rent slightly over time in return for her help with yard work and other small chores.

Homeowners and tenants of informal second units have to be careful about their relationships with neighbors as well. To be discreet, homeowners try to minimize the impact of the additional unit and its residents on their neighbors, particularly by being careful about street parking. A student (Student #10 communication 2018) in one of my courses noted that her mother had two unpermitted units at her house, and she constantly reminded her tenants to be cautious and courteous about their neighbors' street parking. Most tenants of informal second units receive similar advice (Student #7 interview 2013b).[15]

Relationships with neighbors, however, can be finicky. Some neighbors can get irritated by a barking dog and complain (Primack 2014). Figure 4.8 shows an example of a complaint case from South Los Angeles. The adjoining neighbors on both sides of the house shown in the picture used to throw footballs from their front yards to each other. When the owners of the middle house built a fence, one of the neighbors complained that the

FIGURE 4.7
A backyard cottage in Venice, Los Angeles. Photo credit: Mark Simpson.

barrier was taller than what the regulations permitted. Unfortunately for the owners, the zoning inspector, upon visiting the home, found an informally converted garage and an outdoor family dining room in the driveway. The owners were required to lower the height of their fence, make the garage usable for parking, and remove all obstructions from the driveway.

INSTITUTIONAL EMBEDDEDNESS

One of the most common strategies employed by homeowners is to get partial permits or formal approval for the construction of a part of their informal second unit (Bell and Rodriguez interview 2014; Wegmann 2015). For example, Participant #3 (interview 2013), who had an internal second unit on the second floor of her home, got a computer room permit for the construction of her second unit. She later informally added a kitchen to it and converted the space to an independent unit. Partial permits can allow homeowners to incrementally develop their second units over time. The permits help ensure that at least a part of their investment in the unapproved units is secure and protected from subsequent code enforcement

FIGURE 4.8
A taller-than-permitted fence, which led to a neighbor's complaint. Photo credit: Author.

action. Another advantage of obtaining permits is that they allow homeowners to hire licensed contractors. The contractors can then complete some of the more challenging construction work, particularly improvements that involve addressing electricity, gas, and sewer connections (Participant #6 interview 2013).

Before the second unit reforms in the mid to late 2010s, it was significantly easier for homeowners in the city of Los Angeles to get permits for guesthouses than for second units. Guesthouses are for short-term guests and do not require a dedicated parking space, but they cannot include a full kitchen. They can include kitchenettes, but the mini-kitchen cannot have a double sink, garbage disposal, or a dishwasher and must have less than 10 sq. ft. of kitchen counters. In our analysis of the real estate listings, we found several examples of permitted guesthouses, which owners had informally converted to second units through subsequent additions of unpermitted kitchens. Similarly, in cities like Portland, Oregon, homeowners can sign second sink agreements, or additional sink covenants, with the municipality to receive permits allowing for the construction of a second kitchen under the condition that they do not rent out their space as an independent second unit. The second sink agreements allow homeowners to hire licensed contractors to complete the construction work safely.[16]

The distinction between formal and informal is not always clear, and some homeowners try to use the ambiguity to conceal the informality of their second units from neighbors and tenants. Some homeowners, for example, call their second units granny flats or in-law units to suggest that a family member is living there. Others claim that their informal second units are legal and "grandfathered-in"[17] because they are old and were built by previous owners before the land use requirements were introduced or became more demanding and mandatory. Since second units used to be a part of the urban fabric, it is feasible to add new secondary units in older neighborhoods discreetly.

Homeowners with resources can use formal institutions to protect their informal investments. For example, a homeowner in Seattle (Participant #16 interview 2014) had an unpermitted second unit, which he euphemistically described as "technically illegal." He found his tenant through a property management firm and signed a rental contract with her, which he drafted after studying standard rental agreements online. He was careful about paying income tax on the rent he received, which he hoped minimized his legal risk. He charged his tenant, who was a professional in the nonprofit sector, 10–20 percent below the market rate. He hoped that she would continue to rent from him for an extended period, saving him the need to search for a new tenant, and that she would follow his advice to avoid parking directly in front of their immediate neighbors' homes.

One of the most interesting examples of the use of formal institutions to protect informal investments is in California, where the California Association of Realtors recognizes the widespread prevalence of informal construction and safeguards sellers of properties with unpermitted additions through language in its residential purchase contract for single-family residential properties (B. Weiss communication 2014). The language specifies that potential buyers cannot cause an inspection by building and safety inspectors during the escrow period: "Without Sellers prior written consent, Buyers shall neither make nor cause to be made ... Buyer Investigations; or (ii) inspections by any governmental building or zoning inspector or government employee, unless required by Law" (California Association of Realtors, n.d.).

THE POTENTIAL AND PRECARITY OF INFORMALITY

Informality's market-driven nature and embeddedness in spatial, social, and institutional conditions suggest that there will be unevenness in how different communities and households benefit from it. Less affluent families do not have the money and space to take advantage of unregulated economic activities in the same way as wealthy families, and low-income tenants are more vulnerable than homeowners.

THE PROMISE OF INFORMAL HOUSING

Wealthy households often have single-family houses with large lots and the space to build new backyard units that they can hide from street view. They are also more likely to have the financial resources to invest in unpermitted housing that is high quality and compliant with safety standards. As a result, their neighbors and tenants file fewer complaints with code enforcement. In the absence of complaints and concerns about potential enforcement, wealthier families can invest even more in their informal housing. Thus, there is a virtuous cycle of more investment allowing for a better quality of informal housing, which results in even fewer complaints (Campbell interview 2013). Figure 4.9 illustrates one such example and shows a converted garage from the outside and inside, as well as its kitchen.

FIGURE 4.9
The outside and inside of an informal second unit in Central Los Angeles. Photo credit: Ned Brown.

Homeowners interested in adding second units cannot easily obtain institutional financing or construction loans. Consequently, homeowners with personal funds have a significant advantage. Martin Brown's (2014; interview 2015) research based on his survey of homeowners with second units in Portland showed that most of the owners paid for the construction of the second units from their personal assets or financial assistance from their families. Irrespective of whether their second units were formally approved or informally built, homeowners could rarely access institutional financing.[18] Homeowners with resources do not have to incrementally develop their houses over time either. They can afford to build and use a unit with a complete set of amenities all at once.

The wealthy, particularly those with liquid assets or cash, have an advantage in the sales market as well. Lenders use public records to compute the assessed values of properties to determine the amount they can lend to home buyers. They cannot explicitly consider the value of unpermitted and unrecorded units or square footage in their appraisal calculations. This constraint, however, is less challenging for all-cash buyers (Agar communication 2014b).

Perhaps most significantly, the well-off can afford to build their informal units to the required safety standards even if they add them without permits. One of my extended family members did something similar recently. They wanted to rent out their three-bedroom, one-bathroom single-family house in West Los Angeles. The market demand is much more robust for homes with two bathrooms, so they decided to add a second bathroom without permits to save time. The contractor they approached for help with the construction work declined the job because he could lose his license for doing work without permits. Still, he suggested that his assistant, an unlicensed handyman, would be happy to lead the project. The assistant, who has significant experience with construction work, followed all the quality standards and code requirements prescribed by the city of Los Angeles and completed the job without permits.

The tenants who rented their house are unaffected by the unregulated status of the construction work. Their second bathroom is unpermitted, but it meets the safety standards and requirements of the code. Thus, for middle-class and upper-middle-class tenants, informality in the housing market adds choices without necessarily increasing the risks (Ferman and Ferman 1973).

This seems to be the case for Participants #1 and #2 (interview 2013). They are young professionals who rented an unpermitted second unit in Highland Park, a hillside neighborhood in the city of Los Angeles, which they found through a posting on Craigslist. Although they believed they were paying a hundred dollars a month more than the rent for similar-sized alternatives in the market, they were happy with their housing choice because they thought the house did not compromise their safety and offered the amenity of incredible sweeping views.

INFORMAL HOUSING AND VULNERABILITY

Less affluent households often have a very different experience. For disadvantaged households, informal housing can lead to a vicious cycle. Because of their lack of wealth, homeowners with fewer resources are likely to invest less in their informal housing, which probably leads to more complaints and code enforcement actions. And owing to the likelihood of inspections and enforcement, they probably feel insecure about their investments and invest even less.[19] As a result, low-capital investments, like temporary kitchen facilities that are easy to dismantle and remove, are more common. Figure 4.10 shows a second unit with such a kitchen in the Sylmar neighborhood on the northern edge of the city of Los Angeles. (It is very different from the kitchen shown in figure 4.9.) The young couple that lived in the Sylmar unit, both of whom were students, found it advertised on Craigslist (Participants #13 and #14 interview 2013). It is a converted garage without a built-in kitchen. The residents used their electric stove and microwave for cooking and washed their dishes in the bathtub in the restroom, which is the only place with full plumbing. The unit does not have smoke alarms, fire sprinklers, or a fire extinguisher. The residents paid $700 a month and doubted they could find a better place for that price.

Students, as I noted in chapter 1, can be particularly vulnerable and subject to unsafe housing. Some UCLA students live in informal housing without basic fire-security features (Dahl 2010). Student #5 (interview 2013), a graduate architecture student, for example, lived in the converted workshop of a single-family house in West Los Angeles. His unit had a sliding door for light and ventilation, and he used the kitchen and bathroom in the main house, where two other graduate architecture students lived as tenants. The unit did not have smoke alarms or other safety features. But

FIGURE 4.10
A makeshift kitchen in an informal second unit in Los Angeles. Photo credit: Carlos Hernandez.

he was satisfied with his home's proximity to UCLA, his independent room, and its affordable rent.

Typically, the conditions of informal housing rented by UCLA students are very different from the conditions of units rented by people with fewer resources and connections. For example, Participant #7 (interview 2013), her husband, and their three kids live in precarious housing in San Fernando Valley (figure 4.5). They saw a flyer for the house while walking in the neighborhood and pay $800 a month for it. The homeowner carved out the unit from a converted garage of 20 ft. by 20 ft. It has jerry-rigged electrical wiring and does not have a proper kitchen. My informant and her family use a camping stove for cooking. The unit does not have smoke alarms. Its roof is uninsulated, and the unit gets very hot in the summer. She shared that there are rats and cockroaches too. But she rarely complained about the conditions and was more concerned that her landlord would find out that she was talking to strangers about her unit. For low-income tenants like her, the fear of losing their homes can outweigh their concerns about poor housing conditions.

Because of the precarious status of undocumented residents, it is difficult for them to complain about their poor housing conditions. Moreover, for many of them, renting informally might be the only option. They can find it challenging to meet all the necessary approval requirements for renting housing in the formal market, including having recorded credit histories. The informal housing market, thus, provides an essential avenue of survival. However, these tenants are vulnerable and dependent on their landlords, so it is unlikely that they would complain about living conditions in their housing.[20]

Some unpermitted second units, particularly in disadvantaged neighborhoods, have severe problems with mold, lead, and asbestos (Podemski communication 2015). In contrast to a typical graduate student occupying a second unit or converted garage, informal units in low-income neighborhoods can have extreme overcrowding issues as well. Community-based housing advocates say that overcrowding in informal housing units has worsened over the past two decades in disadvantaged communities (Romero-Martínez communication 2019). Stories about fire tragedies in Los Angeles's informal housing are not unusual in the *Los Angeles Times* (see, for example, Reyes 2015; Rocha 2017; Serna 2015; Winton 2014). Zoning inspector Jonathan Pacheco Bell (communication 2016a) often found substandard and hazardous housing in his work and was amazed at the high rents that unsafe housing can command. He found people living in dangerously dilapidated trailer homes as well as in cargo trailers, garden sheds, and poorly converted garages (figure 4.11). As an inspector, he was often tasked with making homeowners remove their unpermitted units and bring their properties into compliance with the zoning requirements. For the most part, though, homeowners he worked with had to abate or remove their informal units because of zoning violations rather than safety reasons (J. P. Bell interview 2016b).

Unfortunately, enforcement actions, even those against units with serious safety risks, do not necessarily help affected tenants find safe housing that they can afford. Enforcement focuses on removing unpermitted units from the market, and there are no institutional practices or procedures for following up with the tenants who get evicted from informal housing during the compliance process. In contrast, there can be multiple follow-up visits by inspectors with homeowners to ensure that they comply with the

FIGURE 4.11
Examples of precarious informal housing. Photo credit: Jonathan Pacheco Bell.

enforcement. In theory, tenants should be protected from "not-at-fault evictions" through relocation assistance and, depending on circumstances, back-rent payments (D. Smith interview 2014). In practice, it is difficult for tenants without formal leases to get relocation assistance (Kettles interview 2016).

As I mentioned earlier, many complaints about informal housing originate from tenants who live in the properties (Bell and Rodriguez interview 2014; 2016). Tired of poor and unsafe living conditions, tenants sometimes lodge these complaints under the assumption that enforcement action will force homeowners to improve their housing. Most of the time, however, owners have to remove the units, and the tenants get displaced. Interestingly, some of the complaints come from homeowners who are keen to get rid of their tenants (Rodriguez interview 2014).

Informal second units in cities like Los Angeles highlight how both conventional land use regulations and zoning enforcement practices deepen the advantages of wealthy households and the disadvantages of less affluent families. Both the formal market based on single-family housing and the zoning-focused enforcement practice based on complaints work for the wealthy. For the less privileged, in the absence of adequate and appropriate housing, informal housing may be the only option. The informal units help address the lack of affordable housing, but living in informal housing can come with considerable risks. Vulnerable tenants have almost no recourse or help from public agencies. To use a phrase often attributed to Truman Capote, "The problem with living outside the law is that you no longer have its protection." While laissez-faire housing markets may work for the elite, for the poor, the lack of minimum standards and enforcement can lead to a high price.

For the less fortunate, the safe housing available on the formal market is unaffordable, and affordable informal housing can be dangerous.

CONCLUSION

In this chapter, I make the case that informal housing has a significant presence in the Global North and needs to be acknowledged and better understood. My analysis suggests that unpermitted second units are common in Los Angeles. I estimate that there are around fifty thousand informal second units on single-family-zoned lots in the city of Los Angeles. In the appendix to this chapter, I also share my estimate of the prevalence of unpermitted second units in the county of Los Angeles and report similar results. While the number and proportion of informal units in Los Angeles are not as high as in many cities in the Global South, the substantial scale of informal housing emphasizes the need for serious academic and policy attention to the issue. Although the lack of robust data on informal housing makes policy making difficult, its discreet nature compounds the challenges—its existence is not a secret. Both policy makers and the general public know about its widespread prevalence. Nonetheless, both policy making and policy-focused academic literature do not adequately acknowledge and address informal second units. Given the substantial magnitude of informal housing in Los Angeles, the lack of attention to it in academic research is particularly surprising.

Second, Los Angeles's informal second units challenge conventional assumptions about the association of informality with low-income households and immigrants from the Global South in the Global North. Unpermitted second units are distributed all over the city and are not confined to low-resourced neighborhoods or disadvantaged residents in the region. While informal housing in the Global South is not limited to low-income households either, the widespread presence of informal settlements with poor infrastructure conveys the misleading association of informality with low-income residents and neighborhoods. The Los Angeles case underlines the complexity of informal housing by clarifying that income and informal economic activities are not necessarily directly associated with each other.

Third, in addition to often being market based, informal housing is spatially, socially, and institutionally embedded in the local conditions and context. Some owners charge below-market rents for their second units because of preexisting social relations with their tenants. While the focus in Southern California—as in the 1987 news story from the *Los Angeles Times*—is on converted garages, other forms of unpermitted second units are more prevalent. These typologically different second units take advantage of the various spatial opportunities available in the malleable structure of single-family-zoned lots and houses, and the institutional possibilities that rental contracts, purchase agreements, and partial permits provide. For example, detached backyard units are more expensive to build, but their inconspicuousness can minimize complaints. It is cheaper and easier to convert garages, but garage conversions are usually less discreet and more visible. They can lead to parking wars with neighbors, which can trigger complaints. Enforcement action is socially constructed too and follows from complaints. Thus, informal housing's material conditions and viability are likely to be contingent on social relationships and socially accepted and tolerated practices.

Fourth, while informal housing is an everyday reality in Los Angeles, it offers significantly diverse living conditions to families from different levels of privilege. Well-resourced households are more likely to benefit from informal housing than are low-income families, including tenants. Wealthy tenants can expect safe housing conditions. Wealthy homeowners face fewer complaints about their unpermitted units and have de facto security for their financial investments in informal housing. In contrast, less affluent families bear a disproportionate burden of the risks associated with unsafe housing. The disparity highlights the multiple advantages of wealthy households and the disadvantages of low-income households related to urban informality. In particular, single-family housing owners can expand their housing options through unpermitted second units while maintaining the social prestige and privileges of their single-family neighborhoods. If they are wealthy, they do not necessarily need building and safety regulations to safeguard the quality of their housing, and the laissez-faire nature of informality does not hurt them. They are not adversely affected by the lack of proactive enforcement either. In contrast, the very presence of housing informality suggests that existing formal land use regulations adversely affect low-income households by limiting the housing supply and making housing less affordable. Restrained safety inspections and enforcement practices focused on zoning regulations do not help protect the most vulnerable from substandard housing conditions. Informality in this context helps to reproduce existing inequalities of privilege and poverty.

Overall, the data and analyses in this chapter add more complexity to the conventional view of informality in the Global North. The prevalence and disparate conditions of unpermitted second units highlight the need for more nuanced and intentional policy responses. It is imperative that informal housing not be criminalized, stigmatized, or ignored.

APPENDIX

In addition to the city of Los Angeles, Los Angeles County includes eighty-seven other incorporated cities with a combined population of around five million and about 825,000 single-family houses (table A.1). My research team examined real estate listings from the spring of 2012 of single-family houses for sale in these cities. After deleting houses under foreclosure or in a short sale, we developed a sample of 5,500 houses for sale in the eighty-seven cities. In them, we identified 431 properties, or over 7.8 percent of the listings, that included or most likely included an unpermitted second unit. The rate is higher than the incidence of 5.4 percent we found for the city of Los Angeles.

The rate of 7.8 percent for the county of Los Angeles extrapolates to almost 65,000 single-family houses with second units. If I follow my strategy of doubling the initial estimate, it is likely that there were about 130,000 informal second units in the other cities of the county. A significant part of the county is unincorporated (i.e., it is not under the jurisdiction of any of the eighty-eight incorporated cities in the county) and, according to my team's analysis of the county assessor's records, included 187,010 single-family houses. We did not analyze the listings of homes for sale in the unincorporated areas. If the unincorporated parts of the county had the same rate of unpermitted second units as the eighty-seven cities, there would have been almost 30,000 more unpermitted second units. Thus, the county of Los Angeles, excluding

Table A.1
Unpermitted second units in other incorporated cities in the county of Los Angeles and their distribution by supervisorial district

District	Population* (2010)	Number of single-family houses†	Number for sale	Unpermitted and likely unpermitted second units	Proportion for sale with unpermitted second units (%)	Median household income of district
1	1,149,722	158,656	1,078	51	4.73	$45,888
2	582,388	74,332	319	20	6.27	$42,528
3	248,048	35,645	728	125	17.17	$63,637
4	1,564,596	280,655	1,786	106	5.94	$66,543
5	1,423,804	275,031	1,589	129	8.12	$71,440
Totals	4,968,558	824,319	5,500	431	7.84	NA

Sources: Author's research of for-sale listings in the spring of 2012; Los Angeles county assessor's records, 2012; and district income data from the Los Angeles County Economic Development Corporation, 2017.
*Population data do not include the city of Los Angeles (3,792,621) and unincorporated parts of the county of Los Angeles (1,057,426).
†The number of single-family houses includes single-family dwellings on multifamily-zoned lots but does not include single-family houses in the unincorporated Los Angeles County (187,010) or the city of Los Angeles (541,259).
NA = Not available.

the city of Los Angeles, likely had 160,000 informal second units. Including the city of Los Angeles's probable 50,000 unpermitted second units, there were likely 210,000 informal second units across the entire county.

We also analyzed the spatial distribution of the unpermitted second units in the county across its supervisorial districts. The districts are used to elect the five-member governing body for the county and have significantly different household incomes. As table A.1 shows, there does not appear to be any clear relationship between household income and prevalence of informal housing at the district level. Figure A.1 shows the boundaries of the five supervisorial districts.

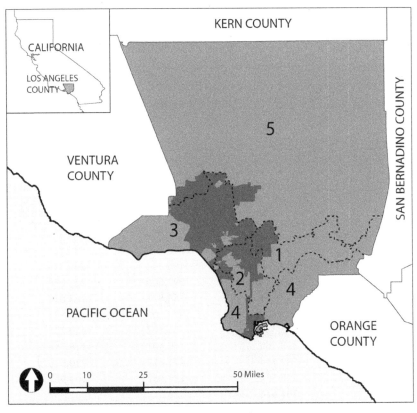

FIGURE A.1
The five supervisorial districts of Los Angeles County. Graphic: Jae-Hyeon Park.

My colleagues and I also examined US Census data for insights on informal housing across the country (Brown, Mukhija, and Shoup 2018, 2020). Table A.2 shows our analysis of informal single-family units in the nation's largest metropolitan statistical areas (MSAs). It follows the methodology of Jake Wegmann and Sarah Mawhorter (2017) and New York's Chhaya Community Development Corporation & Citizens Housing and Planning Council (2008) and compares the "increase" in the number of single-family housing units reported in the US Census with municipal data on the number of single-family building permits issued. Both data sets count second units as single-family housing units. Table A.2 offers strong evidence of the nationwide prevalence of informal housing. However, it would be wrong to conclude that all the unpermitted units are "new" and were added after 2000. According to the late Leobardo Estrada (interview 2018), my former colleague and US Census expert, the counting of the actual number of housing units significantly improved since the 2000 Census. It is likely that many unpermitted units existed previously but were not enumerated before the 2000 Census.[21] It would be incorrect to conclude that the Los

Table A.2
Unpermitted single-family units in the largest MSAs, 2000–2014

MSA	"Increase" in number of single-family units (1)	Number of single-family building permits (2)	Number of "new" single-family units without permits (3) = (1) − (2)
New York	566,167	235,846	330,321
Los Angeles	454,728	155,344	299,384
Chicago	514,888	292,800	222,088
Philadelphia	317,891	153,821	164,070
Dallas	608,604	459,609	148,995
Boston	205,337	86,102	119,235
Washington, DC	398,169	279,401	118,768
Atlanta	582,114	471,479	110,635
Miami	298,554	188,632	109,922
Houston	581,674	526,312	55,362
Total	**4,528,127**	**2,849,346**	**1,678,781**

Sources: (1) US Department of Housing and Urban Development 1985–2013, 2015; (2) and US Census Bureau 2000, 2015 data from Brown, Mukhija, and Shoup 2020. Note: Both data sets count second units as single-family housing units and account for housing loss from demolition and unintentional loss through fire or disasters.

Angeles MSA, which includes Los Angeles and Orange Counties, added almost three hundred thousand unpermitted second units in 2000–2014. But it would be fair to infer that the Census data indicate that there are at least three hundred thousand informal second units in Los Angeles and Orange Counties. Similarly, the Census data suggest that informal housing is common across the US.

III Formal Second Units and Institutional Changes in Single-Family Housing

5 ENFORCEMENT AND FORMALIZATION OF UNPERMITTED SECOND UNITS IN LOS ANGELES

In December 1996, a fire killed five children in a converted garage in Watts, South Los Angeles. A few months later, in March 1997, two children and their grandmother died in a garage fire in Sun Valley, a neighborhood in the northeast part of the city of Los Angeles. Both garages were on single-family-zoned lots and led to respected urban planning commentator William Fulton ruefully noting, "What you have in Los Angeles is First World zoning and Third World reality" (S. Bernstein 1997a). On March 21, 1997, the Los Angeles City Council approved a motion led by Mark Ridley-Thomas, the councilmember representing parts of South Los Angeles, asking the Department of Building and Safety to develop a proactive code enforcement program and report to the city's Public Safety Committee. However, about a week later, the city council approved a different motion proposed by Councilmember Richard Alarcon, who represented parts of northeast Los Angeles in San Fernando Valley. Alarcon asked the city council to establish an interdepartmental Garage Housing Task Force under the housing department's leadership to examine the issue from a broader housing affordability perspective (Los Angeles Housing Department 1997). Alarcon had lived in garage housing, was more sympathetic to the subject, and shared his experience with the task force (Richman interview 2017).[1]

The task force's work was challenging. Some converted garages had dangerous electrical connections, open electrical conductors, risky gas piping, and unvented heaters. Moreover, many older homes have hazardous exposure to lead-based paints and asbestos, which requires abatement or removal (Romero-Martinez interview 2017). The task force also faced political challenges. While Alarcon favored finding a way to preserve the garage units by relaxing or making some of the regulations more flexible, most councilmembers supported stricter enforcement of existing single-family zoning requirements. Like Ridley-Thomas, some endorsed the construction of subsidized apartments instead of preserving garage housing and worried that accepting informal housing was a slippery slope toward normalizing substandard housing conditions (Richman interview 2017).

The task force (Los Angeles Housing Department 1997) adopted a sympathetic position on informal housing. It recommended that the city implement a plan to immediately reduce hazards, provide owners with interim occupancy permits as a step to formalization, and initiate a permanent program for legalizing garage housing on single-family-zoned lots. The recommendations, however, were controversial and were rejected.

The task force's recommendations were consistent with the conventional policy approaches for responding to informal housing. I stylize the possibilities into two main choices, which form the title of this chapter: enforcement and formalization. Enforcement often takes the form of shutting down or demolishing informal units, as in slum clearance, ostensibly to protect residents of substandard and dangerous housing but often merely displaces them to worse living conditions. However, planners can implement enforcement more sensitively through the strategic removal or elimination of the most dangerous hazards.

Formalization covers a wide variety of policy options to address informality. It can include the legalization of previously informal practices through deregulation. For example, changing the rules of conventional single-family zoning to allow homeowners to convert garages and build second units is a form of legalization through deregulation. In the context of informal housing, legalization takes the form of new property rights for homeowners. Formalization can also include the regularization of informal activities through public support for upgrading them. Regularization involves a de facto acknowledgment of informal property claims. Temporary or interim occupancy permits, as the task force recommended, fall short of full legal recognition but indicate an acceptance of the legitimacy of garage housing.

Formalization, legalization, and regularization are not always clearly demarcated in practice. These policies often overlap and are frequently implemented in conjunction with each other.[2] Moreover, not responding to informal activities or tolerating them can be seen as a separate and implicit policy option. My main task in part III is to focus on how Global North cities have responded to informal housing, particularly unpermitted second units, and the underlying issue of increasing the housing supply. In this chapter, I discuss how single-family zoning and the American Dream it embodies are changing through land use reforms in the city of Los Angeles and California. The policy goal to remake single-family living runs counter to how many Angelenos imagine their housing and faces intense hostility. As a result of local opposition, California's state government intervened in municipal land use regulations to make building second units on single-family-zoned lots easier. State government policy focused on developing formal market-based second units through legalization and zoning reform. I argue that in addition to the policy emphasis on diversifying the housing supply, planners and policy makers need to address widespread informal housing directly. Much-needed policies to formalize existing second units through regularization and proactive support for upgrading housing conditions are missing. The enthusiasm for top-down state preemption in local land use regulations may conceal the need for the state government to help local governments financially with the upgrading of informal housing units. The state government may also have an integral role in helping less affluent households access construction finance for adding second units.

INTERPRETING AND RESPONDING TO THE INFORMAL ECONOMY

There are varying perspectives on informal economic activities in the academic literature. I identify five schools of interpretation in the scholarship—structuralist, critical governance, empowerment and insurgency, neoliberal, and reformist—emphasizing different aspects of informality and offering diverse directions for public policy.

INTERPRETING INFORMALITY

Structuralist scholars, building on the Marxian perspective of market exploitation, led the challenge to the old dualist informal sector theory by showing that informal economic activities overlap with and link to formal economic activities through the deepening of global capitalism, transnational labor markets, weakening of labor standards and government enforcement of regulations, and employers' interest in circumventing state regulations governing workplace conditions and wages (Bernhardt et al. 2008; Portes, Castells, and

Benton 1989; Portes and Sassen-Koob 1987; Sassen 1991; Sassen-Koob 1989). They emphasize the market-based exploitation inherent in unregulated economic activities. They argue for structural changes in the economy, stronger labor unions to provide countervailing power, and a new social contract with stricter laws and better enforcement of regulations by governments.

While sympathetic to the structuralist approach, the *critical governmentality* perspective, influenced by postcolonial theory, distrusts state institutions. It focuses on epistemological challenges in contemporary governance and planning (Roy 2005, 2009a, 2009b; Yiftachel 2009). Critical governmentality scholars indict state complicity and public malfeasance as central in producing informality. My colleague Ananya Roy (2009a, 2009b), for example, has systematically criticized the use of state power in the arbitrary enforcement of regulations as a mode of governance that produces and determines informality. Orin Yiftachel (2009) shared similar concerns about the role of government regulations in creating new colonial relations through informality and discretionary enforcement to highlight the potential dark side of planning. Relatedly, scholars note that government agencies often hire informal workers to save costs (Miraftab 2005). Critical governmentality scholars remind planners that informality's underlying issues are significant economic and political power disparities, and meaningful responses must address such differences through more profound social changes.

Some scholars, while concerned about market and government exploitation, see the heroic and anarchist-inspired potential of *empowerment and insurgency* in the informal economy (Holston 2007; Scott 1998; Turner 1977; Turner and Fichter 1972). Social development scholars, for example, note the radical potential of everyday resistance (Kudva 2009), inclusive urban citizenship (Watson 2011), and new community-based economics (Gibson-Graham 2006) nestled within the informal economy. Similarly, urban design scholars in the Global North see radical possibilities of liberation in the informal or unauthored city and advocate for a hands-off approach. My colleague Anastasia Loukaitou-Sideris and I identified four major themes driving the urban design literature (Loukaitou-Sideris and Mukhija 2016, 581):

> First, inspired by Michel de Certeau (2002) and Henri Lefebvre (1991), everyday urbanists see subversive power in ordinary activities and the potential for fundamental change in the everyday tactics of the underrepresented (Chase, Crawford, and Kaliski 2008; Kamel 2014). Second, guerilla urbanists see a similar possibility of insurgence and alternative social and spatial relationships through the

active role of minority groups in placemaking (Hou 2010). Third, Do-It-Yourself-Urbanists (DIY-Urbanists) see the prospects of radical and greater freedom in the autonomy afforded by limited planning (Campo 2013; Douglas 2013; Franck and Paxson 2007; Franck and Stevens 2007; Hughes and Sadler 2000). Finally, advocates of tactical or pop-up urbanism question the faith in long-term strategies and master plans and advocate for temporary uses (Bishop and Williams 2012).

In similar ways to the above progressive approach, scholars following a market-based perspective criticize excessive regulations and argue for legal recognition and empowerment of actors in the informal economy through formal property rights and limited government involvement (De Soto 1989, 2000). Scholars with such a *neoliberal* approach hold unrealistic regulations and legal standards responsible for the informal economy's growth. In particular, the World Bank and international development scholars associated with it in the 1980s and 1990s promoted legalization through deregulation and land titles for improving housing conditions in informal settlements in developing countries as a strategy for enabling markets (De Soto 1989; Jimenez 1983, 1984; Malpezzi and Mayo 1987; World Bank 1993). The property rights legalization approach became the accepted wisdom and guided policy across the Global South.

Finally, scholars from the *reformist* perspective are sympathetic to the governance challenges in informality (Peattie 1979). They see structural reasons for the existence of informality and do not expect it to disappear. In contrast to the neoliberal approach, they call for upgrading and addressing informal activities through the active support of government and civil society institutions (Iskander and Lowe 2010; Peattie 1987; Piore and Sabel 1984; Sanyal 2008). Reformist scholars view informality as simultaneously productive and exploitative. For example, Hernan Ramirez and Pierrette Hondagneu-Sotelo (2009, 86) noted that both "entrepreneurship and subjugation coexist under conditions of informality." They focus on public interventions in response to informality and expect policies to be nuanced, complicated, and seemingly contradictory (Mukhija 2001; Ward 1999). Reformist perspective scholars highlight the importance of new institutional arrangements in addressing the vulnerability of participants in the informal economy. See, for example, the work on day labor worker centers in the US, their role in protecting workers' rights, and importance in providing a forum for organizing, training, and empowerment (Theodore 2020; Theodore, Valenzuela, and Meléndez 2009; Valenzuela 2014).

RESPONSES TO INFORMAL HOUSING IN THE GLOBAL SOUTH

Around the middle of the twentieth century, many countries initiated slum clearance programs, particularly in central city locations, ostensibly to help slum residents. Modernist principles in architecture and urban planning—the belief that slums and their unsanitary housing units needed to be demolished and replaced with bright, airy, and modern housing—guided these projects. Similar to subsequent scholars following a structuralist approach, critics of slum housing saw market-based exploitation of renters in substandard units, called for enforcement against such units, and proposed to create better living conditions through public housing. Typically, however, clearance-based enforcement programs made a bad situation worse. At best, the former slum dwellers were resettled in new houses in distant locations away from their jobs and social networks (Jane Jacobs 1961). More often, slum residents were displaced because it was much easier to demolish slums than to build replacement housing (Abrams 1964). Some scholars questioned the arbitrary characterization of the houses of poor residents as slums (Gans 1962) and argued that public policy interest in redeveloping centrally located real estate land was the primary driver of clearance programs (Abrams 1964). Partly because of these criticisms, slum clearance became less prominent in global housing policies.[3]

Architect John Turner and anthropologist William Mangin (Mangin 1967; Mangin and Turner 1968; Turner 1972, 1977) researched populist land invasions in Lima, Peru, and argued that given enough time, informal housing settlements transform into thriving neighborhoods. They exemplified the empowerment approach in interpreting informal housing. As Turner (1972) famously suggested, housing should be seen through a temporal lens and as an active enterprise of dwelling—or as he elegantly put it, as a verb rather than a noun. Turner and his colleagues supported informal housing as a potential solution for the acute affordable housing shortage (Mangin and Turner 1968; Turner 1972; Turner and Fichter 1972). They argued that the incremental development inherent in informal housing is a creative approach to balance the constraints of affordability and the requirements of housing standards. They recommended that policy makers allow owners to meet required standards over an extended timeline to support gradual improvements.

A related avenue of inquiry (Leeds 1968; Peattie 1968; Perlman 1976; Turner 1968) empirically challenged the negative stereotype of informal housing residents as an underclass deeply linked in a culture of poverty and with little interest in or capacity for economic progress and social integration (O. Lewis 1966). Alejandro Portes (1971), for example, argued that not only were cherished social values like community orientation, solidarity, and trust common among residents of informal settlements, but they affected the prospects for collective action and grew over time with the successful upgrading of their houses and neighborhoods.

Some scholars questioned the radical claims underlying Turner and his colleagues' enthusiasm for self-help and informal housing (Burgess 1978). While Turner emphasized the bottom-up, communitarian aspects of life in informal settlements and was skeptical of active government involvement, critics noted that most developments were rarely a result of populist land invasions. Instead, most unpermitted subdivisions were market based, organized by commercially motivated entrepreneurs, and more likely to serve moderate-income households (Angel et al. 1983; Baross 1990; Payne 1989; Ward 1982). Impoverished families tended to be tenants with more precarious housing and limited prospects of benefiting from the consolidation of their settlements (Gulyani and Talukdar 2008; Kumar 1996).

Though there is consensus among scholars on the need to increase investments in informal housing to improve living conditions, there is no agreement about the best planning strategies for achieving this. The conventional wisdom championed by the Peruvian economist Hernando de Soto (1989, 2000) follows the neoliberal approach and supports legalization through private property rights to increase private investment. De Soto and other property rights advocates build on Turner's insights and argue for legal recognition and security of tenure through individual land titles (Friedman, Jimenez, and Mayo 1988). Land titles, they claim, allow residents to invest their savings in their houses without being worried about the persistent threat of demolition. Moreover, the argument goes, titles through legalization can be used as collateral to access low-cost loans for home improvements. Titles, to paraphrase De Soto, unlock the "dead capital" of slum housing.

Critics of the neoliberal argument describe it as simplistic and overreliant on market-based processes (Doebele 1987; Fernandes and Varley 1998; Gilbert 2002; Varley 2002). In particular, scholars following the reformist approach question the conventional emphasis on land titles for informal housing. They advocate for public investments as a formalization strategy for recognizing the legitimacy of informal housing and call for governments to be directly involved in upgrading efforts. They argue that land titles are neither necessary, nor sufficient, nor always beneficial for upgrading (Payne 2001b; Sanyal 1996; Varley 1987, 2007).

First, critics question the assumption that title-based legalization approaches are the only avenue for making residents of informal housing feel secure about their investments in housing (Payne 2001a). William Doebele (1987), for example, argued that instead of the security of tenure, squatters needed the perception of security of tenure. He suggested that public investments in infrastructure and amenities help create de facto security of tenure. Public investments, particularly in infrastructure, signal to residents that their neighborhoods are stable, that state-sponsored demolition drives are unlikely, and that it is safe for them to spend resources on housing additions and improvements (Imparato and Ruster 2003; Strassmann 1984).

Second, critics argue that land titles in the Global South are insufficient for offering loans for housing investments. Property-based lending is typically limited to higher-income households (Ferguson and Smets 2010; Smets 1997). Formal titles may be correlated with housing investments in the Global South, but they do not necessarily lead to access to credit (Field 2005; Galiani and Schargrodsky 2010). Erica Field (2005), for example, examined a nationwide titling program in Peru and found an increase in housing investments before and after the program. However, the majority of the improvements were financed without credit but followed the lower threat of eviction. Relatedly, Sebastian Galiani and Ernesto Schargrodsky (2010) surveyed homeowners in a poor peripheral area of Buenos Aires, Argentina. They found that most owners, regardless of their property rights, lacked access to credit. The entitled families, however, had invested substantially more in their housing.

Third, title-based formalization approaches may lead to higher rents for tenants (Lemanski 2009). To protect tenants, governments may need to include rent stabilization measures along with formalization programs. Alternatively, gradual improvements in infrastructure and legal status may lead to slower increases in rents for tenants. In a related strategy to slow gentrification, the slum upgrading program in Surabaya, Indonesia, prevented four-wheeled vehicles from accessing the interiors of low-income neighborhoods (UN Millennium Project 2005).

The contrarian scholars suggest that policy makers should consider alternative forms of legal recognition and legitimacy for formalization (Payne

2001a; Payne, Durand-Lasserve, and Rakodi 2009). These other formalization options include customary titles, collective leases, concessions or use rights, temporary or interim occupancy permits, and long-term moratoria or guarantees against clearance. The alternative tenure forms might allow for creative ways to structure rights for tenants, including protection against arbitrary eviction and partial ownership rights.[4]

RESPONDING TO INFORMAL HOUSING IN THE GLOBAL NORTH

What about policy responses to informal housing in the US? As I discussed in chapter 4, scholars argue that informal housing does not receive enough attention from practitioners or researchers in the US (Durst and Wegmann 2017; Mukhija 2014). The main exception is the policy attention to poorly serviced subdivisions in the border region, or *colonias*, and the related scholarship of Peter Ward (1999). Ward and his colleagues critically examined a range of policy responses to infrastructure-poor subdivisions that mirror the conventional practice in the Global South. State and federal policies include legal recognition of property lots and clear titles in the subdivisions and changes to land development regulations to allow for similar subdivisions with better infrastructure (Durst 2019; Durst and Ward 2014, 2016; Ward 1999; Ward and Carew 2001; Ward, de Souza, and Giusti 2004). While policy responses include some public investments for upgrading infrastructure, the support level was inadequate and typically did not include funding support for individual property owners to improve their houses (Donelson and Esparza 2010; Mukhija and Mason 2013; Mukhija and Monkkonen 2006; Ward 1999). Ward and his colleagues argued for more substantial public investments in upgrading.

There is not yet a similar scholarship on unpermitted second units and related policy responses. Nonetheless, the limited research indicates that several jurisdictions actively discourage unpermitted second units in single-family-zoned neighborhoods through zoning and building code enforcement. In addition to soliciting calls and complaints against unpermitted housing, as in the city of Los Angeles, many Southern California cities proactively target zoning violations through inspection programs. Some jurisdictions, like South Gate and Redondo Beach (Los Angeles County), have presale inspection programs. The programs mandate homeowners to have home inspections before they sell them, or they require potential buyers to obtain a report from the building and safety department about the property's permits as a disclosure requirement (Leong 1991).

In a few cases, cities formalized unpermitted units through legalization and amnesty programs. In New York City, for example, owners of unpermitted residential lofts in industrial areas or manufacturing zones were allowed to formalize their units through the 1982 Loft Law. In return, the law required owners to commit to upgrading their units while providing tenants with rent-stabilized housing (Shkuda 2015). Similarly, the town of Babylon, a New York City suburb on Long Island, offered an amnesty program for unpermitted accessory apartments and formalized fifteen hundred of an estimated four thousand informal second units (Rudel 1984). The town limited the initiative to second units carved out of owner-occupied single-family houses.

Along similar lines, policy makers in Daly City, located immediately south of San Francisco, used California's enactment of the 1983 Companion Unit Act (Senate Bill 1534) to legislate a second unit ordinance to respond to the high number of unpermitted second units in the city (Cabansagan 2011). Almost two-thirds of Daly City's housing units were single-family houses, most of them two-story dwellings. It was relatively easy to carve out second units informally without changing the appearance of the neighborhood. The city's planners changed its single-family zoning rules to enable legally approved second units by reducing the parking requirements and allowing parking in the driveway. As in Babylon, they required that the second units be carved out of existing houses, and owners had to occupy one of the two dwellings. Subsequently, in the early 1990s, Daly City introduced a second unit legalization initiative—Project Homesafe—in two rounds. The city extensively marketed a simple checklist, set up an anonymous phone line to answer questions from homeowners, removed its penalties and development fees, and even made loans available for upgrading. The process relied heavily on one building inspector in particular. He was a minister of a local church, and the community members deeply trusted him. Thanks to these efforts, the city legalized over a thousand informal units (Cabansagan 2011).[5]

ENFORCEMENT AND LEGALIZATION OF GARAGE HOUSING

In the late 1980s, the *Los Angeles Times* (Chavez and Quinn 1987) helped focus public attention on informal and precarious housing. It motivated Tom Bradley, the mayor of the city of Los Angeles, to form the Blue Ribbon Committee for Affordable Housing. A report by the committee noted the significant reduction in federal support for affordable housing and recommended the city create a new organization to focus on preserving existing affordable units and building new ones (Blue Ribbon Committee for Affordable Housing 1988; Goetz 1993). The *Los Angeles Times* (1989) followed up with an investigative series on substandard housing, "Los Angeles' Slums: A Growth Industry." With the continued attention on inadequate housing, the Los Angeles City Council adopted the committee's recommendations and instituted a new housing department and affordable housing commission in 1990. The new public institutions, along with the local Community Redevelopment Agency, provided an impetus for the development and rehabilitation of affordable housing units. The focus of these endeavors, however, was on multifamily buildings.

Policy makers did not form any new initiatives to address unpermitted garage apartments or second units on single-family-zoned properties until two tragic garage fires in low-income neighborhoods forced them to revisit the issue. At the city council's direction, the Los Angeles Housing Department assembled a task force to study the issue.

The Garage Housing Task Force recognized the informal units' significance in the city's housing stock and rejected enforcement as the primary approach. It offered four formalization policy options:

(1) Regularization of informal units citywide;
(2) Regularization of unpermitted units on a geographical basis using overlay zones;
(3) Legalization of second units through deregulation of single-family zoning on a geographic basis; and most ambitiously,
(4) Legalization of second units citywide through zoning deregulation.

While the housing department supported implementing all four options, the Department of City Planning rejected the last two possibilities, which involved the deregulation of zoning and the legalization of second units. The planning department was unwilling to support significant changes to the city's single-family neighborhoods (Los Angeles Housing Department 1997). Ultimately, the task force focused on the regularization of existing unpermitted units. It recommended a hazard reduction program, an interim occupancy program of three years to give owners time and a deadline to upgrade their unpermitted units, a requirement for units to follow the city's Rent Stabilization Ordinance to protect tenants from excessive rent increases, and relocation assistance for tenants whose units were deemed hazardous and demolished. The task force acknowledged that finding adequate funding for the necessary improvements and upgrading of poorly built units was challenging (Los Angeles Housing Department 1997).

For many critics of second units in single-family neighborhoods, the task force's recommendations were unacceptable. They perceived second units as a substantial departure from single-family housing norms and worried that higher density would adversely affect their neighborhoods and hurt their homes' property values. Representatives of many homeowners' associations in the city, including the leaders of the Homeowners Associations of Studio City and Encino, actively opposed the recommendations (S. Bernstein 1997b). A member of the Van Nuys Homeowners Association, for example, argued that "neighborhoods like hers will be plagued with traffic congestion, parking problems, and diminished property values" (Martin 1997). City Councilmember Hal Bernson, chair of the influential Planning and Land Use Management (PLUM) Committee, rejected the task force's recommendations and instead pushed for enforcement. He proposed to give homeowners three months to come forward, abate their second units (or get permits if they could meet the prevailing zoning requirements), or face fines and criminal liability (McGreevy 1997).[6]

Gradually, the task force lost all political support for its progressive recommendations. Even Councilmember Alarcon became wary of supporting formalization of second units without additional information. Along with Mayor Richard Riordan, he proposed the institution of an "ad hoc committee on Safe Housing" to study how to address safety issues in unpermitted garage units in the short term (McGreevy 1997; Richman interview 2017). Bernson and the PLUM Committee, however, rejected the suggestion. They pushed for enforcement and removing hazards through a public education campaign for owners and tenants with funding from the Los Angeles Fire Department and the Department of Water and Power (Los Angeles Housing Department 1997; McGreevy 1997; Richman interview 2017). Instead of formalization, the city's focus shifted to enforcement.[7]

SUPPORT FOR AND OPPOSITION TO FORMAL SECOND UNITS IN LOS ANGELES

Local opposition to second units was not limited to the Los Angeles region. It was a statewide phenomenon. In 2002, a few years after the task force considered formalization and legalization of converted garages and second units in the city of Los Angeles, the California state legislature approved Assembly Bill 1866 to nudge cities to allow second units in their single-family neighborhoods more liberally. In 2003, as I discussed in chapter 3, the city of Los Angeles responded by allowing second units by right instead of through its cumbersome and unpredictable discretionary approvals process (City of Los Angeles 2003). The Department of City Planning's records show that the regulatory change had a positive impact and that permits for second units modestly increased from a handful to around thirty ADUs per year (Los Angeles Department of City Planning 2016a).[8]

In late 2009, the city of Los Angeles organized three workshops to solicit public input for a new second unit ordinance. While the planning department was conducting the workshops, the city council's PLUM Committee instructed the department to study and propose how to formalize "previously unpermitted converted units in conjunction with permanent development regulations for Accessory Dwelling Units that consider the character and scale of the City of Los Angeles and are in compliance with AB 1866" (Los Angeles City Council 2009). Councilmembers Paul Koretz and Bill Rosendahl and Council President Eric Garcetti proposed the motion. Other councilmembers, including Alarcon, seconded it.

The city council motion inflamed opposition to second units in the city. Although unpermitted second units are common and hardly a secret (see, for example, figure 5.1), public policy discussion of formalizing them draws the ire of many residents. City Attorney Carmen Trutanich told a group of about sixty angry neighborhood activists, including members of the Hillside Federation, "that nothing in the state law requires the city to open the floodgates to granny flats throughout most of the city's residential areas" (Kaye 2009). As I noted in chapter 3, in light of the vocal opposition, the planning department put off the development of a new second unit ordinance but also stated that "in the interim, the city will comply with the parameters established by State Law" (Goldberg 2009).

Subsequently, in 2010, the city's chief zoning administrator wrote a memorandum and issued an interpretation based on AB 1866—"ZA Memorandum NO. 120" (City of Los Angeles 2010)—that liberalized the rules for second units in the city of Los Angeles. It allowed homeowners to add second units of up to 1,200 sq. ft. on standard-sized lots of 5,000 sq. ft. The previous interpretation, issued in 2003 by the zoning administrator and the zoning engineer (City of Los Angeles 2003), had changed the discretionary

FIGURE 5.1
A truck advertising service for obtaining permits for informal garage conversions. Photo credit: Elsa Rodriguez.

permit process to a by-right approval process but kept the city's more restrictive rules from 1985. Under the 1985 rules, owners needed a minimum lot size of 7,500 sq. ft. and were only permitted to add units of up to 640 sq. ft.

In 2013, Council President Garcetti succeeded Antonio Villaraigosa as mayor and declared that he wanted to add one hundred thousand housing units in the next eight years (Logan 2014).[9] He saw an opportunity to increase the number of second units added each year and was particularly interested in the potential of building units for less than $150,000. Mayor Garcetti asked his Innovation Team (i-team), which was established through a $2.5 million grant from the Bloomberg Foundation, to explore possible policy changes to encourage ADU construction (Neville communication 2016).

Although the city of Los Angeles's 2010 interpretation made it easier for homeowners to get formal permits for second units, there were still significant regulatory constraints. For fire safety, for example, the city required a clear passageway from the front street to the main door of the second unit. The driveway could not serve as the passageway, and it was challenging to fit both on 5,000 sq. ft. lots (Mukhija, Cuff, and Serrano 2014). The city required two covered parking spaces for the main house and additional parking (covered or uncovered) for the second unit and mandated rear and side setbacks, which made permitted garage conversions almost impossible (Blumenfeld interview 2013). The city had embarked on a process of reforming its zoning regulations—recode: LA—and planners and housing activists hoped that some of the regulatory hurdles, particularly the passageway requirement, could be addressed through the reform (Coleman communication 2015; Vallianatos interview 2016).

The mayor's i-team analyzed the second units permitted in the city since the 2010 regulatory changes and conducted focus groups with homeowners who had developed formal second units. It found that most of the second units were being built in the San Fernando Valley, where large lots of 7,500 sq. ft. were more common. Similar to my analysis of the typology of unpermitted units from the sales listings (chapter 4), the i-team found that roughly two-thirds of the permitted second units were backyard structures, and about one-third were formed through garage conversions or carve-outs from the main unit. Homeowners were relying on personal savings or home equity loans to finance the construction. Moreover, in many cases, small entrepreneurs were acquiring single-family houses to build second units of the maximum allowed size of 1,200 sq. ft. to rent both properties or flip them after the addition (Daflos and Neville interview 2016).

AN EMERGING CULTURAL CHANGE

In 2016, the mayor's i-team proposed a second unit pilot program as a "social opportunity" for all stakeholders to learn together (Daflos communication 2016). It hoped that the project would help streamline the city's regulations and create a pathway for homeowners to access loans to finance the construction of second units. It invited LA Más, an urban design nonprofit organization on whose board of directors I served, and UCLA's cityLAB to separately design and build two one-bedroom second units on 5,000 sq. ft. lots. The i-team would help both projects obtain their permits, including the necessary zoning variances from current requirements (Leung and Timme interview 2016). It planned to demonstrate through the two pilot projects that the city's passageway, setback, and covered parking requirements were excessive and unnecessary, and that second units built without these requirements would not have an adverse effect on neighbors.

The i-team also asked Genesis LA Economic Growth Corporation, a local community development financial institution (CDFI), to provide financing for both projects. Genesis LA hoped to sell the loans to a commercial bank (De Simone communication 2016). LA Más set out to build a unit in northeast Los Angeles, and cityLAB targeted Pacoima in the north San Fernando Valley. LA Más (2016) emailed over forty community leaders, posted flyers in more than twenty locations, and made four presentations in the community. UCLA's cityLAB partnered with Pacoima Beautiful, a community-based organization focused on environmental justice in Pacoima and Sun Valley, to organize a workshop on second units to solicit interest from homeowners (see figure 5.2; Blumenfeld communication 2019).

In a parallel process, cityLAB's Dana Cuff and Jane Blumenfeld started working with Assemblymember Richard Bloom (Democrat from Santa Monica) to develop state legislation to remove the city's cumbersome passageway requirement (Daflos and Neville interview 2016).

While the mayor's i-Team, LA Más, UCLA cityLAB, and Genesis LA worked on expanding the feasibility and popular acceptance of second units, there were two additional noteworthy developments: the formalization of informal apartments and the rise of multigenerational housing.

Formalization of Unpermitted Units in Apartments: The city of Los Angeles made an important effort to formalize informal apartments in multifamily housing through its unpermitted dwelling unit (UDU) ordinance. The city created a process to formalize nonconforming units, provided that property owners agreed to keep the units as affordable or maintain at least one low- or moderate-income affordable housing unit in their building for each formalized unit.[10] Introduced by Councilmember Felipe Fuentes of Council District 7, the UDU ordinance garnered support from tenants' groups and landlords and was endorsed by the *Los Angeles Times* (2014). Although there was opposition from some neighborhood groups, the final ordinance was adopted unanimously by the city council in May 2017 (Reyes 2017). It illustrated a pragmatic acceptance of informal housing and its contributions to the city.

Multigenerational Housing: The Great Recession and the increase in the number of multigenerational families transformed the market for single-family housing. In response to changing economic and demographic conditions, several of the largest home builders in the country, including Lennar, Toll Brothers, PulteGroup, Meritage Homes, and Ryland Homes, started redesigning the floor plans of their single-family houses to make them more suitable

MODEL BACKYARD HOME WORKSHOP

**JUNE 2, 2016
6:00-8:00PM**

**PACOIMA CITY HALL
ROOM 200**

**Want to build an extra apartment unit in your yard?
Have an existing unit you would like to upgrade?**

If you have any interest in adding an additional unit to your property, or feel you have a unit that could use upgrading, come to our model backyard home workshop from 6:00-8:00pm on June 2, 2016, in Room 200 of Pacoima City Hall. There, we will be providing information about loans, construction, upgrades, and the feasibility of projects specific to your property.

For more information about the workshop and program, please contact Max Podemski or Yvette Lopez at Pacoima Beautiful. All are welcome.

Yvette Lopez & Max Podemski
(818) 899-2454
ylopez@pacoimabeautiful.org
mpodemski@pacoimabeautiful.org

FIGURE 5.2
A flyer announcing the second unit or Backyard Home workshop in Pacoima. *Source*: Pacoima Beautiful.

for multigenerational families. The new layouts gave buyers the option to have connected but independent second units with discrete entrances. For example, Lennar marketed its new line of multigenerational, family-friendly single-family houses as "Next Gen—The Home within a Home" (Green 2012). "The houses feature a completely separate unit—with own entry, kitchen, bathroom, bedroom and living area—attached to the main house with a double door similar to adjoining hotel rooms" (Kalita 2012).

An article in *Builder Magazine*, a trade publication for home builders, discussed the top "design trends in single-family living" and noted, "Multigenerational living has become part of our culture. Families are staying together longer for various reasons, economic as well as cultural. Lower-level living suites with their own entrance, living spaces, and kitchenette are becoming more prevalent" (Lehnert 2013).

The growth of home-builder-led multigenerational single-family housing with second units was particularly significant in Southern California, where the strong market showed how demand for housing was evolving. According to Phil Bodem (interview 2017) of Meritage Homes and Bradley Hare (interview 2017) of Toll Brothers, their companies were not building multigenerational housing before the recession, but in the ten years since, it had become a central part of their development portfolios. Similarly, Pardee Homes' Matt Sauls and Mike Taylor (interview 2017) estimated that between a quarter and a fifth of their homebuyers in the Southern California region were interested in multigenerational housing, which they marketed as the "GenSmart Suite" option of having a private home within a home. While most buyers of multigenerational housing were family members who pooled their resources, some were older buyers who anticipated the need for home care providers or family members living with them (Han interview 2017). The multigenerational housing segment received a boost in demand with the COVID-19 pandemic as many prospective homeowners wanted their elderly parents to live with them rather than in senior-living facilities (K. McLaughlin 2020).

Figures 5.3, 5.4, and 5.5 illustrate three different arrangements of second-unit-based, multigenerational housing built by the New Home Company, a luxury home builder, in a subdivision in Irvine, Orange County, California. Figure 5.3 shows a detached guest house of about 800 sq. ft., including a service bar kitchenette, separated from the main house by a covered outdoor patio. Figure 5.4 depicts a one-bedroom suite. The company called it "private quarters." It can be closed off from the rest of the house and accessed from a private external entrance. Figure 5.5 shows the two-home compound. It has two adjacent units without a separating wall or fence. The houses share a yard, have separate accessory quarters, and together were the most expensive housing option in the subdivision (Lansner 2012; Spivak 2012). In essence, the high-end housing market was changing to include second units.

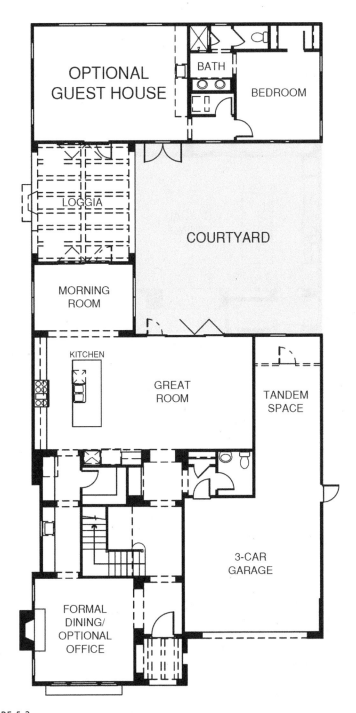

FIGURE 5.3
First-floor plan of the New Home Company's single-family house with a detached guest suite at Lambert Ranch, Irvine, California (not to scale). *Source*: Based on a plan by the New Home Company. Graphic: Jae-Hyeon Park.

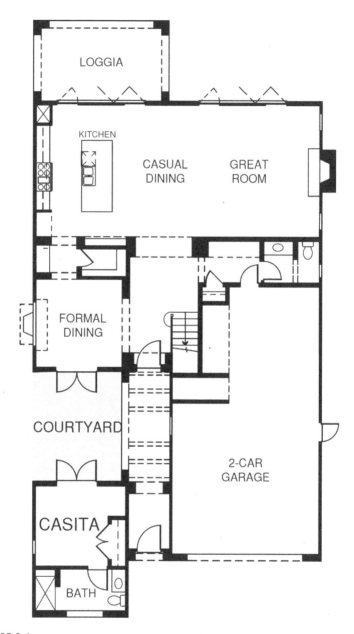

FIGURE 5.4
First-floor plan of the New Home Company's single-family house with an attached private suite at Lambert Ranch, Irvine, California (not to scale). *Source*: Based on a plan by the New Home Company. Graphic: Jae-Hyeon Park.

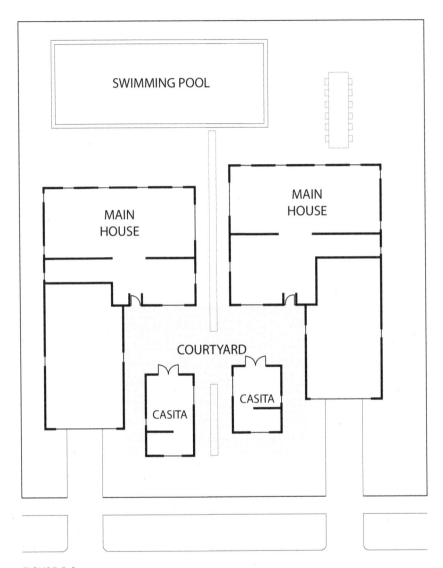

FIGURE 5.5
Schematic plan of the New Home Company's "Compound Home" at Lambert Ranch, Irvine, California (not to scale). *Source*: Based on a plan by the New Home Company. Graphic: Jae-Hyeon Park.

LOCAL CHALLENGES TO SECOND UNITS

Although cityLAB and Pacoima Beautiful volunteers were actively looking for a pilot project site in Pacoima, they found the task extremely difficult. It seemed like everyone who wanted a second unit already had an unpermitted one (Podemski communication 2019), and homeowners' friends or family members often occupied the units (Lopez-Ledesma communication 2019). Houses with converted garages were particularly challenging for the pilot project because the homeowners would have had to remove their unpermitted units and turn their garage apartments back into car storage areas (Daflos and Neville interview 2016). Furthermore, even though Genesis LA agreed to provide financing for the second unit, homeowners who were interested typically had too much existing debt and could not qualify for the loan (Blumenfeld communication 2019; Podemski communication 2019).

Meanwhile, after narrowing down the list of potential homeowners from three to one for its pilot project, LA Más started construction in mid-2017. Its project faced unexpected hurdles. Contrary to the original idea of a more affordable and modest second unit, the selected homeowner was interested in a two-bedroom ADU of about 1,000 sq. ft., which would cost considerably more. LA Más determined that it was feasible to design a project on the selected site within the existing regulatory constraints, as it became clear that it would be too time-consuming to get variances to show how some of the city's regulatory requirements were unnecessary. Although the pilot project was unlikely to be particularly affordable or helpful in pushing the boundaries of second unit regulations, it still had the potential to positively impact citywide conversations on second units and demonstrate a new financing model. The i-team, LA Más, and Genesis LA continued to be enthusiastic about the effort. In late 2017, however, the project got delayed owing to unanticipated foundation work challenges in its hillside location (Leung and Timme interview 2017).

But the biggest institutional challenge was a lawsuit against the city of Los Angeles by the respected public interest and environmental justice attorney Carlyle Hall. As I mentioned in chapter 3, Hall had successfully litigated against the city in 1984 for not updating its zoning to be consistent with its General Plan. In 2016, a neighbor began building a 900 sq. ft. second unit in front of Hall's home in Cheviot Hills, an affluent single-family neighborhood on the west side. Hall was so upset by this that he founded Los Angeles Neighbors in Action in 2016 and sued the city for not following stricter rules for allowing second units in single-family neighborhoods (Hall 2016b). He criticized the second unit's approval and argued, "It doesn't fit into the neighborhood. It's really changing the character, and you can see it from everywhere" (Badger 2016). His complaints about the changing physical character of his neighborhood directly related to his complaints about potential changes to the social composition of his community. With candid prejudice against tenants, Hall criticized second units as "multifamily rental property smack in the middle of what had been an owner-occupied single-family neighborhood," and noted that "the Planning Department's current effort to promote rental housing in single-family neighborhoods, abetted by terrible ongoing advice from the City Attorney, leaves one wondering whether the City Council even understands the ramifications of its decisions, much less whether it really listens to or cares about its single-family neighborhoods" (Hall 2016a).

Hall argued that the city had not formally rolled back its 1985 ordinance on second units. Consequently, he claimed, it needed to stop using ZA Memorandum NO. 120 and the state's default standards on second units and go back to the stricter standards it had originally adopted in 1985 and reaffirmed in 2003, including the maximum allowed unit size of 640 sq. ft. The court agreed with Hall. In February 2016, the Superior Court invalidated ZA Memorandum NO. 120 and asked the city to pass a new ordinance or follow the older, more demanding standards that preceded the zoning administrator's interpretation in 2010 (Hall 2016a, 2016b). The ruling was a significant setback to the city's efforts to encourage the construction of more second units.

STATE GOVERNMENT INTERVENTION AND MANDATES

Despite Hall's successful lawsuit, at an informal salon on second units—irreverently called "Much ADU about Nothing"—at the LA Más office in mid-2016, there was tremendous enthusiasm about two bills making their way through the state legislature in Sacramento. Assembly Bill 2299 by Assemblymember Bloom, with whom Cuff and Blumenfeld of cityLAB had been working, and Senate Bill 1069 by State Senator Bob Wieckowski (Democrat from Fremont). Local second unit advocates like Ira Belgrade (communication 2016) discussed plans for mounting a publicity campaign to highlight second units' positive attributes after the bills were approved.

Second unit enthusiasts saw the two state legislative bills as game changers. They reduced regulatory barriers, streamlined the approval processes, and curtailed cities' ability to impose stricter requirements on second units. Both measures reduced parking mandates, particularly in transit-rich areas. While the maximum parking requirements could be up to one space for a second unit, the bills together mandated that ADUs in transit areas, historic districts, or residential permit districts and second units carved out of the main house or built through garage conversions have no required parking. AB 2299 increased the allowed size of second units to up to 50 percent of the primary residence or a maximum of 1,200 sq. ft. SB 1069 targeted development fees and mandated that cities could not impose the same costs on second units as new housing units. The fees needed to be proportionate to the burden the units imposed on local infrastructure. Both bills made it easier to legalize existing unpermitted units. They prohibited setback requirements for converted garages and mandated that cities do not require sprinklers in second units if they were not required for the primary residence (Wieckowski interview 2018, 2019).

A third bill, Assembly Bill 2406, by then assemblymember Tony Thurmond (Democrat from Richmond), received less attention. It allowed homeowners to carve out "junior accessory dwelling units," or JADUs, of up to 500 sq. ft. from the primary unit without paying additional development fees or meeting any parking requirements. Because of its constraints on parking requirements and development fees, the legislation likely created a legalization pathway for homeowners with modest-sized unpermitted second units carved out of the main dwelling. The bill, however, required homeowners to live on-site in the primary unit or the JADU.

Cuff and Blumenfeld were instrumental in cowriting AB 2299 by collaborating with Assemblymember Bloom (Bennett, Cuff, and Wendell 2019; Blumenfeld communication 2019; Cuff communication 2018). According to Blumenfeld, Senator Wieckowski consulted with Karen Chapple at the University of California, Berkeley, who has conducted influential research on second units (Chapple 2014; Chapple et al. 2011; Wegmann and Chapple 2014). The Northern California group was particularly concerned about cumbersome parking requirements and excessive development fees, and the Southern California collaborators were keen to address parking regulations and prohibit the city of Los Angeles's passageway requirement. Both groups coordinated and reconciled the differences across the two bills (Blumenfeld communication 2019). They were aware of Carlyle Hall's successful lawsuit against the city of Los Angeles, which forced the city to revert to the stricter standards in its 1985 ordinance. Consequently, the bills also categorically stated that all existing second unit ordinances were null and void unless they complied with the new state legislation. Local governments could develop second unit ordinances in compliance with the state or follow the state's default standards. Collectively, the three bills outlawed many of the tactics that localities had used to prevent the construction of second units in single-family-zoned neighborhoods.

Opposition to the legislation was mostly based on a desire to maintain local control over land use and zoning. For example, the Los Angeles County division of the League of California Cities opposed SB 1069 and criticized it for usurping local control and limiting utility connection fees (Chen 2016). The bills faced opposition in the city of Los Angeles too. Through the Rules, Elections, and Intergovernmental Relations Committee of the city (Los Angeles City Council 2016), Councilmembers Nury Martinez and Joe Buscaino introduced a resolution in June to oppose SB 1069. The city's chief legislative analyst (Tso 2016) recommended that the city adopt the Martinez-Buscaino resolution opposing the bill for "undermining local land use control."

Mayor Garcetti, however, endorsed the state legislative efforts and provided letters of support for the bills (Dillon and Khouri 2016). Martinez and Buscaino's city council colleagues also saw the legislative efforts to legalize second units as a pragmatic approach for adding new housing and formalizing existing informal units and did not adopt their resolution either. The *Los Angeles Times* (2016) wrote a supportive editorial too: "Welcome Back 'Granny Flats.'"[11]

The state legislature approved the bills in late August 2016, and Governor Jerry Brown, who had endorsed them earlier (Dillon 2016a), signed them the next month (Dillon 2016b). The new legislation, which formally changed the official terminology from second units to Accessory Dwelling Units to emphasize their subsidiary status, went into effect on January 1, 2017. To guide cities across the state in addressing and implementing the state's new laws, the California Department of Housing and Community Development (2016) released a detailed memorandum on ADUs.[12]

THE EFFECTS OF STATE ACTIVISM AND CHANGING HOUSING MARKETS IN LOS ANGELES

While state legislators debated the breakthrough ADU bills in 2016, planners and policy makers in the city of Los Angeles were trying to determine how to respond to the Superior Court's ruling in the Carlyle Hall lawsuit. After the verdict, the city put permits for second units on hold (Reyes 2016a). In May 2016, the Department of City Planning recommended that the city council simply repeal the city's 1985 ordinance and clear the way for following ZA Memorandum NO. 120 (Los Angeles Department of City Planning 2016a). The city council did not repeal the old city law, but in late August it directed the planning department to develop a new ADU ordinance (Reyes 2016b).[13] Soon after the city council's resolution, Governor Brown approved the new state ADU bills, which went into effect in January 2017.

With the impending state legislation in mind, the planning department prepared interim plans for the city. As in 2003, the city formally adopted its more restrictive 1985 second unit rules without the provision of discretionary approval (City of Los Angeles 2016). However, the city noted that the rules would expire at the end of the year. From January 1, 2017, the city would default to the state's more permissive ADU regulations. Thus, within a matter of months, the city would have ADU regulations that were more liberal than the standards struck down by the Superior Court in February 2016 (Los Angeles Department of City Planning 2016b).

Throughout 2017 and 2018, planners and policy makers discussed how to develop an appropriate ADU ordinance. Whether and how to allow second units in hillside areas was a particularly contentious issue. The Hillside Federation recommended a blanket ban against second units in the city's designated hillside areas (Mims 2018). According to the planning department, the hillside limitation would affect about 28 percent of the single-family-zoned lots in the city (Los Angeles Department of City Planning 2018). It proposed that the city allow second units carved out of existing primary residences. In November 2018, the city planning commission—consisting of commissioners appointed by the mayor—approved the ordinance and recommended its approval by the city council. The city council adopted an ADU ordinance in December 2019 that allowed the units in hillside areas but imposed more restrictive requirements, including one additional parking space for the accessory unit, fire sprinklers, and a minimum front street width (City of Los Angeles 2019).

Meanwhile, the city continued to follow the state's standards, and the market response to the relaxed standards was nothing short of tremendous. In 2017, the city received 3,818 applications requesting construction permits for second units (Los Angeles Department of City Planning 2019). In contrast, in 2015 and 2016, the city received an annual average of 278 ADU applications

(Bertolet and Gabode 2019). In 2018, 2019, and 2020 the number of permit applications for second units increased even more (see table 5.1).

Formal second units became an integral and important part of the local housing market. As table 5.2 shows, there was a sharp increase in the number of construction permits issued for second units in 2017 and 2018 from previous years in the city of Los Angeles. In 2018, moreover, permits issued for constructing second units increased to account for a fifth of the housing units permitted in the city. The effects of the state's legislative efforts to legalize ADUs in the housing market were evident in the increase in permit applications statewide (see table 5.3). That said, the effects were most dramatic in the city of Los Angeles because the city did not impose an owner-occupancy requirement for second units and had relatively low development or impact fees.

The excitement about second units in the city of Los Angeles extended beyond what the permit numbers reflect. Second units entered the cultural imagination and were being appreciated for their avant-garde design

Table 5.1
Applications for second unit permits in the city of Los Angeles, 2017–2020

Applications for permits	2017	2018	2019	2020	2017–2020
Conversion/Alteration	1,884	2,427	2,343	2,602	9,256
Addition	1,310	1,963	2,091	1,864	7,228
New construction	624	1,039	1,185	1,269	4,117
Total	**3,818**	**5,429**	**5,619**	**5,735**	**20,601**

Sources: Los Angeles Department of City Planning 2019, 2020, 2021.

Table 5.2
Permits issued for second units in the city of Los Angeles, 2013–2018

Year	Total housing unit construction permits	Second unit construction permits	Second units as share of housing permits (%)
2013	8,392	84	1.0
2014	14,817	128	0.9
2015	17,307	226	1.3
2016	13,696	117	0.9
2017	14,019	2,326	16.6
2018	20,831	4,171	20.0

Source: Bertolet and Gabode 2019.

Table 5.3
Permit applications for second units in various California cities, 2015–2017

Jurisdiction	2015	2016	2017
City of Los Angeles	299	257	3,818
Long Beach	0	1	42
Oakland	33	99	247
Sacramento	17	28	34
San Diego	16	17	64
San Francisco*	41	384	593*
San Jose	28	45	166

Source: Bertolet and Gabode 2019.
*Data for 2017 are for the first three quarters only.

FIGURE 5.6
A second unit under construction in West Los Angeles. Photo credit: Matthew Hartzell.

potential. Several small architectural design firms and home builders started focusing on the second unit market. Figure 5.6 shows a second unit project under construction by Modative, an architectural design firm that offers design and construction services in the Los Angeles region. In June 2019, the LA Design Festival showcased a self-guided ADU home tour of newly constructed second units in the city (figure 5.7), including LA Más's pilot project.[14]

CHALLENGES IN LEGALIZING AND UPGRADING SECOND UNITS

Although state intervention in second unit regulations and its acceptance in cities like Los Angeles led to noteworthy progress in formalizing second units, several challenges in legalizing and upgrading accessory units persisted.

FIGURE 5.7
Second units in the ADU home tour organized for the 2019 LA Design Festival (clockwise from top left: outside and inside views of Bunch Design's second unit in Highland Park; and inside and outside views of Paul and Yuki's second unit in Echo Park). Photo credit: Author.

MUNICIPAL RELUCTANCE

Many homeowners interested in adding second units continued to face institutional obstacles from their local governments. Costa Mesa, an affluent Orange County city near the coast, exemplified some cities' attempts to use regulatory workarounds to maintain local control over land use and avoid complying with state legislation on second units. In 2017, the city's planning commission responded to AB 2299 and SB 1069 by recommending that the city reduce the minimum lot size requirement for adding second units on single-family-zoned lots from 8,500 sq. ft. to 7,500 sq. ft. Explaining the proposed change, Byron de Arakal, vice chair of the commission, noted, "I think it is reasonable enough to keep the jackals in the marble halls of Sacramento from coming down and hassling us" (Money 2017). The city's ADU rules posted on its website indicated that the Costa Mesa City Council thought the commission's recommendation was too liberal, and set the minimum lot size to 7,900 sq. ft. instead (City of Costa Mesa 2018).[15]

In Los Angeles County, Pasadena tried to limit second units by requiring homeowners to live in either the primary residence or the ADU. Additionally, it had high development or residential impact fees ranging from $23,000 for second units built from conversions to almost $29,000 for new construction (City of Pasadena 2018).[16] The city also required a minimum lot size of 7,200 sq. ft. and restricted second units to 800 sq. ft.

Similarly, the city of Pico Rivera, located in southeastern Los Angeles County, imposed a minimum lot size requirement of 6,000 sq. ft., even though only 37 percent of its single-family-zoned lots qualified for the threshold. If the city reduced the minimum lot size to 5,000 sq. ft., 89 percent of its single-family-zoned lots would be eligible (S. Hernandez 2018). Pico Rivera limited second units to a maximum size of 500 sq. ft. Many cities followed this strategy to discourage second units. For example, in Los Angeles County, Burbank and Glendale restricted second units to 500 sq. ft.; Culver City allowed second units of up to 600 sq. ft.; and Beverly Hills and Santa Monica limited them to 650 sq. ft.

In response to these kinds of municipal shenanigans designed to restrict second units, state legislators approved additional legislation in 2019.[17] Collectively, the bills removed minimum lot size requirements, reduced the maximum setbacks to 4 ft., and increased the maximum allowed size of ADUs to 800 sq. ft. They also eliminated the owner-occupancy requirement for second units for the next five years and drastically reduced impact fees (including eliminating them for units under 750 sq. ft.). They prohibited cities from legislating lot coverage and floor area requirements that prevent second units and barred homeowners' associations from instituting rules that effectively ban second units. The bills significantly eroded single-family zoning in the state by making it feasible for homeowners to have three units on their lots: the main dwelling, an ADU, and a JADU.

ACCESS TO CONSTRUCTION FINANCE

The cost of constructing a new second unit can be high. Jan Breidenbach (communication 2018), a well-known housing policy expert, estimated that it would cost $200,000, or around $370 per square foot, to add a 540 sq. ft. one-bedroom unit to her house in 2018. Jeff Wilson (interview 2016) of Kasita, a high-end, prefabricated manufactured home builder, estimated construction costs of $300–$400 per square foot (plus foundation and infrastructure work, and permit expenses) for his units. Modative, which I mentioned above, estimated total construction cost of $350,000 for a two-bedroom, one-and-a-half-bath second unit of 1,000 sq. ft. ($350 per square foot) on the city of Los Angeles's west side in 2020.[18] The executive directors of LA Más estimated a cost of $300,000 for a new three-bedroom unit of 1,200 sq. ft. (about $275 per square foot) in 2021 (Leung communication 2021). They also estimated a cost of $100,000 to convert a garage to a studio.[19]

No matter the cost of adding a second unit, many homeowners lack the resources to finance their construction. Scholars note that accessing the necessary financing to build second units is a barrier for many homeowners (Chapple et al. 2017; Wegmann 2015). As in the Global South's title-based legalization experience, less affluent households find it challenging to take advantage of legalization. Well-off homeowners draw on personal savings and family resources, or have enough equity in their homes to secure traditional financial products like home equity loans, home equity lines of credit, and cash-out refinancing to pay for their second units. But low-income homeowners with less equity in their homes cannot access affordable financing. Typically, banks and lenders are unwilling to extend construction loans for second units because they lend based on existing collateral, not on the projected future value of a property after the second unit has been added. Similarly, lenders assess borrowers' creditworthiness based on their current income and disregard future rental income. They will not consider a second unit's rental income until it establishes a two-year rental history.

To address the lack of institutional financing for second units, market-based firms like United Dwelling and Dweller offer to build, manage, and pay for second units for homeowners with limited equity. In return, however, the firms require a fifteen- or twenty-five-year lease and a majority share of the rents—64 percent to 70 percent—over the leasehold period to recover their investments (figure 5.8).

FIGURE 5.8
Screenshot of the website of United Dwelling, a second unit developer with a land-lease-based business model. *Source*: uniteddwelling.com.

LA Más aimed to address the lack of access to finance for less affluent homeowners. It launched a new program called the Backyard Homes Project in partnership with Genesis LA and Self-Help Federal Credit Union, a leading national CDFI. Self-Help would provide selected homeowners with a loan, and Genesis LA would provide the CDFI with a financial guaranty. Self-Help's loan would be based on the credit union refinancing a homeowner's existing mortgage to include additional financing to fund the new second unit's construction. Because the loan amount would exceed the value of the existing collateral, Genesis LA agreed to provide a guaranty to Self-Help to mitigate the risk. In exchange for access to financing, and design and construction support from LA Más, homeowners who build second units through the Backyard Homes Project agree to rent the units to a Section 8, or rental subsidy, voucher holder for five years (De Simone communication 2018; Leung and Timme interview 2017). Although the program innovatively opened up access to credit for less affluent homeowners, Genesis LA's guaranty facility of $650,000 with Self-Help could finance the construction of only four to six second units at a time (Mukhija and Meyer 2019). LA Más received more than two hundred applications in 2019 and 2020. It found that many homeowners needed small grants to evaluate the feasibility of building second units on their properties, and awarded planning grants to several applicants. By mid-2021, five projects were completed or under construction (De Simone interview 2021).[20]

THE LACK OF PUBLIC SUPPORT FOR UPGRADING

The state legislature's efforts focused on zoning reforms to legalize second units and increase the supply of new ADUs. While zoning reforms to allow second units encourage new ADU construction, they are an inadequate solution for most working-class homeowners and neighborhoods with existing unpermitted second units requiring investments and improvements. There was not an associated state-level push for regularization and upgrading of existing unpermitted second units.

One important exception was Senate Bill 13 by Senator Wieckowski in 2019, which provided additional time and a pathway to bring informal second units up to code.[21] It afforded homeowners a five-year amnesty to bring their informal units into compliance with zoning and building code requirements that did not relate to health and safety. The five-year horizon provided them with the security to invest in their unpermitted units, improve their conditions, and gradually upgrade them to the required standards (Wieckowski interview 2019).

None of the state's legislative endeavors, however, provided funding to local governments or homeowners for help in upgrading housing conditions in informal second units. As the city of Los Angeles's Garage Housing Task Force noted in 1997, many second units have unsafe living conditions. Homeowners need additional time, funding, and public support to remove hazards and make improvements. Neighborhoods like Pacoima, where it was difficult to find a second unit pilot project site because of existing unpermitted second units and residents' limited capacity to borrow loans, illustrate the significant need for grants, subsidized loans, and technical assistance. Not surprisingly, the cofounders and executive director of Pacoima Beautiful emphasize the need for substantial funding support and public assistance to upgrade informal housing in their community (Grossman communication 2019; Padilla communication 2019; Romero-Martinez communication 2019).

Public support for private housing is not unusual. There are several examples of financial support by the state government for private housing improvements in California to guide future policy. For example, owners of single-family houses can receive grants of up to $3,000 from the California Earthquake Authority, a state agency, to retrofit their homes through the Earthquake Brace + Bolt program (Lin 2018). The authority helps homeowners avoid the cost of hiring a structural engineer to prepare plans for retrofitting by providing ready-to-use retrofit designs. Residents of disadvantaged neighborhoods, however, often miss out on such public assistance programs because their homes are often not up to code and do not qualify.[22] Any effort by the state legislature to help homeowners improve their informal housing will have to ensure that funding from a public assistance program targets and meets low-income households' needs and that affluent beneficiaries do not capture it.

Policy makers can require new rights and protections for tenants in return for public assistance and support for upgrading. There is a need for public funding for legal mediation between tenants of substandard unpermitted second units and property owners. Mediators can help them discuss and address substandard housing conditions, including gas leaks, faulty wiring, poor plumbing, leaking roofs, and broken windows. Currently, nonprofit legal aid agencies are reluctant to pursue mediation and typically favor code enforcement and relocation benefits for their clients. If public funding support were available for upgrading, it is more likely that mediation efforts would be more successful (Haffner interview 2014; Sayeed interview 2014).

Local governments also have a significant role to play in successful regularization and upgrading efforts. They can provide funding to homeowners for foundation work, improving ventilation and insulation, upgrading utilities, safer electrical wiring, and smoke alarms. They can offer fee waivers, fee deferrals, and lower fees for permits, and access to technical assistance, advice, and information on regulatory processes and available funding. As envisioned in SB 13, local governments can provide homeowners additional time for making the necessary improvements through temporary permits and guarantees against enforcement action for a specified period. Since the spatial context and local conditions of informal housing vary across and within jurisdictions, local governments can play an essential role in developing and instituting alternative or flexible rules and standards based on the existing conditions of unpermitted units in their communities.

While it is wrong to equate informal housing with slums, unregulated units can be risky. The most dangerous and unsafe dwellings likely house the poorest and most vulnerable residents. Ignoring informal housing perpetuates the risks associated with substandard units. Moreover, in the case of catastrophic outcomes, it can lead to knee-jerk policy reactions aimed at enforcement and the removal of unregulated units. The corresponding loss of essential housing can only make the situation worse.

CONCLUSION

In the late 1990s, ten years after an important *Los Angeles Times* article on unpermitted garage housing in Los Angeles County (Chavez and Quinn 1987), a series of tragic garage fires killed eight residents in the city of Los Angeles. The fires underscored the precarity of unregulated housing. In the aftermath of the tragedies, the city assembled a task force to develop policy responses. The Garage Housing Task Force was led by the housing department, which was the department most aware of the city's desperate need for affordable housing, the widespread prevalence of informal housing, and the necessity to increase the housing supply through land use reforms. Although the city council initially wanted to focus on enforcement against unpermitted housing, the task force recommended other avenues of action. It proposed changing the city's zoning code to formally allow garage apartments and second units (Los Angeles Housing Department 1997). However, the Department of City Planning and several local policy makers summarily rejected the suggestion to reform single-family zoning. The task force also recommended direct and immediate attention to the city's unpermitted garage apartments and policies to make them safe and livable. City of Los Angeles policy makers ignored this suggestion too. Unpermitted second units, some of which are unsafe, persist in the city and provide precarious but much-needed affordable housing.

Two decades later, single-family zoning, nonetheless, was formally changed through land use reforms in the city of Los Angeles and California. The process of institutional change was slow and incremental. It started with state-led policy changes in the early 1980s to potentially allow second units. Many single-family housing owners contested the changes and opposed what they considered a profound remaking of the American Dream. Several jurisdictions in Southern California fought second units and looked for strategies and ways to slow down their development. However, the land use reforms continued. In the mid-2010s the state government intervened more directly and forcefully in local land use regulations to allow homeowners to add second units. Locally, the city of Los Angeles was at the vanguard of permitting ADUs. While several homeowner groups, including the Hillside Federation, persisted in opposing second units and looking for ways to prevent their development, permit applications for second units increased and accounted for a significant share of the new housing being built in the city of Los Angeles. Although state intervention was crucial, the city of Los Angeles's second unit pilot program likely helped create support and contributed to the city's success with ADU applications and permits.

State and local policy makers focused on formalizing second units through legalization by changing single-family zoning requirements. In addition to expecting deregulation to increase the housing supply and help address the affordable housing shortage, policy makers surmised that legalization would allow homeowners to access loans to invest in their unpermitted second units. However, the Global South literature indicates that mere legalization does not help and can harm disadvantaged households. The experience with deregulation and legalizing second units in California suggests similar lessons. First, legalization is likely insufficient because homeowners with unpermitted second units often need more specific land use exemptions, additional time to meet the requirements, and, perhaps most importantly, access to finance and funding and technical assistance to upgrade their units. Second, from the perspective of tenants of informal housing, legalization may have adverse effects. Without rent stabilization measures, tenants may get displaced in the legalization process owing to rent increases. Tenants are more likely to benefit if homeowners have obligations toward them in return for deregulation and public assistance to upgrade unpermitted units.

While the city of Los Angeles's task force recommended public funding for removing hazards in unpermitted garage conversions, subsequent efforts, including at the state level, paid inadequate attention to upgrading. While SB 13 provided homeowners with additional time to improve their units, the legislation did not include any funding support for upgrading. Policy makers and planners need to acknowledge the widespread prevalence of unpermitted second units, recognize that many may have unsafe living conditions but provide affordable housing to the most needy, and proactively support their regularization and upgrading with financial and technical assistance.

More positively, California became one of the national leaders in remaking single-family zoning through state preemption in local land use regulations. The state's incremental intervention helped overcome many local obstacles to land use reform, particularly homeowners' associations. It made it feasible for homeowners to build three units on single-family-zoned lots: the primary residence, an ADU, and a JADU. In California, many housing activists looked to the state government to continue its interventions and further deregulate local zoning requirements, particularly single-family zoning, to allow duplexes, triplexes, and fourplexes. In September 2021, state policy makers followed up with additional legislation to allow up to four units on single-family-zoned lots statewide.

Given the hold of the ideology of single-family living and the resistance to change by many homeowners, decisive state intervention may have been necessary. However, the city of Los Angeles's progress in mainstreaming second units, the Neighborhood Council survey suggesting some openings in homeowners' opinions in chapter 3, and the likelihood that single-family housing owners gain in property values through upzoning (or zoning changes that allow them to build more on their lots) indicate that they may have been missed opportunities for the state to push for local deliberation and locally led land use reforms. Meaningful and successful local action would still be challenging without state financial support for local efforts to engage residents and governance support through effective regional collaboration and planning institutions.

Top-down state preemption in local land use regulations offers a quicker alternative. But state preemption may have unintended consequences and unpredicted costs. It might help conceal other affordable housing needs and opportunities in the state. For example, the state government may need to push local governments to support upgrading unpermitted units and provide financial support for help with upgrading. It may need to protect tenants and provide grants and subsidized financing to homeowners willing to rent their second units affordably. It may also need to be actively involved in housing finance markets to improve access of low-income households to affordable construction finance for building second units. To make the housing and property market more inclusive, it could learn from the Backyard Homes Project and, like Genesis LA, provide financial guaranties to lenders for second unit construction financing. It could also start an affordable mortgage insurance program to make it easier and less risky for credit unions and banks to lend to households with modest incomes and outstanding debt based on the projected value of their second units. Like LA Más, it could provide modest planning grants to homeowners interested in evaluating the feasibility of adding second units to their lots.

6 THE FORMALIZATION OF SECOND UNITS: THE ROLE OF LOCAL GOVERNMENTS

Minneapolis experienced double-digit population growth during the 2010s. As its housing market became tighter, planners and policy makers became concerned about increasing the housing supply. In mid-2013, the Minneapolis planning department started looking seriously at ADUs and the possibility of expanding an existing pilot program to allow secondary units on single-family- and duplex-zoned lots citywide. Planners decided to research cities in the US and Canada that had successfully reformed their land use regulations to allow second units.

They focused on Santa Cruz, California, Seattle, Portland, Oregon, and Vancouver, Canada (Minneapolis Community Planning & Economic Development 2014). At that time, these cities were considered the leaders of a growing second unit movement. Santa Cruz had received widespread recognition for its ADU program in the early 2000s, which started a nationwide conversation on second units. Since 2009, Seattle had allowed single-family homeowners to add an attached or detached second unit. Portland, which probably had the most liberal ADU regulations among major US cities, allowed second units without additional parking requirements or owner-occupancy restrictions. In 2010, Portland incentivized second units by exempting them from development charges. Of these four cities, Vancouver led in progressive ADU regulations and allowed three units on most single-family-zoned lots. It legalized second units citywide in 2004, and in 2009 it permitted homeowners to add a laneway apartment.

Following up on its research of leading second unit programs, the Minneapolis planning department launched a public engagement program of workshops and an online survey to share its findings and recommendations and receive feedback. The public response suggested overwhelming support for allowing second units. In December 2014, a near-unanimous city council approved second units citywide (City of Minneapolis 2014a). The city's success with ADU legislation and openness to tenants in single-family neighborhoods set the stage for more radical land use reforms four years later. In December 2018, the Minneapolis City Council approved a new comprehensive plan (City of Minneapolis 2018a) that eliminated single-family zoning by allowing triplexes on any residentially zoned lot, and gave property owners the right to sell each of the three units separately. It proposed to transform the purely residential character of single-family neighborhoods by allowing mixed land uses and retail opportunities within a twenty-minute walk of any residence (City of Minneapolis 2020). Minneapolis became the first major city to end single-family zoning and a model for planners and housing supply activists. The *New York Times* (2019) summarized the sentiment with a supportive editorial, "Americans Need More Neighbors."

In this chapter, I focus on Santa Cruz, Seattle, Portland, Minneapolis, and Vancouver to examine the potential, promise, and limitations of locally driven policy approaches for changing single-family housing. These cities are recognized as the vanguard of single-family zoning reforms. They have relaxed their planning regulations to allow second units by reducing their standards for minimum lot sizes, reducing or eliminating off-street parking requirements, reducing building setbacks, and increasing allowed household density, height limits, and unit sizes. Their experiences throw into sharp relief the experience of state preemption from the city of Los Angeles and California. In some of these cities, such as Minneapolis, the widespread acceptance of single-family zoning reforms has allowed the jurisdictions to go beyond second units and explore more dramatic changes in their land use regulations to allow greater density and diversity of housing. The cases suggest that there are alternative, locally driven policy pathways to institutional reform of single-family zoning that may offer advantages over the state-level approach implemented in California.

My aim in this chapter is to explore how cities can implement policies for formalizing informal second units, including deregulation of zoning and upgrading of unpermitted housing. To my disappointment, however, I did not find substantial evidence of direct public support for upgrading of unpermitted second units, or significant efforts to protect the rights of existing tenants in legalized units, in any of the case studies. As in Los Angeles, these cases highlight the need for more policy emphasis on directly improving conditions in informal housing through public support and institutional innovations instead of complete reliance on market-based, private investments.

OVERCOMING LOCAL CONCERNS ABOUT DENSITY AND DEVELOPMENT: WHAT IS THE RIGHT SCALE OF INTERVENTION?

Academic criticism of exclusionary zoning has conventionally focused on affluent suburbs, where local governments prohibit denser developments, including multifamily housing (Davidoff, Davidoff, and Gold 1970; Orfield 1997; Rusk 1999). Scholars hold exclusionary zoning in suburbs significantly responsible for the persistent and increasing economic and racial segregation across jurisdictions, particularly between cities and their outer districts (Logan, Zhang, and Chunyu 2015; Trounstine 2018). Spatial segregation, they argue, fosters inequality (Massey and Denton 1998), and as it worsens, wealth-based segregation is likely to deepen (Bischoff and Reardon 2014).

Regionalists argue that addressing hostility to housing diversity and greater density in suburban jurisdictions requires a regional framework and metropolitan governance (Basolo 2003). Since regional governance is weak in the US, regionalists argue for establishing strong metropolitan institutions (Katz 2000; Orfield 1997; Rusk 1999; Wheeler 2002). They claim that state governments have the legal authority to intervene and create metropolitan institutions (Frug 2002). Critics, however, argue that the political impediments to the redistribution of authority and power away from local governments to a centralized regional level make the establishment of strong metropolitan institutions nearly impossible (Feiock 2007; Norris 2001; Ostrom, Tiebout, and Warren 1961).

In the suburban exclusionary zoning framework, cities are regarded as more open to development. Progressive scholars typically consider markets and pro-growth interests in cities, mainly the landed elite and real estate developers, the biggest obstacle to social and urban justice (Gottdiener 1985; Mollenkopf 1983). Scholars in this vein see contradictory interests between market-based developers and the general public and argue that their divergent interests are difficult to reconcile (Harvey 1997; Purcell 2008). They contend that local governments and local business interests collaborate to manufacture support for growth as a public good and a solution for all.

Such coalitions have collectively been termed the "Growth Machine" by Harvey Molotch and John Logan (Logan and Molotch 1987; Molotch 1976). Growth Machine proponents see a conflict between market-dominated political economies and genuine democracy, especially between elite interests and community planning (Angotti 2008; Hall and Hubbard 1998). They celebrate efforts to challenge the Growth Machine and take back community power (Ferman 1996) and see opportunities for alternative spatial visions in neighborhood progressivism, particularly civic efforts to oppose public subsidies for private developments (Purcell 2000, 2008). They consider opposition and challenges to growth as an important expression of local autonomy and economic democratization (Molotch 1993). Many believe that community and neighborhood-based opposition to market-based development is an "essential countervailing force to the interests of Capital" (Lake 1993, 92).

While critics classify such opposition to real estate development projects as NIMBYism, for scholars suspicious of the market forces, the NIMBY label overlooks reasonable concerns about democratic processes, government accountability, and environmental sustainability (Dear 1992; Lake 1993; Molotch 1993; Wolsink 2006). Many community-oriented scholars in urban studies take a sympathetic approach to NIMBYism and find it more complex (Schively 2007). They point to projects with regional benefits that ignore local costs, distrust in both government institutions and private market actors, and the belief in more significant social and environmental causes as the basis for NIMBY opposition (Burningham 2000; Kraft and Clary 1991; Wolsink 2006). While acknowledging that homeowners' concerns about their property values play an essential part in NIMBY opposition to new development, scholars point out that their surveys show that renters have similar neighborhood character and congestion concerns (Hankinson 2018; Pendall 1999).[1] The self-interest that drives neighborhood-level opposition, they argue, includes place-based identity processes and quality-of-life issues that affect the everyday life of neighborhood residents (Devine-Wright 2009; Purcell 2001).

However, scholars from both market-oriented and social housing-based perspectives have become skeptical and more critical of neighborhood-based opposition to new housing developments in cities. They build on Mike Davis's (1990) critique of the Los Angeles Hillside Federation's fight for the preservation and exclusivity of its neighborhoods as the region's most powerful social movement. Economist Edward Glaeser and his colleagues

(Glaeser, Gyourko, and Saks 2005) argued that homeowners opposing new residential developments collectively act as "homeowners' cooperatives." They limit who lives in their community by controlling the level of new development and benefit from constraining the housing supply through substantial increases in their property values. Others have described homeowner groups as cartels, and cities as the new arena for exclusionary zoning (J. Mangin 2014). In their empirical analysis of the power of homeowners, Vicki Been and her colleagues (Been, Madar, and McDonnell 2014) examined parcel-level data in New York City and decisions of the city's planning commission. They found that the probability of upzoning was correlated inversely with the prevalence of owner-occupied parcels. In a related vein, planners Corianne Scally and Rosie Tighe (2015) criticized organized opposition against affordable housing. They argued that NIMBYism is not about democratic processes; on the contrary, it shows how more privileged groups of homeowners and residents have captured these practices. Indeed, political scientists have found that the urban "neighborhood defenders" who disproportionately participate in planning meetings and oppose new housing developments tend to be white and wealthy and unrepresentative of their communities (Einstein, Glick, and Palmer 2019).

Similarly, affordable housing advocates like Randy Shaw (2018) in *Generation Priced Out* held baby-boom-generation homeowners, particularly in California, responsible for pricing millennials out of big cities through their environmental and neighborhood activism against new housing developments. In *Golden Gates*, news reporter Conor Dougherty (2020) blamed the housing crisis in San Francisco and California on hypocritical homeowners making a progressive cause of their fight against new developments. Scholars warn that racial prejudice plays a central role in neighborhood-based opposition to new developments and new neighbors (Hubbard 2006; Rothstein 2017). Thus, the growing consensus in the literature is that elite homeowners dominate decision-making in many urban neighborhoods and restrict new housing developments. They have matched, if not replaced, the Growth Machine (Been 2018; Schleicher 2013).

Given the federalism context in the US and the lack of strong metropolitan institutions, scholars and policy makers concerned about the housing supply in cities see state government intervention in zoning and land use policy as the most promising arena for addressing local barriers (Glaeser 2017; Infranca 2019). The Tenth Amendment of the Constitution reserves certain powers for the federal government and grants the rest to state governments. States devolve some powers to the local level but have tremendous latitude to intervene in local matters.[2] Noteworthy examples of state government intervention include New Jersey's fair-share housing legislation, which sets affordable or below-market-rate housing quotas for local jurisdictions, and Massachusetts' so-called anti-snob zoning legislation, which allows housing developers with projects with a minimum proportion of affordable housing units to circumvent local governments that deny them permits (Bratt and Vladeck 2014). As the previous chapter detailed, California's state government intervened in local land use regulations to allow second units. Similarly, through Assembly Bill 744, the state government mandated lower parking requirements for California's affordable housing developments in 2015 (Williams, Sturtevant, and Hepner 2017).

Because of the growing affordable housing challenges, calls for state legislatures to intervene and deregulate land use regulations, particularly single-family zoning, have increased in states across the US (Infranca 2019; Lemar 2019). For scholars (Wegmann 2020) and journalists (*Economist* 2015), state government preemption and curtailing local land use authority in land use decision-making has become the new orthodoxy. However, it is less clear how willing state governments are to intervene in this manner and what are the political limits of state preemption of local land use authority. There are also questions about the most effective way for state legislatures to intervene in local land use regulations.

The new enthusiasm for state government preemption in local land use regulations is in conflict with urban planning's normative preference for community participation in decision-making (Arnstein 1969; J. Friedmann 1987; Purcell 2008). Citizen participation in land use planning can offer several advantages. First, it can provide possibilities for residents to be directly involved in decision-making (J. Friedmann 2011), make it easier to reflect local preferences in plans (Tiebout 1956), help plans conform to the specificity of the local context (Alexander, Ishikawa, and Silverstein 1977; Lynch 1981), and allow locally important countervailing ideas and institutions to emerge (A. Fung 2012; Fung and Wright 2003). Second, stakeholder involvement and local knowledge can make it more likely for plans to be implemented (Burby 2003). And third, participation in planning decision-making, scholars argue, has potentially broader benefits, including mobilization and empowerment of communities, the building of civic and problem-solving capacity, and the deepening and strengthening of democracy (Briggs 2008; A. Fung 2004; Rajan 2019).

In recognition of the local advantages, some scholars recommend state governments develop more procedural interventions that establish housing goals or quotas for local governments with credible consequences for noncompliance (Camacho and Marantz 2020; Elmendorf 2019; Elmendorf et al. 2020; Hills and Schleicher 2015). Such indirect interventions that preserve local control over zoning and land use while requiring they meet certain goals may lead to less conflict with local governments (Brinig and Garnett 2013) and allow for more creative and effective programs for addressing unpermitted second units from cities (Cho 2016).

Can local governments in major cities create support for the legalization and upgrading of second units? Can they broaden public participation in planning decision-making beyond the most vocal and elite stakeholders? Will local control help them generate useful policy ideas? If so, under what conditions are local governments likely to reform single-family zoning, allow ADUs, and provide support for improving living conditions in unpermitted second units? The following case studies examine these questions.

SANTA CRUZ: BUILDING SUPPORT FOR LOCAL REFORM

The city of Santa Cruz started the second unit movement in California in the early 2000s (Groom 2013) when city policy makers and housing advocates embraced second units as a pragmatic strategy for increasing the housing supply in a community with widespread informal housing but opposition to growth. Its ADU program, which paired relaxed zoning regulations with proactive administrative and financial support for homeowners who agreed to rent out their units at affordable prices, received national media attention (Moffat 2004; F. Bernstein 2005; El Nasser 2004) and won major awards from the American Institute of Architects, the American Planning Association (APA), the Environmental Protection Agency, the League of California Cities, and the Environmental Design and Research Association.

Unfortunately, the city's efforts to encourage new ADU construction were accompanied by a crackdown on existing unpermitted housing. Unlike homeowners considering building new ADUs, owners of existing unpermitted second units were not supported with financing or guidance to help upgrade their units. The enforcement effort removed seventy units, most of which were safe and solely in violation of zoning rules, from the market.

THE PLANNING CONTEXT FOR SECOND UNITS IN SANTA CRUZ

Santa Cruz is located about seventy-five miles south of San Francisco and occupies a picturesque and narrow coastal shelf between the Santa Cruz Mountains and the Monterey Bay. San Jose—the center of Silicon Valley—is around thirty miles north, across the Santa Cruz Mountains. Santa Cruz has grown from a small beach resort community to a modest-sized city of about sixty-five thousand residents in 2020. The University of California, Santa Cruz (UCSC), founded in 1965 and with almost twenty thousand students in 2020, has been a key catalyst in Santa Cruz's growth and is the city's largest employer. With a land area of about 12.7 sq. mi., Santa Cruz has a moderate density of slightly over five thousand people per square mile and few high-rise buildings. For comparison, the city of Los Angeles's estimated density in 2020 was eighty-five hundred people per square mile. Despite a large number of UCSC students in the city, three-quarters of its residential land was zoned for single-family housing, across roughly eighteen thousand parcels (City of Santa Cruz 2016).[3]

Santa Cruz is a center of liberal and progressive activism and has been admiringly called "the Leftmost City" (Gendron and Domhoff 2008). Environmental issues are significant to many Santa Cruz residents, and in the late 1970s, after a referendum, the city established a clearly defined growth boundary as a commitment against sprawl. Many residents consider opposing the Growth Machine of new development an important progressive virtue (Rotkin interview 2014). While the city's policies and local opposition to new developments constrain the supply of housing, demand for housing continues to grow because of Santa Cruz's location and high quality of life. Consequently, housing is costly, and unpermitted housing units, particularly second units on single-family lots, are common. In the early 2000s, less than 7 percent of the city's residents could afford to buy a median-priced home of almost half a million dollars (City of Santa Cruz 2002). Former city councilmembers estimated two thousand to three thousand unpermitted second units in the city (Primack interview 2014; Rotkin interview 2014), or that between 11 and 17 percent of the city's single-family-zoned lots had an informal unit. While some in the city saw informal housing as a heroic countercultural response to the market economy, others criticized it as an exploitative "black market in affordable housing" (Primack interview 2014).

Santa Cruz adopted its first ADU ordinance in July 1983 in response to state legislation—Senate Bill 1534, the Companion Unit Act (Beatty 1983). Like many other cities, Santa Cruz created strict regulations that severely limited the number of ADUs that could be built in the city. It only allowed attached second units of up to 500 sq. ft., limited them to a maximum of five per census tract (including just one for every 500 ft. along any one street), and imposed restrictions on the maximum allowed rent (City of Santa Cruz 1983). In 1986, the city council acknowledged the widespread existence of unpermitted detached second units and agreed to permit detached units (City of Santa Cruz 1986). Permitted second units, however, continued to be rare. The city made small changes incrementally to improve the ordinance over the next several years, including lifting the rent restrictions and the census tract-level cap and allowing ADUs of up to 800 sq. ft. and tandem parking (City of Santa Cruz 1989, 1994, 1999). However, the city added a citywide cap of twenty-five units per year (City of Santa Cruz 1994).

BUILDING SUPPORT FOR SECOND UNITS
Santa Cruz significantly amended its second unit program in the early 2000s through broad-based support from the city council, the city's planning department, and grassroots advocates. According to several sources, Mark Primack, a former councilmember, was the program's crucial champion (F. Bernstein 2005; Chang 2011; Foster interview 2014; Primack interview 2014). Primack, an architect, previously served on Santa Cruz's zoning board and planning commission. He was elected to serve on the city council from 2001 to 2004. At a town hall meeting on affordable housing in 2001, many argued that the city needed to do more to legalize existing second units (Boerner 2001). Primack decided to focus his political term on second units. He formed the ADU subcommittee with two other councilmembers, Ed Porter and Scott Kennedy, to encourage more second unit development. Primack collaborated actively with the planning department to explore the deregulation of zoning requirements and worked with the fire chief to develop more liberal requirements for firewall separations and sprinklers (Berg interview 2014; Primack interviews 2014, 2018).

There was grassroots-based community support for zoning changes too. David Foster, later the executive director of Habitat for Humanity, Santa

Cruz, and other affordable housing advocates formed a grassroots group called Affordable Housing Advocates. It lobbied for more liberal policies for second units in the city and statewide through concept papers and op-eds in the *Santa Cruz Sentinel*, the local newspaper (Foster 2000, 2001, interview 2014; D. Lane 2001).

Subsequently, the city council revised Santa Cruz's rules for second units in 2002. First, it removed the requirement of covered parking. It also relaxed the on-site location restriction for the parking and allowed for up to three parking spaces to be provided in tandem, permitting the spaces to be located in the front and side yards. Second, for single-story detached units, the ordinance reduced the side and rear setback requirements to 3 ft. Third, it limited the fire sprinkler requirement to the second unit. Previously, a homeowner was required to add fire sprinklers to both the new unit and the main house. Finally, the city allowed second units on lots with a minimum size of 5,000 sq. ft., which—in comparison with the city of Los Angeles's contemporaneous requirement of 7,500 sq. ft.—was radical for its time.

While the city council liberalized several regulatory constraints, it maintained the owner-occupancy requirement, mandating owners to live in the main house or the second unit. In Santa Cruz, with its large population of students and exaggerated fear of student renters, policy makers saw the owner-occupancy requirement as politically indispensable.[4]

Santa Cruz received a competitive grant from the California Pollution Control Financing Authority's Sustainable Communities Grant and Loan Program to facilitate education and outreach for the revised ADU ordinance. It held five public workshops and developed two design manuals and a set of prototype plans (City of Santa Cruz 2003a, 2003b, 2006) (figure 6.1). The richly illustrated documents are designed to provide interested homeowners with comprehensive guidance by walking them through the planning permission, design, construction, construction loan, and tenant selection processes. The manuals discuss various design prototypes (see figure 6.2 for an example of a single-story second unit prototype), show how garage conversions can reduce the cost of development (City of Santa Cruz 2006), and include a sample residential lease agreement (City of Santa Cruz 2003a). According to Carol Berg (interviews 2014, 2018), who, as a principal planner in the city, led the development of the manuals and plan sets, the original idea was for the prototype plan sets to serve as preapproved, off-the-shelf blueprints. However, the plans became more significant as templates and informational documents because of rapid changes in building codes and requirements. Only three houses were

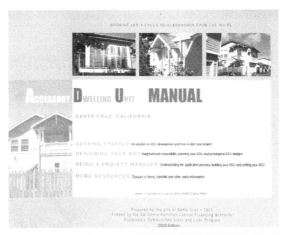

FIGURE 6.1
City of Santa Cruz's design manuals, including the "Accessory Dwelling Unit Manual" (*Source*: City of Santa Cruz 2003a); the "Garage Conversion Manual" (*Source*: City of Santa Cruz 2006); and "Prototype Plan Sets" (*Source*: City of Santa Cruz 2003b).

SECTION FIVE: Sample Floor Plans

In Section Five, we provide sample plans for various types of garage conversion ADUs. Each example provides a summary of site, orientation, parking, and floor plan. As discussed in previous parts of the manual, you have to consider both your own and your tenant's needs. However, these can help you kick-start your thinking about your ADU.

Sample Floor Plans:

ADU 1: Suburban Front Attached

ADU 2: Suburban Side Attached

ADU 3: Suburban Under Attached

ADU 4: Suburban Corner Attached

ADU 5: Traditional Rear Drive Detached

ADU 6: Traditional Side Detached

ADU 7: Traditional Alley Detached

ADU 8: Traditional Corner Detached

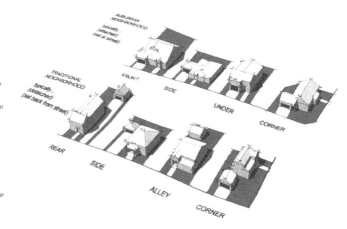

FIGURE 6.2
Summary of the sample floor plans in city of Santa Cruz's "Prototype Plan Sets."
Source: City of Santa Cruz 2003b, 34.

built on the basis of the prototypes, but the city sold several hundred manuals, including many to other local governments interested in learning from its experience.

Santa Cruz offered a technical assistance grant program that allowed interested homeowners to meet with planning department officials for help with understanding the zoning requirements, and outside design professionals to get guidance on design prototypes for their sites. With the support of the Santa Cruz Community Credit Union and its affordable housing trust fund, the city initiated a program of subsidized construction loans for homeowners willing to house low-income residents in their second units. The credit union's loans were available at a low-interest rate of 4.5 percent per year (the prevailing market rate for mortgages in 2003 was about 6.0 percent per annum) and required a fifteen-year affordability deed restriction. Borrowers could remove the deed restriction before fifteen years by paying back the subsidy. The city's efforts created a buzz around second units.

Affordable housing activists like Foster helped expand the community's excitement and acceptance of second units (figure 6.3). He invited his

FIGURE 6.3
The construction of a straw bale ADU in Santa Cruz as a community event for family, friends, and neighbors. Photo credit: David Foster.

friends and neighbors to assist in constructing a straw bale second unit for his parents. His contractor offered a weekend workshop in straw bale construction, and over seventy people participated (Litchfield 2011). Volunteers took hundreds of poems written by friends, family members, and well-wishers and placed them in the straw bale walls during construction of the second unit (Foster interview 2014).

More recently, following California's push for further deregulation of zoning for second units through Assembly Bill 2299 and Senate Bill 1069 in 2016, the city liberalized its rules but not entirely in keeping with the spirit of state law (Primack interview 2018). The city increased the maximum ADU size to 1,200 sq. ft., eliminated discretionary permits for two-story units, and waived the fee for water and sewer connection charges for units carved out of the main unit or an existing accessory building, saving homeowners almost $8,000. It also eliminated the parking requirement for units located within a half mile of the downtown transit center or one block of a car share vehicle (City of Santa Cruz 2016). The state legislation required parking requirements to be waived for all second units located within a half mile of public transit but did not define public transit. While cities like Los Angeles interpreted public transit to include bus lines, Santa Cruz did not. It did not reduce parking requirements near high-frequency bus stops.

Although the number of formally built second units in Santa Cruz increased since the city revised its ADU program in the early 2000s, the annual production was relatively modest. The number of houses built through the program reached a high of forty-three units in 2007 (Donovan communication 2018).

ENFORCEMENT AND FORMALIZATION OF INFORMAL UNITS
The policy emphasis in Santa Cruz was on deregulating zoning requirements to legalize second units. The city did not focus on upgrading and regularizing unpermitted units. Instead, the city created a new enforcement program for proactively inspecting all residential units annually (City of Santa Cruz 2010). Although the program's implementation was delayed, by early 2014 inspectors had uncovered about seventy unpermitted second units that could not be legalized and had to be removed (Khoury interview 2014). Critics like Primack (2014; interview 2014), then a city planning commissioner, noted that only a small minority of the abated units were unsafe. But the overwhelming majority could not meet the city's zoning requirements,

usually the owner-occupancy condition and minimum lot size stipulations. In late 2014, the city council agreed to make small regulatory changes to the second unit rules. It reduced the minimum lot size requirement from 5,000 sq. ft. to 4,500 sq. ft. and offered existing detached ADUs exceptions from setback and lot coverage requirements to reduce the number of livable units lost through the inspection program (City of Santa Cruz 2015). The city maintained its owner-occupancy condition but allowed owners a two-year exception and time to move in or sell their properties to someone who would live on-site (City of Santa Cruz 2015; York 2015). Following multiple state legislative efforts to further liberalize the rules for second units in 2019, including prohibitions on owner-occupancy requirements between 2020 and 2025 through Senate Bill 13, the Santa Cruz planning commission started an effort to loosen the city's regulations and make it easier for owners to receive permits for second units facing abatement (Primack 2019).

SEATTLE: LOCALLY LED UPZONING

In 2019, Seattle significantly reformed its second unit law to permit three units on single-family-zoned lots and earned acclaim as the "best in the nation" (Fester 2019). Over a twenty-five-year period, it incrementally progressed from first allowing attached second units in 1994 to accepting two ADUs—one attached and one detached. It made the progression gradually and slowly through pilot projects, research and evaluation of upzoning efforts, broadening engagement beyond neighborhood councils, and using second units as a gateway for political acceptance of greater density. The city relaxed its land use regulations to make it easier for owners of unpermitted units to legalize them. But it did not provide financial or technical assistance to help homeowners upgrade their units.

THE PLANNING CONTEXT FOR SECOND UNITS IN SEATTLE

Seattle is the largest city in the Pacific Northwest region. New technology firms in software, cloud computing, e-commerce, artificial intelligence, and biotechnology have helped drive the city-region's impressive growth. Seattle's population increased from 516,259 in 1990 to an estimated 737,015 in 2020. Correspondingly, its density reached over 8,800 people per square mile, a little more than the density of the city of Los Angeles. The Seattle metropolitan region's population grew from around 1.5 million people in 1960 to an estimated 4.0 million in 2020. Although the Seattle region is celebrated for its environmental values, critics argue that the ecological narrative conceals the significant financial and social injustices forced on the area's native population (Klingle 2007; Lyons 2004). Housing advocates argue that the city's affluent residents in single-family neighborhoods routinely deploy environmental justifications to oppose new construction (Bertolet 2017; A. Durning 2012–2013).

As Seattle's economy, based on logging, shipbuilding, and the Klondike Gold Rush, boomed in the early twentieth century, it turned to zoning as a tool to manage its growth. In 1923, Seattle approved its first zoning ordinance, prepared with the help of St. Louis, Missouri, based Harland Bartholomew. Bartholomew has been described as the "Dean of Comprehensive Planning" (Cook 1989) and criticized for perpetuating racial, economic, and social segregation in cities through zoning (Benton 2017). The ordinance institutionalized separation of land uses, including housing types, and introduced single-family zoning in the city through the "First Residence District" (City of Seattle 1923). However, the imposed zoning was significantly different from the reality on the ground and created many nonconforming uses. Unrealistically, the ordinance required all nonconforming uses to discontinue within five years (City of Seattle 1923). Subsequent comprehensive planning efforts expanded single-family zoning even more aggressively and further downzoned the city (City of Seattle 1957). Consequently, three-quarters of the city's residentially zoned land, or about 48 percent of all zoned land (City of Seattle 2018a; Rosenberg 2018), was reserved for single-family houses and consisted of approximately 125,000 single-family-zoned parcels (Petzel 2008; Seattle Department of Planning and Development 2016).

In the early 1990s, according to estimates from the city, 3–5 percent of the housing stock was subdivided informally (Moudon 1995). In the *Seattle Times*, a contemporaneous newspaper report shared the planning department's estimate of five thousand to six thousand unpermitted second units (Buck 1992). Similarly, Alan Durning (interview 2014) of Seattle's Sightline Institute, a research center, estimated that 5 percent of the city's single-family houses had informal second units.

SLOW, INCREMENTAL, LOCALLY LED UPZONING

Seattle adopted its first ordinance on second units in July 1994 (City of Seattle 1994a). Washington state's Housing Policy Act of 1993, which required local governments to plan for and provide more affordable housing options (including second units), triggered the ordinance (Infranca 2019). The act directed cities with over twenty thousand residents and counties subject to the state's Growth Management Act to develop second unit ordinances based on their local context. Seattle adopted a morphological or built-form approach to minimize changes in the physical fabric and only allowed attached second units through carve-outs or additions to the primary dwelling. With a fear of renters, the city required homeowners to live in one of the two units, mandated two parking spaces, and permitted only one street-facing entrance (Chapman and Howe 2001; City of Seattle 1994a).

In acknowledging the presence of informal second units in the city, the ordinance allowed for existing units built before October 1979 to have a lower minimum ceiling height of 6 ft. and 8 in. Additionally, while the city allowed a maximum size of 1,000 sq. ft. for second units, the ordinance provided homeowners an eighteen-month window to receive discretionary approval from the planning director for existing larger units. Within the next five years, the city issued permits for approximately 1,027 second units, including 241 new units and 786 previously existing ones (City of Seattle 1999).

In 1998, to explore the possibility of detached ADUs (DADUs) and test their likely impact, Seattle created a demonstration program in which it allowed up to ten detached cottages in the city (City of Seattle 2003; Murdock and Press 2018). The program achieved positive results, and in 2006 the city launched a pilot program to allow DADUs in southeast Seattle, which houses many immigrant communities (De Jong 2014). Mayor Greg Nickels proposed calling the detached second units backyard cottages (Langston 2005; Nickels interview 2014). Although the program was presented as a pilot project, its implementation area covered around a fifth of the city (A. Durning interview 2014). It allowed backyard cottages of up to 800 sq. ft. on lots of 4,000 sq. ft. or larger and required 5 ft. setbacks and two parking spaces (City of Seattle 2010). It also allowed existing accessory structures, including garages, that were built before June 1, 1999, to be converted without adhering to the setback requirements if their footprint was not expanded (City of Seattle 2006; Parker interview 2014).

After a successful evaluation based on door-to-door surveys of neighbors of newly constructed backyard cottages (Seattle Department of Planning and Development 2009), Seattle expanded the backyard cottage program citywide in late 2009 (City of Seattle 2010) (figure 6.4). To assist homeowners, the city released *A Guide to Building a Backyard Cottage*, with the

FIGURE 6.4
An alley-facing backyard cottage under construction in Seattle's Queen Anne neighborhood. Photo credit: Author.

help of Carol Berg of Santa Cruz (City of Seattle 2010). The city reduced the off-street parking requirements by not requiring additional parking for second units in designated urban villages, where residents have better access to public transit (City of Seattle 2010).[5] The city asked owners of unpermitted backyard cottages to apply for permits by June 2010 but allowed them up to two years, until December 2011, to meet the zoning and code requirements (De Jong 2014).

Although the zoning reforms helped increase demand for permits for second units, the numbers were modest.[6] Concerned with the limited progress, the city council in 2014 directed the planning department to explore policy changes to increase the production of second units (City of Seattle 2014). Planners discussed allowing attached and detached units on single-family lots, removing the owner-occupancy requirement, and reducing the minimum lot size (Podowski interview 2014; Seattle Department of Planning and Development 2015).

In January and February 2016, Councilmember Mike O'Brien, the land use committee chair, and the Office of Planning and Community Development cohosted two community meetings on second units (City of Seattle 2016). The councilmember was keen to add new housing without losing or replacing existing units through redevelopment and had become the leading advocate of second units (Levy interview 2018; O'Brien 2015). With the information gleaned from the public meetings, he and the planning department advocated for removing the owner-occupancy requirement, reducing the minimum lot size to 3,200 sq. ft., increasing the maximum size for backyard cottages to 1,000 sq. ft. (same as attached ADUs) from 800 sq. ft., and allowing both detached and attached secondary units (Gross 2016; O'Brien 2017; Seattle Department of Planning and Development 2016).

However, the proposal was stalled by a legal appeal from the Queen Anne Community Council. It represented a well-established, wealthy neighborhood on a hill northwest of downtown Seattle. It claimed that the city had not adequately analyzed the bill's environmental impacts, particularly parking and the risk of displacement due to development (Feit 2016a, 2016b). A hearing examiner agreed with the appeal and asked the city to produce a detailed environmental impact statement. Concerned ADU supporters formed an interest group called More Options for Accessory Residences (MOAR) to advocate for the bill (Cohen 2017; Hutchins interview 2018; MOAR 2017). Although the city's impact statement in 2018 found that the feared outcomes of adverse parking effects and speculative development were unfounded, it did not subdue the opposition (Murdock and Press 2018). The editorial board of *Seattle Times* (2018) criticized the proposal, asked for a "review of impacts neighborhood by neighborhood," and argued, "Don't upzone Seattle neighborhoods."

While the legal challenge delayed the adoption process, the city council tweaked Councilmember O'Brien's proposal and unanimously approved the bill in mid-2019 (Fester 2019). The approved ordinance allowed both attached and detached ADUs and had no owner-occupancy requirement. It imposed a maximum primary unit size equal to half of the lot size, or up to 2,500 sq. ft., to limit mansionization. It created an incentive for owners to maximize buildable floor area through second and third units (Bertolet and Morales 2019). The council also asked the Seattle Department of Construction and Inspections to create an amnesty program for unpermitted ADUs, and directed the Seattle Department of Transportation to provide bike parking in single-family neighborhoods as infrastructure support for second units. Subsequently, the city launched a web-based central resource to guide residents through the process for creating ADUs, allowing them to envision possible configurations on their lots, and provided preapproved DADU designs (City of Seattle 2020).

In early 2019, when Seattle legislators were still deliberating second unit reforms, Washington state legislators tried to move the city forward with two bipartisan efforts: House Bill 1797 and Senate Bill 5812 (M. Morales 2019a). They were inspired by what was happening in Seattle and state preemption in California and Oregon. (I discuss Oregon in the next subsection.) The bills would have prohibited owner-occupancy mandates, removed off-street parking requirements for the accessory units, and allowed two ADUs per lot (M. Morales 2019a, 2019b). The proposed legislation would also have removed minimum lot size requirements, capped impact fees, and expanded the reforms statewide to all cities with more than 2,500 residents. Although the bills died in the legislature in April, their legislators planned to introduce similar bills in subsequent legislative sessions (M. Morales 2019b).

SECOND UNITS AS A GATEWAY TO HIGHER DENSITY IN SINGLE-FAMILY NEIGHBORHOODS

Simultaneously, as the efforts to reform second unit rules progressed, Seattle mayor Ed Murray, who was elected in 2014, and the city council convened a Housing Affordability and Livability Agenda (HALA) advisory committee to provide policy ideas and recommendations on making housing in Seattle more affordable. It was constituted in September 2014 and had twenty-eight members consisting of renters, homeowners, labor and social justice advocates, and housing developers and experts. Mayor Murray expected the committee to craft a compromise or "Grand Bargain" between supporters of the housing supply and advocates of more targeted approaches for building affordable housing (Bicknell 2019). The committee developed a broad-based strategy consisting of sixty-five recommendations for increasing the housing supply, streamlining regulations, adding resources for affordable housing, and addressing displacement (Seattle HALA 2015).

Mayor Murray wanted the HALA committee to include single-family neighborhoods in its purview (Beekman 2015b). The committee recommended allowing more variety of low-density housing "such as small lot dwellings, cottages, courtyard housing, duplexes, and triplexes in single-family zones" citywide (Seattle HALA 2015, 8). It recommended expanding designated urban villages based on walkable access to transit, increasing the density of single-family-zoned lots further within the redefined villages, and combining the upzoning with a new mandatory inclusionary housing program requiring developers to build a modest proportion of affordable units in all projects or pay in-lieu fees (Seattle HALA 2015). The proposed zoning change would affect around 6,500 single-family-zoned lots, covering approximately 800 acres of land, and allow small lot zoning and low-rise multifamily housing (Seattle HALA 2015). As with Councilmember O'Brien's proposal, the committee recommended allowing both attached and detached ADUs on one lot and removing parking and owner-occupancy requirements (Seattle HALA 2015). In recognition of the "large number of unpermitted informal ADUs and DADUs," it suggested that the city "develop a clemency program to legalize undocumented ADUs and DADUs" (Seattle HALA 2015, 26).

The public backlash against the proposal was intense. Critics of the proposal argued that the HALA process was flawed and relied too much on private meetings without adequate public participation (Cruickshank 2015; Westneat 2015). Facing criticism, Mayor Murray withdrew the part of the proposal to allow greater housing diversity in single-family neighborhoods citywide (Beekman 2015a). Instead, he decided to focus on the suggestion to upzone single-family neighborhoods in the urban villages with inclusionary zoning (Beekman 2015a).

The city council introduced the urban villages proposal as the Mandatory Housing Affordability (MHA) program (City of Seattle 2018b). A coalition of neighborhood groups, small businesses, and other HALA opponents led by Seattle Fair Growth formed the Seattle Coalition for Affordability, Livability, and Equality. The coalition appealed MHA on environmental impact grounds, citing adverse effects on historic homes and the city's tree canopy (Hellmann 2017; Trumm 2017).[7] But in December 2018, a local judge ruled in favor of MHA (Beekman 2018; Trumm 2018). In March 2019, the unanimous city council and the mayor approved the program (Beekman 2019; Bicknell 2019).

ENFORCEMENT AND FORMALIZATION OF INFORMAL UNITS

To facilitate the legalization of unpermitted units in the city, policy makers allowed lower ceiling heights for existing units than the minimum required, larger floor areas than the maximum permitted, and smaller setbacks than mandatory. Both the HALA advisory committee and the city council acknowledged the need for formalizing informal units and advocated for amnesty programs. The city council offered homeowners additional time for upgrading their units to the standards necessary for legalization. While homeowners collected the resources to improve their units, the extra time provided a moratorium against enforcement action. The city council also asked for bike-parking infrastructure investments in single-family neighborhoods to support second units' residents, including those in unpermitted ones. However, the city did not offer any grant or loan programs to financially help owners of informal second units improve their units.

PORTLAND: SECOND UNITS AND THE END OF SINGLE-FAMILY ZONING

In the early 2010s, Portland had the most liberal regulations for second units of any major US city (Peterson 2018). Its success was mostly locally driven. It first allowed internally carved-out ADUs as rental properties citywide in 1991 and permitted detached backyard units in 1998. Beginning in 1998, the city did not require owner occupancy or off-street parking for second units. In 2010, it waived additional development charges for new accessory units. Second unit advocates helped create support for ADUs through original research, tours, and workshops. Although Portland's efforts to replace single-family living with duplexes, triplexes, and fourplexes appeared stalled in 2019, the Oregon state legislature adopted similar legislation to reform single-family zoning statewide. In 2020, the Portland City Council approved dramatic changes to single-family zoning. It voted to allow duplexes, triplexes, and fourplexes on almost all single-family-zoned lots citywide (Bliss 2020; City of Portland 2020; Trumm 2020). And it decided to allow up to six units per lot if at least half of the units were restricted as affordable.

THE PLANNING CONTEXT FOR SECOND UNITS IN PORTLAND
Portland is the largest city in Oregon. In 1980 its population was 366,383, slightly below its earlier peak of 382,619 in 1970. The census estimate for 2020 was over 650,000, an increase of almost 80 percent in about four decades. Even with the remarkable population growth, the city's estimated density in 2020 was under five thousand people per square mile, similar to Santa Cruz's. Correspondingly, almost 150,000 lots, covering over 85 percent of the city's

residentially zoned land, were earmarked for single-family housing (City of Portland 2017; Tracy communication 2018a).

Portland has been described as "America's Whitest big city" (Kaleem 2017) and called out for its racist history (Semuels 2016). To avoid the sale of houses in white neighborhoods to people of color, Portland's Realty Board, until 1955, followed a bigoted code of ethics of not completing residential sale transactions without neighbors' consent (Abbott 2011). While the city has become more heterogeneous over time—the share of its non-Hispanic white population dropped from about 83 percent in 1990 to around 72 percent in 2010—gentrification in the city is an ongoing concern (Darby Smith 2015). In particular, scholars worry about the displacement of the city's Black population (Bates 2013).

Planners celebrate the city, its region, and the state for their leadership in land use planning (Abbott 1997; Adler 2012; Ozawa 2004). In 1973, Senate Bill 100, which the APA recognized as a National Planning Landmark, created a new state agency, the Land Conservation and Development Commission (LCDC), to adopt statewide land use planning goals and ensure that local governments comply with state and regional goals. Subsequently, Governor Tom McCall, a Republican, cofounded 1000 Friends of Oregon as a nonprofit watchdog and advocacy organization of SB 100. The extraordinary emphasis on regional governance and growth management in the Portland region followed LCDC's goal of limiting sprawl to preserve agricultural land, forests, and open spaces while making local plans to encourage housing diversity (Adler 2012). Since 1979, Metro, a directly elected regional government, which was earlier known as the Metropolitan Service District, has been responsible for regional planning.

After Portland's residents narrowly rejected zoning through referendums in 1919 and 1920, it was adopted in 1924 with four zones, including single-family housing (Abbott 2011). In 1959, planners comprehensively revised Portland's zoning code and downzoned many multifamily neighborhoods to single-family areas. Second units were disallowed in single-family areas, except on very large lots (City of Portland 1959).

Informal second units are common in Portland. Eli Spevak (interview 2015), a small-scale housing developer and second unit advocate, estimated that 10 percent of the city's single-family houses had an unpermitted second unit. He noted that because Portland had many nonconforming land uses due to the downzoning in 1959, it was difficult to distinguish between informal and formal units. Also, Portland has allowed duplexes on corner lots in single-family neighborhoods since 1991 (City of Portland 2017), leading to neighbors being unclear about unpermitted and permitted second units. Martin Brown (2009; interview 2015), another advocate of second units in Portland, estimated that there were likely two or three unpermitted second units for every permitted one. Kol Peterson (2018), the author of a detailed and trailblazing book about building ADUs, taught workshops on them in Portland. In 2015, he estimated that three-fourths of the second units in the city were unpermitted (Peterson communication 2015a). He also noted that half the inquiries he received for ADU construction were to assess whether an existing second unit could obtain a permit (Peterson interview 2015b). Realtor Niki Rondini (interview 2015), who had significant experience selling houses with second units, told me that unpermitted second units were common enough for buyers not to shy away from them. As in Santa Cruz, an overwhelmingly white city, unpermitted second units are sometimes celebrated as an expression of the place's do-it-yourself and libertarian culture (Gabbe interview 2015).

FROM A REGIONAL NUDGE TO LOCAL ENTHUSIASM

The LCDC and Metro prohibited local governments from banning second units in the Portland region (Liebig, Koenig, and Pynoos 2006). With a new zoning code overhaul in 1981, the city started allowing accessory units carved out from larger single-family dwellings (City of Portland 1980; Nameny communication 2018b). In 1991, planners modified the rules slightly. Second units could be carved out of existing living space, including basements and attics, and rented, but owners had to occupy one of the units (Nameny 2015; Peterson 2018). Interestingly, perhaps because of Portland's low density and abundance of street parking, owners were not required to provide additional off-street parking (City of Portland 2003). The lack of a parking requirement made it easier to build second units and put Portland on a different trajectory than most other cities.

In 1989, planners started developing the Albina Community Plan (City of Portland 1993b). Historically, the Albina district in northeast Portland was one of the few areas where Black residents were allowed to live. Its neighborhoods housed many who had come for shipbuilding jobs during World War II (Gibson 2007). Planners hoped to increase investment and the housing supply in the district while preserving existing housing. In addition to the upzoning of some commercial corridors, they proposed to liberalize rules for accessory rentals in single-family neighborhoods. Initially, planners suggested allowing garage conversions and detached accessory units but faced strong opposition from residents (Mayer 1993a, 1993b). The eventual plan in 1993 modestly changed the existing rules and permitted owners to expand their houses to create attached accessory units (City of Portland 1993b; Nameny 2015). The regulations for second units in Albina were incorporated into a new overlay zone known as the "a" overlay (City of Portland 1993a). In 1996, planners expanded the "a" overlay to cover areas within a quarter mile of transit corridors in the Outer Southeast neighborhoods as part of the community plan update (City of Portland 1996).

In the mid-1990s, Metro made another push for second units (Metro 2000). It mandated that they be permitted but allowed local jurisdictions to develop the requirements. In response to the mandate, and the limited effectiveness of existing regulations, the city started preparing an ordinance.[8] Planners proposed allowing second units through additions citywide, including detached structures, and eliminating the owner-occupancy requirement. They would allow garage conversions, but owners would go through a discretionary review process (City of Portland 1997).

Neighborhood associations across the city opposed the idea and complained of new renters and absentee landlords.[9] Opponents in the Outer Southeast argued that they had just participated in a planning process to accept more density and should be exempted. In December 1997, a divided city council voted three to two to adopt the new regulations while allowing neighborhoods in Albina and the Outer Southeast to continue with the more restrictive "a" overlay zone (City of Portland 1997; Nameny interview 2018a).

In 2004, following up on a monitoring report on second units and recommendations by the planning department (City of Portland 2003), the city council decided to adopt a single set of rules for the entire city. It eliminated the "a" overlay zone, removed owner-occupancy and additional parking requirements citywide, and allowed detached second units and garage conversions within setback boundaries by right (City of Portland 2004). With these changes, Portland had some of the most liberal regulations for second units in the country. Still, while the city allowed for second units of up to 800 sq. ft., it limited them to a third of the main dwelling unit's size, which was a significant constraint. The number of permit applications only modestly increased from the 1998–2003 average of twenty-eight applications a year to about thirty-five applications annually between 2004 and 2008. With the Great Recession, demand for housing permits dropped (Nameny communication 2018b).

In 2010, the city decided to boost the second unit market and provide a financial incentive. It approved a three-year temporary waiver of its System Development Charges (SDC), onetime fees for water and sewer connections and the impact on parks and transportation infrastructure (City of Portland 2010b, 2010c). The SDC waiver saved homeowners $8,000 to $12,000 (Peterson communication 2015a). The city agreed to modify the maximum size regulation too. While keeping the upper limit of 800 sq. ft., it allowed owners to build up to three-fourths of the main dwelling unit's size (City of Portland 2010a).

Around the same time, a small group of green building and tiny homes enthusiasts came together to increase the public information available on second units and advocate for supportive policies. In 2012, Martin Brown, Kol Peterson, and Eli Spevak started a website—accessorydwellings.org—with a treasure trove of information (Peterson 2018). All three were covered in a *New York Times* article on second units (Keenan 2014) and were active in advocating for ADUs nationally. Brown built an ADU and conducted original research on second units (Brown 2009, 2014; Brown and Watkins 2012). Peterson (2018), in addition to writing a comprehensive book with practical advice on building ADUs, built a detached second unit in 2011, lived in it, and rented out the main unit (interview 2015b). He regularly taught a well-received daylong class on building second units. I joined a class in March 2015 (figure 6.5), which included enthusiastic homeowners, prospective home buyers, and realtors. By 2018, over a thousand participants had attended his classes (Peterson 2018). Peterson also taught a half-day class for realtors and organized and led a popular tour of second unit projects (figure 6.6). Finally, Spevak authored a policy brochure on ADUs for the AARP (Spevak and Stanton 2019) and served on the city's Planning and Sustainability Commission.

According to Spevak (interview 2015), the tours, classes, and network of advocates helped create enthusiasm for second units in the city. With the growing number of homeowners with second units, about a hundred designers with second unit projects, and numerous contractors and subcontractors building ADUs, the city had an increasing constituency of stakeholders interested in second units (Spevak interview 2018).

FIGURE 6.5
Portland's ADU Workshop, including site tour, organized by Kol Peterson. Photo credit: Author.

FIGURE 6.6
Poster for Portland's ADU tour, spring 2015. *Source*: accessorydwellings.org.

SECOND UNITS AS A GATEWAY TO ENDING SINGLE-FAMILY ZONING

In 2015, city planners started examining how to increase infill units in single-family neighborhoods to allow more households with a greater range of incomes to live in them. Planners also wanted to address the redevelopment trend of modest single-family houses as mega-sized dwellings or mansionization. The effort was launched as the Residential Infill Project (RIP), pronounced "rip" (Tracy interview 2018b). After a series of public workshops and hearings citywide, planners released a discussion draft in October 2017. They proposed to allow duplexes on lots near urban centers, transit services, and other amenities, and triplexes on corner lots. The upzoning to duplexes would affect approximately 58 percent of all single-family-zoned lots. They proposed permitting two ADUs—one attached and one detached—on all other single-family-zoned lots (City of Portland 2017). RIP received support from Portland for Everyone (n.d.), which was sponsored by 1000 Friends of Oregon and included a broad coalition of housing advocates, progressive neighborhood associations, planners, builders, designers, and environmentalists. In early 2019, the Planning and Sustainability Commission narrowly voted in support of the infill plan (Njus 2019b).

However, the project was overtaken by House Bill 2001, similar legislation in the state legislature advanced by the Oregon House Speaker Tina Kotek, a Portland resident. HB 2001 received bipartisan support. The bill preempted local zoning and legalized duplexes in cities of more than ten thousand residents, and allowed triplexes, fourplexes, attached town homes, and cottage clusters in cities of more than twenty-five thousand residents and within the Portland Metropolitan Area (Andrews 2019; Njus 2019a; Short 2019). Governor Kate Brown (Dillon 2019) and 1000 Friends of Oregon (Mapes 2019) supported the legislation. In mid-2020, Oregon's LCDC started developing the administrative rules and guidance for implementing the state mandate.

By spring 2020, Portland's planners revised RIP and updated their recommendations to comply with HB 2001. They recommended that the city allow duplexes, triplexes, and fourplexes on almost all single-family-zoned lots in the city (Bliss 2020; Trumm 2020). They proposed an incentive for deeper affordability and recommended allowing six units per lot if owners agreed to keep three or more units as affordable. In August 2020, Portland's city council approved the infill project by a vote of three to one (City of Portland 2020).

ENFORCEMENT AND FORMALIZATION OF INFORMAL UNITS
Portland emphasized legalization of informal housing through deregulation. It made it feasible to convert garages to second units because there were no minimum setbacks or parking requirements. In addition, the city waived SDC for second units and did not require owners to occupy one of the two units. But owners did not receive extra time or financial support for upgrading their unpermitted second units. Unlike Santa Cruz, however, Portland did not embark on a potentially counterproductive drive to eliminate informal second units through enforcement. Unlike Seattle, with one key exception, it did not provide or discuss amnesty or opportunities for formalizing unpermitted units through more flexible rules. The important exception was for second units in existing buildings, where it instituted a minimum ceiling height of 6 ft. and 8 in. (Portland Bureau of Development Services 2016).

MINNEAPOLIS: A SWIFT TRANSITION FROM SECOND UNITS
TO THE END OF SINGLE-FAMILY ZONING

In December 2018, the Minneapolis City Council voted to end single-family zoning citywide (City of Minneapolis 2018a). Just four years earlier, the city council had voted to allow second units throughout the city. After a short but seemingly effective public engagement program through meetings and an online survey, the city council adopted new legislation on ADUs within eighteen months (City of Minneapolis 2014a). The city's success in allowing second units set the stage for more radical changes to single-family zoning (Fletcher interview 2019; A. Johnson interview 2019). Planners, planning scholars, and the national media enthusiastically welcomed Minneapolis's innovation (J. Johnson 2019; Kauffman 2018; *Los Angeles Times* 2018; Schuetz 2018), but there was little attention to the political process of the institutional change and its incremental, locally led nature.

THE PLANNING CONTEXT FOR SECOND UNITS IN MINNEAPOLIS
With an estimated population of over 425,000 residents in 2020, Minneapolis is the largest city in Minnesota. Along with Saint Paul, its neighbor to the east and the state capital, the metropolitan region is commonly known as the Twin Cities. With almost 3.7 million people, it is the third-largest metropolitan area in the Midwest; between 1990 and 2020, it added over a million residents. In urban planning, Minneapolis is renowned for its excellent

park system (Garvin 2002). Planners also celebrate the metropolitan region's progressive regional tax-base sharing program through which local governments partially share the growth in their commercial and industrial property tax base (Orfield 1997).[10] Like other contemporary US cities, Minneapolis adopted a zoning code in the mid-1920s (Cecchini 2015). Notably, before the city implemented zoning in 1924, its population, according to the 1920 Census, was over 380,000. The introduction of zoning and subsequent revisions to emphasize single-family housing created a regulatory framework that was significantly more restrictive than the pre-zoning built form. Consequently, nonconforming land uses—for example, duplex homes in single-family-zoned districts—are common, particularly in older neighborhoods.

According to my former students who lived in Minneapolis (Holland communication 2019; Kamp communication 2019) and local planners (Ellis and Mogush interview 2019), informal second units were not common, but they were aware of some. This may be partly because Minneapolis requires a Truth in Sale of Housing (TISH) evaluation and disclosure by independent and certified evaluators when houses are sold (Sether interview 2019).[11] In addition, some of the city's neighborhood associations, like the Lowry Hill East Neighborhood Association, were notorious for their members actively searching for unpermitted units through field surveys by volunteers and complaining to the planning department to remove them through enforcement (Edwards 2016). However, Councilmember Jeremiah Ellison (interview 2019), who represents the less affluent Ward 5 covering the neighborhoods of North Minneapolis, told me that informal housing was more common in his district.

Minneapolis's population peaked in 1950 at nearly 522,000, when it had a density of around 9,650 people per square mile. Its 2020 density of almost 7,900 people per square mile was slightly less than the density of the city of Los Angeles. As with most US cities, most of its zoned land—53 percent—was reserved for single-family houses (City of Minneapolis 2018d). Additionally, 14 percent of the zoned land was earmarked for duplexes (City of Minneapolis 2018d). Thus, Minneapolis's recent land use policy changes have been in the context of over two-thirds of its land reserved for single- and two-family dwellings.

As the city's population started stabilizing in the 1980s and growing more rapidly in the 2010s, there was more pressure on the city's housing market. Adding to housing demand was a change in its demographic structure through smaller households. The average household size decreased from 3.08 in 1950 to 2.23 in 2010 (Roper 2014). In the late 2010s, the housing rental vacancy rate dropped to just 2 percent (Trautman 2018). The city adopted an overlay district in North Phillips / Ventura Village to allow second units, including detached units, on single-family- and duplex-zoned lots to increase the housing supply in the early 2000s. Owners had to occupy one of the units and apply for permits through a discretionary process. The overlay area was just south of the city's central business district. A majority of its residents were renters and people of color (City of Minneapolis 2001; Minneapolis Community Planning & Economic Development 2014).

UNEXPECTEDLY STRONG SUPPORT FOR SECOND UNITS
In mid-2013, Minneapolis's planners began exploring strategies to increase the city's housing supply, including a citywide expansion of the North Phillips / Ventura Village ADU program (Jacobson 2013; M. Smith interview 2018). Meanwhile, Lisa Bender, who earned a master's in city and regional planning from the University of California, Berkeley, joined the city council race to represent Ward 10, a district where most of the electorate are renters. She voiced her strong support for secondary units citywide (Neighbors for Lisa Bender, n.d.). Bender won the election and became a champion for ADUs. Newly elected mayor Betsy Hodges, who envisioned the city's growth from just under four hundred thousand residents to a population of half a million, also backed the concept (Lindeke 2014; Roper 2014).

Planning department staff researched best practices from other North American cities, specifically Santa Cruz, Portland, Seattle, and Vancouver. The department planned four open houses or community workshops to share its research and receive feedback (M. Smith interview 2018). Although four public workshops are not a lot, they exceeded the three organized by the city of Los Angeles, a jurisdiction ten times the size of Minneapolis. The four workshops were organized in August and September 2014 and were well attended. Because of the interest in the topic, the planning department organized a fifth workshop in October 2014. A total of 137 public attendees participated in the workshops (Minneapolis Community Planning & Economic Development 2014). According to Senior City Planner Mei-Ling Smith (interview 2018), the workshop attendees supported allowing second units. Still, many shared their concerns about properties with multiple tenants and absentee landlords.

The planning department developed a survey instrument to understand the opinions of Minneapolis residents. In addition to surveying the workshop attendees, it posted the questionnaire online. Only around two hundred survey questionnaires were completed—ninety-eight by the workshop attendees and an additional ninety-nine by online respondents. Over 90 percent of the survey respondents agreed or strongly agreed that second units should be allowed citywide, and over 70 percent were interested in constructing one. A simple majority of the respondents (54 percent) agreed or strongly agreed in favor of requiring owner occupancy for permitting second units (Minneapolis Community Planning & Economic Development 2014).

Building on the positive response from the public engagement process, Councilmember Bender introduced an amendment in June 2014 to revise the city's zoning code and allow ADUs on single-family- and duplex-zoned properties citywide (Minneapolis Community Planning & Economic Development 2014). The planning department drafted the ordinance based on the feedback from the workshops and the online survey. It proposed allowing attached, detached, and internal secondary units (through carve-outs of existing space) of 1,000 sq. ft. citywide with no minimum lot size or additional parking requirements, and rear and side yard setbacks of only 3 ft. for detached units. The ordinance included an owner-occupancy provision (Minneapolis Community Planning & Economic Development 2014).

The public response to allowing second units was mostly positive. For the planning commission's hearing in November 2014, fifteen letters supported the ordinance, including those from AARP-Minnesota, Minneapolis Senior Citizens Advisory Committee, and Preservation Alliance of Minnesota, and two letters opposed it. All the speakers favored the ordinance, and the commission approved it unanimously (City of Minneapolis 2014b). Soon after, with just one dissenting vote, the city council adopted the law (City of Minneapolis 2014a).

The pace of adoption of the ordinance was remarkably fast. Even the city's planning staff were surprised by how warmly residents received the reform and how quickly the city could adopt it (Sether interview 2019; M. Smith interview 2019). The number of applications and formally approved units, however, remained modest. A year and a half after the ordinance was approved, only fifty units had received approval (Minneapolis Community Planning & Economic Development 2016). After reviewing the ordinance, and with Councilmember Bender's support, planners proposed to increase the maximum size of detached ADUs to 1,300 sq. ft. or 16 percent of the lot area, whichever was greater, but not to exceed 1,600 sq. ft., and eliminate side setbacks (Minneapolis Community Planning & Economic Development 2016). The planning commission approved the changes in August 2016, and the city council followed in September 2016 (City of Minneapolis 2016). Even with the revisions, however, the demand for permits was limited. By March 2019, 138 ADUs had been approved, including 75 internal, 11 attached, and 52 detached units (Ellis and Mogush interview 2019). Interestingly, planning staff estimated that a third of the approved units—most of which were internally carved-out ones—were existing unpermitted units (Sether interview 2019).

MPLS 2040 AND THE TRANSFORMATION
OF SINGLE-FAMILY NEIGHBORHOODS
In April 2019, Lisa Bender (communication 2019), who was by then the council president, opened a well-attended session of the APA's national conference in San Francisco by noting to loud applause, "We eliminated Single-Family Zoning!" Earlier, in December 2018, the Minneapolis City Council made the seemingly impossible change of allowing at least three dwelling units on all residentially zoned lots citywide by approving a new comprehensive plan—MPLS 2040 (City of Minneapolis 2018a).[12] Minneapolis's radical innovation received well-deserved and widespread acclaim in the national media, including the *Los Angeles Times* (2018), the *New York Times* (Mervosh 2018), *Slate* (Grabar 2018), and the *Wall Street Journal* (Kauffman 2018). The editorials and news stories highlighted the need for greater density and deregulation of single-family zoning.

The news accounts, however, mostly missed the complex institutional processes underlying the city's achievement. For example, the reporting did not discuss Minneapolis's success in approving secondary units as a significant stepping-stone for allowing triplexes. In the APA session, City Council President Bender noted that planners and policy makers saw allowing three units as incremental progress from permitting ADUs citywide (also see City of Minneapolis 2018b; Minneapolis Community Planning & Economic Development 2018). The political acceptance of ADUs paved the way for a more progressive city council supportive of housing production in the city's November 2017 elections (A. Johnson interview 2019). The new council strongly supported the proposed upzoning in the comprehensive plan and voted overwhelmingly twelve to one in favor (Mervosh 2018). Senior planning staff told me that they thought the previous council would have supported the plan too, but the vote would have been much closer (Ellis and Mogush interview 2019).

Second, while the news coverage noted that Minneapolis developed the new plan because of state law that required local governments to submit a plan every ten years for how they expect to change, it ignored Minnesota's environmental governance context. Unlike California, the state does not have an environmental protection law with a low bar for opponents to fight and stall urban development. MPLS 2040 was litigated, but because Minnesota did not have a law like California's Environmental Quality Act, which could be used to disrupt development projects, the lawsuit was summarily dismissed (Mannix 2019).

Third, Council President Bender noted in the APA session that the key to Minneapolis's success was avoiding a coalition of NIMBY activists and housing advocates worried about the displacement of low-income residents through redevelopment. To receive the support of housing advocates, planners and policy makers emphasized the racist origins and lasting exclusionary effects of single-family zoning, more than doubled the city's housing budget, committed to partnerships with affordable housing and other mission-based organizations to preserve existing affordable housing units in the city, and agreed to develop a citywide mandatory inclusionary zoning program (Brennan communication 2019; Schroeder interview 2019).

Housing activists concerned about the adverse effects of upzoning welcomed policy makers and planners' willingness to step back from their draft proposal. The plan's initial draft in March 2018 indicated that the city was considering allowing four units on every residential lot (Belz 2018; City of Minneapolis 2018b). Mayor Jacob Frey had run on a platform to increase housing, particularly fourplexes (Grabar 2018; Trickey 2019). But several city councilmembers worried about losing existing affordable housing units through extensive redevelopment (Mannix and Ibrahim 2018). The plan's second draft in September 2018 lowered the proposed density to triplexes (City of Minneapolis 2018c; W. Morris 2018). Newspaper reports suggested that planners dropped the density based on the feedback they received through over ten thousand comments (Mannix and Roper 2018). Planners told me that as they developed the proposal, they realized that since most of the city's residential lots were 40 ft. wide, it would be significantly easier to fit three units in the allowed building envelope rather than four (Ellis and Mogush interview 2019). Additionally, Councilmember Jeremiah Ellison (interview 2019) of Ward 5 told me that while he was concerned about redevelopment and displacement in his community, his North Minneapolis district had several vacant lots due to the city's past population loss. He thought the empty lots were more likely to be built before affordable units were demolished and redeveloped.

Because of the positive engagement experience with ADUs, planners focused on expanding public participation and access to information through public meetings, community events, and online forums (Buhayar 2019; Edwards 2018). While a coalition of neighborhood groups under the paradoxically named umbrella group Minneapolis for Everyone opposed upzoning, YIMBY supporters of the proposal formed Neighbors for More Neighbors to counter the opposition and galvanize neighborhood-level support (Lee 2018; Trickey 2019). School integration proponents supported the plan as well (Kahlenberg 2019).

Finally, MPLS 2040 had other noteworthy aspects. For example, because the city's residential lots can be developed by right with three units and rented out, the owner-occupancy requirement initially included with the ADU ordinance in 2014 became moot (Mogush interview 2019a). The plan proposed to transform the purely residential nature of single-family and duplex neighborhoods by encouraging mixed land uses through retail opportunities within walking distance of all residents (Ellis and Mogush interview 2019). The retail development would be on neighboring transit corridors, where the plan significantly increased the allowed density (Mogush communication 2019b).

ENFORCEMENT AND FORMALIZATION OF INFORMAL UNITS
I found limited information about informal housing in Minneapolis compared with the other cities in this chapter. Unpermitted units may be less prevalent in the city because it has an active enforcement system through its at-sale disclosure requirement. Most planners in the city think that informal housing is less prevalent. Some residents, like Councilmember Ellison, however, disagree with the conventional wisdom. There is some evidence to support his contrarian view. For example, the city's experience with permitting secondary units suggests that about a third of the newly approved ADUs

were existing units. The city's ADU regulations limit internal and attached secondary units to a maximum of 800 sq. ft. However, in recognition of likely informal housing, Minneapolis allowed internal and attached ADUs in structures existing before January 1, 2015, to exceed 800 sq. ft. (City of Minneapolis 2016).

VANCOUVER: MAKING ROOM FOR MORE HOUSING UNITS

Along with the US and Australia, Canada is one of the few countries where urban single-family living dominates. The Canadian Dream is also based on owning a house on its own lot (Condon 2010), and scholars argue that the country's proximity to the US offers underappreciated policy lessons (Tomalty and Mallach 2016). Vancouver, in particular, has an interesting history of radically remaking single-family housing in the postwar era from one to two units, subsequently from two to three dwellings, and since 2018 from three to four units by allowing duplexes with their separate second units (City of Vancouver 2019a). The city's land use transformation was incremental and locally led. Its context is somewhat unusual owing to the widespread prevalence and acknowledgment of informal second units, or "secondary suites," in single-family neighborhoods. According to the city's estimates (Vancouver City Council 2017), there were twenty-five thousand secondary suites without permits in Vancouver's approximately sixty-eight thousand single-family houses. Although there was no public financial support for upgrading unpermitted housing units, policy makers sustained other policy avenues for making them safer.

THE PLANNING CONTEXT FOR SECOND UNITS IN VANCOUVER

Like Portland and Seattle, Vancouver lies in the Cascadia region. It is known for its natural harbor and hills, and the associated industries of tourism, forestry, and shipping. From its founding in 1886 with fewer than a thousand residents (Macdonald 2008) to a population of over 630,000 in 2016, Vancouver became a diverse global city. According to Statistics Canada (2016), 50.6 percent of the population belonged to visible minority groups. With over fourteen thousand residents per square mile, it is Canada's densest city. Scholars criticize its early spatial expansion, based on the dispossession of Indigenous or First Nations reserves, as municipal colonialism

(Stanger-Ross 2008). However, the contemporary city is more celebrated for its central city density, high residential towers, and emphasis on sustainable urbanization (Boddy 2005; McCann 2011; Punter 2003). Its beautiful natural and built environment have made Vancouver an attractive destination for residents and investments from around the world (particularly China), and one of the world's most expensive cities (*Economist* 2016; Kwan 2021; Surowiecki 2014).

As in other contemporary Canadian and US cities, single-family zoning played a crucial part in Vancouver's development. Over 60 percent of the city's zoned land was reserved for Residential Single (RS) Zones or single-family use (City of Vancouver 2009b, 2019b). However, lot sizes are comparatively small, most commonly 33 ft. by 120 ft. on the east side and 50 ft. by 120 ft. on the west side, making Vancouver's single-family neighborhoods denser than in other cities (Berelowitz 2005; Hirt 2014). Moreover, unpermitted secondary suites are ubiquitous (figure 6.7) and help further increase the density (City of Vancouver 2009b; Vancouver City Council 2017). Most of the city's single-family houses are built above a space for storage and heating equipment and protection from moisture which is often converted to an unpermitted secondary suite (Condon interview 2013). These secondary spaces were typically 18 in. below the ground level, enough to protect from Vancouver's relatively high frost line, and around 6½ ft. in height. Changes in heating technology from wood-fueled furnaces to electric and air heating, and regulations allowing full height for the secondary spaces in the 1950s and 1960s, made it easy to use the secondary space as an additional unit and for single-family houses to function as informal duplexes (Bula 2012; Lauster 2016; Suttor 2017; Terriss 2008).

Housing affordability is an important and polarizing issue in Vancouver politics (Bula 2018; Fumano 2019; Jang interview 2013). The city's policy focus has been on increasing the supply of housing through deregulation and upzoning and, to an extent, by allowing informal housing. However, several scholars find fault with the reliance on redevelopment and densification by highlighting concerns of displacement and gentrification (Moos and Mendez 2015; Wood 2012). They point to the relative lack of social housing in the city and criticize Vancouver for its hyper-commodified real estate market, austerity in public spending on housing, and extreme mismatch between local wages and housing prices (Blomley 2003; Lee-Young 2017).

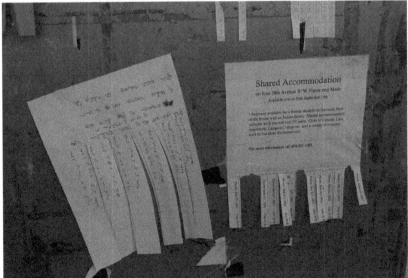

FIGURE 6.7
Advertising for secondary suites and other informal housing arrangements in Vancouver. Photo credit: Neal LaMontagne.

THE LEGALIZATION OF SECONDARY SUITES: NEIGHBORHOOD LEVEL TO CITYWIDE

The Vancouver Town Planning Commission hired Harland Bartholomew and Associates to prepare the city's first comprehensive plan, which was completed in 1928 (Macdonald 2008). It built on the existing dominance of Vancouver's single-family housing, codified it as single-family zoning, and declared, "That the one-family dwelling is the desirable unit for happy living is the general consensus of opinion of all authorities" (Harland Bartholomew and Associates 1928, 234). During World War II, the city council temporarily suspended Vancouver's bylaws and encouraged residents to share their accommodations, particularly basements, with those who lacked shelter (Wartime Prices and Trade Board 1949). As the war ended, Harland Bartholomew and Associates (1946) argued that unpermitted basement units caused overconcentration and congestion and recommended enforcement against them.

Policy makers and planners struggled with enforcing single-family living and addressing the reality of occupied basement suites. In 1956, the city council made secondary suites in single-family zones illegal but created a temporary moratorium for closing units constructed before 1956 (City of Vancouver 2004). In 1960, it adopted a ten-year time frame to close all suites, and by 1966 over two thousand suites had been removed (City of Vancouver 2009b). The city council developed policies for granting "hardship" exceptions on suites occupied by parents, grandparents, or children of owners and extensions based on the owners' or tenants' financial or medical needs (L. Cheng 1980; City of Vancouver 2009b). While affluent west side neighborhood groups lobbied for closing secondary suites, the Vancouver Homeowners Suites Association and the Vancouver Housing Association advocated for lenient policies. They recommended closing "only those suites found to be hazardous to health and safety" (Vancouver City Council 1961a, 657) and providing replacement housing for residents of closed suites (Vancouver City Council 1961b).

As a new group of city councillors, then called aldermen, took office in 1973, they decided to get community input on secondary suites through a plebiscite of homeowners in a limited section of Vancouver neighborhoods known to have a concentration of secondary suites: the east side's Cedar Cottage and the west side's Kitsilano and Grandview-Woodland (L. Cheng 1980). After a series of public meetings, planners asked property owners in

November 1975 if they favored allowing self-contained secondary suites in their subareas (Vancouver City Council 1976). Following the plebiscite, planners rezoned areas in Cedar Cottage and Kitsilano to allow secondary suites based on five-year conditional use permits, on-site owner occupancy, a minimum ceiling height of 7 ft. and 6 in. (though the planning director had discretion to approve down to 7 ft.), and at least one additional off-street parking space (Vancouver City Council 1977).

In the 1980s, judicial courts began to question the fairness of the hardship appeals process. The city council decided that it was necessary to increase public engagement for making decisions about secondary suites (City of Vancouver 2009b). While it solicited public input in 1987, it would only enforce against unpermitted suites built before 1986 if their conditions threatened the life and safety of occupants (Vancouver City Council 1987a). It decided to start with a pilot program of neighborhood secondary suites' review in Joyce Station (east side). This time, rather than hold a plebiscite, the city council agreed to democratically survey both owners and renters on whether the city should allow only an extra family suite per house or permit either family or nonfamily suites. Nonfamily suites were also known as revenue suites. Fifty-six percent of respondents favored allowing revenue suites (Vancouver City Council 1987b, 2767). Subsequently, the city council approved the rezoning of Joyce Station as RS-1S to allow "a second dwelling in a new or existing house providing the house has only one front door, and maintains an internal connection between units" (Thomsett, n.d.).

Following the Joyce Station neighborhood review, the city council decided to allow family suites by right in all single-family neighborhoods in the late 1980s (City of Vancouver 2004; Thomsett, n.d.).[13] It also decided to hold public engagement meetings and conduct citywide polling as part of the 1988 municipal election and ask all residents if they favored a neighborhood review to discuss nonfamily suites in their neighborhoods (City of Vancouver 2009b; Thomsett, n.d.). In areas where nonfamily suites were not permitted, owners would have ten years to phase them out (City of Vancouver 2004; Thomsett, n.d.).

Public meetings regarding the citywide polling were contentious. Mainly homeowners protesting the extension of the vote to all residents spoke. In Riley Park's neighborhood review, for example, several members of the review committee resigned over racist and sexist remarks against Indo-Canadian and Chinese Canadian residents (Fayerman 1988). At one meeting, 150 people publicly commented, and 148 were opposed to the voting structure. As one resident complained, "Why do 10 illegal people get a vote and only one neighbour who owns his house?" (Kavanagh 1988). In the November 1988 civic election, 76 percent of participants representing the majority of respondents in about three-fourths of the neighborhoods voted in favor of considering secondary suites (Thomsett, n.d.; Whitlock interview 2013).

Subsequently, planners conducted neighborhood reviews and surveys by subareas between 1989 and 1992 (City of Vancouver 2009b). Figure 6.8 shows a copy of an opinion survey and public information announcement from 1990. About two-thirds of the neighborhoods that voted in favor of considering secondary suites supported allowing secondary suites in their communities. As a result, 47 percent of all single-family residential neighborhoods were rezoned as RS-1S to allow nonfamily secondary suites (Joe interview 2013; Thomsett, n.d.; Whitlock interview 2013). The requirement for legalizing a secondary suite in the early 1990s included fire sprinklers, one additional off-street parking space, a minimum ceiling height of 6 ft. and 10 in., and an annual business license and water service fees of about $60 (City of Vancouver 1990).

In July 1999, the ten-year phase-out period enacted after the citywide plebiscite began to come to a close, and so-called phase-out suites in some neighborhoods could now be shut down (City of Vancouver 2004). As earlier, these units provided an important housing stock for the city. The city council decided to withhold enforcement for another three years (City of Vancouver 2004; Whitlock interview 2013).

Meanwhile, planners responsible for soliciting input from Vancouver's residents through its CityPlan (1995–2006) and City Vision (1998–2010) programs found support for increasing housing choices, including nonfamily suites, citywide (McAfee 2013; interview 2013). The support suggests that the city's incremental legalization reforms and its democratic process for soliciting public opinion on secondary suites had helped erode the opposition against them. Also, some reluctant homeowners realized that nonfamily suites in Vancouver helped increase property values and became in favor of allowing them in their neighborhoods.

During two public hearings in March 2004, most participants, including representatives from Smart Growth British Columbia and the Tenants Resource and Advisory Centre (TRAC), spoke in favor of allowing nonfamily suites citywide. Subsequently, the city council legalized them in all

THE FORMALIZATION OF SECOND UNITS 221

City of Vancouver
PLANNING DEPARTMENT

Renfrew / Collingwood
Secondary Suites Opinion Survey

Area 1

Public Information Meeting

AREAS 1, 2 & 3

TIME: 7:30 p.m., Tuesday

DATE: May 29, 1990

PLACE: Windermere School
School Auditorium
3155 E. 27th Ave.,
Vancouver

THE OPINION SURVEY

The City is carrying out neighbourhood reviews in single-family (RS-1) zoned areas to consider either phasing out or permitting secondary suites.

By answering the question on the enclosed ballot, you can voice your opinion on this important matter. Your opinion will help City Council decide what to do.

When you have answered the question, return the ballot to the Vancouver Planning Department using the enclosed self-addressed envelope. No postage is needed.

To Have Your Opinion Count, You Must Return
The Ballot In the Enclosed Envelope by June 20, 1990.
Your Response is Completely Confidential.

THE PUBLIC INFORMATION MEETING

The Planning Department will explain the Renfrew / Collingwood neighbourhood review on secondary suites and the opinion survey. Staff will also explain and answer your questions about typical building code and parking requirements for suites, the difference between RS-1 and RS-1S zoning and the ten-year phase-out program for existing suites under certain conditions.

INFORMATION ABOUT SECONDARY SUITES

A SECONDARY SUITE is a second dwelling unit, with its own kitchen, in a house. Single-family (RS-1) zoning permits only one dwelling unit per house. However, the Planning Department estimates that about 30% of all houses in Renfrew / Collingwood contain secondary suites. Most of these suites have not been created legally.

There are two types of secondary suites: Family Suites and Revenue Suites.

A FAMILY SUITE is a secondary suite which is occupied by immediate family members (parents, children,

FIGURE 6.8

An opinion survey and public information meeting announcement from 1990 for changing the zoning to allow secondary suites in Vancouver. *Source*: City of Vancouver 1990.

single-family neighborhoods (City of Vancouver 2009b; Vancouver City Council 2004). Additionally, it made the terms "family suite" and "phase-out suite" redundant (City of Vancouver 2019b). In a series of legislative decisions between March 2004 and April 2005, the city council eliminated the previous requirement for access to secondary suites from inside the main dwelling or "internal access," removed the off-street parking space requirement for secondary suites in buildings constructed before April 2004, allowed homeowners to install hardwired smoke alarms with carbon monoxide detection (instead of a sprinkler system), and reduced the minimum ceiling-height requirement for suites in existing basements to just 6 ft. and 6 in. in at least 80 percent of the suite (figure 6.9) (City of Vancouver 2019b; Whitlock interview 2013). Thus, Vancouver adopted some of the most realistic regulations for legalizing unpermitted second units in North America.

FROM SECONDARY SUITES TO MAKING ROOM FOR DUPLEXES WITH SECOND UNITS

In 2008, the Vancouver City Council adopted the EcoDensity Charter to promote sustainable growth practices and address climate change (City of Vancouver 2008). The charter committed Vancouver to promoting "gentle" (e.g., row houses), "hidden" (e.g., lane-oriented housing), and "invisible" (e.g., secondary suites) forms of densification. The strategies drew from the feedback that planners received during the CityPlan and City Vision public engagement programs (McAfee 2013; interview 2013).

The city council asked the planning department to explore regulations for laneway housing—a detached dwelling built at the rear of a lot facing an alley or lane, where a garage would typically go. The planning department recommended allowing laneway housing on 94 percent of the city's single-family lots, specifically on parcels "10.0m (33′) and wider, with access to an open lane, or on a corner site with lane dedication, or a double fronting lane" (City of Vancouver 2009a, 7). In July 2009, the city council approved the recommendation and allowed laneway housing of up to 750 sq. ft. with one additional off-street parking space in most of the city's single-family neighborhoods (Bula 2009; City of Vancouver 2013). Now, most single-family lots could accommodate three units: the main dwelling, a secondary suite, and a laneway house. The city council structured the laneway housing program like a pilot initiative and directed the planning department to report back after one hundred permits were issued. In its assessment, planners found that the covered parking built with laneway housing

THE FORMALIZATION OF SECOND UNITS

FIGURE 6.9
Inside a secondary suite in Vancouver. The regulations allow for a minimum ceiling height of 6 ft., 6 in. for habitable spaces for existing basement units. Photo credit: Author.

often had insulated floors and walls and was being informally converted to habitable space after the units were inspected and occupied (Burpee and Roth interview 2013). They recommended eliminating the enclosed parking requirement and increasing the permitted floor area to a maximum of 900 sq. ft. (City of Vancouver 2013). The city council accepted the recommendations. By 2018, the city had approved over three thousand permits for laneway houses, including over five hundred permits in both 2016 and 2017 (City of Vancouver 2018a). Figure 6.10 shows examples of laneway houses.

FIGURE 6.10
New laneway houses of different styles in Vancouver. Photo credit: Author.

High housing prices, however, continued to be a challenge in Vancouver. Critics called for taxes and other policies to dampen the insatiable demand for housing, particularly from global investors (Dougherty 2018).[14] The city's supply-focused approach received a boost from YIMBY groups like Abundant Housing Vancouver (Bula 2016; LaMontagne interview 2018). In November 2017, the city council and the mayor approved the Housing Vancouver Strategy for exploring zoning changes in single-family neighborhoods to allow duplex, triplex, and multifamily buildings (City of Vancouver 2018c). The strategy set a ten-year target of seventy-two thousand new houses (City of Vancouver 2018b).

As a quick-start action for implementing the housing strategy, in September 2018 the outgoing city council approved by a vote of seven to four to allow duplexes in 99 percent of Vancouver's single-family neighborhoods (Larsen 2018; Lee-Young and Padgham 2018).[15] The zoning reform, named Making Room, did not change the allowed intensity of development on single-family lots but increased the permitted density of development by allowing owners to build duplexes with secondary suites or lock-off units (City of Vancouver 2018b). With duplexing, owners could build four units on their lots and sell the duplex units (along with their accessory units) separately.

In December 2018, the new city council agreed to retain the policy and continue to allow duplexes with accessory units on a trial basis in the city's single-family neighborhoods (City of Vancouver 2019a; O'Connor 2018).

ENFORCEMENT AND FORMALIZATION OF INFORMAL UNITS

After World War II, planners and policy makers in Vancouver made concerted efforts to enforce single-family zoning regulations by banning secondary suites and closed thousands of them in the 1950s and 1960s. Nonetheless, compared with the other cities discussed in this chapter, Vancouver did significantly more to formalize informal housing.

Planners and policy makers supported informal housing through exceptions and extensions and created conditions for owners to invest in them. They carved out hardship exceptions for broad categories of suites, including owners and tenants facing financial and medical challenges and suites occupied by immediate family members. They also provided owners with multiyear extensions for shutting down their unpermitted units. For example, after the 1988 plebiscite, owners of phase-out suites received ten years for shutting them down and another three-year extension after the ten-year period ended. The city council shifted the enforcement focus to suites with life-threatening conditions.

The city's acknowledgment of its vast number of unpermitted units helped create a perception of tenure security for informal housing owners. With data from Statistics Canada and the British Columbia Assessment Authority, planners estimated that there were twenty-five thousand unpermitted secondary suites in Vancouver in the late 2010s (Vancouver City Council 2017). Similarly, the regional district's planners estimated seventy-seven thousand to eighty-five thousand secondary suites in the Vancouver metropolitan area, most without building permits (City of Vancouver 2009b; Metro Vancouver 2018).[16] Vancouver's planning reports are consistently open about the number of unpermitted units in the city, rarely discuss enforcement, and focus on deregulation and legalization strategies.

Vancouver's reforms to legalize secondary suites include no parking requirements, allowance for existing suites to have ceiling heights of 6 ft. and 6 in. (and even lower in 20 percent of the unit), and smoke alarms rather than more expensive sprinkler systems. Such realistic regulations have made it feasible for many owners to receive permits or feel confident that they can obtain permits if necessary.

Finally, although there is no significant public financial support program for owners to improve and upgrade their unpermitted units, policy makers have created important institutional avenues to enable upgrading. These opportunities signal to owners the safety of their financial investments and provide access to resources for investment.

First, the Vancouver Fire Department offers risk-free fire safety checks for secondary suites to owners irrespective of their permit status (Bellett 2014). As part of the program, the department provides all participating owners with free smoke alarms for installing in secondary suites.

Second, owners of secondary suites, including unpermitted units, can receive loans and mortgages based on their rental income from institutions like Vancity, Canada's largest credit union (McKinley interview 2013).[17]

Third, the provincial government and nonprofit organizations provide legal support for tenants in unpermitted housing. As I discussed in chapter 4, tenants in unpermitted units find it difficult to protest their living conditions. If they complain to municipal governments, they often find their homes shut down owing to enforcement. However, tenants of unpermitted units in British Columbia can approach the local Residential Tenancy Branch (RTB), a department of the provincial government with responsibility for

FIGURE 6.11
A pamphlet on tenants' rights produced by TRAC. *Source*: TRAC.

tenancy laws, for dispute resolution with the owners of the units. In Vancouver, TRAC, a nonprofit organization, provides legal information and education on tenants' rights (figure 6.11) and represents tenants in RTB's dispute resolution hearings. RTB and TRAC deal directly with property owners, ask them to make improvements, and provide an avenue for intervention and mediation without the municipal government's involvement (T. Durning interview 2013).

CONCLUSION: THE POTENTIAL, PROMISE, AND LIMITATIONS OF LOCAL INTERVENTIONS

Many scholars and commentators argue that attempts to reform single-family zoning locally are doomed to failure. These critics have looked to places like Los Angeles, where local attempts to relax the city's strict second unit permitting rules were met with resistance by furious homeowners, lawsuits over supposed environmental impacts, and grumbling over parking, and concluded that residents of single-family neighborhoods would never support greater density or affordable rental units. Having concluded that local efforts are hopeless, scholars and activists have shifted their focus to supporting state-level legislation that preempts local land use to force cities to accept more density. The cases discussed in this chapter suggest that this emerging conventional wisdom may be misguided.

First, with the right process and outreach efforts, local policy makers can persuade homeowners in single-family neighborhoods to change their minds and support second units. To illustrate, Santa Cruz started the ADU movement in the early 2000s before the California legislature became more active in land use reform. Seattle first allowed attached second units in 1994 and started permitting two ADUs in 2019. It had the nation's most supportive regulations for accessory units. Portland used to have the country's most liberal ADU regulations. It started allowing carved-out second units in 1991, and in 2004 it made it easier for homeowners to have an attached or detached ADU by not requiring additional parking or on-site owner occupancy. The city waived development charges for second units in 2010 and helped create vested stakeholders with enthusiasm for them. In 2014, Minneapolis expanded a pilot project for ADUs from the early 2000s to a citywide program. Vancouver allowed second units citywide in 2004 and started permitting laneway apartments, or alley-facing third units, in 2009. Together the cases show the success of locally led land use regulation changes and suggest a diversity of pathways to second unit reforms.

Moreover, local second unit reforms can be the gateway to more ambitious land use conversations and outcomes. For instance, Seattle expanded the areas covered in its designated urban villages and upzoned all the parcels, including single-family-zoned lots. Portland initiated and later approved RIP, a citywide upzoning initiative, which became the catalyst for Oregon's state preemption through HB 2001. The reform allowed property owners to build market-rate fourplexes or below-market-rate sixplexes with affordable housing restrictions on single-family-zoned lots. Minneapolis became the first major US city to eliminate single-family zoning through MPLS 2040. And Vancouver implemented Making Room, a zoning reform program, to allow duplexes with their secondary suites, or four units, on all single-family-zoned parcels.

It might be more feasible for local governments in major cities to create support for second units and additional density on single-family-zoned lots because homeowners can benefit directly and financially as developers while living in their homes. While many homeowners oppose denser housing and retail developments in their neighborhoods because of traffic congestion concerns and fears of adverse effects on their property values, they might be more open to upzoning on their own lots because of increases in their property values. The process is likely to be incremental as various stakeholders, particularly homeowners, understand how they are affected by and benefit from the changes. In Vancouver, for example, initially, only half the neighborhoods supported allowing secondary suites. Ten years later, owners in the city's other half realized that their property values would increase with upzoning and became more supportive.

Second, the cases illustrate that local governments, as in the city of Los Angeles, face significant challenges in changing single-family urbanism. To achieve success, they must broaden public participation. They are more likely to succeed through widespread public workshops, opinion surveys, and plebiscites that make it easier for tenants and low-income residents to participate. Minneapolis showed how to effectively conduct public hearings and opinion surveys in a short period. Vancouver conducted neighborhood-level workshops and plebiscites over a more extended period. Its planners and policy makers made what many homeowners considered a radical decision in the 1980s to include tenants and residents of informal secondary suites in the process. Additionally, pilot projects followed by evaluations or monitoring reports—as in Seattle and Portland—are likely to provide practical, constructive information and demonstrate and create support for second units.

Although locally led reforms can take time, broadening participation in land use decision-making can create opportunities for deepening democracy. For instance, Vancouver's neighborhood-level second unit plebiscites empowered many Indo-Canadian and Chinese Canadian residents to participate in an important land use decision. Cities that openly and inclusively discuss housing and land use decisions by a broader range of stakeholders, particularly disadvantaged and underrepresented communities, can create an urban culture of public participation and collective decision-making.

Third, locally led planning strategies are essential because they are more likely to be informed by local conditions and context. For example, in recognition of the local built environment, planners in Seattle, Portland, and Vancouver created significant minimum ceiling height exceptions—6 ft. and 8 in. in Seattle and Portland and 6 ft. and 6 in. in Vancouver—for existing informal second units to enable their legalization and upgrading. In Minneapolis, for instance, after initially proposing upzoning of single-family lots to four units, planners concluded that it was easier to build three units on the city's 40 ft. wide lots. Local planners are also more aware of diversity across their neighborhoods. Because some communities have older housing stock and informal housing units, which tend to be more affordable, local planners are more likely to develop strategies to maximize the number of new housing units added while minimizing the loss of existing low-rent housing.

Fourth, while the case studies show progress in upgrading informal housing, much more is needed, particularly public funding for improving substandard unpermitted units. The cities have made the most progress in carving out regulatory exceptions like smaller lot sizes, larger floor areas, lower ceiling heights, and shorter setbacks in their land use requirements to allow the legalization of informal units. Some helped homeowners with extensions and additional time for legalization. For example, Vancouver provided moratoria against closure and extensions for informal units identified for phasing out. In Seattle, after allowing detached backyard cottages citywide, planners allowed homeowners with unpermitted dwellings extra time to bring their units up to the required standards. The city's policy makers also showed an openness to supporting informal housing by advocating for a clemency program.

Relatedly, Vancouver led the way with a radical public acknowledgment of the magnitude of its informal housing stock and a recognition of its contributions to the city's supply of affordable housing. It was transparent about the vast number of unpermitted secondary suites in the city. Additionally, its policy makers enabled upgrading and helped protect tenant safety by supporting the city's fire safety and free smoke alarm program, allowing credit unions and banks to lend based on rental income from unpermitted units, and not interfering with the mediation support provided by nonprofit organizations to tenants of informal housing. However, there were no significant public funding or assistance programs for homeowners interested in improving the quality of their informal units. There was no public investment in neighborhood-level social or physical infrastructure in communities with large numbers of informal units. Government investments can improve the public realm and signal to owners that their unpermitted units are legitimate and that their private investments in upgrading them are likely to be secure. Seattle may have taken a small step in this direction by adding bike infrastructure in its single-family neighborhoods and acknowledging that residents of unpermitted units will use it.

Finally, while the case studies illustrate the success of local changes to single-family zoning, they also show how state governments can play an important role in enabling local reform. States can push local governments to broaden participation in housing and land use decision-making. Local governments are likely to be motivated if there is a regional framework for planning and collaboration. State governments will need to strengthen regional governance institutions, address how property taxes are distributed fairly within and across regions, and reform environmental protection regulations that opponents of infill housing development misuse to promote sprawl. State governments can also provide financial and institutional support for making the changes to single-family neighborhoods more inclusive. Their support can include funding for upgrading existing informal housing, subsidized loans for homeowners willing to add units for low-income households, funding for nonprofit organizations interested in affordable housing development opportunities in single-family neighborhoods, and public infrastructure investments. They can also take a proactive role in strengthening tenants' rights. As in British Columbia, state governments can mediate and resolve disputes between owners and tenants.

Overall, policy makers need more creative ways for state and local governments to cooperate and collaborate. The conventional wisdom that state governments' primary role is to preempt and directly intervene in single-family zoning and enable the housing market to deliver more equitable outcomes is severely limited and bound to be disappointing.

IV The New American Dream

7 REMAKING THE SUBURBAN CITY

As the 2020 presidential election campaign in the US heated up, President Donald Trump attempted to shift the political focus to the suburbs with blatant overtures to racial and class prejudice. The president promised to preserve single-family zoning, protect the suburbs from the crime and chaos of cities, fight the Democrats' plan "to remake the suburbs in their image," and stop "the Left [which] wants to take that American Dream from you" through its "dystopian version of building low-income housing units next to your suburban house" (Trump and Carson 2020). The president expected the elections to be decided in the suburbs, which most Americans—including urban residents of single-family neighborhoods—identify with and describe as their communities (Kolko 2015, 2018). He was appealing to his perceived Republican suburban base.[1] But President Trump lost the election, and "the suburbs moved away from him" (Badger and Bui 2020). According to the *New York Times* (Badger and Bui 2020), President Joe Biden received almost 5 percent more votes than former secretary of state Hillary Clinton in the 2016 elections in about four hundred suburban counties, which the newspaper identified based on their low density and where the vote margin changed the most between the two presidential elections.

President Biden's success in the 2020 elections may signal a new willingness for change in US suburban neighborhoods, which are increasingly diverse. I have documented changes to single-family zoning in Los Angeles, Santa Cruz, California, Seattle, Portland, Oregon, Minneapolis, and Vancouver, Canada, and statewide in California and Oregon. When I started my research for this book, Vancouver, Portland, and Seattle were at the forefront of zoning reforms to allow ADUs on single-family-zoned lots. As I completed the book, those cities, along with Minneapolis, were at the vanguard of ending single-family zoning and remaking their single-family neighborhoods as denser, more urban places. Meanwhile, cities as diverse as Austin, Boston, Chicago, Denver, Raleigh, Tucson, and Washington, DC, allowed or strongly considered allowing ADUs in their single-family neighborhoods. In California, the state legislature intervened in local land use regulations to allow three units (the main house, an ADU, and a junior ADU [JADU]) on single-family-zoned lots in 2017. Subsequent legislation made it significantly easier for property owners across the state to add ADUs and JADUs, which I prefer to refer to as second and third units. In early 2021, unanimous city councils in Berkeley, Oakland, and Sacramento took initial steps to allow up to four units on single-family-zoned lots (Dillon 2021; Orenstein 2021; Ravani 2021). To cap it all, Governor Gavin Newsom of California approved legislation to allow for up to four units on single-family-zoned lots statewide through duplexing and lot splitting in September 2021 (Office of Governor Gavin Newsom 2021).

ADUS AS A RATIONAL PLANNING RESPONSE

Single-family housing is a defining feature of postwar US urbanism and a potent symbol of American exceptionalism and affluence. More than 60 percent of American households lived in detached single-family houses. In most cities, local governments reserved an overwhelming majority of the residentially zoned land for single-family neighborhoods. Many residents guarded their antiurban lifestyles of avoiding social contact and conflict with both neighbors and strangers by routinely objecting to denser housing developments. Planners, policy makers, private entrepreneurs, architects, urban designers, and other cultural influencers collaborated in building the ideology of single-family living for almost a century.

However, homeowners needing additional living space or rental income subverted the consensus and built unpermitted dwelling units on their single-family-zoned lots. Many of these units contributed to the supply of affordable housing in their communities, and local governments limited enforcement action against them. Throughout the 2010s, policy makers and planners in cities across the country recognized the value of second units in single-family neighborhoods and changed or considered changing single-family zoning regulations to formally allow property owners to add multiple accessory units. The American Planning Association (APA) saw adding ADUs in single-family neighborhoods as a feasible solution to increase the housing supply and diversity. It indicated that this was a "high priority topic" for the profession (Morley communication 2019). For many reasons, second units became an acceptable planning response and are likely to gain traction across the US.

First, it is often spatially feasible and architecturally easy to accommodate second units of varying types on most single-family-zoned lots. While Reyner Banham (1971) optimistically observed that Los Angeles's residents, if needed, could increase the city's low-density built form through infill development at the neighborhood scale, the same holds for single-family housing lots. Their backyards provide ample room for building backyard cottages. Additionally, underused garages, basements, and attics offer an opportunity for conversion to independent dwellings. Single-family houses are malleable (Moudon and Sprague 1982) and can be subdivided or added to and carved into multiple units.

Homeowners adopted these spatial strategies to create informal housing units in Los Angeles and cities throughout the US and Canada. Many property owners converted their basements into secondary suites in cities like Vancouver, where semibasements are typical. These owners ingeniously created thousands of new housing units by adding extra living space, converting underused spaces, and creatively carving out space. Policy makers in the US and Canada followed their lead to legalize second units of varying built forms with corresponding formal names, including backyard cottages, detached ADUs, attached ADUs, JADUs, semibasement secondary suites, and laneway apartments.

Second, there is market support for changing single-family housing norms and regulations because the demand for housing is changing. Sociologists note that small, one-person households (Klinenberg 2012b) and large, multigenerational families (Newman 2012) are becoming more common in the US. Single-family houses do not serve the needs of these households or many others that depart from the nuclear family structure. The existing stock of single-family dwellings is a poor fit for their needs and budgets. The dearth of affordable housing, including missing-middle housing, has increased the demand for lower-priced housing, which homeowners have filled with informal units. Though policy making has been slow to confront the issue, this is not a new problem. In the late 1980s, the *Los Angeles Times* asked my former UCLA colleague, the late Leobardo Estrada, to explain the unpermitted garage conversions in Los Angeles County's outlying suburban areas. Leo had a simple explanation: in job-rich, peripheral areas of the region, "garages are plentiful and cheap apartments are not" (Chavez and Quinn 1987).

The rise of informal housing units illustrates the economic value of the rent they can generate for property owners. When homeowners and realtors prepare real estate listings, many sellers disclose the unpermitted second units on the single-family-zoned properties they are selling, even though they are not required to do so. This widespread practice indicates that many homeowners do not consider informal units a liability in the real estate market. On the contrary, they believe informal second units can help increase the sale value of their homes. Nonetheless, other homeowners often oppose zoning changes to allow accessory units because they worry that the quality of life in their neighborhoods and their property values might decline. Indeed, additional dwelling units may lower property values in communities where buyers are willing to pay a premium for the amenity of low density (Lang 2005; Sirmans, Macpherson, and Zeitz 2005). However, in most single-family neighborhoods in cities and inner suburbs with high housing prices and unmet demand for housing, permitting second units likely leads to higher property values for homeowners.

Consequently, it is economically advantageous and rational for homeowners to support changes to their single-family zoning to permit accessory units. Upzoning should help increase the housing supply in the long run, and the price of housing units might grow less steadily or decline. However, owners of upzoned single-family houses, who are also the landowners, can expect their property values to rise because of the development capacity on their single-family-zoned lots increasing from one to two units.

Third, accessory units may be slowly becoming culturally acceptable to single-family homeowners. Some homeowners' resistance to upzoning their lots is cultural. The prospect of tenants in their neighborhood full of owner-occupied houses disrupts the accepted ideology of single-family living. ADUs, however, offer the possibility of slow, incremental changes that provide immediate benefits to property owners without significantly altering the physical form of their neighborhoods. Homeowners are subject to the same demographic changes discussed in this book. Many directly benefit from the flexibility of having a second unit for family members or caretakers on their single-family-zoned property. With accessory units, they can decide who their tenants are. Neighbors may feel that their neighborhood's transformation is limited and incremental. They can exercise some control beyond their lot boundaries, particularly when their neighbors have informal units and are concerned about complaints against them. Finally, even after planners change the underlying zoning to allow multiple accessory units, their neighborhoods maintain their physical character and continue to be known as single-family communities. For example, in California, where homeowners could build an ADU and a JADU; in Seattle, where they could have an attached and a detached ADU; and in Vancouver, where laneway apartments and secondary suites were permitted, planning documents and residents still described the neighborhoods as single-family communities.

Fourth, given the dominance of single-family zoning in urban land use, accessory units are a rational response for governments trying to manage the conflict between the need to increase the housing supply and homeowner opposition to upzoning in their single-family neighborhoods. As more homeowners see economic benefits from accessory units, the political opposition to them weakens. As ADUs become politically and culturally acceptable, the institutional challenge of reforming single-family zoning becomes more manageable for policy makers. Moreover, affordable housing advocates often oppose conventional upzoning because existing market-based affordable housing units can be lost through demolition and redevelopment. The possibility of multiple accessory units through infill development, conversions, and carve-outs of the existing building stock limits the loss of "naturally occurring" affordable housing. With less opposition from homeowners and affordable housing advocates, it is easier for governments to pursue this land use reform.[2] Additionally, policy makers are attracted to changing zoning to legalize ADUs because it is a deregulation-based approach for addressing informal housing and does not require public funds.

However, the growing acceptance of accessory units as a planning response poses a challenge for expanding access to homeownership. Suppose single-family housing homeowners support plans to allow ADUs because their property values will increase. These increased property values come at a cost: their homes are now less affordable for new home buyers.[3] The challenge suggests a need for more diversity in the supply of homes for sale. A simple way forward would be to allow property owners to sell their second and third units separately, through either easy land subdivision regulations or shared property rights. I prefer to call ADUs "second units"—and JADUs "third units"—to emphasize the possibility that if the conveyance rules changed, owners could sell them separately, and they could be independent, nonaccessory housing units. The state government of California took a step in this direction in 2021 by approving Senate Bill 9 by Senate president pro tempore Toni Atkins. While the legislation does not allow property owners to sell their ADUs and JADUs separately, it makes it feasible for owners of single-family houses to subdivide their homes and lots to sell them under certain conditions.

Rules prohibiting accessory units from being sold independently incentivize informal property ownership arrangements. If laws prevent prospective buyers from buying the units individually, then in some cases friends and family members will need to collaborate to afford single-family houses with second and third units. However, they will informally subdivide the ownership interests and own the different units separately in practice.[4]

URBAN INFORMALITY AND INFORMAL HOUSING IN THE GLOBAL NORTH

My desire to understand the nature of unpermitted second units and the remaking of single-family housing in Los Angeles is connected to my research interest in informal economic activities and policies to address them. Previously, I researched informal housing in the Global South and in California's agricultural communities. It took me some time to grasp the extensive scale of informal housing units interspersed with formal dwellings in the Los Angeles region. In part, this is because academic literature on informal housing in US cities has been mostly nonexistent. Outside academia, policy makers and planners in US cities rarely discussed unpermitted housing units except in enforcement actions. Both academics and policy makers see informal housing in the Global North as an anomaly to be ignored or eliminated. They likely associate informal economic activities with the Global South.

While living conditions in informal housing in the Global South and the Global North can be significantly different, unpermitted housing often offers many residents the only alternative and viable option. While policy makers have tried to limit and discourage new residents by restricting the supply of housing units in cities in both the Global South and the Global North, they have failed for similar reasons. The pull of jobs and economic opportunities in vibrant cities is so strong that housing supply restrictions are ineffective in curbing migration. Unless there are draconian and stringent enforcement policies against urban informality, property owners and entrepreneurs are likely to develop informal housing to provide disadvantaged new urban residents with living options. Inevitably, some of these options are unsafe and dangerous. My research has identified key arguments and policy lessons for informal housing in the Global North.

First, contrary to conventional wisdom, informal housing is common in cities of the Global North. According to my analysis of real estate listings of single-family houses for sale, there were around fifty thousand unpermitted second units in single-family neighborhoods in the city of Los Angeles. More than one in ten of the single-family-zoned lots in the city probably had an unpermitted second unit. Unpermitted second units are likely even more common on multifamily-zoned lots with single-family houses and in the much larger Los Angeles County. Vancouver had the highest incidence of informal housing in unpermitted secondary suites among the cities I researched for this book. According to the city's estimates (Vancouver City Council 2017), there were seventy thousand single-family houses in the city, and twenty-five thousand of them likely included an unpermitted secondary suite, or more than one in three single-family houses had an informal second unit.

Furthermore, real estate sales listings and complaints to the Department of Building and Safety in the city of Los Angeles show informal second units are not limited to disadvantaged or immigrant neighborhoods. Informal housing is distributed across cities in both low-income and wealthy communities. Unpermitted units are not easily visible from streets and sidewalks. However, as my survey of the Neighborhood Councils in the city of Los Angeles indicated, neighbors are often aware of them. As public documents, newspaper reports, and my interviews suggest, policy makers know about them too. Nonetheless, they tend to avoid them in planning and policy making. I argue that their widespread prevalence means that they need more public acknowledgment, policy consideration, and research attention from scholars.

Second, my research expands the conventional understanding of the nature and characteristics of urban informality by highlighting its territorially or spatially embedded nature. Although the original academic literature saw informality through a dualist lens and emphasized structural barriers to regular wage earning in the formal sector (Hart 1973; International Labour Organization 1972), subsequent scholars questioned the dualist logic inherent in its early conceptualization (Bromley 1978; Moser 1978). It is now generally accepted in the literature that while informal economic activities are unregulated, separating them distinctly from formal economic activities is difficult. Informal and formal economic activities have linkages, often overlap, and are integrated into the global economy's framework of international trade and financial institutions (Peattie 1987; Portes, Castells, and Benton 1989; Portes and Sassen-Koob 1987; Sanyal 1988). Scholars argue that economic activities and informal exchanges are often market based and commercially driven (Angel et al. 1983; Burgess 1978; Geertz 1978; Kim 2004; Ward 1982, 1999). Increasingly, it is accepted that social relations, networks, and norms play an essential part in sustaining informal markets, usually to pool resources and reduce uncertainty and transaction costs (Axelrod 1984; Fawaz 2008; Razzaz 1993; Saunders 2012). Thus, the existing literature highlights the complex nature of informal activities, suggesting that informality is economically, institutionally, and socially embedded. It posits that recognizing the embeddedness is key to developing appropriate policy responses.

Using the grounded example of Los Angeles's unpermitted second units, I build on the literature to show how urban informality is also spatially embedded in the built environment. I suggest that informal housing's territorially embedded nature stems from local housing markets, cultural housing preferences, prejudices and political intolerance or acceptance of unregulated housing in different places, place-specific social relations that enable unpermitted housing to function without complaints and enforcement, and the spatial configuration of housing and neighborhoods that makes it easier for certain forms of informal housing—such as garage conversions or backyard additions or basement retrofits—to develop discreetly. In contrast to conventional scholarship's focus on informal activities' global economic connections, I emphasize informality's corresponding local linkages and influences. The spatially embedded nature of informality suggests that not only do informal economic activities differ between the Global South and the Global North, but there are likely important and understudied differences in informal housing from place to place. These differences have policy implications.

Third, living conditions within Los Angeles's unpermitted second units are unequal and vary significantly. The wide variation of living conditions within the city's informal housing stock illustrates both the potential and the precarity of urban informality. While some scholars celebrate informal activities for their radical potential of everyday resistance and survival (Kudva 2009) and promise of inclusive urban citizenship (Watson 2011), others criticize them for their dangerous living and working conditions, exploitation of labor, associated economic uncertainty, and the prospect of the unaccountable use of state discretionary power (Bernhardt et al. 2008; Roy 2005, 2009b; Yiftachel 2009). Capturing these two perspectives, William Mangin (1967) saw in the squatter settlements of Lima, Peru, both a problem and a solution. Similarly, Li Tian (2008) described China's unregulated urban villages as a boon and a bane for residents. Like them, I see urban informality as paradoxical and contradictory. Los Angeles's unpermitted second units represent the potential of a more appropriately located, designed, and affordable housing supply, as well as the risks and dangers of unsafe housing with few protections and rights for tenants.

Moreover, because informal housing is spatially, economically, institutionally, and socially embedded, it provides households from different socioeconomic backgrounds with disparate and divergent living conditions. In this context, disadvantaged, low-income, immigrant, undocumented, and families of color are likely to bear the burden of dangerous and substandard informal housing. They are likely to be more vulnerable to informal housing because it is more difficult for them to afford safe and decent market-based housing. Wealthy households, in contrast, have multiple advantages. They are less adversely affected by the exclusionary nature of single-family zoning. Their informal housing is more prone to be safe and livable. There will likely be fewer complaints against their unpermitted units, less negative attention from enforcement agencies, and more confidence for owners to invest in improving them. Laissez-faire works well for them.

Fourth, instead of ignoring, enforcing against, or primarily addressing informal housing through deregulation to attract private investments, there is a significant need for public support and public funding to upgrade unpermitted units. The conventional enforcement practice makes it difficult for tenants of informal housing to complain about their living conditions. Cities need a new institutional focus. The living conditions of the unpermitted units should be as important a municipal function as zoning enforcement. In contrast to enforcement, improving living conditions will require considerably more public expenditure. The city of Los Angeles's

Garage Housing Task Force recognized this necessity in the late 1990s. It recommended public funding for removing hazards in unpermitted garages to make them safe and livable. Policy makers can signal government support for informal housing by acknowledging its presence, noting its essential contribution to the housing supply, providing financial support and technical assistance for upgrading, and implementing locally informed policies to support upgrading.

Policy programs to improve and upgrade the living conditions in informal housing will be more successful when they recognize and build on its spatially, economically, institutionally, and socially embedded nature. For example, Vancouver planners recognized that many of the city's informal secondary suites were in basements with low ceiling heights. The planners significantly reduced the minimum height requirement citywide to 6 ft. and 6 in. to match the existing height conditions of Vancouver's secondary suites. I have not seen such a low minimum ceiling height requirement anywhere else, but it was the only feasible response to existing conditions in the city. The planners also promoted the installation of smoke alarms, and policy makers encouraged the fire department to provide free smoke alarms to any interested household, irrespective of their basements' legal status. These policies signaled to homeowners that they could safely invest in improving conditions in their secondary suites and helped make them safer and more livable. However, like most Global North cities, Vancouver did not provide any significant funding support to homeowners for upgrading their basements. If it had, the city could have required owners to accept rent stabilization agreements to protect vulnerable tenants from rent increases likely from the upgrading of their secondary suites.

Informal second units for well-off households raise different policy issues than informal housing for modest-resourced and working-class families. While informal second units by disadvantaged households emphasize the need for state-supported upgrading to address dangerous or substandard conditions, informal ADUs by wealthy families more starkly highlight the need for housing deregulation and zoning changes.

LOCAL GOVERNMENTS AND SINGLE-FAMILY HOUSING

Like informal economic activities, formal institutions are territorially and socially embedded. In Douglass North's (1990, 3) words, they are the "rules of the game" that constrain human behavior. To issue permits for second units, planners and policy makers have to change single-family zoning regulations in a cultural context that often uncompromisingly reveres the ideal of single-family living. As a consequence of strong neighborhood-based opposition to development, even the *Economist* (2015), the weekly newspaper known for its social and economic liberalism and support for decentralization and less government involvement, called for top-down land use planning interventions. The conventional academic literature suggests that local planners and policy makers do not have the power to effect such significant changes (Glaeser 2017; Infranca 2019; Lemar 2019; Wegmann 2020). But top-down changes to single-family housing regulations are not only controversial but also challenging to implement. This book shows that even when local communities strongly support single-family housing and oppose additional density, they can accept second units. There are important reasons for planners, policy makers, and housing advocates to persevere with local reforms.

First, while the state legislature pushed California's ADU reforms, my secondary cases show that local governments can lead policy changes to remake single-family zoning through second units. Urban studies scholars are divided on the question of power and control of development decision-making in cities. In the late twentieth century, the conventional wisdom on political economy and growth politics in the US viewed cities as Growth Machines driven by coalitions of local government interests and land-based, elite business interests (Logan and Molotch 1987; Molotch 1976). While the criticism of the pro-development perspective still holds significant standing in contemporary urban studies (Angotti 2008; Moskowitz 2017), it has been joined and to some extent supplanted by a narrative of intense neighborhood-based activism and opposition to density and development, which scholars usually characterize as NIMBY sentiment (Fulton 2001; Schively 2007; Tighe 2012). According to Edward Glaeser and his colleagues, organized homeowners, or "homeowners' cooperatives," have replaced the pro-development Growth Machine with their focus on maintaining and enhancing their private home values by opposing property development in and near their neighborhoods (Glaeser, Gyourko, and Saks 2005).[5] In contrast to the Growth Machine and homeowners' cooperatives perspectives, John Mollenkopf (1983) explained urban growth as a contest between the conflicting interests of different elite groups in his classic, *The Contested City*. His scholarship may better explain how city growth trajectories can favor neighborhood stability and antigrowth sentiment at times and property development, including second units and single-family zoning reforms, at other times. Thus, it may be feasible for local governments to persuade owners of single-family housing, particularly in major cities and their inner suburbs, to support second units, third units, and upzoning of their lots because homeowners can benefit directly. Consequently, as the cases show, there are a diversity of institutional pathways to second unit reforms, including the locally led remaking of single-family zoning.

Second, the cases discussed in this book show the significance of formal and informal public engagement in addressing single-family zoning and demonstrate a range of institutional possibilities for engagement-based institutional change (A. Fung 2004, 2012). Successful public engagement strategies included public workshops and advocacy by a nonprofit group in Santa Cruz, pilot neighborhood upzonings and evaluations of backyard cottages in Seattle, ADU tours organized by housing and environmental sustainability activists in Portland, and public hearings and online opinion surveys in Minneapolis. Collectively the cases show the value of policy dialogue, pilot projects, and incrementalism for creating institutional change (Roland 2004). Correspondingly, the three ADU workshops organized by the planning department in the city of Los Angeles in 2009 were woefully inadequate. In contrast, the second unit pilot project facilitated by the mayor's office in 2016 probably played a central role in generating attention, discussion, and the subsequent enthusiasm for and success of ADUs in the city's formal housing market. Along the same lines, the most interesting participation model may be in Vancouver, where the local government organized neighborhood forums and a citywide referendum followed by neighborhood-based workshops and opinion surveys. Its experience with direct democracy suggests that planners and policy makers have opportunities to go directly to residents to gauge their interests in supporting second units and institutional changes to single-family zoning at both the neighborhood and city levels.

Third, while locally led zoning reforms and initiatives can be challenging, they have several advantages and imperatives. Local governments and housing advocates need to pursue them because it is unlikely that state governments will be interested in preempting local land use regulations in many states. For example, Minneapolis policy makers and planners did not expect the Minnesota state legislature's intervention to help them change the city's single-family zoning. Locally led processes create more robust opportunities for residents to participate in decision-making and for policy makers to broaden participation opportunities. In Vancouver, planners sought all residents' opinions, including tenants of unpermitted secondary suites. Though there are likely to be differences and disagreements among stakeholders, land use and housing deliberation can be the basis of invigorated civic life. Policy making and planning based on local knowledge and contextual understanding, including spatial conditions, will likely be more nuanced and successful. Local governments should take the lead in pushing state governments to implement their reforms regionally. Local engagement may lead to broader benefits, including empowering disadvantaged communities, local problem-solving capacity, a more profound democracy, and the more ambitious and inclusive remaking of single-family neighborhoods.

Although decentralized land use decision-making can allow second units in single-family housing, such direct democracy might not work well for all controversial land use decisions. In the case of secondary units and upzoning of single-family-zoned lots, property owners are likely to be motivated by the possibility of additional units, their potential rent, and higher property values. In other cases, such as making neighborhoods more open to unhoused residents, it is less likely that any community will volunteer to be more accepting. In such contexts, the countervailing power of top-down decision-making is necessary (Ehrenfeucht and Loukaitou-Sideris 2014; Young 1990). However, state governments' countervailing ability in zoning reform does not need to be in the form of direct decision-making. They can push, support, and enable local governments to broaden and deepen public engagement for land use reforms. They can provide strong regional institutions for collaboration, including incentives for jurisdictions to meet their share of housing production and penalties and enforcement against communities that fail to meet their obligations. California's attempt to strengthen its framework for the regional allocation of housing goals and responsibilities and state enforcement of local actions through changes in its Regional Housing Needs Assessment model is a noteworthy step in this direction (Camacho and Marantz 2020; Elmendorf et al. 2020).

HOUSING AS A SOCIAL DREAM

My central claim is that the ideal of single-family living is slowly and gradually evolving through informal and formal changes. There are multiple institutional pathways to neighborhood change, including informal interventions by homeowners and zoning reforms led by local and state governments. Several writers have called for moving away from the conventional model of single-family housing for aesthetic reasons (Huxtable 1964; Keats 1956; Lerup 1987), environmental reasons (Mumford 1961; Real Estate Research Corporation 1974), and social justice reasons (Fishman 1987; Hayden [1984] 2002; G. Wright [1981] 1983), including the challenge of affordable housing (Manville, Monkkonen, and Lens 2020; Wegmann 2020). My research, however, suggests that the need for additional space and homeowners' parochial economic interests, particularly the potential for rental income and higher property values, are driving the transformation of single-family housing. Correspondingly, policy makers may welcome second unit reforms because they are a market-based planning strategy for increasing the housing supply that does not require increased government investment in affordable housing or active involvement in the housing market.

The rational nature of these housing transformations should not obscure their promise and possibility of something bigger and more radical. These changes to single-family neighborhoods offer opportunities to remake US urbanism's suburban and private nature and replace it with the sharing and cosmopolitanism optimistically associated with cities and urban living. Scholars have suggested that single-family housing's predictable ethic is at the root of the fetish for control and superficial order in American planning (Garnett 2009; Wilson 1991). They argue this orthodoxy not only robs cities of urban vitality but also marginalizes low-income households, particularly families of color, and households that depart from the nuclear-family norm. The eclipse of single-family living, even its waning, may lead to more flexibility in land use regulations, more open and inclusive cities, and a pathway to more just cities.

SPATIAL AND INSTITUTIONAL DIVERSITY IN HOUSING

Affordable housing is a significant challenge in the US because housing costs have increased while inflation-adjusted wages have flatlined for most households and public subsidies have not increased. It will be impossible to address the housing challenge adequately without reversing the trend on all three fronts. I have focused on a small part of the housing challenge with second units because many homeowners have informally adopted this strategy. Second and third units on single-family-zoned lots help reduce housing costs and add diversity to the housing supply. I like second and third units because they are a creative spatial strategy for upzoning and adding housing density through small-scale infill or carve-outs while minimizing the loss of existing housing units from demolition and redevelopment. The low-rent housing units occupied by low-income households are often the most attractive for redevelopment. These properties might include unpermitted units. Losing them would cause more pain and housing struggles for the most disadvantaged groups. In jurisdictions like the city of Los Angeles, most single-family-zoned lots are 5,000 sq. ft. or bigger and large enough to add second and third units through infill and carve-outs. The micro-infill approach's focus on adapting the old built environment fabric instead of replacing the building stock is environmentally friendly too. The scale may enable small, locally owned businesses and residents to get more involved in housing construction activities. Governments can help builders access construction finance and create business development programs for contractors in disadvantaged communities. They can also organize workforce development and training programs focused on construction and trade skills. Additionally, second and third units can provide an unprecedented opportunity for public agencies to make direct incremental investments in subsidized affordable housing units in single-family neighborhoods, which dominate urban land use.

The shared amenities, including kitchens, toilets, and laundry rooms, in many informally modified single-family houses suggest opportunities for new spatial designs and diversity in housing layouts. Like single-family homeowners with informal units, several of the country's largest home builders have innovated new housing designs for multigenerational housing with shared spaces. Building off these examples, architects and urban designers have the opportunity and responsibility to develop more radical arrangements for transforming single-family living for a new urban culture.

In pioneering scholarship, Dolores Hayden (1980) proposed gender-equity retrofits to single-family neighborhoods based on sharing in her article "What Would a Non-sexist City Be Like?" Similarly, my former colleague at UCLA, the late Jacqueline Leavitt, developed several new gender-equity housing designs that privileged sharing. Jackie designed the Double Dream, which "combined two single-family attached houses using a variety of flexible spaces" (Leavitt 1996, 70). Figure 7.1 shows her New American House Concept. It includes six town houses with street-facing, single-story offices

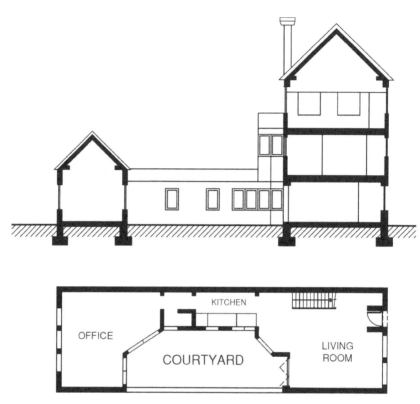

FIGURE 7.1
Section and first-floor plan of the award-winning New American House (1984) by Troy West and Jaqueline Leavitt (not to scale). *Source*: Based on an illustration in Schoenauer 2003. Graphic: Jae-Hyeon Park.

and workspaces, which could serve as neighborhood childcare centers and other shared amenities, and private living quarters at the back. A kitchen and a private courtyard link the front and back of each house. The layout allows parents in both the private living area and the public workspace to share domestic responsibilities, such as cooking in the kitchen or supervising children playing in the courtyard (Leavitt 1996; Rowe 1991). Planning and zoning requirements need to be flexible enough to allow and incentivize such design innovations.

In addition to new spatial forms, there are opportunities and a need for new institutional arrangements of property rights and ownership. As I noted earlier, ADU and upzoning reforms can make single-family-zoned lots more valuable and therefore less affordable. By making secondary units tenure neutral and allowing homeowners the right to sell them separately, governments can increase access to homeownership by lowering its cost. Homeowners should have the ability to transfer the right to build and sell or rent second units in their backyards. Similarly, if the jurisdictions allow third units, homeowners should have the ability to sell the dwellings or rights to the units separately. Assembly Bill 587 by Assemblymember Laura Friedman (Democrat from Glendale), which the California state legislature adopted in 2019, was a limited move to enable the sale of secondary units. It allowed nonprofit organizations to develop ADUs on single-family- and multifamily-zoned lots and sell them separately as independent units. Policy makers should extend this right of property conveyance to all homeowners. Correspondingly, they should replace the terminology of "accessory units" with "second units" and "third units."

Public agencies and community-based organizations have a significant opportunity to expand social and nonmarket housing alternatives in single-family neighborhoods by investing directly in second, third, and fourth units. In return for rent-stabilization agreements, they can provide homeowners with funding to upgrade their existing informal units. Like the Santa Cruz Community Credit Union, they can offer below-market-rate loans to homeowners willing to add accessory units with rent restrictions and affordable housing covenants. They can provide grants to homeowners who agree to significantly restrict their rents and keep units affordable or reserve them for families receiving rental subsidies. Los Angeles County offered homeowners grants and construction finance if they agreed to rent the units to Section 8 voucher holders. The program, however, had limited funding and needs to be expanded.

Suppose conventional ADU zoning rules were to change to allow homeowners to sell second and third units separately. In that case, public agencies could work with the owners to build new scattered-site, publicly owned housing units or pay for the right to expand and carve out units from existing single-family houses. The strategy would allow cities to distribute affordable housing units more widely, potentially sidestepping neighborhood opposition to larger affordable housing projects. Crucially, it would enable cities to build affordable housing at a much lower cost than the current system. In 2020, the average cost of building a single unit of homeless housing in the city of Los Angeles was $531,000 (Oreskes 2021a). In several cases, housing developers built these projects on publicly owned land, and the actual cost of development was significantly higher. Even the city's program to acquire motels and adapt their rooms as studios for emergency housing costs about $230,000 per unit (Oreskes 2021b). Second units can be built for a much lower cost per unit: LA Más, the Los Angeles–based nonprofit organization, estimated in 2021 that it could convert garages of almost 400 sq. ft. to studios for $100,000 and to one-bedroom units for $120,000, and build new two-bedroom, one-and-a-half-bath units of 710 sq. ft. for $220,000 (LA Más 2021; Leung communication 2021).

Along the lines of my suggestion to allow homeowners the property right to sell their second and third units, California's SB 9 permits them to split their lots into two and carve out two dwellings from their single-family houses for sale. However, the legislation includes several conditions that are likely to limit its effectiveness. For example, in its quest for planning order, the legislation requires owners to divide their lots roughly equally. This stipulation will make it difficult for homeowners with significant front setbacks to split their lots nearly evenly. The legislation would have been more effective if it had been based on the spatial diversity of single-family-zoned lots across the state. Take the case of the community of Pacoima in Los Angeles. Its single-family-zoned lots are long and deep. They often contain three units, two of which are informal, in a straight line. Homeowners will be unable to take advantage of the legislation without losing one of the existing units. Other conditions put limitations on homeowners with tenants. The protection is well intended but unlikely to address fears of gentrification and displacement in disadvantaged communities. Moreover, it will not protect tenants of informal units and might incentivize more homeowners to rent their properties informally.

Many community members in places like South Los Angeles recognize the need for more housing but are genuinely worried about displacement in their communities (E. Smith 2021). To address their fears of redevelopment and displacement, governments need to go beyond zoning deregulation. They need to get more actively involved in housing and property markets to demonstrate that the outcomes can be inclusive. Finding planning approaches to preserve existing informal housing and expanding the institutional diversity of new housing can help. Building on SB 9, governments can provide grants and subsidized loans to homeowners interested in expanding and then subdividing their single-family houses to sell to nonprofit organizations and community-based groups for affordable housing. Similarly, they can provide financial support for community-based organizations to acquire housing units for their community members. Like Portland, they can level the playing field for nonprofit housing developers by allowing six dwellings instead of four if developers agree to restrict the price of some of the houses and earmark them for affordable housing.

State governments in particular have a role in expanding access to housing loans and mortgages for residents of disadvantaged communities. There is race- and ethnicity-based inequality in access to mortgages, and Black and Latinx home buyers are disproportionately channeled into high-cost loans (Loya and Flippen 2021). State governments can build on the federal model of providing mortgage insurance to expand equitable access to mortgages, including homeowners interested in sharing property ownership opportunities to transform single-family lots.

SHARING THE CITY: BEYOND PRIVATE LOT LINES

America's single-family neighborhoods were built to provide white, middle-class, heterosexual nuclear families with a single male breadwinner an ideal setting to raise their children. For decades, scholars and activists have criticized these neighborhoods on environmentalist, racial justice, gender equality, and affordability grounds. There is a growing recognition that they no longer serve most people's needs. Individual homeowners have led the way in adapting their single-family houses for modern life by building or carving out informal second units in garages, backyards, and basements. Forward-thinking cities have recognized these informal innovations to single-family housing and responded by legalizing the construction of second and third units in single-family-zoned neighborhoods. Widespread homeowner acceptance of these modest, incremental changes to the character of their communities challenges the conventional wisdom around the political sanctity of single-family zoning. These reforms to single-family zoning represent a fundamental transformation of American urbanism and the American Dream itself.

Along with the possibility of spatial and institutional diversity in housing forms and property rights at the lot level, additional units on single-family-zoned lots suggest openings for innovative designs, shared infrastructure, and collaborative processes that cross private lot lines and work at the scale of blocks and neighborhoods.

There are opportunities for new design thinking, mixed land uses, and shared amenities. Earlier, I mentioned that the workspaces in the New American House Concept could provide neighborhood-serving uses. Los Angeles has several inspiring built and unbuilt precedents along these lines. Early twentieth-century housing forms in Los Angeles were known for their bungalow courts and shared courtyards (Hayden [1984] 2002). Architect and urbanist Clarence Stein (1951) originally designed community kitchens for the celebrated Baldwin Hills Village (now Village Green) housing development. Another innovative example is LA Más's proposal for shared Community ADUs (figure 7.2). The nonprofit organization speculated that some homeowners might not have big enough backyards to build detached second units. It proposed that neighboring homeowners be allowed to build dwellings across private lot lines, and neighborhoods could have a network of jointly owned and used Community ADUs. The structures could also serve other nonresidential, community-serving uses.

As single-family neighborhoods get denser and more diverse with additional housing and residents, they will need more shared amenities and infrastructure.

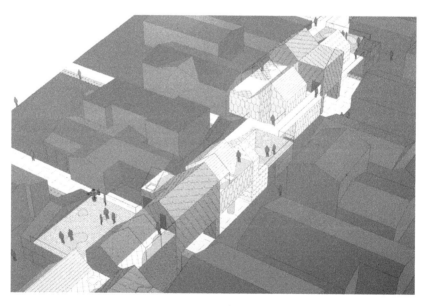

FIGURE 7.2
LA Más's Community ADU proposal for the 2015 exhibition *Shelter: Rethinking How We Live in Los Angeles* at the A+D Museum. Courtesy of LA Más.

The COVID-19 pandemic highlighted the value of neighborhood-level public investments in small open spaces, playgrounds, and community gardens. Other useful and necessary social infrastructure in neighborhoods includes childcare centers, senior centers, community kitchens, health-care facilities, resiliency centers, libraries, and language and learning centers for immigrants and adult learners. Public agencies should invest in these shared neighborhood amenities. Moreover, public commitment for physical and social infrastructure investments in communities can help create additional support for upzoning and neighborhood change.

Policy makers should prioritize public investments in disadvantaged neighborhoods. With the rise of the Black Lives Matter and racial justice movements across the country, the recognition of disproportionate deaths from COVID-19 in Black, Latinx, and Indigenous communities, and the reckoning with historical and continuing racial injustices, there is growing interest in social and racial justice and critically revisiting how jurisdictions spend their resources on policing and community health and safety. Communities are making commitments to increase public investment in social housing and disadvantaged neighborhoods. In Los Angeles County, voters approved Measure J in November 2020. The ballot measure diverts public spending to social services and commits at least 10 percent of the county's revenue for community investments and incarceration alternatives. Some of the most encouraging debates about reimagining policing, public spending, and social justice have occurred in Minneapolis, Portland, and Seattle, where local governments and activists helped create a more open culture by democratically discussing housing issues. These modest but hopeful beginnings may portend significantly more public investment in disadvantaged communities' social infrastructure.

Finally, like single-family zoning reforms, public neighborhood investments provide a promising avenue for fostering direct democracy and citizenship. Neighborhood residents can participate in discussions, forums, workshops, and voting to decide a community's social infrastructure and amenity priorities. Neighborhood-level deliberations can provide an opportunity for neighbors to learn about their communities' needs and make decisions collectively. In the process, there will likely be many surprises, unexpected possibilities, and wonders. Gradually, cities and neighborhoods that reposition inclusive access to housing, social infrastructure, and participation and collaboration in decision-making at the center of urbanism can emerge.

NOTES

CHAPTER 1: THE CHANGING NORMS AND REGULATIONS OF SINGLE-FAMILY HOUSING

1. When groups of immigrant workers in meatpacking plants became infected with COVID-19, Secretary Azar ignored their factories' working conditions and blamed their housing arrangements. On the contrary, the global experience, particularly from Asia, and planning research showed that the fears about multifamily housing and the pandemic are irrational, and that density is not related to COVID-19 infection or mortality rates (Hamidi, Sabouri, and Ewing 2020).

2. The 2017 American Housing Survey by the US Census replicated Trulia's survey with a larger household sample. It found similar results: 52 percent of respondents described their neighborhoods as suburban, 26 percent urban, and 21 percent rural (Kolko 2018). For example, the survey indicated that 54 percent of residents identified their neighborhoods as suburban in the Los Angeles Metropolitan Statistical Area.

3. Federalism in the US has typically implied that the federal government has a less direct role in local land use policy. While the federal government can significantly affect urban development patterns, it has, since the modern small government movement and the neoliberal market-based reforms of the 1980s under the Republican president Ronald Reagan, focused on changing local land use policy through advocacy. See, for example, the *Not in My Backyard: Removing Barriers to Affordable Housing* report by Kean, Ashley, and the Advisory Commission on Regulatory Barriers to Affordable Housing (1991) for HUD secretary Jack Kemp and President George H. W. Bush and the *Housing Development Toolkit* released by President Barack Obama's administration (White House 2016).

4. I refer to housing unregulated by governments as informal housing and follow Manuel Castells and Alejandro Portes's (1989, 15) widely accepted lead of describing

informal economic activities as "the unregulated production of otherwise licit goods and services."

5. The association among homeownership, single-family housing, and the American Dream is a prominent theme in urban planning and housing studies and evident in several books' titles: in addition to Dolores Hayden's ([1984] 2002) *Redesigning the American Dream: The Future of Housing, Work, and Family Life*, cited earlier, important examples include Gwendolyn Wright's ([1981] 1983) classic, *Building the Dream: A Social History of Housing in America*; Charles Haar and Jerold Kayden's (1989) *Zoning and the American Dream: Promises Still to Keep*; and the Southern California focused *Re: American Dream—Six Urban Housing Prototypes for Los Angeles* (Sherman 1995). Similarly, more recent examples include *Chasing the American Dream: New Perspectives on Affordable Homeownership* (Rohe and Watson 2007); *The Option of Urbanism: Investing in a New American Dream* (Leinberger 2007); *Foreclosed: Rehousing the American Dream* (Bergdoll and Martin 2012); *The End of the Suburbs: Where the American Dream Is Moving* (Gallagher 2013); *Rebuilding a Dream: America's New Urban Crisis, the Housing Cost Explosion, and How We Can Reinvent the American Dream for All* (Shashaty 2014); *Detroit: The Dream Is Now—the Design, Art, and Resurgence of an American City* (Arnaud 2017); and *Predatory Lending and the Destruction of the African-American Dream* (Sarra and Wade 2020).

6. Paul Mangin and John Turner (Mangin 1963, 1967; Mangin and Turner 1968; Turner 1967) were among the first scholars to observe and celebrate community-led squatting and land invasions in Peru. Subsequent researchers, however, argue that the era of free land in the Global South is over. Market actors start most unpermitted subdivisions, and commercial interests drive the informal housing process (Angel et al. 1983; Payne 1989; Ward 1982).

7. Scholars often choose between single- and multiple-case research. I am partial to single-case research because it is more feasible to collect in-depth data and more comprehensive information about the case. However, it is more challenging to theorize from one case. I like to examine secondary cases because they guide me in my primary case research and allow me to be more certain about my data collection strategy and my findings' robustness (internal validity) and generalizability (external validity). In the past, I have described this alternative strategy of conducting single-case research as "N of One Plus Some" (Mukhija 2010).

CHAPTER 2: THE IDEOLOGY OF SINGLE-FAMILY LIVING

1. Springdale is a neighborhood of Stamford, a city of about 135,000 residents in the Greater New York Metropolitan area. It is around thirty miles northeast of Manhattan and offers easy commuter rail access to New York City through the Springdale train station on the New Canaan Branch (a branch of the New Haven Line).

2. Hoover served as the honorary chair of the Better Homes in America movement. He "equated homeownership with citizenship, good citizenship with a stable workforce, and both with an improved social order" (Hise 1999, 38).

3. Leigh Gallagher (2013, 76), for example, recounted a study by the real estate website Trulia based on the site's biannual online American Dream survey in 2011, two years after the housing market crash and Great Recession of 2007–2009, that "showed that 70 percent of Americans still consider homeownership a central part of the American Dream." Trulia's 2015 survey, conducted after the housing market had recovered significantly, showed even greater optimism and faith in homeownership. It found that 75 percent of respondents agreed that homeownership was part of the American Dream (R. McLaughlin 2015). Similarly, the National Association of Realtors' 2018 consumer survey data revealed that among those polled, approximately 75 percent of nonhomeowners believed homeownership is part of the American Dream, while nine in ten current homeowners said the same (National Association of Realtors 2019).

4. According to the 2018 Housing Aspirations Report by Zillow, an online real estate website, 94 percent of its survey respondents were interested in homeownership, about 64 percent agreed that owning a home was necessary to live the American Dream, and 82 percent preferred living in single-family houses (Terrazas 2018).

5. In the wake of the Great Recession and its housing foreclosures, several large-scale investors and Wall Street firms acquired over two hundred thousand single-family houses to develop portfolios of single-family rental properties. Many observers predict that private equity groups, hedge funds, and global investors will continue investing in single-family rentals as a new asset class (Charles 2020; Mari 2020; Dezember 2020).

6. Nelson's estimate of single-family housing units includes manufactured housing or mobile homes. According to the Manufactured Housing Institute (2020), a trade industry group, manufactured housing accounts for about 10 percent of new single-family housing starts.

7. Originally, when the Constitution was amended in 1913 to enable the collection of income taxes, taxpayers were allowed to deduct all of their interest payments from their taxable income, and MID was called an "accidental" housing policy (Ventry 2010). Its role was explicitly institutionalized in 1959. The Tax Cuts and Jobs Act of 2017, also known as the Trump tax cuts, reduced the MID cap from $1 million to $750,000. The act doubled the standard deduction too, which made itemized deductions like the MID less attractive. Overall, however, the 2017 tax cuts were regressive and reduced the tax rate for affluent Americans. By cutting the use of the deduction, the act further concentrated its benefits to high-income households. Moreover, for loans originated before December 14, 2017, homeowners could continue to deduct interest on mortgage debt up to $1 million and up to $100,000 on home-equity loans for first and second homes. Homeowners continued to benefit from a lack of taxes on their imputed rental income and capital gains tax allowances in addition to lower tax rates.

8. Levittown, New York, is a planned community that was built on Long Island between 1947 and 1951. It included 6,000 houses and is considered the model for postwar suburban development (Kelly 1993). Lakewood, California, is in Los Angeles

County. It is considered Levittown's West Coast counterpart and was built between 1949 and 1953 with 17,500 dwellings at a record-breaking pace (Waldie 1996).

9. For homebuilders, the trade journals *American Builder* and *House & Home* were similarly instrumental in disseminating information on trade associations like the National Association of Home Builders—which was founded in 1942 and is still active—as well as new ideas about building materials and products, construction best practices, design innovations, and management strategies (James Jacobs 2015).

10. However, as Christopher Silver (1997, 25) noted, racial zoning was not limited to the South: "Select Northern and Western cities, especially those where the Black population increased rapidly, also experimented with racial zoning."

11. Urban studies scholars argue that local zoning's ability to guarantee exclusively single-family housing districts is a central reason for its popularity and public acceptance in a country with deep regard for private property rights (Babcock 1969; Hirt 2014; Perin 1977; Siegan 1972). Whereas zoning's German, English, French, and other European precedents were more technocratic and included opportunities for discretionary decisions by public officials—for example, planners could permit grocery stores in residential neighborhoods—the US version catered to the American sensibility of distrust in government. By reducing opportunities for discretion, single-family zoning in the US, even though it is stricter and relies on absolute prohibitions, seems to involve less government control or involvement (Babcock 1969; Hirt 2014).

12. Per the Bureau of Labor Statistics Bulletin No. 1231 (*New Housing and Its Materials 1940–56*), the average size of a new single-family house was 1,177 sq. ft. in 1940 and 1,170 sq. ft. in 1955 (Murphy 1958). Most of the houses in Lakewood, California, built shortly after World War II, were around 1,100 sq. ft. (Waldie 1996). In 2015, according to the US Census Bureau (US Department of Commerce 2015), the average size of a new US single-family house set a new record of 2,687 sq. ft. Relatedly, the Urban Land Institute (2019), a real estate think tank, reported that the share of newly constructed houses over 2,400 sq. ft. had increased from 32 percent in 1999 to 50 percent in 2017.

13. In contrast, Andres Rodriguez-Pose and Michael Storper (2022) questioned the impact of housing markets on the mobility of low-skilled workers from low-opportunity regions to booming regions. They claimed that upgrading the skills and training of low-skilled workers was more significant than deregulating housing markets.

14. Reeves (2017) criticized the US upper-middle class, which he described as consisting of those earning over $120,000 annually and constituting the top 20 percent of households, for controlling the housing market and separating itself from the rest of the country. He also criticized the upper-middle class for perpetuating their social and economic status by capturing opportunities for access to education through legacy admissions in colleges, internships, and other job opportunities through social networks and nepotism. His arguments echo earlier criticism by Robert Reich (1991) in which he was critical of the "secession of the fortunate fifth" through its residential

patterns, particularly isolated suburban subdivisions. Reeves argued that almost all the income gains in the past thirty years have accrued to the top quintile.

15. The US is not unique in this demographic shift. In Sweden, for example, 47 percent of households have just one occupant, and in its capital city, Stockholm, "a staggering 60 percent of all dwellings are occupied by someone who lives alone" (Klinenberg 2012b, 213).

16. Relatedly, Katherine Newman (2012) documented the rise of the so-called accordion family. She noted that accordion families—parents sharing their homes with adult children—are emerging all over the Global North. She estimated that 3.5 million US parents live with their adult children, whom she described as the boomerang generation living off their parents' retirement savings. Newman considered these households as victims of the neoliberal global economy and noted that they are increasingly common in affluent countries where lower-resourced households have to pool their resources in the absence of adequate state support for affordable housing and subsidized education.

CHAPTER 3: CITY OF DREAMS: SINGLE-FAMILY HOUSING AND SECOND UNITS IN LOS ANGELES

1. The Greater Los Angeles area—or the so-called Los Angeles–Long Beach Combined Statistical Area—which includes three additional counties of Ventura, Riverside, and San Bernardino, grew from about a quarter-million population in 1900 to about 18.7 million in 2020.

2. Late in the nineteenth century, the Los Angeles region had a significant number of Chinese American residents. As Carey McWilliams (1946, 85) wrote, "In 1880 there were about twenty thousand Chinese in Southern California, and, at that time, they constituted a sizeable proportion of the total population."

3. Overall, the city had five districts or zones: A for single-family housing, B for all other residences, C for nonindustrial uses, D for non-noxious industries, and E for unlimited uses. The city's zoning system, like several early examples of zoning, was pyramidal or cumulative rather than exclusive. Single-family housing was at the top of the pyramid and could be built in all the other zones. Similarly, in addition to Zone B, multifamily housing could be built in all other zones except for Zone A, and so on.

4. For example, "from 1936 to 1938 the council moved 14.3 miles of street frontage from multifamily designations into single-family R-1" (Whittemore 2012b, 111).

5. The antidensity battles of homeowners' associations were common throughout the county of Los Angeles. For example, in Monterey Park, a suburban city east of Downtown Los Angeles, the Residents Association of Monterey Park (RAMP), which was derisively known as Residents Against More People, led a slow-growth movement and fought for moratoria against permits for multifamily housing in the late 1970s and 1980s (Fong 1994).

6. The controversy over Proposition 14, which sought to overturn California's fair housing law through a statewide ballot in 1964, is an example of the toxic racial environment at that time. In June 1963, California's legislature approved the Rumford Fair Housing Act to prohibit landlords of multifamily housing (defined as five units or more) from discriminating based on race. This led to an uproar by the California Real Estate Association and the California Apartment Owners' Association. They promoted Proposition 14 to invalidate the act (Nicolaides 2002). California governor Democrat Pat Brown opposed the proposition, which he described as legalized bigotry. The proposition, however, was supported by Republican Ronald Reagan, who called the state's fair housing law an assault on private property. Almost two-thirds of the state's voters agreed with Reagan and approved the proposition. The debate contributed to Brown's defeat and Reagan's election as governor in 1966. However, in 1966 the state court declared the proposition unconstitutional for violating the equal protection clause (14th Amendment), and it reinstated the Rumford Fair Housing Act. The state court's decision was upheld by the US Supreme Court the following year (Nicolaides 2002).

7. The McCone Commission, which was headed by John A. McCone, the former head of the Central Intelligence Agency, was criticized by scholars for not discussing police brutality or examining in depth housing discrimination and the need for a fair housing code in the wake of Proposition 14 (Fogelson 1967b).

8. Zero Population Growth, an antigrowth citizen's group, was active in the city at that time. Its members wanted a cap of four million residents for the city of Los Angeles and argued that growth could be capped by denying housing permits (Fanucchi 1970; Ray 1970).

9. In November 1974, a few months after the Centers Plan was adopted by the Los Angeles City Council, Proposition A, a ballot proposition to add a half-cent sales tax surcharge for funding a rail and bus transit plan for the region, was rejected by Los Angeles County voters (Elkind 2014). Soon after, in 1976, two ballot measures to add half-cent sales tax surcharges for expanding the rail and bus transit system, Measures R and T, were rejected by county voters. While Proposition A was approved by county voters with 54 percent support in November 1980, in order to build a successful coalition of support, its backers agreed to scale back their rail plans and dedicate a smaller proportion of the funds to rail transit (Elkind 2014).

10. In 1978, the California state legislature approved Assembly Bill 283, which requires the city of Los Angeles to make its zoning consistent with its General Plan (Alperin 1987). Previously, only General Law cities, which have less autonomy than Charter cities, were required to maintain consistency. AB 283, as initially proposed, required all Charter cities to do the same. However, the League of California Cities and affected cities opposed the bill for its associated planning costs and erosion of home rule. The amended bill applied to cities with more than two million residents, a categorization that only applied to the city of Los Angeles (Diener 1979).

11. Kaplan noted that public planning was in danger of hitting another low. In the footsteps of the Hillside Federation's legal victory, city of Los Angeles residents were getting ready for a ballot initiative against new development. Proposition U, or "the initiative for reasonable limits on commercial buildings and traffic growth," was proposed by City Councilmembers Zev Yaroslavsky, Joel Wachs, and Marvin Braude and had the support of the president of the city's planning commission, Daniel Garcia, and a newly formed citizens' group, Not Yet New York (Kaplan 1986). The initiative covered most of the city but exempted Downtown, Century City, the Hollywood redevelopment area, and the Wilshire corridor. In November 1986, with a two to one margin, the electorate voted to cut in half the allowed intensity of commercial zoning in a majority of the city. In response to the successful initiative, the city's zoning ordinance was revised, but the rezoning made it impossible for many of the proposed centers in the General Plan to develop at their planned density (Fulton 2001).

12. In 1997, the Hillside Federation sued the city for the insufficiency of its environmental impact report and its measures to mitigate traffic. The following year, the Superior Court ruled against the city and vacated its approval of the Framework Element (Federation of Hillside & Canyon Associations v. City of Los Angeles 2000). Four years later, the planning department submitted a revised plan, which was readopted by the city council in 2001 (Los Angeles Department of City Planning 2001).

13. According to the US Decennial Census, between 1950 and 2010, Riverside County's population increased from 170,046 to 2,189,641, and San Bernardino County's population climbed from 281,642 to 2,035,210. This regional expansion has contributed to the phenomenon of super commuters, daily commuters with one-way commutes over ninety minutes (Dougherty and Burton 2017; McPhate 2017).

14. As discussed in chapter 2, unaffordable housing and constraints in the housing supply dampen the economy and adversely affect incomes. The McKinsey Global Institute estimated that California's housing shortage costs the state $140 billion in lost economic output each year (Woetzel et al. 2016). These losses are through the housing sector's backward linkages of lost construction-related jobs and forward linkages of foregone consumption of goods and services for new housing.

15. De La Cruz-Viesca and her colleagues analyzed wealth data from the National Asset Scorecard for Communities of Color, which collects original survey-based data on assets and debts among US subpopulations according to race, ethnicity, and country of origin. They noted, "Among nonwhite groups, Japanese ($592,000), Asian Indian ($460,000), and Chinese ($408,200) households had higher median wealth than whites. All other racial and ethnic groups had much lower median net worth than white households—African Blacks ($72,000), other Latinx ($42,500), Koreans ($23,400), Vietnamese ($61,500), and Filipinos ($243,000)" (De La Cruz-Viesca et al. 2016, 5–6).

16. Mello served two decades in the state legislature, in part as the state senate majority leader, and had a remarkable legislative record. In addition to the Companion Unit Act, his accomplishments include the "Granny Bill" (Senate Bill 1160) and the "Mello Coastal Act" (Senate Bill 626), which also went into effect in 1982 and established a minimum requirement for affordable housing within the California coastal zone.

17. We obtained a directory of email addresses from the Los Angeles Department of Neighborhood Empowerment. The directory contained over fourteen hundred email addresses, which we narrowed down to the addresses of 372 board members. Before launching the survey, we piloted the survey instrument with two East Hollywood Neighborhood Council members. The survey included space for open-ended comments and the option to contact us to discuss the issue of second units in more detail. We followed up with emails in mid-July to improve the response rate to the survey and closed the survey on August 8, 2012. We received forty-one responses from thirty-four Neighborhood Councils. In our follow-up emails with the board members, we made it clear that we were only expecting one response per Neighborhood Council. From the forty-one original responses, we removed the seven multiple responses from the same Neighborhood Councils and retained the responses from the more senior board members, typically the presidents of the councils.

18. One respondent's sole positive attribute of second units was the facetious response of housing for UCLA faculty and students. Thus, more accurately, ten of the thirty-four survey respondents, almost 30 percent of the group, did not think that second units make any positive contribution.

CHAPTER 4: THE EVERYDAY PREVALENCE OF INFORMAL SECOND UNITS

1. Another indicator of the prevailing toxic environment in the state, including Southern California, was Proposition 187 in 1994. The statewide proposition, popularly known as the Save Our State initiative, proposed to deny undocumented immigrants access to publicly funded social services, including schools and nonemergency health care. It mandated the establishment of a state government-run citizenship screening system. In a solid turnout of over 60 percent of the electorate, the proposition was handily approved by 59 percent of California's voters. With the exception of a few counties in the Bay Area, it received majority support across the state. Republican governor Pete Wilson was a prominent supporter. In spite of his low approval ratings, he successfully rode the xenophobic proposition to reelection. The subsequent law, however, was found unconstitutional by a federal district court in 1999, and Democratic governor Gray Davis halted the state's appeal of the ruling (Bowler, Nicholson, and Segura 2006).

2. Racial privilege and discrimination, as well as gendered ideas of work, have played an important role in the country's labor struggles by limiting their gains to privileged groups. The Fair Labor Standards Act of 1938, for example, created the right

to a minimum wage and the provision of overtime pay but did not cover the labor rights of farmworkers and domestic workers, many of whom were people of color.

3. There are, however, noteworthy exceptions. The sociologist Sudhir Alladi Venkatesh (2006, 2013), for example, extensively researched illegal activities involving gangs, drugs, and prostitution through the lens of informality.

4. Although past research notes that informal activities in the Global South can be found across all income groups, including the elite (Azuela de la Cueva 1987; Roy 2009b, 2011; Varley 1985), the overwhelming emphasis in the literature is on disadvantaged groups and their economic challenges.

5. I found limited research and details on informal housing in Europe. The literature, nonetheless, notes that informal housing settlements can be found in eastern Europe (Slaev and Hirt 2016) and southern Europe, where they are known as *abusivi* in Italy, *afthereta* in Greece, and *clandestinos* in Portugal (Allen et al. 2004).

6. The reporters' estimate of 3.2 percent of single-family houses with garage conversions in the county from a sample of five hundred homes has a margin of error of ±1.5 percent, indicating that the number of converted garages could range from 1.7 percent to 4.7 percent (or from around twenty-two thousand to over sixty-two thousand).

7. Gage-Babcock & Associates, a planning consulting firm in Vancouver, Canada, used a similar approach to estimate the number of informal second units in the city in the early 2000s (City of Vancouver 2009b). Martin Brown and Taylor Watkins (2012) did the same for Portland, Oregon.

8. This section of the chapter builds on previously published research (Mukhija 2014) in my coedited book *The Informal American City: Beyond Taco Trucks and Day Labor* (Mukhija and Loukaitou-Sideris 2014).

9. Previous research based on hedonic modeling of sales data from twenty-one counties spanning the region from central New Jersey to northern Maryland indicated that additional density and intensity on single-family-zoned lots, including second units, can detract from the perceived value of detached single-family houses in suburban neighborhoods where privacy is highly valued and reduce their sale price (Lang 2005).

10. In the 1980s, the San Francisco Planning Department staff surveyed the sales records of single-family properties in the city and concluded that 10–15 percent of them included an informal second unit. A decade later, the department staff conducted a field-based survey of a representative sample of single-family houses on both single-family- and multifamily-zoned lots in the city and found that 23–29 percent of them, or about twice the previous estimate, had unpermitted units (SPUR 2001). Unpermitted second units were more common with single-family houses on multifamily-zoned lots.

11. If I were to also consider single-family houses on multifamily-zoned lots, the actual number of unpermitted second units in the city is higher. While the county

assessor's data indicated over 462,000 single-family houses on lots zoned for single-family housing, data from the American Community Survey suggested there were 541,259 single-family dwellings in the city (US Census Bureau 2013a). Thus, there were about 80,000 single-family houses on lots zoned for a higher density. According to Eric Agar, a former student who is now a realtor, informal second units are more common on multifamily-zoned lots with single-family houses. Agar estimated 15–25 percent of such lots in the city of Los Angeles had an unpermitted second unit (Agar interview 2014a; communication 2014c).

12. Previous research on second units in the Bay Area found detached construction accounted for almost a third of the informal second units (Chapple et al. 2011). While my findings are slightly different, both studies suggest a greater variety of second unit forms, including a significant proportion of backyard construction.

13. Perhaps for similar reasons, at a workshop on second units, Jason Neville (communication 2016), from the city of Los Angeles's Mayor's Office, noted that even among newly permitted second units in the city, two-thirds were backyard structures. A study of thirty-two middle-class, dual-income families living in single-family houses in Los Angeles found that only a quarter of the households parked their cars in the garages (Arnold et al. 2012). The garages, however, were highly prized and heavily used for storage. In contrast, the researchers found that the families hardly used their backyards. Thus, homeowners may value their garages even though they do not use them for storing cars. Similarly, two large surveys in 1949 and 1950 conducted by the Small Homes Council of the University of Illinois, Urbana-Champaign, and the Institute for Social Research at the University of Michigan, Ann Arbor, found that "a very high percentage of buyers . . . wanted an attached garage, but very few of them wanted to use the garage only for the car. Other planned uses for the garage included storage and laundry" (B. Lane 2015, 188–189).

14. We considered analyzing the category coded as MISC, "Miscellaneous." It is a catchall category and might include complaints about second units. But the number of complaints coded as MISC is very high (3,581 in 2011), and because the likelihood of complainants referring to unpermitted second units under this classification is low, we did not analyze the MISC category. After identifying addresses with GARCV and ILUSE complaints from the CSR request data, we reviewed each address's LADBS Property Activity Report (subsequently called the Permit & Inspection Report). The report details both permit and code enforcement activity related to the complaint and the status of the city's code enforcement action. For instance, if an inspector investigated the complaint and did not find a violation, they marked "No Violation." Depending on the notation preferences of the inspector, there is much variability in the level of detail provided for each property in the LADBS Property Activity Report. In some cases, inspectors' notes are incredibly detailed, describing exact dimensions of second units. In other cases, they do not provide any information beyond the status of the complaint, meaning it is impossible to determine whether the property included an unpermitted second unit.

15. This everyday diplomacy with neighbors about parking is not limited to Los Angeles. While conducting fieldwork, I stayed in an unpermitted secondary suite in Kitsilano, Vancouver. My host requested I not leave my rental car parked in front of a neighbor's house for more than a day (Participant #6 interview 2013).

16. Second sink agreements can be a source of confusion. For example, a friend of a former student of mine bought a single-family house in Portland and thought that it had a formally permitted second unit (Participant #17 interview 2015). The house, however, came with a second sink agreement. To formally use the additional space as a second unit, the homeowner had to pay the city's system development charges to remove the second sink agreement.

17. As I noted earlier, planning regulations often consider existing land uses nonconforming but legal and exempt them from new rules and requirements. Such land uses are considered to have been grandfathered in and their owners have grandfather rights. While the terminology is commonly used in contemporary planning, it has racist origins in late nineteenth-century legislation. In the period following the American Civil War, several Southern states created literacy requirements for voting as a strategy to deny Black voters their voting rights. To create a workaround for white voters who did not meet the literacy requirement, the states exempted those whose ancestors or grandfathers had voting rights before the Civil War.

18. The lack of availability of formal financing reduces the incentive for homeowners to build formally approved second units. As I explain in part III, the availability of formal financing is slowly changing. However, formal financing was usually unavailable to owners with less equity in their single-family houses (De Simone communication 2016). Lenders typically want to see an executed lease in place before they consider the future income of rental properties in their loan calculations, which is nearly impossible in the case of an unbuilt second unit. Only homeowners with substantial equity in their houses can do a cash-out refinance, acesss home equity loans, or use a home equity line of credit to finance the construction of their second units.

19. Public investments can follow a similar pattern. At a discussion on affordable housing in the city of Los Angeles, Councilmember Felipe Fuentes (communication 2015) of Council District 7 described how his constituents in the working-class neighborhood of Pacoima were initially very enthusiastic about a public program to install solar panels on private houses. However, when the homeowners realized that the installation process would involve building inspectors visiting their homes, and possibly seeing their unpermitted additions and units, they withdrew their interest in the program.

20. To illustrate, the *Los Angeles Times* shared a sad and macabre story highlighting the vulnerability of a couple without immigration documents living in an informally converted garage (Mejia 2015; Goldenstein 2015). The couple were the caregivers of a relative who died. But because of their undocumented status, they were afraid of contacting the authorities and did not know what to do with the body. They ended up placing the body in their refrigerator, where it remained for over a year.

I suspect tenants like them would rarely complain about their housing conditions. It is worth noting that substandard conditions are common in formal housing too, and because of extreme poverty, vulnerability, and lack of better options, many tenants are reluctant and afraid to complain (Desmond 2016).

21. News reports suggested that because of President Donald Trump's interest in including a citizenship question on the decennial census and not counting undocumented immigrants for reallocating congressional seats, the 2020 Census count was likely flawed. The heightened deportation threats, the COVID-19 global pandemic, and the rushed schedule for counting likely resulted in an undercount of hard to enumerate groups and categories, including informal housing (Galvan and Schneider 2021; Jordan 2020).

CHAPTER 5: ENFORCEMENT AND FORMALIZATION OF UNPERMITTED SECOND UNITS IN LOS ANGELES

1. A student in UCLA's Department of Urban Planning interviewed Richard Alarcon for her two-week capstone examination and found that he had "lived in a converted garage, illegal non-conforming unit, as a newlywed" (Martinez 2013, 35).

2. Indeed, some scholars use the terms "formalization," "legalization," and "regularization" interchangeably (Varley 2007).

3. Some scholars worry that slum clearance remains attractive to policy makers and is likely to be implemented in more indirect ways (Mayne 2018).

4. In addition, scholars emphasize the need to increase the housing supply. One of the more interesting planning supply responses based on lessons from incremental development in informal housing was the widespread introduction of sites and services schemes in the Global South during the 1970s (Dunkerley 1983; Sanyal 1987). Sites and services projects kept housing costs low through small lots with minimal housing and services and the expectation that owners and governments would improve housing conditions and infrastructure over time. However, as the demands of affordability pushed for lower standards, sites and services projects became challenging to implement. Politicians were wary of being accused of developing slums by their middle-class constituents (Peattie 1994). Besides, high land costs made it difficult to implement the strategy in most primary cities (Angel et al. 1983; Baross 1990). With a few exceptions in Honduras, Nicaragua, and El Salvador, state-assisted sites and services projects disappeared with growing land costs and the rise of neoliberalism in the 1990s (UN Millennium Project 2005). However, scholars have shown that several sites and services projects successfully met their housing affordability and urban planning goals, and that policy makers need to reconsider the strategy (Owens, Gulyani, and Rizvi 2018).

5. The literature mentions other cases of legalization of informal housing through changes or exceptions to the underlying zoning. For example, San Mateo County,

California, had an initiative for legalizing informal second units during the 1990s (Wasserman 2002b); Barnstable, Massachusetts, the largest community in area and population on Cape Cod, had a seemingly successful amnesty program for unpermitted second units in the early 2000s (Sage Computing 2008); and Marin County, California had an amnesty program for second units between 2007 and 2008 (Chapple et al. 2011). I have not, however, found detailed accounts of these cases.

6. Hal Bernson was a conservative Republican and a leading proponent of the San Fernando Valley seceding from the city of Los Angeles. In the mid-1980s, he led an unsuccessful effort, which many considered racially motivated, to evict almost three thousand, mostly Latinx, tenants of substandard apartments in the Northridge neighborhood of his district (Simon 1985).

7. Mayor Riordan formed a citizens' committee—Blue Ribbon Citizens' Committee on Slum Housing—later that year to address the continuing concerns of substandard housing. The committee, however, focused on multifamily housing and advocated for proactive enforcement in its report, *The Slum Housing Problem in Los Angeles and the Department of Building and Safety* (Blue Ribbon Citizens' Committee on Slum Housing 1997). The mayor and the city council accepted the committee's main recommendation of regular inspections of multifamily rental housing and instituted the Systematic Code Enforcement Program (SCEP). They decided to implement SCEP in association with the existing Rent Escrow Account Program (REAP), in which tenants of substandard multifamily housing units paid their rents to the city and a public agency used the money to pay for improvements in their housing. The underlying idea was that regular inspections through SCEP would uncover poor-quality housing units, and the city could redirect tenants' rents collected through REAP to upgrade the units without using public funding.

8. In 2004, the county of Los Angeles adopted a second unit ordinance for the unincorporated areas to comply with AB 1866. Its production of permitted second units doubled and increased to about sixty ADUs per year (Chung communication 2016). In a land use strategy brief prepared for the jurisdiction's Homeless Initiative Policy Summit, planners noted, "Since 2004, when the County adopted its Second Unit Ordinance, 719 second units have been permitted in the unincorporated area. The County's second unit production reached an annual high of 137 in 2007 right before the Great Recession" (County of Los Angeles 2015, 1–2). In most of the region, however, AB 1866 had limited effect. The policy emphasis continued to be on enforcement. The city of Long Beach, for example, adopted new legislation in 2011 called the Aviles Law to clear and remove unpermitted garage conversions and encourage residents to report unpermitted conversions (Yee 2013). The law commemorated three central Long Beach girls killed in a horrendous fire in a converted garage. The Aviles sisters were between six and ten years old and died from burns and carbon monoxide poisoning. In 2013, the state legislature passed a resolution in recognition and support of the Aviles Law, and the *Long Beach Press-Telegram* (2013) advised other municipalities to "be watchful" and diligently enforce their second unit laws.

9. Mayor Garcetti's goal was to add 12,500 units per year between 2014 and 2021. It was an ambitious goal that had only been achieved once, in 2008. Between 1991 and 2013, on average, the city added only 5,500 housing units each year (Logan 2014).

10. SCEP, which I discussed in note 7, received awards and recognition for directing substantial private investment to the upgrading of substandard housing, but its efforts had an unintended outcome. Every year, its inspectors unearthed five hundred to six hundred unpermitted use units carved out of parking spaces, common areas, and existing apartments in multifamily buildings. Most of these units did not conform to the existing regulations—usually density limits and parking requirements—and had to be shut down, removing significant affordable housing stock from the city (Fuentes communication 2015). According to the city's estimates, almost half the units revealed through the inspections and removed each year were in small multifamily buildings with four or fewer units (Los Angeles Department of City Planning 2015). The UDU ordinance focused on preserving and formalizing these informal units.

11. The *Los Angeles Times* (2016), however, was not entirely convinced by the direction of the state bills and emphasized its support for smaller and discreet units by endorsing the approach of the city's old ordinance. It noted, "The city's original ordinance in 1985 allowed second units of not more than 640 square feet. They had to be located behind the main building on the lot and not visible from the street." The newspaper cautioned against provisions in the state legislations for allowing larger second units and limited its enthusiasm to smaller ADUs. It added, "While the city is appropriately eager to generate more affordable housing, shoehorning oversized second units behind single family homes is not an effective way to accomplish that."

12. The following year, Assemblymember Bloom and Senator Wieckowski authored two follow-up bills—Assembly Bill 494 (Bloom) and Senate Bill 229 (Wieckowski)—to help implement their landmark 2016 ADU bills. Cuff and Blumenfeld also helped Assemblymember Bloom write AB 494 (Blumenfeld interview 2017). The two follow-up bills were approved by the legislature and the governor in 2017 and went into effect on January 1, 2018. Both follow-up bills clarified the original bills' intent and improved various provisions of the law to promote the development of ADUs. They allowed ADUs to be built concurrently with new single-family houses, expanded the areas where ADUs can be built to include all zoning districts that allow single-family uses, and modified and limited fees from utilities, such as special districts and water corporations. They addressed tandem parking too. The original ADU bills allowed for tandem parking of multiple cars to make it easier for homeowners to meet their parking requirements. Some cities, however, were keen to limit tandem parking to two cars. AB 494 and SB 229 explicitly clarified that homeowners could arrange more than two parking spaces in tandem (Blumenfeld interview 2018; Wieckowski interview 2018). Subsequently, both Senator Wieckowski and Assemblymember Bloom continued to propose new ADU legislation to make it easier for homeowners to add second units and formalize prevailing unpermitted ones. For example, Senator Wieckowski proposed Senate Bill 831 in 2018 (which was approved by the Senate

but was unsuccessful in the Assembly) and authored Senate Bill 13 in 2019 (which was approved by the legislature and signed into law by the governor).

13. The planning department had also asked the city council to clarify the ambiguous legal status of hundreds of second units that had been permitted before the ruling, including several that were midway through construction. The council agreed to affirm their legal status, allowing affected property owners to proceed without uncertainty (Reyes 2016b).

14. The 2020 LA Design Festival in September featured a 3D-printed second unit in the Future of Housing tour. Mighty Buildings (http://mightybuildings.com), a California-based start-up, built the ADU. The company used prefab designs and 3D printing to construct the second unit in eight weeks.

15. Additionally, the City of Costa Mesa (2018) had an owner-occupancy requirement, limited second units to 800 sq. ft., and required the units to follow its residential design guidelines.

16. The city reduced the impact fees to about $3,500 for conversions and around $9,500 for new construction for homeowners committing to rent their second units to family members or low-income tenants for seven years (City of Pasadena 2018).

17. In addition to follow-up bills by Assemblymember Bloom (Assembly Bill 881) and Senator Wieckowski (Senate Bill 13), the governor and the legislature approved Assembly Bill 68 (authored by Phil Ting, Democrat from San Francisco) and Assembly Bill 670 (by Laura Friedman, Democrat from Glendale).

18. The firm also projected a rent of $4,300 per month for the unit. Because of such high rent estimates, scholars like Darrel Ramsey-Musolf (2018) argue that California's state legislature made a policy mistake by allowing cities to count second units toward their low-income housing need obligations.

19. The nonprofit organization noted that it was tricky to estimate garage conversion costs. Costs can increase because of structural limitations of the garage, complicated access to sewer lines, the need to increase the electric panel's capacity, additional site preparation work, and some homeowners' desire to separate utilities between the existing house and the new second unit (LA Más 2021; Leung communication 2019).

20. Additionally, LA Más managed a pilot project for the county of Los Angeles as part of its homelessness strategy. Through the pilot project, the county would offer selected homeowners access to financing and grants of $75,000 each for a commitment to house a formerly homeless individual or family. But the pilot project was limited to three homeowners (Leung communication 2018).

21. SB 13 built on Senator Wieckowski's efforts to pass similar legislation in 2018. Senate Bill 831, his previous measure, was identical to SB 13 but required local governments to waive all impact fees for second units. While the Senate approved it, the bill did not make it out of committee in the Assembly (Barbosa and Montes interview 2019). I wrote an op-ed with Senator Wieckowski in the *Sacramento Bee* to support

SB 13 while it was being debated in the legislature (Wieckowski and Mukhija 2019). At the senator's invitation, I provided expert testimony to the Assembly's Local Government Committee in support of the bill.

22. This was unfortunately the case with the noise abatement funds for neighborhoods close to the Los Angeles International Airport. The Federal Aviation Administration and Los Angeles World Airports distributed the funds to provide support for soundproofing and other noise abatement measures, particularly for homes in the vicinity of the airport. However, the funding was disproportionately allocated to wealthier neighborhoods, often away from the airport, and with less exposure to the noise (D. Smith 2019). The houses of low-income residents were typically not compatible with the zoning—which had been revised to reduce the number of residents close to the airport—and not up to the building and safety code standards, and therefore failed to qualify for the funding support. Although more affluent residents had less exposure to the noise, their houses conformed to the zoning and met the code standards. They received grants for installing air conditioners and double-paned windows.

CHAPTER 6: THE FORMALIZATION OF SECOND UNITS: THE ROLE OF LOCAL GOVERNMENTS

1. There is evidence that renters, particularly in expensive cities, are more open to new housing development than homeowners. Still, like homeowners, they oppose new projects in their neighborhoods (Hankinson 2018).

2. States fall into two categories in the US: those that follow Dillon's Rule, which limits local powers, and those that are home rule states, which have more authority at the local level. In California, the overwhelming majority of the state's 58 counties and 482 cities fall under Dillon's Rule (i.e., the state's 44 General Law counties and 361 General Law cities). Its minority Charter cities and counties follow home rule. However, even in home rule jurisdictions, the state government can intervene directly in local matters related to broad public benefits.

3. According to my calculations based on the city's zoning map (City of Santa Cruz 2017), 76 percent of residentially zoned land is reserved for single-family houses.

4. The city maintained a discretionary review requirement for permitting second units. However, it eliminated the condition in 2003 in response to the state government's adoption of Assembly Bill 1866, which prohibited discretionary reviews for second units. Subsequently, it offered as-of-right permits for single-story second units but maintained discretionary reviews for two-story second units and eliminated its annual cap on permits (City of Santa Cruz 2003c, 2003d).

5. Seattle's 1994 Comprehensive Plan (City of Seattle 1994b) identified six urban centers and twenty-four urban villages (six hub urban villages and eighteen residential urban villages).

6. In 2010, permits for new second units reached 122 (76 attached and 46 detached); the previous high had been 78 in 1998 (all attached). In 2014, the permits increased to 128 (75 attached and 53 detached) (Welch communication 2018). While the city collected data on legalization of existing second units from 1994 to 1999, it did not collect similar data after 1999.

7. Some pro-development advocates were unhappy with MHA because of its inclusionary housing requirements and threated to bring additional legal challenges (Valdez 2018).

8. Between 1981 and 1997, only about fifty second units were formally permitted (City of Portland 1997).

9. The Centennial Neighborhood Association, for example, argued that the new citywide ordinance would "lower property values, double density, create traffic and parking problems, undermine homeownership which stabilizes neighborhoods, increase rentals and lead to poorer maintenance of those properties and code violations, [and] turn single-family zones into double family or multiple family" (Cody 1997).

10. The regional tax-base sharing program is known as the Fiscal Disparities Program and was implemented in the seven-county Twin Cities metropolitan region in 1971. Accordingly, all local governments contribute 40 percent of the growth in their commercial and industrial property tax base to a common pool, which is distributed across the region's jurisdictions according to their need (as a function of their population and existing property tax base). The program reduced tax-base disparity across the region by limiting corrosive competition among local governments for commercial and industrial land uses (Orfield 1997).

11. The evaluation is posted online by the evaluators and shared with buyers. TISH is supposed to disclose all required repairs as well as discrepancies with city records about the number of permitted units.

12. After receiving approval from the Metropolitan Council, the regional planning agency, in September 2019 (Roper 2019), the city council completed its final adoption of MPLS 2040 in October 2019, which went into effect in January 2020 (City of Minneapolis 2020).

13. Planners estimated that immediate family members occupied only 5–15 percent of the city's secondary suites (Hunter 1988).

14. To curb foreign buyers and speculators, the province of British Columbia and Vancouver increased taxes and introduced new taxes. As of 2020, taxes in Vancouver include the province's additional property transfer tax for foreigners of 20 percent of the sale value and a 2 percent speculation and vacancy tax, as well as Vancouver's annual Vacant Home Tax, equal to 1 percent of the assessed taxable value (Lindeman 2019; Yan communication 2020).

15. The city council was criticized for not caring about public opinion and approving a significant land use policy change just days before the municipal election

(M. Anderson 2018). Its actions followed two days of public hearings and testimony from 306 letters in opposition and 186 in support of duplexes (Lee-Young and Padgham 2018).

16. In addition to building permits, owners of formal secondary suites in Vancouver need to pay a business license fee. According to Andy Coupland (communication 2013), a former city planner, only around two thousand suites had business licenses in 2013.

17. Vancity, headquartered in Vancouver, was remarkably accepting of informal housing. It also offered mixer mortgages, which allowed multiple parties to receive joint loans (Penner and Sinoski 2013). It is not unusual for friends and family members in the city to collectively buy two-unit (primary unit and secondary suite) or three-unit (primary unit, secondary suite, and laneway housing) properties with the intention of informally owning and using the individual units separately (Fry interview 2013).

CHAPTER 7: REMAKING THE SUBURBAN CITY

1. According to the Pew Research Center, political polarization is evident in Americans' housing and neighborhood preferences. Reporting on the results of a nationwide survey of over ten thousand adults, the center's researchers noted that "the differences between right and left go beyond disagreements over politics, friends and neighbors. If they could choose anywhere to live, three-quarters of consistent conservatives prefer a community where 'the houses are larger and farther apart, but schools, stores, and restaurants are several miles away.' The preferences of consistent liberals are almost the exact inverse, with 77% saying they'd choose to live where 'the houses are smaller and closer to each other, but schools, stores, and restaurants are within walking distance'" (Pew Research Center 2014, 13).

2. Some planners and policy makers may consider accessory units a strategic and potential gateway to more dramatic zoning changes, as in several of the book's cases. Correspondingly, some homeowners may be suspicious of accessory units, view them as a slippery slope and an incremental step to higher density, and oppose them even more stridently.

3. In May 2021, California's median price of single-family houses reached a new record high of $818,260 (Kamin 2021). Observers noted that the price increase was probably due to low mortgage interest rates, buyers' interest in more space for home offices during the COVID-19 pandemic, and the state's historical housing shortage. The increase was likely also fueled by an increase in the value of single-family houses due to their upzoning and owners' potential to add accessory units.

4. As I noted in the previous chapter, family members and friends partnered to buy houses with secondary suites and laneway apartments in Vancouver. Although they

owned the properties jointly, many partners planned to use and own the multiple units separately (Fry interview 2013).

5. Mark Purcell's (2000) contrarian Los Angeles–based research on homeowner activism added to the debate by suggesting that while homeowners are often opposed to neighboring developments, they are not necessarily driven by a narrow interest in preserving their property values. He argued that homeowners have multiple motivations and are driven by a broader set of interests, including quality-of-life concerns over density, traffic, and congestion. Purcell, nonetheless, agreed that homeowner activism had eroded the pro-development Growth Machine in cities.

REFERENCES

AARP and APA. 2000. *Accessory Dwelling Units: Model State Act and Local Ordinance.* Washington, DC: AARP.

Abbott, Carl. 1997. "The Portland Region: Where City and Suburbs Talk to Each Other—and Often Agree." *Housing Policy Debate* 8 (1): 11–51.

Abbott, Carl. 2011. *Portland in Three Centuries: The Place and the People.* Corvallis: Oregon State University Press.

Abelson, Jenn. 2014. "Illegal Apartment, with Only One Way Out, Claims a Life." *Boston Globe*, May 3.

Abrams, Charles. 1964. *Housing in the Modern World: Man's Struggle for Shelter in an Urbanizing World.* Cambridge, MA: MIT Press.

Adams, James Truslow. 1931. *The Epic of America.* Boston: Little, Brown.

Adler, Sy. 2012. *Oregon Plans: The Making of an Unquiet Land Use Revolution.* Corvallis: Oregon State University Press.

Alexander, Christopher, Sara Ishikawa, and Murray Silverstein. 1977. *A Pattern Language: Towns, Buildings, Construction.* New York: Oxford University Press.

Allen, James P., and Eugene Turner. 1997. *The Ethnic Quilt: Population Diversity in Southern California.* Los Angeles: Center for Geographical Studies, California State University Northridge.

Allen, Judith, James Barlow, Jesús Leal, Thomas Maloutas, and Liliana Padovani. 2004. *Housing and Welfare in Southern Europe.* Oxford: Blackwell.

Alperin, Anthony Saul. 1987. "AB 283—a Zoning Consistency Odyssey." *Southwestern University Law Review* 17 (1): 1–22.

Anderson, Elijah. 2015. "The White Space." *Sociology of Race and Ethnicity* 1 (1): 10–21.

Anderson, Michael. 2018. "Duplexes Are Now Legal on 99% of Vancouver's Low-Density Lots." Sightline Institute, September 20. https://www.sightline.org/2018/09/20/duplexes-are-now-legal-on-99-of-vancouvers-low-density-lots/.

Andrews, Jeff. 2019. "Oregon Just Effectively Banned Single-Family Zoning." *Curbed*, July 1. https://archive.curbed.com/2019/7/1/20677502/oregon-yimby-single-family-zoning-nimby-rent-control.

Angel, Shlomo, Raymon Archer, Sidhijai Tanphiphat, and Emiel Wegelin, eds. 1983. *Land for Housing the Poor*. Singapore: Select Books.

Angotti, Tom. 2008. *New York for Sale: Community Planning Confronts Global Real Estate*. Cambridge, MA: MIT Press.

Antoninetti, Maurizio. 2008. "The Difficult History of Ancillary Units: The Obstacles and Potential Opportunities to Increase the Heterogeneity of Neighborhoods and the Flexibility of Households in the United States." *Journal of Housing for the Elderly* 22 (4): 348–375.

Arnaud, Michael. 2017. *Detroit: The Dream Is Now—the Design, Art, and Resurgence of an American City*. New York: Abrams.

Arnold, Jeanne E., Anthony P. Graesch, Enzo Ragazzini, and Elinor Ochs. 2012. *Life at Home in the Twenty-First Century: 32 Families Open Their Doors*. Los Angeles: Cotsen Institute of Archaeology Press, UCLA.

Arnstein, Sherry R. 1969. "A Ladder of Citizen Participation." *Journal of the American Institute of Planners* 35 (4): 216–224.

Asian Law Caucus. 2013. "Our Hidden Communities: Secondary Unit Households in the Excelsior Neighborhood of San Francisco." A Report by the Asian Law Caucus, San Francisco, March 23. https://archive.advancingjustice-alc.org/wp-content/uploads/2013/05/Report-Excelsior-in-law-units-final_0.pdf.

Averitt, Robert T. 1968. *The Dual Economy: The Dynamics of American Industry Structure*. New York: W. W. Norton.

Avila, Eric. 2014. *The Folklore of the Freeway: Race and Revolt in the Modernist City*. Minneapolis: University of Minnesota Press.

Axelrod, Robert. 1984. *The Evolution of Cooperation*. New York: Basic Books.

Azuela de la Cueva, A. 1987. "Low Income Settlements and the Law in Mexico City." *International Journal of Urban and Regional Research* 11 (4): 522–542.

Baar, Kenneth K. 1996. "The Anti-apartment Movement in the US and the Role of Land Use Regulations in Creating Housing Segregation." *Netherlands Journal of Housing and the Built Environment* 11 (4): 359–379.

Babcock, Richard F. 1969. *The Zoning Game: Municipal Practices and Policies*. Madison: University of Wisconsin Press.

Badger, Emily. 2016. "The Next Big Fight over Housing Could Happen, Literally, in Your Back Yard." *Wonkblog, Washington Post*, August 7.

Badger, Emily. 2018. "How 'Not in My Backyard' Became 'Not in My Neighborhood.'" Upshot, *New York Times*, January 3.

Badger, Emily, and Quoctrung Bui. 2019. "Cities Start to Question an American Ideal: A House with a Yard on Every Lot." *New York Times*, June 18.

Badger, Emily, and Quoctrung Bui. 2020. "How the Suburbs Moved Away from Trump." Upshot, *New York Times*, November 16.

Baer, William. 1986. "The Shadow Market in Housing." *Scientific American* 255 (5): 29–35.

Bairoch, Paul. 1973. *Urban Unemployment in Developing Countries: The Nature of the Problem and Proposals for Its Solution*. Geneva: International Labour Organization.

Banham, Reyner. 1971. *Los Angeles: The Architecture of Four Ecologies*. New York: Harper & Row.

Baross, Paul. 1990. "Sequencing Land Development: The Price Implications of Legal and Illegal Settlement Growth." In *The Transformation of Land Supply Systems in Third World Cities*, edited by Paul Baross and Jan van der Linden, 57–82. Aldershot: Avebury.

Bartholomew, Harland. 1932. *Urban Land Uses: Amounts of Land Used and Needed for Various Purposes by Typical American Cities*. Cambridge, MA: Harvard University Press.

Basolo, Victoria. 1999. "Passing the Housing Policy Baton in the US: Will Cities Take the Lead?" *Housing Studies* 14 (4): 433–452.

Basolo, Victoria. 2003. "US Regionalism and Rationality." *Urban Studies* 40 (3): 447–462.

Bates, Lisa K. 2013. "Gentrification and Displacement Study: Implementing an Equitable Inclusive Development Strategy in the Context of Gentrification." For City of Portland Bureau of Planning and Sustainability.

Beatty, Paul. 1983. "SC Developing Guidelines for 'Granny Units.'" *Santa Cruz Sentinel*, May 6.

Beauregard, Robert. 2006. *When America Became Suburban*. Minneapolis: University of Minnesota Press.

Beekman, Daniel. 2015a. "Mayor Murray Withdraws Proposal to Allow More Density in Single-Family Zones." *Seattle Times*, July 29.

Beekman, Daniel. 2015b. "Rethink Single-Family Zoning? Seattle Officials Open to Some Changes." *Seattle Times*, July 7.

Beekman, Daniel. 2018. "Here's When the City Council Could Upzone Seattle Neighborhoods." *Seattle Times*, December 3.

Beekman, Daniel. 2019. "Seattle Upzones 27 Neighborhood Hubs, Passes Affordable-Housing Requirements." *Seattle Times*, March 18.

Been, Vicki. 2018. "CITY NIMBYS." *Journal of Land Use & Environmental Law* 33 (2): 217–250.

Been, Vicki, Ingrid Gould Ellen, and Katherine O'Regan. 2018. "Supply Skepticism: Housing Supply and Affordability." *Housing Policy Debate* 29 (1): 25–40.

Been, Vicki, Josiah Madar, and Simon McDonnell. 2014. "Urban Land-Use Regulation: Are Homevoters Overtaking the Growth Machine?" *Journal of Empirical Legal Studies* 11 (2): 227–265.

Belk, Russell W., John F. Sherry Jr., and Melanie Wallendorf. 1988. "A Naturalistic Inquiry into Buyer and Seller Behavior at a Swap Meet." *Journal of Consumer Research* 14 (4): 449–470.

Bell, Jeannine. 2013. *Hate Thy Neighbor: Move-In Violence and the Persistence of Racial Segregation in American Housing*. New York: New York University Press.

Bellett, Gerry. 2014. "Man Dies from Burns Sustained in East Vancouver Garage Fire." *Vancouver Sun*, March 6.

Belz, Adam. 2018. "Draft Plan, Including Fourplex Proposal, Released by Minneapolis." *Star Tribune*, March 23.

Bennett, Alysia, Dana Cuff, and Gus Wendell. 2019. "Backyard Housing Boom: New Markets for Affordable Housing and the Role of Digital Technology." *Technology|Architecture+Design* 3 (1): 76–88.

Benton, Mark. 2017. "'Just the Way Things Are Around Here': Racial Segregation, Critical Junctures, and Path Dependence in Saint Louis." *Journal of Urban History* 44 (6): 1113–1130.

Berelowitz, Lance. 2005. *Dream City: Vancouver and the Global Imagination*. Vancouver: Douglas & McIntyre.

Bergdoll, Barry, and Reinhold Martin. 2012. *Foreclosed: Rehousing the American Dream*. New York: Museum of Modern Art Publications.

Berger, Alan, and Joel Kotkin, eds. 2017. *Infinite Suburbia*. New York: Princeton Architectural Press.

Bernhardt, Annette, Heather Boushey, Laura Dresser, and Chris Tilly, eds. 2008. *The Gloves-Off Economy: Workplace Standards at the Bottom of America's Labor Market*. Champaign, IL: Labor and Employment Relations Association.

Bernstein, Fred. 2005. "In Santa Cruz, Affordable Housing without Sprawl: Granny Flats for Cool Grannies." *New York Times*, February 6.

Bernstein, Sharon. 1997a. "City Officials Grapple with Illegal Garage Apartments." *Los Angeles Times*, April 21.

Bernstein, Sharon. 1997b. "Plan Would Allow Some Garage Housing." *Los Angeles Times*, May 3.

Bertolet, Dan. 2017. "Washington's State Environmental Policy Act Has Become a Bane to Sustainable Urban Development." Sightline Institute, November 7. https://www.sightline.org/2017/11/07/washingtons-state-environmental-policy-act-has-become-a-bane-to-sustainable-urban-development/.

Bertolet, Dan, and Nisma Gabobe. 2019. "LA ADU Story: How a State Law Sent Granny Flats off the Charts." Sightline Institute, April 5. https://www.sightline.org/2019/04/05/la-adu-story-how-a-state-law-sent-granny-flats-off-the-charts/.

Bertolet, Dan, and Margaret Morales. 2019. "Seattle Says Yes to the Best Rules in America for Backyard Cottages." Sightline Institute, July 1. https://www.sightline.org/2019/07/01/seattle-approves-best-backyard-cottages-rules-united-states/.

Bhatia, Neeraj, and Shawn Komlos, eds. 2015. *Urbanism from Within*. San Francisco: Urban Works Agency, California College of the Arts.

Bicknell, Natalie. 2019. "How We Got Here: A (Brief) History of Mandatory Housing Affordability in Seattle." The Urbanist, March 18. https://www.theurbanist.org/2019/03/18/how-we-got-here-a-brief-history-of-mandatory-housing-affordability-in-seattle/.

Birkinshaw, Jack. 1982. "Cities May Open Door to 'Granny Housing.'" *Los Angeles Times*, July 18.

Bischoff, Kendra, and Sean F. Reardon. 2014. "Residential Segregation by Income, 1970–2009." In *Diversity and Disparities: America Enters a New Century*, edited by John R. Logan, 208–234. New York: Russell Sage Foundation.

Bishop, Peter, and Lesley Williams, eds. 2012. *The Temporary City*. New York: Routledge.

Blais, Pamela. 2010. *Perverse Cities: Hidden Subsidies, Wonky Policy, and Urban Sprawl*. Vancouver: University of British Columbia Press.

Blake, Peter. 1964. *God's Own Junkyard: The Planned Deterioration of America's Landscape*. New York: Holt, Reinhart & Winston.

Bliss, Laura. 2020. "How Portland's Landmark Zoning Reform Could Work." Bloomberg CityLab, August 13. https://www.bloomberg.com/news/articles/2020-08-13/how-portland-dethroned-the-single-family-home.

Blomley, Nick. 2003. *Unsettling the City: Urban Land and the Politics of Property*. New York: Routledge.

Blue Ribbon Citizens' Committee on Slum Housing. 1997. *The Slum Housing Problem in Los Angeles and the Department of Building and Safety*. Los Angeles: Office of the Mayor.

Blue Ribbon Committee for Affordable Housing. 1988. *Housing Los Angeles: Affordable Housing for the Future*. Los Angeles: Office of the Mayor.

Bobrowsky, Joshua. 2007. "Second Units: The Experience of Local Jurisdictions in Los Angeles County in Complying with AB 1866." Term paper, Public Policy Clinic, UCLA Law, University of California, Los Angeles.

Boddy, Trevor. 2005. "Vancouverism vs. Lower Manhattanism: Shaping the High Density City." Insight, ArchNewNow, September 20. http://www.archnewsnow.com/features/Feature177.htm.

Boerner, Heather. 2001. "Housing, Environment Top Concerns at Community Forum." *Santa Cruz Sentinel*, March 21.

Bohn, Sarah, Caroline Danielson, and Patricia Malagon. 2021. "Poverty in California." Fact Sheet, July 2021, Public Policy Institute of California, San Francisco. https://www.ppic.org/wp-content/uploads/JTF_PovertyJTF.pdf.

Borchert, James. 1980. *Alley Life in Washington: Family, Community, Religion, and Folklife in the City, 1850–1970*. Urbana: University of Illinois Press.

Boudreaux, Paul. 2011. *The Housing Bias: Rethinking Land Use Laws for a Diverse New America*. New York: Palgrave Macmillan.

Bowler, Shaun, Stephen P. Nicholson, and Gary M. Segura. 2006. "Earthquakes and Aftershocks: Race, Direct Democracy, and Partisan Change." *American Journal of Political Science* 50 (1): 146–159.

Brandt, Nadja, and John Gittelsohn. 2014. "Housing Woes Worse in L.A. Than New York, San Francisco." *Bloomberg*, September 3.

Bratt, Rachel G., and Abigail Vladeck. 2014. "Addressing Restrictive Zoning for Affordable Housing: Experiences in Four States." *Housing Policy Debate* 24 (3): 594–636.

Briggs, Xavier de Souza, ed. 2005. *The Geography of Opportunity: Race and Housing Choice in Metropolitan America*. Washington, DC: Brookings Institution Press.

Briggs, Xavier de Souza. 2008. *Democracy as Problem Solving: Civic Capacity in Communities across the Globe*. Cambridge, MA: MIT Press.

Brinig, Margaret F., and Nicole Stelle Garnett. 2013. "A Room of One's Own? Accessory Dwelling Unit Reforms and Local Parochialism." *Urban Lawyer* 45 (3): 519–569.

Brodsly, David. 1981. *L.A. Freeway: An Appreciative Essay*. Berkeley: University of California Press.

Bromley, Ray. 1978. "Introduction—The Urban Informal Sector: Why Is It Worth Discussing?" *World Development* 2 (9/10): 1034–1035.

Brooks, Andre. 1979. "Legal or Not, Single-Family Homes Adding Apartments." *New York Times*, June 3.

Brooks, Richard R. W., and Carol M. Rose. 2013. *Saving the Neighborhood: Racially Restrictive Covenants, Law, and Social Norms*. Cambridge, MA: Harvard University Press.

Brown, Anne, Vinit Mukhija, and Donald Shoup. 2018. "Zoning to Promote Garage Apartments." *Zoning Practice*, May, 1–7.

Brown, Anne, Vinit Mukhija, and Donald Shoup. 2020. "Converting Garages into Housing." *Journal of Planning Education and Research* 40 (1): 56–68.

Brown, Martin J. 2009. "People in Portland Want and Build ADUs—with or without Permits." *Architectural Therapy*, October 13. https://architecturaltherapy.files.wordpress.com/2009/10/portland-adus-permitted-and-not-2009-10-13.pdf.

Brown, Martin J. 2014. "Accessory Dwelling Units in Portland, Oregon: Evaluation and Interpretation of a Survey of ADU Owners." Oregon Department of Environmental Quality, June 1. https://accessorydwellings.files.wordpress.com/2014/06/adusurveyinterpret.pdf.

Brown, Martin J., and Taylor Watkins. 2012. "Understanding and Appraising Properties with Accessory Dwelling Units." *Appraisal Journal* 80 (40): 297–309.

Buck, Richard. 1992. "Mother-in-Law Units: Benefit or Blight?—Washington's Growth Management Act Renews Debate over Accessory Housing." *Seattle Times*, October 25.

Buhayar, Noah. 2019. "To Fix Its Housing Crunch, One US City Takes Aim at the Single-Family Home." *Bloomberg Businessweek*, July 31.

Buhayar, Noah, and Christopher Cannon. 2019. "How California Became America's Housing Market Nightmare." *Bloomberg*, November 6.

Bula, Frances. 2009. "The Laneway House: A Novel Solution to Vancouver's Real-Estate Crunch." *Globe and Mail*, July 27.

Bula, Frances. 2012. "Vancouver's Budding Romance with Row Houses." *Globe and Mail*, June 8.

Bula, Frances. 2016. "Advocates Want Developments Instead of Single-Family Houses in Vancouver." *Globe and Mail*, July 14.

Bula, Frances. 2018. "Vancouver Mayor Gregor Robertson Pushes to Allow Multiunit Housing in Low-Density Neighborhoods." *Globe and Mail*, July 9.

Burby, Raymond J. 2003. "Making Plans That Matter: Citizen Involvement and Government Action." *Journal of the American Planning Association* 69 (1): 33–49.

Burgess, Rod. 1978. "Petty Commodity Housing or Dweller Control? A Critique of John Turner's Views on Housing Policy." *World Development* 6 (9–10): 1105–1133.

Burnham, Linda, and Nik Theodore. 2012. *The Invisible and Unregulated World of Domestic Work*. New York: National Domestic Workers Alliance.

Burningham, Kate. 2000. "Using the Language of NIMBY: A Topic for Research, Not an Activity for Researchers." *Local Environment* 5 (1): 55–67.

Cabansagan, Clarrissa. 2011. "Project Homesafe: From the Bay to LA. Lessons of Granny Flat Legalization in Daly City." Master's applied research project, University of California, Los Angeles.

California Association of Realtors. n.d. "California Residential Purchase Agreement and Joint Escrow Instructions." Revised December 2021. https://www.car.org/-/media/CAR/Documents/Transaction-Center/PDF/Standard-Forms/2021-December-Update/2020-RPA-VERSION-142-DRAFT.pdf?la=en&hash=CE6B78B1BD6AEB5D265D9CEF2B99F0FE532C64F9.

California Department of Housing and Community Development. 2016. *Accessory Dwelling Unit Memorandum*. Sacramento, CA: Department of Housing and Community Development.

California Housing Partnership Corporation. 2014. *How California's Housing Market Is Failing to Meet the Needs of Low-Income Families*. Los Angeles: California Housing Partnership Corporation.

California Legislative Analyst's Office. 2015. *California's High Housing Costs: Causes and Consequences*. Sacramento, CA: Legislative Analyst's Office.

Calthorpe, Peter. 1993. *Next American Metropolis: Ecology, Community, and the American Dream*. New York: Princeton Architectural Press.

Camacho, Alejandro E., and Nicholas Marantz. 2020. "Beyond Preemption, Toward Metropolitan Governance." *Stanford Environmental Law Journal* 39 (2): 125–198.

Campo, Daniel. 2013. *The Accidental Playground: Brooklyn Waterfront Narratives of the Undesigned and Unplanned*. New York: Fordham University Press.

Cancryn, Adam, and Laura Barrón-López. 2020. "Azar Faulted 'Home and Social' Conditions for Meatpacking Outbreaks." *Politico*, May 7.

Carr, Marilyn, Martha Alter Chen, and Jane Tate. 2000. "Globalization and Home-Based Workers." *Feminist Economics* 6 (3): 123–142.

Carson, Rachel. 1962. *Silent Spring*. Boston: Houghton Mifflin.

Castells, Manuel, and Alejandro Portes. 1989. "World Underneath: The Origins, Dynamics, and Effects of the Informal Economy." In *The Informal Economy: Studies in Advanced and Less Developed Countries*, edited by Alejandro Portes, Manuel Castells, and Lauren A. Benton, 11–37. Baltimore: Johns Hopkins University Press.

Cecchini, Alex. 2015. "Zoning's Impact on Minneapolis Form." Streets.mn, February 12. https://streets.mn/2015/02/12/zonings-impact-on-minneapolis-form/.

Chang, Aron. 2011. "Beyond Foreclosure: The Future of Suburban Housing." *Places*, September. https://placesjournal.org/article/beyond-foreclosure-the-future-of-suburban-housing/.

Chapman, Nancy J., and Deborah J. Howe. 2001. "Accessory Apartments: Are They a Realistic Alternative for Aging in Place?" *Housing Studies* 16 (5): 637–650.

Chapple, Karen. 2014. *Planning Sustainable Cities and Regions: Towards More Equitable Development*. New York: Routledge.

Chapple, Karen, Jake Wegmann, Farzad Mashhood, and Rebecca Coleman. 2017. "Accessory Dwelling Units: Lessons Learned from Portland, Seattle, and Vancouver." Terner Center for Housing Innovation, UC Berkeley.

Chapple, Karen, Jake Wegmann, Alison Nemirow, and Colin Dentel-Post. 2011. *Yes in My Backyard: Mobilizing the Market for Secondary Units*. Berkeley: Center for Community Innovation, University of California.

Charles, Suzanne Lanyi. 2020. "The Financialization of Single-Family Rental Housing: An Examination of Real Estate Investment Trusts' Ownership of Single-Family Houses in the Atlanta Metropolitan Area." *Journal of Urban Affairs* 42 (8): 1321–1341.

Chase, John L., Margaret Crawford, and John Kaliski, eds. 2008. *Everyday Urbanism*. New York: Monacelli Press.

Chavez, Stephanie, and James Quinn. 1987. "Substandard Housing: Garages: Immigrants in, Cars Out." *Los Angeles Times*, May 24.

Chen, Carol. 2016. "Notice of Opposition: SB 1069 (Wieckowski) Accessory Dwelling Units (As Amended April 26)." Carol Chen, President, Los Angeles County Division, League of California Cities, June 29.

Cheng, Lai-Sum Lisa. 1980. "Secondary Suites: Housing Resource or Problem, the Vancouver Case." Master's thesis, University of British Columbia.

Cheng, Wendy. 2013. *The Changs Next Door to the Díazes: Remapping Race in Suburban California*. Minneapolis: University of Minnesota Press.

Chetty, Raj, and Nathaniel Hendren. 2015. *The Impacts of Neighborhoods on Intergenerational Mobility: Childhood Exposure Effects and County-Level Estimates*. Cambridge, MA: Harvard University and National Bureau of Economic Research.

Chetty, Raj, Nathaniel Hendren, and Lawrence Katz. 2016. "The Effects of Exposure to Better Neighborhoods on Children: New Evidence from the Moving to Opportunity Project." *American Economic Review* 106 (4): 855–902.

Chhaya Community Development Corporation & Citizens Housing and Planning Council. 2008. *Illegal Dwelling Units: A Potential Source of Affordable Housing in New York City*. New York: New York City's Department of Housing Preservation and Development.

Cho, Jane. 2016. "Second Units in the Silicon Valley." *Urban Lawyer* 48 (3): 459–488.

City and County of San Francisco. 2014. "Legalization of Dwelling Units Installed without a Permit." Information Sheet, Department of Building Inspection, City and County of San Francisco, May 21.

City of Costa Mesa. 2018. "Accessory Dwelling Units—Frequently Asked Questions." Ordinance 18–03, effective February 17.

City of Los Angeles. 2003. "Second Dwelling in Single Family Zone Pursuant to AB 1866." Inter-departmental correspondence from Chief Zoning Administrator and Zoning Engineer, Los Angeles, June 23.

City of Los Angeles. 2010. "ZA Memorandum NO. 120: Second Dwelling Units Pursuant to AB 1866." Office of Zoning Administration, Los Angeles Department of City Planning, May 6.

City of Los Angeles. 2016. "Zoning Administrator's Interpretation." Case No. ZA 2016–4167, Office of Zoning Administration, Los Angeles Department of City Planning, November 2.

City of Los Angeles. 2019. "Ordinance No. 186481." Adopted December 11.

City of Minneapolis. 2001. "Minneapolis City Council Official Proceedings, Regular Meeting of May 18, 2001."

City of Minneapolis. 2014a. "Minneapolis City Council Official Proceedings, Regular Meeting of December 5, 2014."

City of Minneapolis. 2014b. "Request for City Council Committee Action from the Department of Community Planning & Economic Development." Referral from the November 10, 2014, City Planning Commission Meeting to Zoning and Planning Committee, November 20.

City of Minneapolis. 2016. "Ordinance No. 2016–060." Adopted September 2.

City of Minneapolis. 2018a. "Authorizing Submittal of the Minneapolis 2040 Comprehensive Plan to the Metropolitan Council." Resolution No. 2018R-411, File No. 2018-00770, December 15 (Passage, December 7). https://lims.minneapolismn.gov/Download/MetaData/11736/2018-00770%20Resl%20411_Id_11736.pdf.

City of Minneapolis. 2018b. "Minneapolis 2040 — The City's Draft Comprehensive Plan." May. https://minneapolis2040.com/media/1406/minneapolis-2040-comprehensive-plan-draft.pdf.

City of Minneapolis. 2018c. "Minneapolis 2040 — The City's Draft Comprehensive Plan." September. https://lims.minneapolismn.gov/Download/FileV2/20139/pdf_minneapolis2040_with_appendices.pdf.

City of Minneapolis. 2018d. "Planning Primary Zoning." GIS Shapefile. http://opendata.minneapolismn.gov/datasets/planning-primary-zoning.

City of Minneapolis. 2020. "Minneapolis 2040 PDF." https://minneapolis2040.com/pdf.

City of Pasadena. 2018. "Accessory Dwelling Units Regulations." April.

City of Portland. 1959. "Ordinance No. 110103." Adopted May 28.

City of Portland. 1980. "Ordinance No. 150851." Adopted October 16.

City of Portland. 1993a. "Adopted Albina Community Plan." Portland Bureau of Planning, October.

City of Portland. 1993b. "Ordinance No. 166786." Adopted July 27.

City of Portland. 1996. "Adopted Outer Southeast Community Plan." Bureau of Planning, March 25.

City of Portland. 1997. "Ordinance No. 171879." Adopted December 17.

City of Portland. 2003. "Accessory Dwelling Unit Monitoring Project: Report to Planning Commission." Portland Bureau of Planning.

City of Portland. 2004. "Ordinance No. 178172." Adopted February 4.

City of Portland. 2010a. "Ordinance No. 183598." Adopted March 10.

City of Portland. 2010b. "Ordinance No. 183679." Adopted April 14.

City of Portland. 2010c. "Ordinance No. 183688." Adopted April 14.

City of Portland. 2017. "Residential Infill Project: An Update to Portland's Single Family Zoning Rules." Discussion Draft. Volume 1: Staff Report and Map Amendments. Portland Bureau of Planning and Sustainability, October.

City of Portland. 2020. "Ordinance No. 190093." Adopted August 12.

City of Santa Cruz. 1983. "Ordinance No. 83–26." Adopted July 26.

City of Santa Cruz. 1986. "City Council Meeting Minutes." October 21, 44–47.

City of Santa Cruz. 1989. "Ordinance No. 89–31." Adopted September 26.

City of Santa Cruz. 1994. "Ordinance No. 94–31." Adopted June 28.

City of Santa Cruz. 1999. "Ordinance No. 99-11." Adopted July 20.

City of Santa Cruz. 2002. *Expanding Housing Options for the City of Santa Cruz*. Santa Cruz: Housing and Community Development Division.

City of Santa Cruz. 2003a. *Accessory Dwelling Unit: Manual*. Santa Cruz: Housing and Community Development Division.

City of Santa Cruz. 2003b. *Accessory Dwelling Unit: Prototype Plan Sets*. Santa Cruz: Housing and Community Development Division.

City of Santa Cruz. 2003c. "Ordinance No. 2003–16." Adopted May 27.

City of Santa Cruz. 2003d. "Ordinance No. 2003–17." Adopted June 10.

City of Santa Cruz. 2006. *Accessory Dwelling Unit: Garage Conversion Manual*. Santa Cruz: Housing and Community Development Division.

City of Santa Cruz. 2010. "Ordinance No. 2010–17." Adopted September 7.

City of Santa Cruz. 2015. "Ordinance 2015–02." Adopted January 15.

City of Santa Cruz. 2016. *City of Santa Cruz: Accessory Dwelling Unit Development Program*. Santa Cruz: Housing and Community Development Division.

City of Santa Cruz. 2017. "Zoning GIS Shapefile Dataset." October 20, 2017. https://data1-cruzgis.opendata.arcgis.com/datasets/282fb222c0464c7ea832d293b31800ad_42.

REFERENCES

City of Seattle. 1923. "Ordinance No. 45382." Introduced as Council Bill No. 34320. Adopted June 18; approved by Mayor June 28; published July 3.

City of Seattle. 1957. "Resolution No. 17488." Adopted by City Council April 29.

City of Seattle. 1994a. "Ordinance 117203." Adopted July 11.

City of Seattle. 1994b. *Toward a Sustainable Seattle: A Plan for Managing Growth, 1994–2014.* Seattle: Seattle City Council.

City of Seattle. 1999. "Ordinance 119617." Adopted August 27.

City of Seattle. 2003. *Evaluation of the 1998–2001 Demonstration Program for Innovative Housing Design: Detached ADUs and Cottages.* Seattle: Department of Design, Construction, and Land Use.

City of Seattle. 2006. "Ordinance 122190." Adopted August 15.

City of Seattle. 2010. *A Guide to Building a Backyard Cottage.* Seattle: Planning Commission & Department of Planning and Development.

City of Seattle. 2014. "Resolution 31547." Adopted October 13.

City of Seattle. 2016. "Encouraging Backyard Cottages." Agenda and meeting packet, February 14.

City of Seattle. 2018a. "Accessory Dwelling Units: Draft Environmental Impact Statement." May 10.

City of Seattle. 2018b. "Mandatory Housing Affordability: Citywide Implementation: Director's Report and Recommendation." Office of Planning and Community Development, Office of Housing, Department of Neighborhoods, and Seattle Department of Construction and Inspections in collaboration with the Mayor's Office, February.

City of Seattle. 2020. "ADUniverse." https://aduniverse-seattlecitygis.hub.arcgis.com/.

City of Vancouver. 1990. "Renfrew/Collingwood: Secondary Suites Neighborhood Survey." Vancouver Planning Department.

City of Vancouver. 2004. "Secondary Suites." Policy Report, Development and Building, Rob Whitlock, Director of the Housing Centre, January 13.

City of Vancouver. 2008. "EcoDensity: Revised Charter and Initial Actions." Policy Report, Urban Structure, Brent Toderian, Ronda Howard, and Thor Kuhlmann, June 10.

City of Vancouver. 2009a. "Implementing Laneway Housing in RS-1 and RS-5 Single Family Areas." Policy Report, June 9.

City of Vancouver. 2009b. "The Role of Secondary Suites: Rental Housing Strategy—Study 4." Social Development—Housing Policy, Community Services Group, December.

City of Vancouver. 2013. "Amendments to the Laneway Housing Regulations and Guidelines and Expansion of the Laneway Housing Program." Policy Report, Development and Building, May 6.

City of Vancouver. 2018a. "Amendments to the Zoning and Development By-law—Laneway Home Regulations." Policy Report, June 5.

City of Vancouver. 2018b. "Amendments to the Zoning and Development By-law for Most RS Zones to Allow Two-Family Dwellings (Duplexes) to Increase Housing Choice." Policy Report, June 27.

City of Vancouver. 2018c. "Making Room Housing Program: Overview and Quick Start Action." Administrative Report, June 5.

City of Vancouver. 2019a. "Amendments to the Zoning and Development By-Law to Revise Design Regulations for 'Outright' Two-Family Dwellings (Duplexes)." From General Manager of Planning, Urban Design and Sustainability, February 6.

City of Vancouver. 2019b. "Secondary Suite Program Update." From Paul Mochrie, Deputy City Manager, September 30.

Clark, Clifford Edward. 1986. *The American Family Home: 1800–1960*. Chapel Hill: University of North Carolina Press.

Clark, Kenneth B. 1965. *Dark Ghetto: Dilemmas of Social Power*. New York: Harper & Row.

Coates, Ta-Nehisi. 2014. "The Case for Reparations." *Atlantic*, June.

Coates, Ta-Nehisi. 2015. *Between the World and Me*. New York: Spiegel & Grau.

Cody, Louise. 1997. "Accessory Rental Code Rewrite: Testimony to City Council on Behalf of the Centennial Neighborhood Association, October 8." In City of Portland 1997, Ordinance No. 171879 file.

Cohen, Josh. 2017. "Urbanists, Architects Say Backyard Cottages Are a Must in Affordable Housing Push." Next City, October 30. https://nextcity.org/urbanist-news/urbanists-architects-backyard-cottages-affordable-housing.

Colburn, Gregg, and Clayton Page Aldern. 2022. *Homelessness Is a Housing Problem: How Structural Factors Explain US Patterns*. Berkeley: University of California Press.

Condon, Patrick M. 2010. *Seven Rules for Sustainable Communities: Design Strategies for the Post-Carbon World*. Washington, DC: Island Press.

Connerly, Charles E. 2005. *The Most Segregated City in America: City Planning and Civil Rights in Birmingham, 1920–1980*. Charlottesville: University of Virginia Press.

Cook, Joan. 1989. "Harland Bartholomew, 100, Dean of City Planners." *New York Times*, December 7.

County of Los Angeles. 2015. "Increase the Number of Accessory Dwelling Units (ADUs)." Strategy Briefs: Land Use, Homeless Initiative Policy Summit, County of Los Angeles.

Crane, Rebecca. 2020. "Is Granny in that Flat?: How Regulations Shape the Construction and Use of Accessory Dwelling Units in Los Angeles." PhD diss., UCLA.

Crawford, Margaret. 2008. "Blurring the Boundaries: Public Space and Private Life." In *Everyday Urbanism*, edited by John L. Chase, Margaret Crawford, and John Kaliski, 22–35. New York: Monacelli Press.

Creswell, Cathy. 2003. "Second Unit Legislation, Effective January 1, 2003 and July 1, 2003." Memorandum for Planning Directors and Interested Parties from Cathy

Creswell, Deputy Director, Division of Housing Policy Development, California Department of Housing and Community Development, August 6.

Cruickshank, Robert. 2015. "Why the HALA Single-Family Upzones Died." The Urbanist, August 3. https://www.theurbanist.org/2015/08/03/why-the-hala-single-family-upzones-died/.

Cuff, Dana. 2000. *The Provisional City: Los Angeles Stories of Architecture and Urbanism*. Cambridge, MA: MIT Press.

Cuff, Dana, Tim Higgins, and Per-Johan Dahl, eds. 2010. *Backyard Homes LA*. Los Angeles: cityLAB, UCLA.

Curtiss, Aaron. 1995. "Panel Adopts City Blueprint for 21st Century Development: Planning Commission Approves Document That Channels Growth into Areas That Can Accommodate It." *Los Angeles Times*, July 28.

Dahl, Per-Johan. 2010. "The Shadows of L.A." *Critical Planning* 17:124–139.

Davidoff, Paul, Linda Davidoff, and Neil Newton Gold. 1970. "Suburban Action: Advocate Planning for an Open Society." *Journal of the American Institute of Planners* 36 (1): 12–21.

Davidoff, Thomas. 2005. "Income Sorting: Measurement and Decomposition." *Journal of Urban Economics* 58 (2): 289–303.

Davis, Mike. 1990. *City of Quartz: Excavating the Future of Los Angeles*. New York: Verso.

Dear, Michael. 1992. "Understanding and Overcoming the NIMBY Syndrome." *Journal of the American Planning Association* 58 (3): 288–300.

De Certeau, Michel. 2002. *The Practice of Everyday Life*. Berkeley: University of California Press.

De Jong, Judith K. 2014. *New SubUrbanisms*. New York: Routledge.

De La Cruz-Viesca, Melany, et al. 2016. *The Color of Wealth in Los Angeles*. Developed for the Ford Foundation's Building Economic Security Over a Lifetime Initiative. Los Angeles: UCLA Asian American Studies Center Policy Report.

Desmond, Matthew. 2016. *Evicted: Poverty and Profit in the American City*. New York: Crown Publishing.

Desmond, Matthew. 2017. "How Homeownership Became the Engine of American Inequality." *New York Times*, May 9.

De Soto, Hernando. 1989. *The Other Path: The Invisible Revolution in the Third World*. New York: Harper and Row.

De Soto, Hernando. 2000. *The Mystery of Capital: Why Capitalism Triumphs in the West and Fails Everywhere Else*. New York: Basic Books.

Devine-Wright, Patrick. 2009. "Rethinking NIMBYism: The Role of Place Attachment and Place Identity in Explaining Place-Protective Action." *Journal of Community & Applied Social Psychology* 19 (6): 426–441.

Devlin, Ryan T. 2011. "'An Area That Governs Itself': Informality, Uncertainty and the Management of Street Vending in New York City." *Planning Theory* 10 (1): 53–65.

Devlin, Ryan T. 2018. "Asking 'Third World Questions' of First World Informality: Using Southern Theory to Parse Needs from Desires in an Analysis of Informal Urbanism of the Global North." *Planning Theory* 17 (4): 568–587.

Dezember, Ryan. 2020. *Underwater: How Our American Dream of Homeownership Became a Nightmare*. New York: Thomas Dunne Books.

Diener, G. Edward. 1979. "Defining and Implementing Local Plan-Land Use Consistency in California." *Ecology Law Quarterly* 7:753–779.

Dillon, Liam. 2016a. "Everything You Need to Know about Gov. Jerry Brown's Housing Plan." *Los Angeles Times*, June 2.

Dillon, Liam. 2016b. "More 'Granny Flats' Moving In." *Los Angeles Times*, September 28.

Dillon, Liam. 2019. "Oregon Vowed Not to Become California—and Passes Sweeping Housing Crisis Legislation." *Los Angeles Times*, July 19.

Dillon, Liam. 2021. "In a First for California, Sacramento Poised to Allow Apartments in Single-Family Home Neighborhoods." *Los Angeles Times*, February 10.

Dillon, Liam, and Andrew Khouri. 2016. "How to Solve California's Housing Shortage? Build 'Granny Flats' in Homeowners' Backyards." *Los Angeles Times*, July 26.

Doebele, William A. 1987. "The Evolution of Concepts of Urban Land Tenure in Developing Countries." *Habitat International* 11 (1): 7–22.

Donelson, Angela J., and Adrian X. Esparza, eds. 2010. *The Colonias Reader: Economy, Housing and Public Health in US-Mexico Border Colonias*. Tucson: University of Arizona Press.

Dougherty, Conor. 2017. "The Great American Single Family Home Problem" *New York Times*, December 1.

Dougherty, Conor. 2018. "In Vancouver, a Housing Frenzy That Even Owners Want to End." *New York Times*, June 2.

Dougherty, Conor. 2020. *Golden Gates: Fighting for Housing in America*. New York: Penguin Press.

Dougherty, Conor, and Andrew Burton. 2017. "A 2:15 Alarm, 2 Trains and a Bus Get Her to Work by 7 A.M." *New York Times*, August 17.

Douglas, Gordon. 2013. "Do-It-Yourself Urban Design: The Social Practice of Informal 'Improvement' through Unauthorized Alteration." *City and Community* 13 (1): 5–25.

Downs, Anthony. 1991. "The Advisory Commission on Regulatory Barriers to Affordable Housing: Its Behavior and Accomplishments." *Housing Policy Debate* 2 (4): 1095–1137.

Duany, Andres, Elizabeth Plater-Zyberk, and Jeff Speck. 2000. *Suburban Nation: The Rise of Sprawl and the Decline of the American Dream*. New York: North Point Press.

Duneier, Mitchell. 2016. *Ghetto: The Invention of a Place, the History of an Idea*. New York: Farrar, Straus and Giroux.

Dunkerley, Harold B., ed. 1983. *Urban Land Policy: Issues and Opportunities*. New York: Oxford University Press.

Durning, Alan. 2012–2013. "Legalizing Inexpensive Housing." Sightline Institute, Series. https://www.sightline.org/series/legalizing-inexpensive-housing/page/11/.

Durning, Alan. 2015. "Open Up Seattle's Single-Family Zoning to Those Who Aren't Rich." Opinion, *Seattle Times*, July 19.

Durst, Noah J. 2019. "Informal and Ubiquitous: Colonias, Premature Subdivisions and Other Unplanned Suburbs on America's Urban Fringe." *Urban Studies* 56 (4): 722–740.

Durst, Noah J., and Peter M. Ward. 2014. "Measuring Self-Help Home Improvements in Texas Colonias: A Ten Year 'Snapshot' Study." *Urban Studies* 51 (10): 2143–2159.

Durst, Noah J., and Peter M. Ward. 2016. "Colonia Housing Conditions in Model Subdivisions: A Déjà Vu for Policy Makers." *Housing Policy Debate* 26 (2): 316–333.

Durst, Noah J., and Jake Wegmann. 2017. "Informal Housing in the United States." *International Journal of Urban and Regional Research* 41 (2): 282–297.

Economist. 2015. "Urban Land: Space and the City." April 4.

Economist. 2016. "Global House Prices: Hot in the City." April 2.

Edwards, John. 2016. "A History of Downzoning." *Wedge Times—Picayune*, February 15.

Edwards, John. 2018. "The Whole Story of Minneapolis 2040." *Wedge Times—Picayune*, December 13.

Ehrenfeucht, Renia, and Anastasia Loukaitou-Sideris. 2014. "The Irreconcilable Tension between Dwelling in Public and the Regulatory State." In *The Informal American City: Beyond Taco Trucks and Day Labor*, edited by Vinit Mukhija and Anastasia Loukaitou-Sideris, 155–171. Cambridge, MA: MIT Press.

Einstein, Katherine Levine, David M. Glick, and Maxwell Palmer. 2019. *Neighborhood Defenders: Participatory Politics and America's Housing Crisis*. New York: Cambridge University Press.

Elkind, Ethan N. 2014. *Railtown: The Fight for the Los Angeles Metro Rail and the Future of the City*. Berkeley: University of California Press.

Ellen, Ingrid Gould, Jeffrey Lubell, and Mark A. Willis. 2021. *Through the Roof: What Communities Can Do about the High Cost of Rental Housing in America*. Cambridge, MA: Lincoln Institute of Land Policy.

Elmendorf, Christopher S. 2019. "Beyond the Double Veto: Housing Plans as Preemptive Intergovernmental Compacts." *Hastings Law Journal* 71:79–150.

Elmendorf, Christopher S., et al. 2020. "Making It Work: Legal Foundations for Administrative Reform of California's Housing Framework." *Ecology Law Quarterly* 47:973–1060.

El Nasser, Haya. 2004. "Granny Flats Finding a Home in a Tight Market." *USA Today*, January 5.

Fan, Stephen. 2014. *SubUrbanisms: Casino Urbanization, Chinatowns, and the Contested American Landscape*. New London, CT: Lyman Allyn Art Museum.

Fanucchi, Kenneth. 1970. "'Concept L.A.' Plan Termed Suicidal at Ecology Program." October 29.

Farragher, Thomas, and Casey Ross. 2014. "Overcrowding Rampant in Student Neighborhoods." *Boston Globe*, May 4.

Fawaz, Mona. 2008. "An Unusual Clique of City-Makers: Social Networks in the Production of a Neighborhood in Beirut (1950–75)." *International Journal of Urban and Regional Research* 32 (3): 565–585.

Fayerman, Pamela. 1988. "Acrimony, Racism Deplete Suites Committee." *Vancouver Sun*, November 18.

Federation of Hillside & Canyon Associations v. City of Los Angeles. 2000. No. B126659. Court of Appeal, Second District, Division Three, California. September 28, 2000. https://caselaw.findlaw.com/ca-court-of-appeal/1402603.html.

Feige, Edgar L. 1990. "Defining and Estimating Underground and Informal Economies: The New Institutional Economics Approach." *World Development* 18 (7): 989–1002.

Feiock, Richard C. 2007. "Rational Choice and Regional Governance." *Journal of Urban Affairs* 29 (1): 47–63.

Feit, Josh. 2016a. "Queen Anne Residents Are Challenging the City's Plan to Make Seattle Denser." *Seattle Met*, October 18.

Feit, Josh. 2016b. "Ruling Puts Hold on Adding Density to Single-Family Neighborhoods." *Seattle Met*, December 14.

Fennell, Lee Anne. 2009. *The Unbounded Home: Property Values beyond Property Lines*. New Haven, CT: Yale University Press.

Ferguson, Bruce, and Peer Smets. 2010. "Finance for Incremental Housing: Current Status and Prospects for Expansion." *Habitat International* 34 (3): 288–298.

Ferman, Barbara. 1996. *Challenging the Growth Machine: Neighborhood Politics in Chicago and Pittsburgh*. Lawrence: University Press of Kansas.

Ferman, Patricia R., and Louis A. Ferman. 1973. "The Structural Underpinnings of the Irregular Economy." *Poverty and Human Resources Abstracts* 8 (1): 3–17.

Fernandes, Edesio, and Ann Varley. 1998. *Illegal Cities: Law and Urban Change in Developing Countries*. London: Zed Books

Fester, Stephen. 2019. "What Seattle's 'Best in the Nation' Mother-in-Law Apartment and Backyard Cottage Reform Does." The Urbanist, July 1. https://www.theurbanist.org/2019/07/03/what-seattles-best-in-the-nation-mother-in-law-apartment-and-backyard-cottage-reform-does/.

Field, Erica. 2005. "Property Rights and Investments in Urban Slums." *Journal of the European Economic Association* 3 (2–3): 279–290.

Finnegan, Michael. 2020. "How Would Trump or Biden Approach Housing and Homelessness?" *Los Angeles Times*, August 17.

Fischel, William A. 2001. *The Homevoter Hypothesis: How Home Values Influence Local Government Taxation, School Finance, and Land-Use Policies*. Cambridge, MA: Harvard University Press.

Fischler, Raphael. 1998. "The Metropolitan Dimension of Early Zoning: Revisiting the 1916 New York City Ordinance." *Journal of the American Planning Association* 64 (2): 170–188.

Fishman, Robert. 1987. *Bourgeois Utopias: The Rise and Fall of Suburbia*. New York: Basic Books.

Flint, Barbara J. 1977. "Zoning and Residential Segregation: A Social and Physical History, 1910–1940." PhD diss., University of Chicago.

Fogelson, Robert M. 1967a. *The Fragmented Metropolis: Los Angeles, 1850–1930*. Cambridge, MA: Harvard University Press.

Fogelson, Robert M. 1967b. "White on Black: A Critique of the McCone Commission Report on the Los Angeles Riots." *Political Science Quarterly* 82 (3): 337–367.

Folts, W. Edward, and Kenneth B. Muir. 2002. "Housing for Older Adults: New Lessons from the Past." *Research on Aging* 24 (1): 10–28.

Fong, Timothy. 1994. *The First Suburban Chinatown: The Remaking of Monterey Park, California*. Philadelphia: Temple University Press.

Foster, David. 2000. "Yes in My Back Yard: How Our Second Unit Program Could Better Address the Affordable Housing Needs of Santa Cruz." Concept paper, Affordable Housing Advocates, Santa Cruz.

Foster, David. 2001, "Granny Units Can Help Ease Housing Crisis." *Santa Cruz Sentinel*, June 10.

Fox, Liana. 2019. "The Supplemental Poverty Measure: 2018." Report Number P60–268, US Census Bureau, US Department of Commerce.

Franck, Karen A., and Lynn Paxson. 2007. "Transforming Public Space into Sites of Mourning and Free Expression." In *Loose Space: Possibility and Diversity in Urban Life*, edited by Karen Franck and Quentin Stevens, 132–153. New York: Routledge.

Franck, Karen A., and Quentin Stevens, eds. 2007. *Loose Space: Possibility and Diversity in Urban Life*. New York: Routledge.

Freishtat, Sarah. 2021. "The City Has Received Applications to Add More Than 160 Coach Houses and Granny Flats. Will They Help Solve Chicago's Affordable Housing Shortage?" *Chicago Tribune*, June 14.

Freund, David M. P. 2007. *Colored Property: State Policy and White Racial Politics in Suburban America*. Chicago: University of Chicago Press.

Friedman, Joseph, Emmanuel Jimenez, and Stephen K. Mayo. 1988. "The Demand for Tenure Security in Developing Countries." *Journal of Development Economics* 29 (2): 185–198.

Friedman, Nicole. 2021. "U.S. Median Home Price Hit New High in June." *Wall Street Journal*, July 22.

Friedman, Robyn A. 2021. "Your Garage May Hold the Keys to a New Rental Opportunity." *Wall Street Journal*, August 25.

Friedmann, John. 1987. *Planning in the Public Domain: From Knowledge to Action*. Princeton, NJ: Princeton University Press.

Friedmann, John. 2011. *Insurgencies: Essays in Planning Theory*. New York: Routledge.

Frug, Gerald E. 2002. "Beyond Regional Government." *Harvard Law Review* 115 (7): 1763–1836.

Fry, Richard. 2019. "The Number of People in the Average U.S. Household Is Going Up for the First Time in Over 160 Years." Pew Research Center, October 1. https://www.pewresearch.org/fact-tank/2019/10/01/the-number-of-people-in-the-average-u-s-household-is-going-up-for-the-first-time-in-over-160-years/.

Fry, Richard, and Jeffery S. Passel. 2014. "Young Adults Driving Growth in Multigenerational Living." Pew Research Center, July 17. https://www.pewresearch.org/social-trends/2014/07/17/young-adults-driving-growth-in-multi-generational-living/.

Fulton, William. 2001. *The Reluctant Metropolis: The Politics of Urban Growth in Los Angeles*. Baltimore: Johns Hopkins University Press.

Fumano, Dan. 2019. "Growth, Density Lead the Debate in Most Council Races in Metro Vancouver." *Vancouver Sun*, September 16.

Fung, Archon. 2004. *Empowered Participation: Reinventing Urban Democracy*. Princeton, NJ: Princeton University Press.

Fung, Archon. 2012. "Continuous Institutional Innovation and the Pragmatic Conception of Democracy." *Polity* 44 (4): 609–624.

Fung, Archon, and Erik Olin Wright, eds. 2003. *Deepening Democracy: Institutional Innovations in Empowered Participatory Governance*. New York: Verso.

Fung, Lisa. 2015. "Working Poor, Working Hard." *UCLA Blueprint*, Fall.

Galiani, Sebastian, and Ernesto Schargrodsky. 2010. "Property Rights for the Poor: Effects of Land Titling." *Journal of Public Economics* 94 (9–10): 700–729.

Gallagher, Leigh. 2013. *The End of the Suburbs: Where the American Dream Is Moving*. New York: Portfolio/Penguin.

Galvan, Astrid, and Mike Schneider. 2021. "Did Census Overlook Communities of Color?" *Los Angeles Times*, August 29.

Ganong, Peter, and Daniel W. Shoag, 2017. "Why Has Regional Income Convergence in the U.S. Declined?" NBER Working Papers 23609, National Bureau of Economic Research, Cambridge, MA.

Gans, Herbert J. 1962. *The Urban Villagers*. New York: Free Press of Glencoe.

Garnett, Nicole Stelle. 2009. *Ordering the City: Land Use, Policing, and the Restoration of Urban America*. New Haven, CT: Yale University Press.

Garvin, Alexander. 2002. *The American City: What Works and What Doesn't*. New York: McGraw-Hill.

Geertz, Clifford. 1978. "The Bazaar Economy: Information and Search in Peasant Marketing." *American Economic Review* 68 (2): 28–32.

Geist, William F.. 1981. "A Suburban Tempest." *New York Times*, December 8.

Gellen, Martin. 1985. *Accessory Apartments in Single-Family Housing*. New Brunswick, NJ: Center for Urban Policy Research, Rutgers University.

Gendron, Richard, and G. William Domhoff. 2008. *The Leftmost City: Power and Progressive Politics in Santa Cruz*. Boulder, CO: Westview Press.

Gibson, Karen J. 2007. "Bleeding Albina: A History of Disinvestment, 1940–2000." *Transforming Anthropology* 15 (1): 3–25.

Gibson-Graham, J. K. 2006. *A Postcapitalist Politics*. Minneapolis: University of Minnesota Press.

Gilbert, Alan. 2002. "On the Mystery of Capital and the Myths of Hernando de Soto: What Difference Does Legal Title Make?" *International Development Planning Review* 24 (1): 1–19.

Gilbert, Alan, and Peter M. Ward. 1985. *Housing, the State and the Poor: Policy and Practice in Three Latin American Cities*. Cambridge: Cambridge University Press.

Gish, Todd. 2007. "Building Los Angeles: Urban Housing in the Suburban Metropolis, 1900–1936." PhD diss., University of Southern California, Los Angeles.

Glaeser, Edward. 2011. *Triumph of the City: How Our Greatest Invention Makes Us Richer, Smarter, Greener, Healthier, and Happier*. New York: Penguin Books.

Glaeser, Edward. 2017. "Reforming Land Use Regulations." Report, Brookings, April 24. https://www.brookings.edu/research/reforming-land-use-regulations/.

Glaeser, Edward, and Joseph Gyourko. 2003. "The Impact of Zoning on Housing Affordability." *Economic Policy Review* 9 (2): 21–39.

Glaeser, Edward, Joseph Gyourko, and Raven Saks. 2005. "Why Have Housing Prices Gone Up?" *American Economic Review* 95 (2): 329–333.

Goetz, Edward G. 1993. *Shelter Burden: Local Politics and Progressive Housing Policy*. Philadelphia: Temple University Press

Goldberg, Gail. 2009. "Status Report on Accessory Dwelling Unit Ordinance." Los Angeles Department of City Planning, December 17.

Goldenstein, Taylor. 2015. "Authorities Identify Body Found in Fridge." *Los Angeles Times*, December 23.

Goldin, Greg. 2003. "The 'Granny Unit' Option for a Rental-Squeezed LA." *Los Angeles Times*, June 1.

Gottdiener, Mark. 1985. *Social Production of Urban Space*. Austin: University of Texas Press.

Gottlieb, Robert, and Simon Ng. 2017. *Global Cities: Urban Environments in Los Angeles, Hong Kong, and China*. Cambridge, MA: MIT Press.

Gowan, Teresa. 2009. "New Hobos or Neoromantic Fantasy? Urban Ethnography beyond the Neoliberal Disconnect." *Qualitative Sociology* 32 (3): 231–257.

Grabar, Henry. 2015. "The Incredible Shrinking Megacity: How Los Angeles Engineered a Housing Crisis." *Salon*, April 5.

Grabar, Henry. 2018. "Minneapolis Confronts Its History of Housing Segregation." *Slate*, December 18.

Granovetter, Mark. 1985. "Economic Action and Social Structure: The Problem of Embeddedness." *American Journal of Sociology* 91 (3): 481–510.

Green, Penelope. 2012. "Under One Roof, Building for Extended Families." *New York Times*, November 29.

Greenhut, Steven. 2020. "Abolish Single-Family-Only Zoning Expands Freedom and Choice." *Reason*, January 10.

Groom, Sean. 2013. "Rise of the ADU." *Fine Homebuilding* 235 (Spring/Summer): 80–85.

Gross, Ashley. 2016. "Seattle City Council Member O'Brien Proposes Changes to Encourage More Backyard Cottages." KPLU-FM, May 19.

Gruber, Jonathan, Amalie Jensen, and Henrik Kleven. 2017. "Do People Respond to the Mortgage Interest Deduction? Quasi-experimental Evidence from Denmark." Working Paper Series No. 23600, National Bureau of Economic Research, Cambridge, MA.

Gulyani, Sumila, and Debabrata Talukdar. 2008. "Slum Real Estate: The Low Quality High-Price Puzzle in Nairobi's Slum Rental Market and Its Implications for Theory and Practice." *World Development* 36 (10): 1916–1937.

Gyourko, Joseph, and Jacob Krimmel. 2021. "The Impact of Local Residential Land Use Restrictions on Land Values across and within Single-Family Housing Markets." Working Paper 28993, National Bureau of Economic Research, Cambridge, MA.

Haar, Charles M. 1959. *Land-Use Planning: A Casebook on the Use, Misuse, and Reuse of Urban Land*. New York: Little, Brown.

Haar, Charles, and Jerold Kayden, eds. 1989. *Zoning and the American Dream: Promises Still to Keep*. Chicago: American Planning Association.

Hagman, Donald G. 1971. *Urban Planning and Land Development Control Law*. St. Paul, MN: West Publishing Company.

Hagman, Donald G. 1983. "The American Dream as Public Nightmare, or, Sam, You Made the Front Yard Too Long." *UCLA Journal of Environmental Law and Policy* 32:219–246.

Hall, Carlyle. 2016a. "On the Brink of Folly: Will City Council Unwittingly Upzone LA's Single-Family Neighborhoods?" Citywatchla.com, July 21. https://www.citywatchla.com/index.php/cw/los-angeles/11502-on-the-brink-of-folly-will-city-council-unwittingly-upzone-la-s-single-family-neighborhoods.

Hall, Carlyle. 2016b. "Second Units and Los Angeles' Broken Planning System." *The Planning Report: Insider's Guide to Planning and Infrastructure*, April 26. https://www.planningreport.com/2016/04/26/second-units-and-los-angeles-broken-planning-system.

Hall, Tim, and Phil Hubbard. 1998. *The Entrepreneurial City: Geographies of Politics, Regime, and Representation*. Chichester: John Wiley & Sons.

Hamidi, Shima, Sadegh Sabouri, and Reid Ewing. 2020. "Does Density Aggravate the COVID-19 Pandemic?" *Journal of the American Planning Association* 86 (4): 495–509.

Hamilton, Calvin S. 1986. "What Can We Learn from Los Angeles?" *Journal of the American Planning Association* 52 (4): 500–507.

Hankinson, Michael. 2018. "When Do Renters Behave Like Homeowners? High Rent, Price Anxiety, and NIMBYism." *American Political Science Association* 112 (3): 1–21.

Hanson, Sandra, and John White, eds. 2011. *The American Dream in the 21st Century*. Philadelphia: Temple University Press.

Hare, Patrick H. 1981. "Carving Up the American Dream." *Planning* 47 (7): 14–17.

Hare, Patrick H. 1982. *Accessory Apartments: A New Housing Option for the Elderly Homeowner*. Washington, DC: Center for the Study of Retirement and Aging of the Catholic University of America.

Hare, Patrick H., Susan Conner, and Dwight H. Merriam. 1981. *Accessory Apartments: Using Surplus Space in Single-Family Houses*. PAS Report No. 365. Chicago: American Planning Association.

Harland Bartholomew and Associates. 1928. *A Plan for the City of Vancouver British Columbia*. St. Louis, MO: Harland Bartholomew and Associates.

Harland Bartholomew and Associates. 1946. *A Preliminary Report upon Zoning: Vancouver, British Columbia*. St. Louis, MO: Harland Bartholomew and Associates.

Harris, Cheryl. 1997. "Whiteness as Property." *Harvard Law Review* 106 (8): 1707–1791.

Harris, Diane. 2012. *Little White Houses: How the Postwar Home Constructed Race in America*. Minneapolis: University of Minnesota Press.

Harris, John R., and Michael P. Todaro. 1970. "Migration, Unemployment and Development: A Two-Sector Analysis." *American Economic Review* 60 (1): 126–142.

Harris, Richard. 1994. "Chicago's Other Suburbs." *Geographical Review* 84 (4): 394–410.

Harris, Richard. 1996. *Unplanned Suburbs: Toronto's American Tragedy, 1900–1950*. Baltimore: Johns Hopkins University Press.

Hart, Keith. 1973. "Informal Income Opportunities and Urban Employment in Ghana." *Journal of Modern African Studies* 11 (1): 61–89.

Harvey, David. 1997. "Contested Cities: Social Process and Spatial Form." In *Transforming Cities: Contested Governance and New Spatial Divisions*, edited by Nick Jewson and Susanne MacGregor, 19–28. New York: Routledge.

Hayden, Dolores. 1980. "What Would a Non-sexist City Be Like? Speculations on Housing, Urban Design, and Human Work." *Signs: Journal of Women in Culture and Society* 5 (S3): S170–S187.

Hayden, Dolores. (1984) 2002. *Redesigning the American Dream: The Future of Housing, Work, and Family Life*. Revised and expanded edition. New York: W. W. Norton.

Healey, Jon, and Matthew Ballinger. 2021. "What Just Happened with Single-Family Zoning in California?" *Los Angeles Times*, September 17.

Hellmann, Melissa. 2017. "Seattle Coalition Appeals Zoning Changes." *Seattle Weekly*, November 28.

Hernandez, Jennifer. 2019. "California Getting in Its Own Way." Research Brief, Center for Demographics and Policy, Chapman University.

Hernandez, Susan. 2018. "State Mandates vs. Local Concerns: Accessory Dwelling Units in Pico Rivera." Master's applied research project, University of California, Los Angeles.

Hilber, Christian A. L., and Tracy M. Turner. 2013. "The Mortgage Interest Deduction and Its Impact on Homeownership Decisions." *Review of Economics and Statistics* 96 (4): 618–637.

Hills, Roderick M., and David Schleicher. 2015. "Planning an Affordable City." *Iowa Law Review* 101:91–136.

Hirt, Sonia A. 2014. *Zoned in the USA: The Origins and Implications of American Land-Use Regulation*. Ithaca, NY: Cornell University Press.

Hise, Greg. 1993. "Home Building and Industrial Decentralization in Los Angeles: The Roots of the Postwar Urban Region." *Journal of Urban History* 19 (2): 95–125.

Hise, Greg. 1999. *Magnetic Los Angeles: Planning the Twentieth-Century Metropolis*. Baltimore: Johns Hopkins University Press.

Hoffman, Jeremy S., Vivek Shandas, and Nicholas Pendelton. 2020. "The Effects of Historical Housing Policies on Resident Exposure to Intra-Urban Heat: A Study of 108 US Urban Areas." *Climate* 8 (1): 12. https://doi.org/10.3390/cli8010012.

Holleran, Max. 2021. "Millennial 'YIMBYs' and Boomer 'NIMBYs': Generational Views on Housing Affordability in the United States." *Sociological Review* 69 (4): 846–861.

Holston, James. 1991. "Autoconstruction in Working-Class Brazil." *Cultural Anthropology* 6 (4): 447–465.

Holston, James. 2007. *Insurgent Citizenship: Disjunctions of Democracy and Modernity in Brazil*. Princeton, NJ: Princeton University Press.

Hondagneu-Sotelo, Pierette. 2001. *Domestica: Immigrant Workers Cleaning and Caring in the Shadow of Affluence*. Berkeley: University of California Press.

Horowitz, Julia Menasce, Ruth Igielnik, and Rakesh Kochhar. 2020. "Most Americans Say There Is Too Much Economic Inequality in the US, but Fewer Than Half Call It a Top Priority." Pew Research Center, January 9. https://www.pewresearch.org/social-trends/wp-content/uploads/sites/3/2020/01/PSDT_01.09.20_economic-inequailty_FULL.pdf.

Hou, Jeffrey, ed. 2010. *Insurgent Public Space: Guerilla Urbanism and the Remaking of Contemporary Cities*. New York: Routledge.

Howe, Deborah A. 1990. "The Flexible House—Designing for Changing Needs." *Journal of the American Planning Association* 56 (1): 69–77.

Hsieh, Chang-Tai, and Enrico Moretti. 2015. "Why Do Cities Matter? Local Growth and Aggregate Growth." Kreisman Working Papers Series in Housing Law and Policy No. 30. https://ssrn.com/abstract=2693282.

Hubbard, Phil. 2006. "NIMBY by Another Name? A Reply to Wolsink." *Transactions of the Institute of British Geographers* 31 (1): 92–94.

Hubka, Thomas C., and Judith T. Kenny. 2000. "The Workers' Cottage in Milwaukee's Polish Community: Housing and the Process of Americanization, 1870–1920." *Perspective in Vernacular Architecture* 8:33–52.

Huerta, Álvaro. 2021. "How Cities Can Boost the Informal Economy: Support Street Vendors and Prioritize Economic Equity." *Planning* (Summer): 34–39.

Hughes, Jonathan, and Simon Sadler, eds. 2000. *Non-plan: Essays on Freedom, Participation and Change in Modern Architecture and Urbanism*. Oxford: Architectural Press.

Hunt, Darnell, and Ana-Christina Ramon, eds. 2010. *Black Los Angeles: American Dreams and Racial Realities*. New York: New York University Press.

Hunter, Justine. 1988. "Council Legalizes Secondary Suites in Single-Residential Communities." *Vancouver Sun*, October 21.

Huxtable, Ada Louise. 1964. "Clusters Instead of Slurbs." *New York Times*, February 9.

Imparato, Ivo, and Jeff Ruster. 2003. *Slum Upgrading and Participation: Lessons from Latin America*. Washington, DC: World Bank.

Industrial Design. 1971. "Getting it All Together." 18 (1): 24–25.

Infranca, John. 2019. "The New State Zoning: Preemption amid a Housing Crisis." *Boston College Law Review* 60 (3): 823–887.

International Labour Organization. 1972. *Employment, Income and Inequality: A Strategy for Increasing Productive Employment in Kenya*. Geneva: International Labour Organization.

Iskander, Natasha, and Nichola Lowe. 2010. "Hidden Talent: Tacit Skill Formation and Labor Market Incorporation of Latino Immigrants in the United States." *Journal of Planning Education and Research* 30 (1): 132–146.

Jackson, Kenneth. 1985. *Crabgrass Frontier: The Suburbanization of the United States*. New York: Oxford University Press.

Jacobs, James A. 2015. *Detached America: Building Houses in Postwar Suburbia*. Charlottesville: University of Virginia Press.

Jacobs, Jane. 1961. *The Death and Life of Great American Cities*. New York: Random House.

Jacobson, Don. 2013. "Carriage Houses Could Be on Their Way Back in Minneapolis." *Star Tribune*, June 20.

Jargowsky, Paul. 2015. *Architecture of Segregation: Civil Unrest, the Concentration of Poverty, and Public Policy*. New York: Century Foundation.

Jimenez, Emmanuel. 1983. "The Magnitude and Determinants of Home Improvement in Self-Help Housing: Manila's Tondo Project." *Land Economics* 59 (1): 70–83.

Jimenez, Emmanuel. 1984. "Tenure Security and Urban Squatting." *Review of Economics and Statistics* 66 (4): 556–567.

Johnson, Anna. 2020. "Raleigh Changes Its Mind about Backyard Cottages—Again." *News & Observer*, July 8.

Johnson, Joshua. 2019. "Across America: How US Cities Are Tackling the Affordable Housing Crisis." *1A*, National Public Radio, August 28.

Johnson, Marilynn. 1993. *The Second Gold Rush: Oakland and the East Bay in World War II*. Berkeley: University of California Press.

Joint Center for Housing Studies of Harvard University. 2013. *America's Rental Housing: Evolving Markets and Needs*. Cambridge, MA: Joint Center for Housing Studies of Harvard University.

Joint Center for Housing Studies of Harvard University. 2016. *Projections & Implications for Housing a Growing Population: Older Household 2015–2035*. Cambridge, MA: Joint Center for Housing Studies of Harvard University.

Joint Center for Housing Studies of Harvard University. 2020. *America's Rental Housing 2020*. Cambridge, MA: Joint Center for Housing Studies of Harvard University.

Joint Center for Housing Studies of Harvard University. 2021. *The State of the Nation's Housing 2021*. Cambridge, MA: Joint Center for Housing Studies of Harvard University.

Jones-Correa, Michael. 2000. "The Origins and Diffusion of Racial Restrictive Covenants." *Political Science Quarterly* 115 (4): 541–568.

Jordan, Miriam. 2020. "In California, It Will Take More Than a Parade to Save an Imperiled Census." *New York Times*, August 9.

Jun, Kyu-Nahm. 2013. "Escaping the Local Trap? The Role of Community-Representing Organizations in Urban Governance." *Journal of Urban Affairs* 35 (3): 343–363.

Kahlenberg, Richard D. 2019. "How Minneapolis Ended Single-Family Zoning." Report (Rights & Justice), Century Foundation, October 24.

Kahlenberg, Richard D. 2021. "The 'New Redlining' Is Deciding Who Lives in Your Neighborhood." *New York Times*, April 19.

Kaleem, Jaweed. 2017. "Even Before the Train Killings, Portland Was Embroiled in Conflicts over Hate and Racism." *Los Angeles Times*, June 1.

Kalita, S. Mira. 2012. "Multiple Families, One Roof: Owners Challenge Zoning to Make Room for Adult Children, Elderly Parents." *Wall Street Journal*, July 18.

Kamel, Nabil. 2014. "Learning from the Margin: Placemaking Tactics." In *The Informal American City: Beyond Taco Trucks and Day Labor*, edited by Vinit Mukhija and Anastasia Loukaitou-Sideris, 119–136. Cambridge, MA: MIT Press.

Kamin, Debra. 2021. "California's Red-Hot Real Estate Market Cools Just a Bit." *New York Times*, June 29.

Kaplan, Sam Hall. 1986. "Citizens Want a Hand in Zoning." *Los Angeles Times*, April 6.

Katz, Bruce, ed. 2000. *Reflections on Regionalism*. Washington, DC: Brookings Institution Press.

Kauffman, Elliot. 2018. "Housing Deregulation in Progressive Clothes." *Wall Street Journal*, December 22–23.

Kavanagh, Jean. 1988. "Planners Predict Prolonged Fight over Illegal Suites." *Vancouver Sun*, November 2.

Kaye, Ron. 2009. "'Granny Flats' Decision Fuels Passions over L.A. Housing Policies." *The Planning Report: Insider's Guide to Planning and Infrastructure*, December 4. https://www.planningreport.com/2009/12/04/%E2%80%98granny-flats-decision-fuels-passions-over-la-housing-policies.

Kean, Thomas H., Thomas Ludlow Ashley, and Advisory Commission on Regulatory Barriers to Affordable Housing. 1991. *Not in My Backyard: Removing Barriers to Affordable Housing*. Washington, DC: US Department of Housing and Urban Development.

Keats, John. 1956. *The Crack in the Picture Window*. Boston: Houghton Mifflin.

Keenan, Sandy. 2014. "Grandma Never Had It So Good." *New York Times*, May 7.

Kelly, Barbara M. 1993. *Expanding the American Dream: Building and Rebuilding Levittown*. Albany: State University of New York Press.

Khouri, Andrew. 2021. "Southern California Home Prices Keep Climbing, Hit New Record in July." *Los Angeles Times*, August 18.

Kim, Annette M. 2004. "A Market without the 'Right' Property Rights." *Economics of Transition* 12 (2): 275–305.

Kiviat, Barbara. 2010. "The Case against Homeownership." *Time*, September 11.

Klinenberg, Eric. 2012a. "Solo Nation: American Consumers Stay Single." *Fortune*, January 25.

Klinenberg, Eric. 2012b. *Going Solo: The Extraordinary Rise and Surprising Appeal of Living Alone*. New York: Penguin Books.

Klingle, Matthew. 2007. *Emerald City: An Environmental History of Seattle*. New Haven, CT: Yale University Press.

Koebel, C. Theodore, Julia Beamish, and Karen A. Danielsen. 2003. *Evaluation of the HUD Elder Cottage Housing Opportunity (ECHO) Program*. Washington, DC: US Department of Housing and Urban Development.

Kolko, Jed. 2015. "How Suburban Are Big American Cities?" *FiveThirtyEight*, May 21. https://fivethirtyeight.com/features/how-suburban-are-big-american-cities/.

Kolko, Jed. 2018. "America Really Is a Nation of Suburbs." Bloomberg CityLab, November 14. https://www.bloomberg.com/news/articles/2018-11-14/u-s-is-majority-suburban-but-doesn-t-define-suburb.

Kolnick, Kathy A. 2007. "Order before Zoning: Land Use Regulation in Los Angeles, 1880–1915." PhD diss., University of Southern California, Los Angeles.

Kotkin, Joel. 2005. "Hands Off My Yard, Mr. Mayor." Opinion, *Los Angeles Times*, December 13.

Kotkin, Joel. 2021. "To Make Homeownership Affordable Again in California, Rethink the Suburbs." *Los Angeles Times*, September 26.

Kraft, Michael E., and Bruce B. Clary. 1991. "Citizen Participation and the NIMBY Syndrome: Public Response to Radioactive Waste Disposal." *Western Political Quarterly* 44 (2): 299–328.

Kraus, Michael W., Julian M. Rucker, and Jennifer A. Richeson. 2017. "Americans Misperceive Racial Economic Equality." *Proceedings of the National Academy of Sciences* 114 (39): 10324–10331.

Kudler, Adrian Glick. 2015. "Los Angeles Housing Prices Have Shot Up More Than Any Other U.S. City's since 2000." Curbed LA, April 2. https://la.curbed.com/2015/4/2/9974380/los-angeles-housing-prices-have-soared-126-percent-since-2000.

Kudva, Neema. 2009. "The Everyday and the Episodic: The Spatial and Political Impacts of Urban Informality." *Environment and Planning A* 41 (7): 1614–1628.

Kumar, Sunil. 1996. "Landlordism in Third World Urban Low-Income Settlements: A Case for Further Research." *Urban Studies* 33 (4): 753–782.

Kurtz, Stanley. 2020. "Biden and Dems Are Set to Abolish the Suburbs." *National Review*, June 30.

Kutz, Jessica. 2021. "Could Casitas Help Prevent Displacement in the West's Cities?" *High Country News*, July 8.

Kwak, Nancy H. 2015. *A World of Homeowners: American Power and the Politics of Housing Aid*. Chicago: University of Chicago Press.

Kwan, Shawna. 2021. "Hong Kong Homes Ranked World's Least-Affordable, Vancouver Second-Worst" *Vancouver Sun*, February 23.

Kyle, Selena. 2000. "There Goes the Neighborhood: The Failure and Promise of Second Units as a Housing Source for the Midpeninsula." Undergraduate thesis, Stanford University.

Lake, Robert W. 1993. "Planners' Alchemy Transforming NIMBY to YIMBY: Rethinking NIMBY." *Journal of the American Planning Association* 59 (1): 87–93.

LA Más. 2016. "Second Unit Prototype Project: NELA Homeowner Selection." Agenda and meeting packet, May 12.

LA Más. 2021. "The Backyard Homes Project: Homeowner Design Package. Floor Plans+Unit Details."

Lane, Barbara Miller. 2015. *Houses for a New World: Builders and Buyers in American Suburbs, 1945–1965*. Princeton, NJ: Princeton University Press.

Lane, Don. 2001. "AHA! Seeks to Keep Housing Affordable." *Santa Cruz Sentinel*, August 12.

Lang, Robert E. 2005. "Valuing the Suburbs: Why Some 'Improvements' Lower Home Prices." *Opolis* 1 (1): 5–12.

Langston, Jennifer. 2005. "Plan Would Legalize Garage Apartments in Southeast Seattle." *Seattle Post-Intelligencer*, November 21.

Lansner, Jonathan. 2012. "Irvine Homes Built to Keep Families Connected." *Orange County Register*, May 6.

Larsen, Karin. 2018. "Vancouver's New Duplex Rules Explained." *CBC News*, September 20.

Lauster, Nathanael. 2016. *The Death and Life of the Single-Family House: Lessons from Vancouver on Building a Livable City*. Philadelphia: Temple University Press.

Lavine, Amy. 2010. "Urban Renewal and the Story of Berman v. Parker." *Urban Lawyer* 42 (2): 423–475.

Leavitt, Jacqueline. 1996. "Designing Women's Welfare: Home/Work." In *Under One Roof: Issues and Innovation in Shared Housing*, edited by George Hemmens, Charles Hoch, and Jana Carp, 63–74. Albany: State University of New York Press.

Lee, Jessica. 2018. "Triplexes, Max Heights and Parking: What to Expect from a Revised Minneapolis 2040 Plan." *MinnPost*, September 18.

Lee, Youngsung, Bumsoo Lee, and Md Tanvir Hossain Shubho. 2019. "Urban Revival by Millennials? Intraurban Net Migration Patterns of Young Adults, 1980–2010." *Journal of Regional Science* 59 (3): 538–566.

Leeds, Anthony. 1968. "The Significant Variables Determining the Character of Squatter Settlements." *América Latina* 12 (3): 44–86.

Lee-Young, Joanne. 2017. "Vancouver Outstrips Rest of Canadian Cities for Highest Percentage of Low-Income Households." *Vancouver Sun*, September 28.

Lee-Young, Joanne, and Massey Padgham. 2018. "Vancouver Council Votes to Rezone Most Single-Family Areas for Duplexes." *Vancouver Sun*, September 19.

Lefebvre, Henri. 1991. *Critique of Everyday Life*. Translated by John Moore. London: Verso.

Lehnert, Nick. 2013. "Top 15 Design Trends in Single-Family Living." *Builder Magazine*, June 10.

Leinberger, Christopher. 2007. *The Option of Urbanism: Investing in a New American Dream*. Washington, DC: Island Press.

Lemanski, Charlotte. 2009. "Augmented Informality: South Africa's Backyard Dwellings as a By-Product of Formal Housing Policies." *Habitat International* 33 (4): 472–484.

Lemar, Anika Singh. 2019. "The Role of States in Liberalizing Land Use Regulations." *North Carolina Law Review* 97 (2): 293–354.

Lemon, Robert. 2019. *The Taco Truck: How Mexican Street Food Is Transforming the American City*. Urbana: University of Illinois Press.

Lens, Michael C., and Paavo Monkkonen. 2016. "Do Strict Land Use Regulations Make Metropolitan Areas More Segregated by Income?" *Journal of the American Planning Association* 82 (1): 6–21.

Leong, Dora K. 1991. "The Conversion of Garages to Residential Use in Los Angeles County: Impacts and Potential as a Housing Resource." Master's thesis, Massachusetts Institute of Technology.

Lerup, Lars. 1987. *Planned Assaults*. Montreal: Canadian Centre for Architecture.

Levine, Jonathan. 2006. *Zoned Out: Regulation, Markets, and Choices in Transportation and Metropolitan Land-Use*. Washington, DC: Resources for the Future.

Levitt, Zach, and Jess Eng. 2021. "Where America's Developed Areas Are Growing: Way Off into the Horizon." *Washington Post*, August 11.

Lewis, Oscar. 1966. "The Culture of Poverty." *Scientific American* 215 (4): 19–25.

Lewis, W. Arthur. 1954. "Economic Development with Unlimited Supplies of Labour." *Manchester School* 22 (2): 139–191.

Liebig, Phoebe, Teresa Koenig, and Jon Pynoos. 2006. "Zoning, Accessory Dwelling Units, and Family Caregiving." *Journal of Aging and Social Policy* 18 (3–4): 155–172.

Liebmann, George W. 1990. "Suburban Zoning: Two Modest Proposals." *Real Property, Probate, and Trust Journal* 25 (Spring): 1–16.

Lillard, Richard G. 1966. *Eden in Jeopardy, Man's Prodigal Meddling with His Environment: The Southern California Experience.* New York: Alfred A. Knopf.

Lin, Rong-Gong, II. 2018. "Making Single-Family Homes Safer in Quakes." *Los Angeles Times*, January 24.

Lindeke, Bill. 2014. "Minneapolis Begins to See the Benefits of 'Granny Flats.'" *MinnPost*, July 23.

Lindeman, Tracey. 2019. "New Taxes and Higher Density Aren't Fixing Vancouver's Housing problem." CityLab, *The Atlantic*, May 7.

Litchfield, Michael. 2011. *In-laws, Outlaws, and Granny Flats: Your Guide to Turning One House into Two Homes.* Newtown, CT: Taunton Press.

Loewen, James W. 2006. *Sundown Towns: A Hidden Dimension of American Racism.* New York: New Press.

Lofquist, Daphne A. 2012. "Multigenerational Households: 2009–2011." *American Community Survey Briefs*, Washington, DC: United States Census Bureau, October.

Logan, John R., and Harvey Molotch. 1987. *Urban Fortunes: The Political Economy of Place.* Berkeley: University of California Press.

Logan, John R., Weiwei Zhang, and Miao David Chunyu. 2015. "Emergent Ghettos: Black Neighborhoods in New York and Chicago, 1880–1940." *American Journal of Sociology* 120 (4): 1055–1094.

Logan, Tim. 2014. "Hitting L.A. Housing Goal Won't Be Easy." *Los Angeles Times*, November 6.

Lombard, Hamilton. 2015. "As Families Decline, Living Alone Is Now the Most Common Type of Household." StatChat, Demographics Research Group, University of Virginia, Richmond, November 30.

Lomnitz, Larissa A. 1988. "Informal Exchange Networks in Formal Systems: A Theoretical Model." *American Anthropologist* 90 (1): 42–55.

Long Beach Press-Telegram. 2013. "'Aviles Law' Born out of Three Girls' Deaths in Illegally Converted Garage." Editorial, October 24.

Los Angeles City Council. 2009. "Motion 09–2589." Planning and Land Use Committee, October 20.

Los Angeles City Council. 2016. "Resolution." Rules, Elections and Intergovernmental Relations Committee, June 7.

Los Angeles County Economic Development Corporation. 2017. LA County Supervisorial Districts 2017. https://laedc.org/research-analysis/search-reports/download-info/la-county-supervisorial-districts-2017/.

Los Angeles Department of City Planning. 1967. *Concepts for Los Angeles.* Los Angeles: Los Angeles Department of City Planning.

Los Angeles Department of City Planning. 1970. *The Concept for the Los Angeles General Plan*. Los Angeles: Los Angeles Department of City Planning.

Los Angeles Department of City Planning. 1995. *The Citywide General Plan Framework: An Element of the City of Los Angeles General Plan*. Adopted by Los Angeles City Council on December 11, 1996.

Los Angeles Department of City Planning. 2001. *The Citywide General Plan Framework: An Element of the City of Los Angeles General Plan*. Readopted by Los Angeles City Council on August 8, 2001.

Los Angeles Department of City Planning. 2009. "Accessory Dwelling Units (ADUs) Workshops." Bilingual information poster.

Los Angeles Department of City Planning. 2015. "Committee Transmittal: Report Back Relative to Unapproved Dwelling Units." June 4.

Los Angeles Department of City Planning. 2016a. "Recommendation Report to City Planning Commission." Case No. CPC-2016–1245-CA, May 12.

Los Angeles Department of City Planning. 2016b. "Recommendation Report to City Planning Commission." Case No. CPC-2016–4345 CA, December 15.

Los Angeles Department of City Planning. 2018. "Report Back Regarding Hillside Impact of the Proposed Accessory Dwelling Unit Ordinance; Council File: 16–1468." Department of City Planning to PLUM Committee, May 10.

Los Angeles Department of City Planning. 2019. "Quarterly Report: October–December 2018." Housing Progress Report, February, Los Angeles Department of City Planning.

Los Angeles Department of City Planning. 2020. "Housing Progress Dashboard: Accessory Dwelling Unit (ADU) Permit Applications January 2017–June 2020." https://planning.lacity.org/resources/housing-reports.

Los Angeles Department of City Planning. 2021. "Housing Progress Dashboard: Accessory Dwelling Unit (ADU) Permit Applications." https://planning.lacity.org/resources/housing-reports.

Los Angeles Department of City Planning and Los Angeles Housing Department. 2020. "City of Los Angeles: Housing Element 2021–2029." City of Los Angeles.

Los Angeles Housing Department. 1997. "Enforcement and Policy Issues, Strategies and Recommendations by the Garage Housing Task Force Regarding Conversion of Garages into Dwelling Units." Garage Housing Task Force Report, May 12.

Los Angeles Times. 1969. "Zoning Plan Protested as $40,000 Slum." June 3.

Los Angeles Times. 1989. "Los Angeles's Slums: A Growth Industry." July 30 (start of series).

Los Angeles Times. 2014. "Amnesty for Bootlegged Apartments." Editorial, August 24.

Los Angeles Times. 2015. "L.A. Has a Serious Housing Crisis and It's Time for City Officials To Do Something About It." Editorial, January 11.

Los Angeles Times. 2016. "Welcome Back 'Granny Flats.'" Editorial, June 29.

Los Angeles Times. 2018. "Minneapolis' Radical Solution." Editorial, December 19.

Los Angeles Times. 2019. "California Finally Acted on the Housing Crisis; Will 2020 Be Even Better?" Editorial, December 29.

Loukaitou-Sideris, Anastasia, and Vinit Mukhija. 2016. "Responding to Informality through Urban Design Studio Pedagogy." *Journal of Urban Design* 21 (5): 577–595.

Loya, Jose, and Chenoa Flippen. 2021. "The Great Recession and Ethno-racial Disparities in Access to Mortgage Credit." *Social Problems* 68 (4): 1026–1050.

Lynch, Kevin. 1981. *A Theory of Good City Form*. Cambridge, MA: MIT Press.

Lyons, James. 2004. *Selling Seattle: Representing Contemporary Urban America*. New York: Wallflower Press.

Maass, Peter. 1996. "20 Silver Bullets: 7. How to Make Housing Affordable: Let People Subdivide Their Homes." *US News & World Report*, December 22.

Macdonald, Elizabeth. 2008. "The Efficacy of Long-Range Physical Planning: The Case of Vancouver." *Journal of Planning History* 7 (3): 175–213.

Mahler, Sarah. 1995. *American Dreaming: Immigrant Life on the Margins*. Princeton, NJ: Princeton University Press.

Malpezzi, Stephen. 1994. "Getting the Incentives Right. A Reply to Robert-Jan Baken and Jan van der Linden." *Third World Planning Review* 16 (4): 451–466.

Malpezzi, Stephen, and Stephen K. Mayo. 1987. "User Cost and Housing Tenure in Developing Countries." *Journal of Development Economics* 25 (1): 197–220.

Mangin, John. 2014. "The New Exclusionary Zoning." *Stanford Law & Policy Review* 25:91–120.

Mangin, William P. 1963. "Urbanization Case in Peru." *Architectural Design* 33:366–370.

Mangin, William P. 1967. "Latin American Squatter Settlements: A Problem and a Solution." *Latin American Research* 2 (3): 65–98.

Mangin, William P., and John F. C. Turner. 1968. "The Barriada Movement." *Progressive Architecture* 49 (5): 154–162.

Mannix, Andy. 2019. "Judge Dismisses Lawsuit against Minneapolis 2040 Plan." *Star Tribune*, May 3.

Mannix, Andy, and Mukhtar M. Ibrahim. 2018. "Feeling the Heat, Minneapolis Council Members Say 2040 Plan Must Change." *Star Tribune*, July 21.

Mannix, Andy, and Eric Roper. 2018. "10,000 Comments Later, Revised Minneapolis 2040 Plan Seeks Balance." *Star Tribune*, September 28.

Manufactured Housing Institute. 2020. "2020 Manufactured Housing Facts: Industry Overview. Updated May." https://www.manufacturedhousing.org/wp-content/uploads/2020/07/2020-MHI-Quick-Facts-updated-05-2020.pdf.

Manville, Michael, Paavo Monkkonen, and Michael Lens. 2020. "It's Time to End Single-Family Zoning." *Journal of the American Planning Association* 86 (1): 106–112.

Mapes, Jeff. 2019. "What Should Oregon Look Like? The Fight over Single-Family Zoning." *Oregon Public Broadcasting*, February 4.

Mari, Francesca. 2020. "A $60 Billion Housing Grab by Wall Street." *New York Times*, March 4.

Marohn, Charles. 2020. "It's Time to Abolish Single-Family Zoning." *American Conservative*, July 3.

Martin, Hugo. 1997. "Crackdown Urged on Illegal Garage Homes." *Los Angeles Times*, May 28.

Martinez, Alma K. 2013. "City of Los Angeles: Accessory Dwelling Unit Ordinance Analysis." Master's two-week examination, University of California, Los Angeles.

Marx, Leo. 1964. *The Machine in the Garden: Technology and the Pastoral Ideal in America*. New York: Oxford University Press.

Massey, Douglas S., and Nancy A. Denton. 1993. *American Apartheid: Segregation and the Making of the Underclass*. Cambridge, MA: Harvard University Press.

Mathews, Jay. 1988. "Los Angeles Discovers a Severe Housing Crunch." *Washington Post*, December 8.

Mattingly, Marybeth, Sarah Bohn, Caroline Danielson, Sara Kimberlin, and Christopher Wilmer. 2019. *Poverty Declines in California, More Than 1 in 3 Are Poor or Nearly Poor*. Stanford, CA: Stanford Center for Poverty and Inequality.

Mayer, James. 1993a. "City Council Surrenders on 'Granny Flat' Plan in Albina." *Oregonian*, June 9.

Mayer, James. 1993b. "Rental Proposal in Albina Plan Stirs Storm of Protests." *Oregonian*, May 6.

Mayne, Alan. 2018. *Slums: The History of a Global Injustice*. London: Reaktion Books.

McAfee, Ann. 2013. "Tools for Change: CityPlan—Vancouver's Strategic Planning Process." *Built Environment* 39 (4): 438–453.

McCann, Eugene J. 2011. "Urban Policy Mobilities and Global Circuits of Knowledge: Towards a Research Agenda." *Annals of Association of American Geographers* 101 (1): 107–130.

McCarty, Maggie, Libby Perl, and Katie Jones. 2019. *Overview of Federal Housing Assistance Programs and Policy*. Congressional Research Service Report, RL 34591.

McCone Commission. 1965. *Violence in the City: An End or a Beginning? A Report by the Governor's Commission on the Los Angeles Riots*. Los Angeles: California Governor's Commission on the Los Angeles Riots.

McGreevy, Patrick. 1997. "Panel Opposes Garage Housing: Officials Call for New Studies of 'Granny Flat' Issue." *Los Angeles Daily News*, May 28.

McLaughlin, Katy. 2020. "Covid-19 Is Giving the Multigenerational Home Business a Big Boost." *Wall Street Journal*, November 12.

McLaughlin, Ralph. 2015. "Pessimism Is Starting to Creep into the US Housing Market." Personal Finance, *Business Insider*, December 3.

McPhate, Mike. 2017. "California Today: The Rise of the Super Commuter." *New York Times*, August 21.

McWilliams, Carey. 1946. *Southern California Country: An Island on the Land.* New York: Duell, Sloan, and Pearce.

Megeriain, Chris, Liam Dillon, and Eli Stokols. 2020. "Trump Repeals Rules Meant to Integrate Neighborhoods, Further Striking Racial Divisions in Campaign." *Los Angeles Times,* July 23.

Mejia, Brittany. 2015. "Body Found in Rental's Refrigerator." *Los Angeles Times,* December 19.

Mervosh, Sarah. 2018. "Minneapolis, Tackling Housing Crisis and Inequity, Votes to End Single-Family Zoning." *New York Times,* December 13.

Metro. 2000. *The Nature of 2040: The Region's 50-Year Plan for Managing Growth.* Portland: Metro, Oregon.

Metro Vancouver. 2018. "Housing Data Book." Revised April. http://nvcan.ca/wordpress1/wp-content/uploads/2018/09/MV_Housing_Data_Book-marked-up.pdf.

Mies, M. 1982. *The Lace Makers of Narsapur: Indian Housewives Produce for the World Market.* London: Zed Books.

Mims, Charley. 2018. "CPC-2016-4345-CA (CF 16–1468), OPPOSE Accessory Dwelling Units in Hillside Areas." Letter to Los Angeles City Planning Commission from President, Federation of Hillside and Canyon Associations, Inc. November 29.

Minneapolis Community Planning & Economic Development. 2014. "Zoning Code Text Amendment Summary." To Allow Accessory Dwelling Units Citywide, CPED Staff Report to City Planning Commission. November 10, CPC Agenda Item #7.

Minneapolis Community Planning & Economic Development. 2016. "Zoning Code Text Amendment Summary." To Amend Regulations Related to Accessory Dwelling Units, CPED Staff Report to City Planning Commission. August 1, CPC Agenda Item #11.

Minneapolis Community Planning & Economic Development. 2018. "Minneapolis 2040: The City's Draft Comprehensive Plan." Draft, May 2018.

Miraftab, F. 2005. "Informalizing the Means of Reproduction: The Case of Waste Collection Services in Cape Town, South Africa." In *Rethinking Informalization: Precarious Jobs, Poverty and Social Protection,* edited by Lourdes Beneria and Neema Kudva, 148–162. Ithaca, NY: Cornell University e-Publishing Program.

MOAR (More Options for Accessory Residences). 2017. "Beyond Backyard Cottages: 10 Ideas to Address Seattle's Housing Shortage." *Medium,* October 15.

Moffat, David. 2004. "EDRA/Places Awards: Accessory Dwelling Units—Santa Cruz, California." *Places* 16 (3): 26–29.

Mohan, Rakesh. 1994. *Understanding the Developing Metropolis: Lessons from the City Study of Bogota and Cali, Colombia.* Washington, DC: World Bank.

Mollenkopf, John H. 1983. *The Contested City.* Princeton, NJ: Princeton University Press.

Molotch, Harvey. 1976. "The City as a Growth Machine: Toward a Political Economy of Place." *American Journal of Sociology* 82 (2): 309–332.

Molotch, Harvey. 1993. "The Political Economy of Growth Machines." *Journal of Urban Affairs* 15 (1): 29–53.

Money, Luke. 2017. "Costa Mesa Commission Advances Rules That Would Allow 'Granny Flats' in More Areas." *Los Angeles Times*, October 10.

Monkkonen, Paavo. 2011. "The Housing Transition in Mexico: Expanding Access to Housing Finance." *Urban Affairs Review* 47 (5): 672–695.

Montgomery, Charles. 2014. *Happy City: Transforming Our Lives through Urban Design.* New York: Farrar, Straus and Giroux.

Moos, Markus, and Pablo Mendez. 2015. "Suburban Ways of Living and the Geography of Income: How Homeownership, Single-Family Dwellings and Automobile Use Define the Metropolitan Social Space." *Urban Studies* 52 (10): 1864–1882.

Morales, Alfonso. 2010. "Planning and the Self-Organization of Marketplaces." *Journal of Planning Education and Research* 30 (2): 182–197.

Morales, Margaret. 2019a. "Can Washington Pass the Country's Most Ambitious Statewide ADU Reform?" Sightline Institute, January 30. https://www.sightline.org/2019/01/30/can-washington-pass-the-countrys-most-ambitious-statewide-adu-reform/.

Morales, Margaret. 2019b. "Washington's Progressive ADU Bill Died this Week." Sightline Institute, April 18. https://www.sightline.org/2019/04/18/washingtons-progressive-adu-bill-died-this-week/.

Morris, Steven Leigh. 2009. "Invasion of the Granny Flat." *LA Weekly*, December 10.

Morris, William. 2018. "New Minneapolis 2040 Draft Eases Off Density." *Finance & Commerce*, October 1. https://finance-commerce.com/2018/10/new-2040-minneapolis-draft-eases-off-density/.

Morrow, Greg. 2013. "The Homeowner Revolution: Democracy, Land Use and the Los Angeles Slow-Growth Movement, 1965–1992." PhD diss., University of California, Los Angeles.

Moser, Caroline. 1978. "Informal Sector or Petty Commodity Production: Dualism or Dependence in Urban Development?" *World Development* 6 (9/10): 1041–1064.

Moskowitz, Peter. 2017. *How to Kill a City: Gentrification, Inequality, and the Fight for the Neighborhood.* New York: Bold Type Books.

Moudon, Anne Vernez. 1995. "The Subdivision of the Single-Family House in the United States." *Nordic Journal of Architectural Research* 8 (3): 59–78.

Moudon, Anne Vernez, and Chester Sprague. 1982. "More Than One: A Second Life for the Single-Family Property." *Built Environment* 8 (1): 54–59.

Mukhija, Vinit. 2001. "Enabling Slum Redevelopment in Mumbai: Policy Paradox in Practice." *Housing Studies* 16 (6): 791–806.

Mukhija, Vinit. (2003) 2017. *Squatters as Developers? Slum Redevelopment in Mumbai.* New York: Routledge.

Mukhija, Vinit. 2010. "N of One Plus Some: An Alternative Strategy for Conducting Single Case Research." *Journal of Planning Education and Research* 29 (4): 416–426.

Mukhija, Vinit. 2012. "The 1970 Centers Concept Plan for Los Angeles." In *Planning Los Angeles*, edited by David Sloane, 36–44. Chicago: APA Planners Press.

Mukhija, Vinit. 2014. "Outlaw In-Laws: Informal Second Units and the Stealth Reinvention of Single-Family Housing." In *The Informal American City: Beyond Taco Trucks and Day Labor*, edited by Vinit Mukhija and Anastasia Loukaitou-Sideris, 39–57. Cambridge, MA: MIT Press.

Mukhija, Vinit, Dana Cuff, and Kimberly Serrano. 2014. *Backyard Homes and Local Concerns: How Can Local Concerns Be Better Addressed?* Los Angeles: cityLAB, UCLA.

Mukhija, Vinit, and Anastasia Loukaitou-Sideris, eds. 2014. *The Informal American City: Beyond Taco Trucks and Day Labor.* Cambridge, MA: MIT Press.

Mukhija, Vinit, and David Mason. 2013. "Reluctant Cities, Colonias and Municipal Underbounding in the U.S.: Can Cities Be Convinced to Annex Poor Enclaves?" *Urban Studies* 50 (14): 2959–2975.

Mukhija, Vinit, and David Mason. 2015. "Resident-Owned, Informal Mobile Home Communities in Rural California: Lessons from Rancho Don Antonio, Coachella Valley." *Housing Policy Debate* 25 (1): 179–194.

Mukhija, Vinit, and Samantha Meyer. 2019. "Small Homes, Big Impact: Encouraging New Accessory Dwelling Units and Naturally Occurring Affordable Housing." JPMorgan Chase, PRO Neighborhoods program grant evaluation report.

Mukhija, Vinit, and Paavo Monkkonen. 2006. "Federal Colonias Policy in California: Too Broad and Too Narrow." *Housing Policy Debate* 17 (4): 755–780.

Mukhija, Vinit, and Paavo Monkkonen. 2007. "What's in a Name? A Critique of Colonias in the United States." *International Journal of Urban and Regional Research* 31 (2): 475–488.

Mumford, Lewis. 1961. *The City in History*. New York: Harcourt, Brace, and World.

Murdock, Vanessa, and Marj Press. 2018. "Seattle Fine-Tunes Backyard Cottages." *Planning*, October.

Murphy, Kathryn Robertson. 1958. *New Housing and Its Materials 1940–56: Bulletin of the United States Bureau of Labor Statistics, No. 1231*. Washington, DC: US Department of Labor, Bureau of Labor Statistics.

Musso, Juliet, Christopher Weare, Nail Oztas, and William E. Loges. 2006. "Neighborhood Governance Reform and Networks of Community Power in Los Angeles." *American Review of Public Administration* 36 (1): 79–97.

Myers, Dowell, and Elizabeth Gearin. 2001. "Current Preferences and Future Demand for Denser Residential Environments." *Housing Policy Debate* 12 (4): 633–659.

Nameny, Phil. 2015. "ADU Regulations: History of Zoning Code Regulations." Portland, OR: Portland Bureau of Planning and Sustainability, February.

National Association of Realtors. 2019. "Homeownership Part of 'American Dream'; Housing Costs Deterrent for Non-owners." National Association of Realtors, Newsroom. https://www.nar.realtor/newsroom/homeownership-part-of-american-dream-housing-costs-deterrent-for-non-owners.

National Research Council. 2002. *Costs of Sprawl: 2002*. Transportation Research Board. Washington, DC: National Academy Press.

NBC Los Angeles. 2020. "Woman Found Dead in Garage Fire in South LA." January 5.

Neighbors for Lisa Bender. n.d. "About Lisa." http://www.minneapolismn.gov/ward10/about-bender. Accessed September 29, 2021.

Nelson, Arthur C. 2006. "Leadership in a New Era." *Journal of the American Planning Association* 72 (4): 393–407.

Nelson, Arthur C. 2013. *Reshaping Metropolitan America: Development Trends and Opportunities to 2030*. Washington, DC: Island Press.

Newman, Katherine S. 2012. *The Accordion Family: Boomerang Kids, Anxious Parents, and the Private Toll of Global Competition*. Boston: Beacon Press.

New York Times. 2019. "Americans Need More Neighbors." June 15.

Nicolaides, Becky. 2002. *My Blue Heaven: Life and Politics in the Working-Class Suburbs of Los Angeles, 1920–1965*. Chicago: University of Chicago Press.

Njus, Elliot. 2019a. "Bill to Eliminate Single-Family Zoning in Oregon Neighborhoods Passes Final Legislative Hurdle." *Oregonian*, June 30.

Njus, Elliot. 2019b. "Controversial Portland Infill Plan Narrowly Advances." *Oregonian*, March 12.

Norris, Donald F. 2001. "Prospects for Regional Governance under the New Regionalism: Economic Imperatives versus Political Impediments." *Journal of Urban Affairs* 23 (5): 557–571.

North, Douglass C. 1990. *Institutions, Institutional Change and Economic Performance*. New York: Cambridge University Press.

O'Brien, Mike. 2015. "Proposed Changes to Single Family Zones." Mike O'Brien District 6, Seattle.gov, July 17. https://obrien.seattle.gov/2015/07/17/proposed-changes-to-single-family-zones/.

O'Brien, Mike. 2017. "Update on Backyard Cottage Legislation & Next Steps." Mike O'Brien District 6, Seattle.gov, March 27. https://obrien.seattle.gov/2017/03/27/update-on-backyard-cottage-legislation-next-steps/.

O'Connor, Naoibh. 2018. "Duplexes Will Remain an Option in Single-Family Neighborhoods on Trial Basis." *Vancouver Courier*, December 20.

OECD. 2009. *Is Informal Normal? Towards More and Better Jobs in Developing Countries*. Paris: OECD Development Centre.

Office of Governor Gavin Newsom. 2021. "Governor Newsom Signs Historic Legislation to Boost California's Housing Supply and Fight the Housing Crisis." September 16. https://www.gov.ca.gov/2021/09/16/governor-newsom-signs-historic-legislation-to-boost-californias-housing-supply-and-fight-the-housing-crisis/.

Orenstein, Natalie. 2021. "Oakland Takes a Step toward Banning Single-Family Zoning." *The Oaklandside*, March 17.

Oreskes, Benjamin. 2021a. "Councilman Kevin de León Wants 25,000 Housing Units for Homeless by 2025." *Los Angeles Times*, January 12.

Oreskes, Benjamin. 2021b. "Program to Buy Hotels for Homeless People Could Get Another Influx of Cash." *Los Angeles Times*, January 8.

Orfield, Myron. 1997. *Metropolitics: A Regional Agenda for Community and Stability.* Washington, DC: Brookings Institution; Cambridge, MA: Lincoln Institute for Land Policy.

Ostrom, Vincent, Charles M. Tiebout, and Robert Warren. 1961. "The Organization of Government in Metropolitan Areas: A Theoretical Inquiry." *American Political Science Review* 55 (4): 831–842.

Owen, David. 2009. *Green Metropolis: Why Living Smaller, Living Closer, and Driving Less Are the Keys to Sustainability.* New York: Riverhead Books.

Owens, Kathryn E., Sumila Gulyani, and Andrea Rizvi. 2018. "Success When We Deemed It Failure? Revisiting Sites and Services Projects in Mumbai and Chennai 20 Years Later." *World Development* 106 (June): 260–272.

Ozawa, Connie P. 2004. *The Portland Edge: Challenges and Successes in Growing Communities.* Washington, DC: Island Press.

Parolek, Daniel. 2012. "Missing Middle Housing: Responding to the Demand for Walkable Urban." *Opticos Design*, April 6. https://opticosdesign.com/blog/missing-middle-housing-responding-to-the-demand-for-walkable-urban-living-2.

Parolek, Daniel. 2020. *Missing Middle Housing: Thinking Big and Building Small to Respond to Today's Housing Crisis.* Washington, DC: Island Press.

Payne, Geoffrey. 1989. *Informal Housing and Land Subdivisions in Third World Cities: A Review of the Literature.* Oxford: Center for Development and Environmental Planning.

Payne, Geoffrey. 2001a. "Lowering the Ladder: Regulatory Frameworks for Sustainable Development." *Development in Practice* 11 (2–3): 308–318.

Payne, Geoffrey. 2001b. "Urban Land Tenure Policy Options: Titles or Rights?" *Habitat International* 25 (3): 415–429.

Payne, Geoffrey, Alain Durand-Lasserve, and Carole Rakodi. 2009. "The Limits of Land Titling and Home Ownership." *Environment and Urbanization* 21 (2): 443–462.

Peattie, Lisa. 1968. *The View from the Barrio.* Ann Arbor: University of Michigan Press.

Peattie, Lisa. 1979. "Housing Policy in Developing Countries: Two Puzzles." *World Development* 7 (11–12): 1017–1022.

Peattie, Lisa. 1982. "What Is to Be Done with the Informal Sector? A Case Study of Shoe Manufacturers in Colombia." In *Towards a Political Economy of Urbanization in Third World Countries*, edited by Helen Safa, 208–232. New Delhi: Oxford University.

Peattie, Lisa. 1987. "An Idea in Good Currency and How It Grew: The Informal Sector." *World Development* 15 (7): 147–158.

Peattie, Lisa. 1994. "An Argument for Slums." *Journal of Planning Education and Research* 13 (2): 136–143.

Pendall, Rolf. 1999. "Opposition to Housing: NIMBY and Beyond." *Urban Affairs Review* 35 (1): 112–136.

Pendall, Rolf. 2000. "Local Land Use Regulation and the Chain of Exclusion." *Journal of the American Planning Association* 66 (2): 125–142.

Pendall, Rolf, Lesley Freiman, Dowell Myers, and Selma Hepp. 2012. *Demographic Challenges and Opportunities for US Housing Markets*. Economic Policy Program. Washington, DC: Bipartisan Policy Center.

Penner, Derrick, and Kelly Sinoski. 2013. "How to Be a Landlord in Metro Vancouver." *Vancouver Sun*, October 4.

Perin, Constance. 1977. *Everything in Its Place: Social Order and Land Use in America*. Princeton, NJ: Princeton University Press.

Perlman, Janice. 1976. *The Myth of Marginality: Urban Poverty and Politics in Rio De Janeiro*. Berkeley: University of California Press.

Peterson, Kol. 2018. *Backdoor Revolution: The Definitive Guide to ADU Development*. Portland, OR: Accessory Dwelling Strategies.

Peterson, M. Nils, Tarla Peterson, and Jianguo Liu. 2013. *The Housing Bomb: Why Our Addiction to Houses Is Destroying the Environment and Threatening Our Society*. Baltimore: Johns Hopkins University Press.

Petzel, Andrea. 2008. "Backyard Cottages: Estimating City-Wide Backyard Cottage Unit Production." Memorandum, December 15, City of Seattle Department of Planning and Development.

Pew Research Center. 2014. *Political Polarization in the American Public*. https://www.pewresearch.org/politics/2014/06/12/political-polarization-in-the-american-public/.

Piore, Michael J., and Charles F. Sabel. 1984. *The Second Industrial Divide*. New York: Basic Books.

Pollak, Patricia B. 1994. "Rethinking Zoning to Accommodate the Elderly in Single Family Housing." *Journal of the American Planning Association* 60 (4): 521–539.

Portes, Alejandro. 1971. "The Urban Slum in Chile: Types and Correlates." *Land Economics* 47 (3): 235–248.

Portes, Alejandro, Manuel Castells, and Lauren Benton, eds. 1989. *The Informal Economy: Studies in Advanced and Less Developed Countries*. Baltimore: Johns Hopkins University Press.

Portes, Alejandro, and Saskia Sassen-Koob. 1987. "Making It Underground: Comparative Material on the Informal Sector in Western Market Economies." *American Journal of Sociology* 93 (1): 30–61.

Portland Bureau of Development Services. 2016. "Program Guide: Accessory Dwelling Units." June 22.

Portland for Everyone. n.d. "The Future of Oregon's Biggest City Depends on You." 1000 Friends of Oregon. https://friends.org/about-us/programs/P4E. Accessed, February 28, 2022.

Powell, Walter W. 1990. "Neither Market Nor Hierarchy: Network Forms of Organization." *Research in Organizational Behavior* 12:295–336.

Pratt Center for Community Development and Chhaya Community Development Corporation. 2008. *New York's Housing Underground: A Refuge and Resource*. New York: Pratt Center and Chhaya.

Primack, Mark. 2014. "Santa Cruz Planners Wrong on Rentals." Opinion. *Santa Cruz Sentinel*, April 26.

Primack, Mark. 2019. "Single Family Zoning Is Our Own Worst Enemy." Opinion. *Santa Cruz Sentinel*, June 24.

Punter, John. 2003. *The Vancouver Achievement: Urban Planning and Design*. Seattle: University of Washington Press.

Purcell, Mark. 2000. "The Decline of the Political Consensus for Urban Growth: Evidence from Los Angeles." *Journal of Urban Affairs* 22 (1): 85–100.

Purcell, Mark. 2001. "Neighborhood Activism among Homeowners as a Politics of Space." *Professional Geographer* 53 (2): 178–194.

Purcell, Mark. 2008. *Recapturing Democracy: Neoliberalization and the Struggle for Alternative Urban Futures*. New York: Routledge.

Queally, James. 2019. "Ghost Ship Verdict: Jury Acquits One Defendant, Deadlocks on Second in Warehouse Fire That Killed 36." *Los Angeles Times*, September 5.

Rajan, Raghuram. 2019. *The Third Pillar: How Markets and the State Leave the Community Behind*. New York: Penguin.

Rakowski, Cathy. 1994. "Convergence and Divergence in the Informal Sector Debate: A Focus on Latin America, 1984–92." *World Development* 22 (4): 501–516.

Ramirez, Hernan, and Pierrette Hondagneu-Sotelo. 2009. "Mexican Immigrant Gardeners in Los Angeles: Entrepreneurs or Exploited Workers?" *Social Problems* 56 (1): 70–88.

Ramsey-Musolf, Darrel. 2018. "Accessory Dwelling Units as Low-Income Housing: California's Faustian Bargain." *Urban Science* 2 (3): 89. https://doi.org/10.3390/urbansci2030089.

Ravani, Sarah. 2021. "Berkeley Vows to End Single-Family Zoning by the End of 2022." *San Francisco Chronicle*, February 24.

Ray, Herbert. 1970. "Planners Put Forth 50-Year Program for City of 5 Million." December 10.

Razzaz, Omar. 1992. "Group Non-compliance: A Strategy for Transforming Property Relations—the Case of Jordan." *International Journal of Urban and Regional Research* 16 (3): 408–419.

Razzaz, Omar. 1993. "Examining Property Rights and Investment in Informal Settlements: The Case of Jordan." *Land Economics* 69 (4): 341–355.

Real Estate Research Corporation. 1974. *The Costs of Sprawl: Environmental and Economic Costs of Alternative Residential Development Patterns at the Urban Fringe*. Vol. 1:

REFERENCES

Executive Summary; Vol. 2: Detailed Cost Analysis; Vol. 3: Literature Review and Bibliography. Washington, DC: US Government Printing Office.

Reeves, Richard V. 2017. *Dream Hoarders: How the American Upper Middle Class Is Leaving Everyone Else in the Dust, Why That Is a Problem, and What to Do about It.* Washington, DC: Brookings Institution Press.

Reich, Robert B. 1991. "Secession of the Successful." *New York Times*, January 20.

Resnikoff, Ned. 2021. "It's Hard to Have Faith in a State That Can't Even House Its People." *New York Times*, July 26.

Reyes, Emily Alpert. 2015. "Blaze Displaces 21 People from 1,000-Square-Foot Pacoima Home." *Los Angeles Times*, January 3.

Reyes, Emily Alpert. 2016a. "'Granny Flats' Left in Legal limbo amid City Hall Debate." *Los Angeles Times*, August 28.

Reyes, Emily Alpert. 2016b. "LA Lawmakers Plan to Grandfather in Hundreds of Granny Flats." *Los Angeles Times*, August 31.

Reyes, Emily Alpert. 2017. "LA Approves a 'Path to Legalization' for Some Bootlegged Apartments." *Los Angeles Times*, May 10.

Reyes, Emily Alpert, and Tim Logan. 2014. "Some Trade Safety for Affordable Rent." *Los Angeles Times*, April 7.

Reyes, Emily Alpert, and Ryan Menezes. 2014. "LA and Orange Counties Are an Epicenter of Overcrowded Housing." *Los Angeles Times*, March 7.

Rocha, Veronica. 2017. "L.A. Teen Dies after Fire Guts Converted Garage He Shared with Three People." *Los Angeles Times*, June 27.

Rodriguez-Pose, Andrés, and Michael Storper. 2022 "Dodging the Burden of Proof: A Reply to Manville, Lens and Mönkkönen." *Urban Studies*, 59 (1): 59–74.

Rohe, William, and Harry Watson, eds. 2007. *Chasing the American Dream: New Perspectives on Affordable Homeownership*. Ithaca, NY: Cornell University Press.

Rojas, James T. 1993. "The Enacted Environment of East Los Angeles." *Places* 8 (3): 42–53.

Rojas, James T. 2014. "Latino Vernacular: Latino Spatial and Cultural Values Transform the American Single-Family House and Street." *Northern News*, November 1, 29–30.

Roland, Gérard. 2004. "Understanding Institutional Change: Fast-Moving and Slow-Moving Institutions." *Studies in Comparative International Development* 38 (4): 109–131.

Roper, Eric. 2014. "'Granny Flats' up for Debate in Minneapolis." *Star Tribune*, June 15.

Roper, Eric. 2019. "Minneapolis' 2040 Plan Wins Met Council Approval." *Star Tribune*, September 25.

Rosen, Andy. 2021. "For Years, In-law Apartments Have Been Discouraged in Greater Boston. The Housing Shortage Is Changing That." *Boston Globe*, July 11.

Rosenberg, Mike. 2018. "Seattle's Housing Crunch Could Be Eased by Changes to Single-Family Zoning, City Report Says." *Seattle Times*, December 3.

Rostow, Walt Whitman. 1960. *The Stages of Economic Growth: A Non-Communist Manifesto*. Cambridge: Cambridge University Press.

Rothstein, Richard. 2017. *Color of Law: A Forgotten History of How Our Government Segregated America*. New York: Liveright.

Rothwell, Jonathan T., and Douglas S. Massey. 2010. "Density Zoning and Class Segregation in U.S. Metropolitan Areas." *Social Science Quarterly* 91 (5): 1123–1143.

Rowe, Peter G. 1991. *Making a Middle Landscape*. Cambridge, MA: MIT Press.

Roy, Ananya. 2005. "Urban Informality: Toward an Epistemology of Planning." *Journal of American Planning Association* 71 (2): 147–158.

Roy, Ananya. 2009a. "Strangely Familiar: Planning and the Worlds of Insurgence and Informality." *Planning Theory* 8 (1): 7–11.

Roy, Ananya. 2009b. "Why India Cannot Plan Its Cities: Informality, Insurgence, and the Idiom of Urbanization." *Planning Theory* 8 (1): 76–87.

Roy, Ananya. 2011. "Slumdog Cities: Rethinking Subaltern Urbanism." *International Journal of Urban and Regional Research* 35 (2): 223–238.

Rudel, Thomas K. 1984. "Household Change, Accessory Apartments, and Low Income Housing in Suburbs." *Professional Geographer* 36 (2): 174–181.

Rugh, Jacob S., and Douglas S. Massey. 2014. "Segregation in Post-Civil Rights America: Stalled Integration or End of the Segregated Century." *Du Bois Review: Social Science Research on Race* 11 (2): 205–232.

Rusk, David. 1999. *Inside Game/Outside Game: Winning Strategies for Saving Urban America*. Washington, DC: Brookings Institution.

Sage Computing. 2008. "Accessory Dwelling Units: Case Study." Prepared by Sage Computing, Reston, VA, for the US Department of Housing and Urban Development, Office of Policy Development and Research.

Saiz, Albert. 2010. "The Geographic Determinants of Housing Supply." *Quarterly Journal of Economics* 125 (3): 1253–1296.

Saltzman, Jonathan. 2014. "City No Match for Scofflaw Landlords." *Boston Globe*, May 5.

Sampson, Robert J. 2012. *Great American City: Chicago and the Enduring Neighborhood Effect*. Chicago: University of Chicago Press.

San Francisco Planning Department. 2021. *2020 San Francisco Housing Inventory*. San Francisco Planning Department. https://sfplanning.org/sites/default/files/documents/reports/2020_Housing_Inventory.pdf.

Santa Barbara News Press. 2002. "Granny Flats as Housing Rx." August 26.

Santos, Boaventura De Sousa. 1977. "The Law of the Oppressed: The Construction and Reproduction of Legality in Pasargada." *Law & Society Review* 12 (1): 5–126.

Sanyal, Bishwapriya. 1987. "Problems of Cost-Recovery in Development Projects: Experience of the Lusaka Squatter Upgrading and Site/Service Project." *Urban Studies* 24 (4): 285–295.

Sanyal, Bishwapriya. 1988. "The Urban Informal Sector Revisited: Some Notes on the Relevance of the Concept in the 1980s." *Third World Planning Review* 10 (1): 65–83.

Sanyal, Bishwapriya. 1996. "Intentions and Outcome: Formalization and Its Consequences." *Regional Development Dialogue* 17 (1): 161–178.

Sanyal, Bishwapriya. 2008. "What Is New in Planning?" *International Planning Studies* 13 (2): 151–160.

Sarra, Janis, and Cheryl L. Wade. 2020. *Predatory Lending and the Destruction of the African-American Dream*. New York: Cambridge University Press.

Sassen, Saskia. 1991. *The Global City: New York, Tokyo, London*. Princeton, NJ: Princeton University Press.

Sassen, Saskia. 1997. "Informalization in Advanced Market Economies." Issues in Development Discussion Paper 20, International Labour Organization, Geneva.

Sassen-Koob, Saskia. 1989. "New York City's Informal Economy." In *The Informal Economy: Studies in Advanced and Less Developed Countries*, edited by Alejandro Portes, Manuel Castells, and Lauren A. Benton, 60–77. Baltimore: Johns Hopkins University Press.

Saunders, Doug. 2012. *Arrival City: How the Largest Migration in History Is Reshaping Our World*. New York: Pantheon Books.

Scally, Corianne Payton, and J. Rosie Tighe. 2015. "Democracy in Action? NIMBY as Impediment to Equitable Affordable Housing Siting." *Housing Studies* 30 (5): 749–769.

Schively, Carissa. 2007. "Understanding the NIMBY and LULU Phenomena: Reassessing Our Knowledge Base and Informing Future Research." *Journal of Planning Education and Research* 21 (3): 255–266.

Schleicher, David. 2013. "City Unplanning." *Yale Law Journal* 122:1670–1737.

Schneider, Benjamin. 2019. "Liberal America's Single-Family Hypocrisy." *The Nation*, May 8.

Schoenauer, Norbert. 2003. *6,000 Years of Housing*. New York: W.W. Norton.

Schuetz, Jenny. 2018. "Minneapolis 2040: The Most Wonderful Plan of the Year." *The Avenue*, Brookings Institution, December 12. https://www.brookings.edu/blog/the-avenue/2018/12/12/minneapolis-2040-the-most-wonderful-plan-of-the-year/.

Schuetz, Jenny. 2019. "Campaign 2020: How to Fix America's Housing Policies." *The Avenue*, Brookings Institution, September 10. https://www.brookings.edu/blog/the-avenue/2019/09/10/campaign-2020-how-to-fix-americas-housing-policies/.

Scott, James C. 1998. *Seeing Like a State: How Certain Schemes to Improve the Human Condition Have Failed*. New Haven, CT: Yale University Press.

Seattle Department of Planning and Development. 2009. "Backyard Cottages Staff Report." March (Attachment to City Ordinance 123141, adopted November 4, 2009).

Seattle Department of Planning and Development. 2015. "Removing Barriers to Backyard Cottages." Report and Analysis, October.

Seattle Department of Planning and Development. 2016. "Removing Barriers to Backyard Cottages & Accessory Dwelling Units." Director's Report, Prepared for Seattle City Council, May.

Seattle HALA. 2015. "Final Advisory Committee Recommendations to Mayor Edward B. Murray and the Seattle City Council." Housing Affordability and Livability Agenda, July 13.

Seattle Times Editorial Board. 2018. "Don't Upzone Seattle's Neighborhoods." Editorial. *Seattle Times*, June 29.

Semuels, Alana. 2016. "The Racist History of Portland, the Whitest City in America." *Atlantic*, July 22.

Serna, Joseph. 2015. "Early Morning Fire Races through 3 El Monte Homes, Displaces 11." *Los Angeles Times*, January 28.

Serna, Joseph. 2016. "Two Bodies Recovered in Lake Balboa Garage Fire." *Los Angeles Times*, February 13.

Shashaty, Andre, ed. 2014. *Rebuilding a Dream: America's New Urban Crisis, the Housing Cost Explosion, and How We Can Reinvent the American Dream for All*. San Rafael, CA: Partnership for Sustainable Communities.

Shaw, Randy. 2018. *Generation Priced Out*. Berkeley: University of California Press.

Sherman, Roger, ed. 1995. *Re: American Dream—Six Urban Housing Prototypes for Los Angeles*. New York: Princeton Architectural Press.

Shkuda, Aaron. 2015. "The Artist as Developer and Advocate: Real Estate and Public Policy in SoHo, New York." *Journal of Urban History* 41 (6): 999–1016.

Short, Aaron. 2019. "TOD-Da! Oregon Blocks Single-Family Zoning." *Streetsblog USA*, July 2. https://usa.streetsblog.org/2019/07/02/tod-da-oregon-blocks-single-family-zoning/.

Shoup, Donald. 2005. *The High Cost of Free Parking*. Chicago: American Planning Association.

Siegan, Bernard H. 1972. *Land Use without Zoning*. Lexington, MA: Lexington Books.

Silver, Christopher. 1997. "The Racial Origins of Zoning in America." In *Urban Planning and the African American Community: In the Shadows*, edited by June Manning Thomas and Marsha Ritzdorf, 23–42. Thousand Oaks, CA: Sage Publications.

Simon, Richard. 1985. "Bernson Backs Off Effort to Evict Tenants of Project." *Los Angeles Times*, October 2.

Sirmans, Stacy, David Macpherson, and Emily Zietz. 2005. "The Composition of Hedonic Pricing Models." *Journal of Real Estate Literature* 13 (1): 1–44.

Slaev, Aleksandar D., and Sonia A. Hirt. 2016. "Informal Settlements and Public Policies in Bulgaria during the Post-Socialist Period." In *Learning from the Slums for the Development of Emerging Cities*, edited by Jean-Claude Bolay, Jérôme Chenal, and Yves Pedrazzini, 189–200. GeoJournal Library, Volume 119, Cham, Switzerland: Springer.

Smets, P. 1997. "Private Housing Finance in India: Reaching Down-Market?" *Habitat International* 21 (1): 1–15.

Smith, Darby Minow. 2015. "The 10 U.S. Cities That Are Gentrifying the Fastest." *Grist*, February 6. https://grist.org/cities/the-10-u-s-cities-that-are-gentrifying-the-fastest/.

Smith, Doug. 2019. "Poor Neighborhood Endures Worst LAX Noise but Is Left Out of Home Soundproofing Program." *Los Angeles Times*, May 23.

Smith, Erika D. 2021. "'We May Lose This.' Despair over Gentrification Reaches New Depths in South L.A." *Los Angeles Times*, September 24.

Smith, Stanley K., Stefan Rayer, and Eleanor A. Smith. 2008. "Aging and Disability: Implications for the Housing Industry and Housing Policy in the United States." *Journal of the American Planning Association* 74 (3): 289–306.

Spevak, Eli, and Melissa Stanton. 2019. *The ABCs of ADUs: A Guide to Accessory Dwelling Units and How They Expand Housing Options for People of All Ages*. Washington, DC: AARP.

Spivak, Jeffrey. 2012. "Making Room for Mom and Dad." *Planning*, October, 8–13.

SPUR. 2001. *Secondary Units: A Painless Way to Increase the Supply of Housing*. San Francisco: San Francisco Planning and Urban Research Association.

Stanger-Ross, Jordan. 2008. "Municipal Colonialism in Vancouver: City Planning and the Conflict over Indian Reserves, 1928–1950s." *Canadian Historical Review* 89 (4): 541–580.

Statistics Canada. 2016. "Census Profile, 2016 Census: Vancouver, British Columbia, and Greater Vancouver, British Columbia." https://www12.statcan.gc.ca/census-recensement/2016/dp-pd/prof/details/page.cfm?Lang=E&Geo1=CSD&Code1=5915022&Geo2=CD&Code2=5915&SearchText=vancouver&SearchType=Begins&SearchPR=01&B1=All&TABID=1&type=0.

Stein, Clarence. 1951. *Toward New Towns for America*. Liverpool: Liverpool University Press.

Stewart, Nikita, Ryan Christopher Jones, Sergio Peçanha, Jeffrey Furticella, and Josh Williams. 2019. "Underground Lives: The Sunless World of Immigrants in Queens." *New York Times*, October 23.

Storper, Michael, Thomas Kemeny, Naji Makarem, and Taner Osman. 2015. *The Rise and Fall of Urban Economies: Lessons from San Francisco and Los Angeles*. Stanford, CA: Stanford University Press.

Strassmann, W. Paul. 1984. "The Timing of Urban Infrastructure and Housing Improvements by Owner Occupants." *World Development* 12 (7): 743–753.

Surowiecki, James. 2014. "Real Estate Goes Global." Financial Page, *New Yorker*, May 26.

Suttor, Greg. 2017. "Basement Suites: Demand, Supply, Space, and Technology." *Canadian Geographer* 61 (4): 483–492.

Tapp, Renee. 2021. "Introducing the YIMBYs: Renters, Housing, and Supply-Side Politics in Los Angeles." *Environment & Planning C* 39 (7): 1511–1528.

Taylor, Brian D. 2000. "When Finance Leads Planning: Urban Planning, Highway Planning, Metropolitan Freeways in California." *Journal of Planning Education and Research* 20 (2): 196–214.

Temin, Peter. 2017. *The Vanishing Middle Class: Prejudice and Power in a Dual Economy*. Cambridge, MA: MIT Press.

Temko, Allan. 1968. "Reshaping Super-City: The Problem of Los Angeles." *Lotus* 5:62–69.

Terrazas, Aaron. 2018. "Homeownership Aspirations: The Enduring and Evolving American Dream." Zillow Research, July 6. https://www.zillow.com/research/homeownership-american-dream-20476/.

Terriss, Kenneth. 2008. "Stucco." In *Vancouver Matters*, edited by James Eidse, Mari Fujita, Joey Giaimo, Lori Kiessling, and Christa Min, 115-130. Vancouver: Blueimprint.

Theodore, Nik. 2020. "Regulating Informality: Worker Centers and Collective Action in Day-Labor Markets." *Growth and Change* 51 (1): 144–160.

Theodore, Nik, Abel Valenzuela Jr., and Edwin Meléndez. 2009. "Worker Centers: Defending Labor Standards for Migrant Workers in the Informal Economy." *International Journal of Manpower* 30 (5): 422–436.

Thomsett, Dave. n.d. "Secondary Suites Neighbourhood Review Program." Vancouver.

Tian, Li. 2008. "The *Chengzhongcun* Land Market in China: Boon or Bane?—a Perspective on Property Rights." *International Journal of Urban and Regional Research* 32 (2): 282–304.

Tiebout, Charles M. 1956. "A Pure Theory of Local Expenditures." *Journal of Political Economy* 64 (5): 416–424.

Tighe, J. Rosie. 2012. "How Race and Class Stereotyping Shapes Attitudes toward Affordable Housing." *Housing Studies* 27 (7): 962–983.

Todaro, Michael. 1969. "A Model of Labor Migration and Urban Unemployment in Less Developed Countries." *American Economic Review* 59 (1): 138–148.

Toll, Seymour I. 1969. *Zoned America*. New York: Grossman.

Tomalty, Ray, and Alan Mallach. 2016. *America's Urban Future: Lessons from North of the Border*. Washington, DC: Island Press.

Trautman, Sarah. 2018. "Fourplex City: Local Politics and Neighborhood Values." *Minnesota Law Review* 103. https://minnesotalawreview.org/2018/11/25/fourplex-city/.

Trickey, Erick. 2019. "How Minneapolis Freed Itself from the Stranglehold of Single-Family Homes." *Politico*, July 11.

Trounstine, Jessica. 2018. *Segregation by Design: Local Politics and Inequality in American Cities*. New York: Cambridge University Press.

Trumm, Doug. 2017. "Homeowner Group Coalition Sues to Block MHA Rezone." *The Urbanist*, November 28. https://www.theurbanist.org/2017/11/28/homeowner-group-coalition-sues-block-mha-rezone/.

Trumm, Doug. 2018. "Mandatory Housing Affordability Rules the Day in Hearing Examiner Decision." The Urbanist, November 27. https://www.theurbanist.org/2018/11/27/mandatory-housing-affordability-rules-the-day-in-hearing-examiner-decision/.

Trumm, Doug. 2020. "Portland Passes Sweeping Zoning Reform." *The Urbanist*, August 12. https://www.theurbanist.org/2020/08/12/portland-passes-sweeping-zoning-reform/.

Trump, Donald J., and Ben Carson. 2020. "We'll Protect America's Suburbs." Opinion. *Wall Street Journal*, August 16.

Tso, Sharon M. 2016. "Report of the Chief Legislative Analyst: Resolution (Martinez-Buscaino) to OPPOSE SB 1069 (Wieckowski), Which Would Replace the Term 'Second Unit' with 'Accessory Dwelling Units (ADU)' and Prescribes the Maximum Standards of an ADU." Council File No. 15–0002-S189; Assignment No. 16-06-0551, City of Los Angeles, July 20.

Turner, John F. C. 1967. "Barriers and Channels for Housing Development in Modernizing Countries." *Journal of the American Institute of Planners* 33 (3): 167–181.

Turner, John F. C. 1968. "Housing Priorities, Settlement Patterns and Urban Development in Modernizing Countries." *Journal of the American Institute of Planners* 34 (6): 354–363.

Turner, John F. C. 1972. "Housing as a Verb." In *Freedom to Build: Dweller Control of the Housing Process*, edited by John F. C. Turner and Robert Fichter, 148–175. New York: Macmillan.

Turner, John F. C. 1977. *Housing by People: Towards Autonomy in Building Environments*. New York: Pantheon Books.

Turner, John F. C. 1982. "Issues in Self-Help and Self-Managed Housing." In *Self-Help Housing: A Critique*, edited by Peter M. Ward, 99–114. London: Mansell.

Turner, John F. C., and Robert Fichter, eds. 1972. *Freedom to Build: Dweller Control of the Housing Process*. New York: Macmillan.

UN-Habitat. 2003. *The Challenge of Slums: Global Report on Human Settlements 2003*. Sterling, VA: Earthscan.

UN Millennium Project. 2005. *A Home in the City*. Lead authors: Pietro Garau, Elliot D. Sclar and Gabriella Y. Carolini; Task Force on Improving the Lives of Slum Dwellers. Sterling, VA: Earthscan.

Urban Land Institute. 2019. *Attainable Housing: Challenges, Perceptions, and Solutions*. Washington, DC: Urban Land Institute.

US Census Bureau. 1950. "Census of Population: 1950 Volume I Number of Inhabitants." https://www.census.gov/library/publications/1952/dec/population-vol-01.html.

US Census Bureau. 2010. "2010 Census Summary File 1. 2010 Census of Population and Housing." https://www2.census.gov/programs-surveys/decennial/2010/technical-documentation/complete-tech-docs/summary-file/sf1.pdf.

US Census Bureau. 2013a. "American Community Survey (2013) 1-Year Estimates." Table S2504—Physical Housing Characteristics for Occupied Housing Units. https://data.census.gov/cedsci/table?text=Table%20S2504&g=1600000US0455000,0644000,0666000,0668000,1714000,3651000,4260000,4819000,4835000,4865000&y=2013&tid=ACSST1Y2013.S2504.

US Census Bureau. 2013b. "American Housing Survey (2013) National Summary Tables." https://www.census.gov/programs-surveys/ahs/data/2013/ahs-2013-summary-tables/national-summary-report-and-tables---ahs-2013.html.

US Census Bureau. 2014. "American Community Survey (2014) 1-Year Estimates." Table S1101. Households and Families (Householder Living Alone). https://data

.census.gov/cedsci/table?t=Household%20Size%20and%20Type&y=2014&tid=ACSST1Y2014.S1101.

US Census Bureau. 2021a. "Annual Characteristics of New Housing. Square Feet of Floor Area in New Single-Family Houses Completed." https://www.census.gov/construction/chars/.

US Census Bureau. 2021b. "Building Permits Survey: New Privately Owned Housing Units Authorized by Building Permits in Permit-Issuing Places." https://www.census.gov/construction/bps/.

US Census Bureau. 2021c. "Table HH-4. Households by Size: 1960 to Present." https://www.census.gov/data/tables/time-series/demo/families/households.html.

US Department of Commerce. 2015. "2015 Characteristics of New Housing." Economics and statistics administration, US Census Bureau. https://www.census.gov/construction/chars/pdf/c25ann2015.pdf.

Valdez, Roger. 2018. "The Mandatory Housing Affordability Program Will Worsen Seattle's Housing Crisis." *Seattle Times*, December 6.

Valenzuela, Abel, Jr. 2003. "Day Labor Work." *Annual Review of Sociology* 29 (1): 307–333.

Valenzuela, Abel, Jr. 2014. "Regulating Day Labor: Worker Centers and Organizing in the Informal Economy." In *The Informal American City: Beyond Taco Trucks and Day Labor*, edited by Vinit Mukhija and Anastasia Loukaitou-Sideris, 261–276. Cambridge, MA: MIT Press.

Valenzuela, Abel, Jr., Nik Theodore, Edwin Melendez, and Ana L. Gonzalez. 2006. *On the Corner: Day Labor in the United States*. Los Angeles: UCLA Center for the Study of Urban Poverty.

Vallianatos, Mark. 2018. "Undo LA's Racist Zoning Legacy." Opinion. *Los Angeles Times*, April 2.

Vancouver City Council. 1961a. "Meeting Minutes." Vol. 75, January 18/24.

Vancouver City Council. 1961b. "Meeting Minutes." Vol. 76, February 13.

Vancouver City Council. 1976. "Meeting Minutes." Vol. 122, February 5.

Vancouver City Council. 1977. "Meeting Minutes." Vol. 125, February 22.

Vancouver City Council. 1987a. "Meeting Minutes." Vol. 179, July 17.

Vancouver City Council. 1987b. "Meeting Minutes." Vol. 180, October 10.

Vancouver City Council. 2004. "Special Council Meeting Minutes." March 1 and 2.

Vancouver City Council. 2017. "Motion on Notice: Reporting Data on Secondary Suites," December 12. https://council.vancouver.ca/20171212/documents/motionb3.pdf.

Varady, David. 1988. "Factors Affecting Middle-Income Elderly Interest in Accessory Apartment Conversion." *Journal of Architectural and Planning Research* 5 (1): 81–87.

Varley, Ann. 1985. "Urbanization and Agrarian Law: The Case of Mexico City." *Bulletin of Latin American Research* 4 (1): 1–16.

Varley, Ann. 1987. "The Relationship between Tenure Legalization and Housing Improvements: Evidence from Mexico." *Development and Change* 18 (3): 463–481.

Varley, Ann. 2002. "Private or Public: Debating the Meaning of Tenure Legalization." *International Journal of Urban and Regional Research* 26 (3): 449–461.

Varley, Ann. 2007. "Gender and Property Formalization: Conventional and Alternative Approaches." *World Development* 35 (10): 1739–1753.

Varley, Ann. 2013. "Postcolonialising Informality?" *Environment and Planning D: Society and Space* 31 (1): 4–22.

Venkatesh, Sudhir Alladi. 2006. *Off the Books: The Underground Economy of the Urban Poor*. Cambridge, MA: Harvard University Press.

Venkatesh, Sudhir Alladi. 2013. *Floating City: A Rogue Sociologist Lost and Found in New York's Underground Economy*. New York: Penguin Press.

Ventry, Dennis J. 2010. "The Accidental Deduction: A History and Critique of the Tax Subsidy for Mortgage Interest." *Law and Contemporary Problems* 73 (1): 233–284.

Waldie, D. J. 1996. *Holy Land: A Suburban Memoir*. New York: W. W. Norton.

Ward, Peter M., ed. 1982. *Self-Help Housing: A Critique*. London: Mansell.

Ward, Peter M. 1999. *Colonias and Public Policy in Texas and Mexico: Urbanization by Stealth*. Austin: University of Texas Press.

Ward, Peter M., and Jeremiah Carew. 2001. "Tracking Land Ownership in Self-Help Homestead Subdivisions in the United States: The Case of Texas 'Colonias.'" *Land Use Policy* 18 (2): 165–178.

Ward, Peter M., Flavio de Souza, and Cecilia Giusti. 2004. "'Colonia' Land and Housing Market Performance and the Impact of Lot Title Regularisation in Texas." *Urban Studies* 41 (13): 2621–2646.

Warner, Sam Bass. 1969. *Streetcar Suburbs: The Process of Growth in Boston, 1870–1900*. New York: Atheneum.

Warner, Sam Bass, and Andrew H. Whittemore. 2012. *American Urban Form: A Representative History*. Cambridge, MA: MIT Press.

Wartime Prices and Trade Board. 1949. "Order No. 200." Canadian war orders and regulations. https://archive.org/stream/canadianwarorde1942v1cana#page/176/mode/2up.

Wasserman, Jim. 2002a. "'Granny Flat' Bill Hits Davis' Desk." *Orange County Register*, August 31.

Wasserman, Jim. 2002b. "New Bill to Spur Secondary Units Draws Fire from Cities." *Berkeley Daily Planet*, July 1.

Watson, Vanessa. 2011. "Engaging with Citizenship and Urban Struggle through an Informality Lens." *Planning Theory & Practice* 12 (1): 150–153.

Weber, Carolyn. 1999. "Everything's Relative." *Builder* 22 (13): 200–201.

Wegmann, Jake. 2015. "Research Notes: The Hidden Cityscapes of Informal Housing in Suburban Los Angeles and the Paradox of Horizontal Density." *Buildings & Landscapes: Journal of the Vernacular Architecture Forum* 22 (2): 89–110.

Wegmann, Jake. 2020. "Death to Single-Family Zoning... and New Life to the Missing Middle." *Journal of the American Planning Association* 86 (1): 113–119.

Wegmann, Jake, and Karen Chapple. 2012. "Understanding the Market for Secondary Units in the East Bay." Working Paper, No. 2012-03, University of California, Berkeley, Institute of Urban and Regional Development.

Wegmann, Jake, and Karen Chapple. 2014. "Hidden Density in Single-Family Neighborhoods: Backyard Cottages as an Equitable Smart Growth Strategy." *Journal of Urbanism: International Research on Placemaking and Urban Sustainability* 7 (3): 307–329.

Wegmann, Jake, and Sarah Mawhorter. 2017. "Measuring Informal Housing Production in California Cities." *Journal of the American Planning Association* 83 (2): 119–130.

Weigel, David. 2020. "The Trailer: Can Trump Sell Fear to the Suburbs?" *Washington Post*, July 19.

Weiss, Marc A. 1986. "Urban Land Developers and the Origins of Zoning Laws: The Case of Berkeley." *Berkeley Planning Journal* 3 (1): 7–25.

Weiss, Marc A. 1987. *The Rise of the Community Builders: The American Real Estate Industry and Urban Land Planning*. New York: Columbia University Press.

Westneat, Danny. 2015. "Get Rid of Single-Family Zoning? These Conversations Shouldn't Be Secret." *Seattle Times*, July 7.

Wheeler, Stephen M. 2002. "The New Regionalism: Key Characteristics of an Emerging Movement." *Journal of the American Planning Association* 68 (3): 267–278.

White House. 2016. *Housing Development Toolkit*. Washington, DC: Office of President Barack Obama.

Whittemore, Andrew. 2010. "The Regulated City: The Politics of Land Use Regulation in Los Angeles, 1909–2009." PhD diss., UCLA.

Whittemore, Andrew. 2012a. "How the Federal Government Zoned America: The Federal Housing Administration and Zoning." *Journal of Urban History* 39 (4): 620–642.

Whittemore, Andrew. 2012b. "One Hundred Years of Land-Use Regulation." In *Planning Los Angeles,* edited by David Sloane, 107–121. Chicago: APA Planners Press.

Whittemore, Andrew. 2012c. "Zoning Los Angeles: A Brief History of Four Regimes." *Planning Perspectives* 27 (3): 393–415.

Whittemore, Andrew. 2018. "The Role of Racial Bias in Exclusionary Zoning: The Case of Durham, North Carolina, 1945–2014." *Environment and Planning A* 50 (4): 826–847.

Wieckowski, Bob, and Vinit Mukhija. 2019. "California's Housing Market Is Overburdened. Loosening Laws on 'Granny Flats' Can Help." Viewpoint, *Sacramento Bee*, September 10.

Wildermuth, John. 2014. "Legalization for S.F. In-law Units Gets Past 1st Hurdle: Controversy Minimal in Planners' Decision." *San Francisco Chronicle*, March 14.

Williams, Stockton, Lisa Sturtevant, and Rosemarie Hepner. 2017. "Yes in My Backyard: How States and Local Communities Can Find Common Ground in Expanding Housing Choice and Opportunity." Washington, DC: Terwilliger Center for Housing,

Urban Land Institute. https://2os2f877tnl1dvtmc3wy0aq1-wpengine.netdna-ssl.com/wp-content/uploads/ULI-Documents/State-Housing-Policy-Report-2017.pdf.

Wilson, Elizabeth. 1991. *The Sphinx in the City: Urban Life, the Control of Disorder, and Women*. London: Virago.

Winton, Richard. 2014. "Converted Barn Owner Charged with Safety Violations after Fire Kills 4." *Los Angeles Times*, June 20.

Woetzel, Jonathan, Jan Mischeke, Shannon Peloquin, and Daniel Weisfield. 2016. *Closing California's Housing Gap*. Los Angeles: McKinsey Global Institute.

Wolsink, Maarten. 2006. "Invalid Theory Impedes Our Understanding: A Critique on the Persistence of the Language of NIMBY." *Transactions of the Institute of British Geographers* 31 (1): 85–91.

Wood, Daniel. 2012. "Vancouver's Density Debate Pits Sullivanism versus the Ideas of Jane Jacobs." *Georgia Straight*, June 6. https://www.straight.com/news/vancouvers-density-debate-pits-sullivanism-versus-ideas-jane-jacobs.

World Bank. 1993. *Housing: Enabling Markets to Work*. Washington, DC: World Bank.

Wright, Frank Lloyd. 1932. *The Disappearing City*. New York: William Farquhar Payson. (Republished in 1945 as *When Democracy Builds* [Chicago: University of Chicago Press])

Wright, Gwendolyn. (1981) 1983. *Building the Dream: A Social History of Housing in America*. Cambridge, MA: MIT Press.

Yee, Greg. 2013. "'Aviles Law' Goes after Illegally Converted Garages." *Long Beach Press-Telegram*, October 21.

Yiftachel, Oren. 2009. "Theoretical Notes on 'Gray Cities': The Coming of Urban Apartheid." *Planning Theory* 8 (1): 88–100.

York, Jessica. 2015. "Unpermitted Santa Cruz Granny Units Get Reprieve: Council Plans May 12 Full Review of Ordinance." *Santa Cruz Sentinel*, April 18.

Young, Iris Marion. 1990. *Justice and the Politics of Difference*. Princeton, NJ: Princeton University Press.

Zasloff, Jonathan. 2020. "I Have Spent My Career Advocating for Fair Housing. It's Good to See Obama's Rule Go." Planetizen, August 12. https://www.planetizen.com/features/110189-i-have-spent-my-career-advocating-fair-housing-its-good-see-obamas-rule-go.

Zaveri, Mihir, and Matthew Haag. 2021. "New York's Storm Deaths Highlight a Shadow World of Basement Apartments." *New York Times*, September 2.

Ziegler, Edward H., Jr. 1983. "The Twilight of Single-Family Zoning." *UCLA Journal of Environmental Law and Policy* 3 (2): 161–217.

INTERVIEWS AND PERSONAL COMMUNICATIONS

Agar, Eric (realtor, Keller Williams). 2014a. Interview (in-person), March 14.

Agar, Eric. 2014b. Communication (email), subject: unpermitted work, March 21.

Agar, Eric. 2014c. Communication (email), subject: accessory units, October 27.

Baker, Andrew (real estate attorney). 2013. Interview (in-person), June 30.

Barbosa, Jeff (communications director, State Senator Bob Wieckowski), and Francisco Montes (legislative aide, State Senator Bob Wieckowski). 2019. Interview (in-person), July 10.

Belgrade, Ira (ADU/housing activist). 2016. Communication (public forum), ADU salon at LA Más, Los Angeles, May 31.

Bell, Jonathan Pacheco (zoning inspector, County of Los Angeles). 2016a. Communication (public forum), ADU salon at LA Más, Los Angeles, May 31.

Bell, Jonathan Pacheco. 2016b. Interview (in-person), September 6.

Bell, Jonathan Pacheco, and Elsa Rodriguez (zoning inspectors, County of Los Angeles). 2014. Interview (in-person), May 14.

Bell, Jonathan Pacheco, and Elsa Rodriguez (zoning inspectors, County of Los Angeles). 2016. Interview (in-person), August 10.

Bender, Lisa (city council president, City of Minneapolis). 2019. Communication (public forum), Annual National American Planning Association (APA) Conference, San Francisco, April 15.

Berg, Carol (principal planner, City of Santa Cruz). 2014. Interview (in-person), February 13.

Berg, Carol. 2018. Interview (phone), July 31.

Blumenfeld, Jane (former deputy director, Department of City Planning, City of Los Angeles). 2013. Interview (in-person), December 18.

Blumenfeld, Jane. 2017. Interview (in-person), August 23.

Blumenfeld, Jane. 2018. Interview (in-person), October 17.

Blumenfeld, Jane. 2019. Communication (public forum), Pacoima Comprehensive Project class at UCLA, Department of Urban Planning, Los Angeles, January 24.

Bodem, Phil (Southern California, division president, Meritage Homes). 2017. Interview (phone), June 9.

Breidenbach, Jan (lecturer, Department of Urban Planning, UCLA). 2018. Communication (email), subject: ADUs and international development, November 8.

Brennan, Andrea (director of Housing Policy and Development, City of Minneapolis). 2019. Communication (public forum), Annual National American Planning Association (APA) Conference, San Francisco, April 15.

Brown, Martin (Portland ADU activist and researcher). 2015. Interview (in-person), March 18.

Burpee, Heather (planner Urban Design and Sustainability, City of Vancouver), and Heike Roth (former senior planner, Urban Design and Sustainability, City of Vancouver). 2013. Interview (in-person), October 2.

REFERENCES

Campbell, James (real estate broker). 2013. Interview (in-person), August 1.

Chung, Connie (supervising regional planner, Los Angeles County Department of Regional Planning). 2016. Communication (public forum), ADU salon at LA Más, Los Angeles, May 31.

Coleman, Erin (assistant planner, Department of City Planning, City of Los Angeles). 2015. Communication (email), subject: update and question on second units, December 27.

Condon, Patrick (professor of urban design, University of British Columbia, Vancouver). 2013. Interview (in-person), October 1.

Coupland, Andy (former city planner, Vancouver). 2013. Communication (email), subject: secondary suite permits, City of Vancouver, December 20.

Cuff, Dana (professor of architecture, director cityLAB, UCLA). 2018. Communication (public forum), Affordable Housing Symposium: The Supply Crisis in Los Angeles, Los Angeles, February 5.

Daflos, Amanda (chief innovation officer, Mayor's Innovation Team, City of Los Angeles). 2016. Communication (public forum), ADU salon at LA Más, Los Angeles, March 10.

Daflos, Amanda, and Jason Neville (Mayor's Innovation Team). 2016. Interview (in-person), April 6.

De Simone, Tom (president and CEO, Genesis LA). 2016. Communication (public forum), ADU salon at LA Más, Los Angeles, July 20.

De Simone, Tom. 2018. Communication (public forum), Affordable Housing Symposium: The Supply Crisis in Los Angeles, Los Angeles, February 5.

De Simone, Tom. 2021. Interview (Zoom), June 29.

Donovan, Katherine (planner, City of Santa Cruz). 2018. Communication (email), subject: permit data for ADUs, August 17.

Durning, Alan (executive director, Sightline Institute, Seattle). 2014. Interview (in-person), August 22.

Durning, Tom (senior staffer, Tenant Resource & Advisory Centre, Vancouver). 2013. Interview (in-person), October 10.

Ellis, Bradley, and Paul Mogush (Community Planning and Economic Development, City of Minneapolis). 2019. Interview (in-person), March 14.

Ellison, Jeremiah (councilmember, City of Minneapolis). 2019. Interview (in-person), March 15.

Estrada, Leobardo (professor, Department of Urban Planning, UCLA). 2018. Interview (in-person), May 8.

Fletcher, Steve (councilmember, City of Minneapolis). 2019. Interview (in-person), March 15.

Foster, David (executive director, Habitat for Humanity, Santa Cruz County). 2014. Interview (in-person), February 11.

Fry, Jake (founder/principal, Smallworks, Vancouver). 2013. Interview (in-person), October 2.

Fuentes, Felipe (councilmember, Council District 7, City of Los Angeles). 2015. Communication (public forum), *Shelter: Rethinking How We Live in Los Angeles*, ADU salon, Los Angeles, October 21.

Gabbe, C. J. (assistant professor, Department of Environmental Studies and Sciences, Santa Clara University). 2015. Interview (in-person), March 22.

Grossman, Marlene (former executive director, Pacoima Beautiful). 2019. Communication (public forum), Pacoima Comprehensive Project class at UCLA, Department of Urban Planning, Los Angeles, January 31.

Haffner, Stephanie (senior litigator, Western Center on Law and Poverty). 2014. Interview (phone), September 23.

Han, Deborah (project manager, Toll Brothers). 2017. Interview (phone), June 1.

Hare, Bradley (senior vice president, Southern California Division, Toll Brothers). 2017. Interview (phone), May 24.

Holland, Taylor (former graduate student, Department of Urban Planning, UCLA). 2019. Communication (email), subject: Minneapolis, August 12.

Hutchins, Matt (More Options for Accessory Residences [MOAR], Seattle). 2018. Interview (phone), July 31.

Jang, Kerry (city councillor, City of Vancouver). 2013. Interview (in-person), October 7.

Joe, Wesley (city planner, City of Vancouver). 2013. Interview (in-person), October 7.

Johnson, Andrew (councilmember, City of Minneapolis). 2019. Interview (in-person), March 15.

Juarez, Gabriela (Department of City Planning, City of Los Angeles). 2019. Interview (phone), June 19.

Kamp, John (former graduate student, Department of Urban Planning, UCLA). 2019. Communication (email), subject: unpermitted second units in Minneapolis, June 19.

Kettles, Gregg (attorney, Best, Best & Krieger). 2016. Interview (in-person), April 26.

Khoury, Andrew (assistant director of planning and community development, City of Santa Cruz). 2014. Interview (in-person), February 13.

LaMontagne, Neal (former senior planner, City of Vancouver). 2018. Interview (in-person), September 28.

Leung, Helen (executive director, LA Más). 2018. Communication (email), subject: follow up on ADU questions, April 18.

Leung, Helen. 2019. Communication (email), subject: your thoughts on the micro-unit, February 20.

Leung, Helen. 2021. Communication (email), subject: follow up, May 3.

Leung, Helen, and Elizabeth Timme (executive directors, LA Más). 2016. Interview (in-person), February 10.

Leung, Helen, and Elizabeth Timme. 2017. Interview (in-person), November 17.

Levy, Susan (legislative aide, Councilmember Mike O'Brien, City of Seattle). 2018. Interview (phone), August 31.

Lopez-Ledesma, Yvette (former deputy director, Pacoima Beautiful). 2019. Communication (public forum), Pacoima Comprehensive Project class at UCLA, Department of Urban Planning, Los Angeles, January 17.

McAfee, Ann (former director of planning, City of Vancouver). 2013. Interview (in-person), October 12.

McKinley, Ryan (mortgage development manager, Vancouver City Savings Credit Union [Vancity]). 2013. Interview (in-person), October 8.

Mogush, Paul (manager of community planning, City of Minneapolis). 2019a. Interview (phone), January 16.

Mogush, Paul. 2019b. Communication (public forum), Annual National American Planning Association (APA) Conference, San Francisco, April 15.

Morley, David (Research Program and Quality Assurance Manager at the American Planning Association). 2019. Communication (public forum), Annual National American Planning Association (APA) Conference, San Francisco, April 13.

Nameny, Phil (city planner, City of Portland). 2018a. Interview (phone), March 12.

Nameny, Phil. 2018b. Communication (email), subject: unpublished ADU permit data, March 13.

Neville, Jason (manager, Mayor's Innovation Team, City of Los Angeles). 2016. Communication (public forum), ADU salon at LA Más, Los Angeles, March 10.

Nickels, Greg (former mayor, City of Seattle). 2014. Interview (in-person), August 20.

Padilla, Veronica (executive director, Pacoima Beautiful). 2019. Communication (public forum), Pacoima Comprehensive Project class at UCLA, Department of Urban Planning, Los Angeles, January 24.

Parker, Bruce (founder and lead designer, Microhouse, Seattle). 2014. Interview (in-person), August 21.

Participants #1 and #2 (tenants). 2013. Interview (in-person), July 18.

Participant #3 (homeowner). 2013. Interview (in-person), July 27.

Participant #4 (tenant). 2013. Interview (in-person), September 2.

Participant #5 (tenant). 2013. Interview (in-person), September 4.

Participant #6 (homeowner). 2013. Interview (in-person), September 30.

Participant #7 (tenant). 2013. Interview (in-person), October 22.

Participant #8 (homeowner). 2013. Interview (in-person), October 26.

Participant #9 and #10 (tenants). 2013. Interview (in-person), October 26.

Participant #11 (homeowner/tenant). 2013. Interview (in-person), October 27.

Participant #12 (homeowner/tenant). 2013. Interview (in-person), November 25.

Participant #13 and #14 (tenants). 2013. Interview (in-person), December 6.

Participant #15 (homeowner). 2014. Interview (in-person), February 8.

Participant #16 (homeowner). 2014. Interview (in-person), October 31.

Participant #17 (homeowner). 2015. Interview (in-person), March 23.

Peterson, Kol (ADU expert and class instructor). 2015a. Communication (public forum), ADU class—Building an ADU in Portland, March 21.

Peterson, Kol. 2015b. Interview (in-person), March 22.

Podemski, Max (planning director, Pacoima Beautiful). 2015. Communication (public forum), ADU salon at LA Más, Los Angeles, December 7.

Podemski, Max (former planning director, Pacoima Beautiful). 2019. Communication (public forum), Pacoima Comprehensive Project class at UCLA, Department of Urban Planning, Los Angeles, February 7.

Podowski, Mike (land use policy manager, Department of Planning and Development, City of Seattle). 2014. Interview (in-person), August 21.

Primack, Mark (former city councilmember, City of Santa Cruz). 2014. Interview (in-person), February 6.

Primack, Mark. 2018. Interview (phone), June 11.

Richman, Sally (former manager, Garage Housing Task Force; public information officer and manager, Housing and Community Investment Department, City of Los Angeles). 2017. Interview (in-person), March 7.

Rodriguez, Elsa (zoning inspector, County of Los Angeles). 2014. Interview (in-person), September 24.

Rojas, James (founder, Place It!). 2015. Interview (in-person), March 25.

Romero-Martínez, Liseth (former executive director, Pacoima Beautiful; program manager, Housing and Community Investment Department, City of Los Angeles). 2017. Interview (in-person), March 7.

Romero-Martínez, Liseth (former executive director, Pacoima Beautiful). 2019. Communication (public forum), Pacoima Comprehensive Project class at UCLA, Department of Urban Planning, Los Angeles, January 31.

Rondini, Niki (real estate broker, Portland Proper Real Estate). 2015. Interview (in-person), March 22.

Rotkin, Mike (former city councilmember and mayor, City of Santa Cruz). 2014. Interview (in-person), February 7.

Sauls, Matt (vice president, marketing and product development, Pardee Homes), and Mike Taylor (Southern California division president, Pardee Homes). 2017. Interview (phone), June 9.

Sayeed, Almas (Skadden Fellow, Inner City Law Center). 2014. Interview (phone), May 30.

Schroeder, Jeremy (councilmember, City of Minneapolis). 2019. Interview (in-person), March 15.

Sether, Shanna (senior city planner, City of Minneapolis). 2019. Interview (in-person), March 15.

Smith, Doug (attorney, public counsel). 2014. Interview (phone), May 22.

Smith, Mei-Ling (senior city planner, City of Minneapolis). 2018. Interview (phone), June 28.

Smith, Mei-Ling. 2019. Interview (phone), January 22.

Spevak, Eli (founder, Orange Splot LLC, Portland). 2015. Interview (in-person), March 18.

Spevak, Eli. 2018. Interview (phone), July 9.

Student #1 (homeowner). 2011. Communication. Urban Planning Applied Research Project, University of California, Los Angeles.

Student #1. 2014. Interview (in-person), February 8.

Student #4 (tenant). 2013. Communication (email), subject: informal second units, May 15.

Student #5 (tenant). 2013. Interview (in-person), July 11.

Student #6 (tenant). 2013. Interview (in-person), July 27.

Student #7 (tenant). 2013a. Interview (in-person), April 10.

Student #7. 2013b. Interview (in-person), October 22.

Student #8 (homeowner). 2014. Interview (in-person), April 10.

Student #9 (tenant). 2014. Interview (in-person), May 13.

Student #10. 2018. Communication (public forum), UP219: Informal City Seminar, Department of Urban Planning, UCLA, Los Angeles, May 17.

Tracy, Morgan (city planner, City of Portland). 2018a. Communication (email), March 14.

Tracy, Morgan. 2018b. Interview (phone), September 6.

Vallianatos, Mark (policy director of the Urban & Environmental Policy Institute at Occidental College). 2016. Interview (in-person), July 20.

Weiss, Barry (realtor, Compass). 2014. Communication (email), subject: Residential purchase contract, November 16.

Welch, Nick (senior planner, Office of Planning and Community Development, City of Seattle). 2018. Communication (email), subject: dataset, City of Seattle, February 1.

Whitlock, Rob (former director of the Housing Centre, City of Vancouver). 2013. Interview (in-person), October 1.

Wieckowski, Bob (state senator, California State Legislature). 2018. Interview (phone), September 10.

Wieckowski, Bob. 2019. Interview (in-person), July 10.

Wilson, Jeff (founder, Kasita). 2016. Interview (in-person), September 29.

Yan, Andy (director of the City Program, Simon Fraser University, Vancouver). 2020. Communication (email), subject: Hedge City question, June 8.

INDEX

AARP, 22, 55, 204
AARP-Minnesota, 211
Accessory Dwelling Units (ADUs), 6–7, 21, 23–25, 55, 78, 80–83, 153–154, 162–170, 173, 176–177, 179–180, 185, 187–188, 191–193, 197–200, 202, 204–408, 210–212, 214–215, 228, 236–240, 244–246, 250–251
community ADUs, 254
detached accessory dwelling units (DADUs), 195–199, 230, 239
junior accessory dwelling units (JADUs), 23, 164, 170, 177, 236–237, 239–240
manuals, 188–190, 196
preapproved designs/plans, 188–190, 198
tours, 168, 204–206, 246
See also second units
Affirmatively Furthering Fair Housing (AFFH), 3, 4. *See also* Fair Housing Act of 1968
affordable housing, 17, 36, 91–92, 96, 151, 156, 175–177, 184, 187, 190, 195, 198, 213, 228, 231, 239, 243, 248–253
challenges, 5, 10, 12–13, 74, 79, 85, 235, 248

diverse housing stock, 6, 21
informal market, 25, 30, 131, 146, 187, 230, 236
naturally occurring, 239
opposition to, 183
trust fund, 190
See also inclusionary housing/zoning
Affordable Housing Advocates (Santa Cruz), 188
aging-in-place, 55
Alarcon, Richard, 141–142, 152–153. *See also* Los Angeles City Council
American Dream, 3–5, 7–10, 21, 33, 37–40, 47–50, 56–57, 143, 175, 235, 253
American exceptionalism, 8, 236
American Housing Survey, 40–41
American Institute of Architects (AIA), 185
American Planning Association (APA), 22, 79, 185, 201, 212–213, 237
amnesty, for informal second units, 94, 150, 173, 197, 199–200, 208, 230
anticommunism, 8, 40
anti-urbanism, 38, 47, 236
Arts and Architecture (magazine), 64
Assembly Bill 587 (2019, California), 251

Assembly Bill 1866 (2002, California), 78, 80, 153
Assembly Bill 2299 (2016, California), 163–166, 169, 192
Assembly Bill 2406 (2016, California), 164–166
Assembly Bill 2702 (2004, California), 79
Atkins, Toni, 240
Atlanta, Georgia, 11, 45, 53, 136
Australia, 37–38, 215
Azar, Alex, 4

baby boomers, 12, 53
backyard cottages, 6, 21–22, 195–197, 230, 237, 246. *See also* second units
Backyard Homes Project, 172–173, 177
Baker, Andrew, 106
balloon-frame construction, 43
Baltimore, Maryland, 45
Banham, Reyner, 63–65, 237
Baross, Paul, 14–15
Bartholomew, Harland, 194, 218
Beauregard, Robert, 5
Been, Vicki, 183
Belgrade, Ira, 163
Bell, Jonathan Pacheco, 115, 129
Bender, Lisa, 210–213
Berg, Carol, 188, 196
Berkeley, California, 44, 62–63, 236
Bernson, Hal, 152. *See also* Los Angeles City Council
Better Homes & Gardens (magazine), 44
Biden, Joseph, 3–4, 235
Blake, Peter, 5
Bloom, Richard, 156, 163–164. *See also* Assembly Bill 2299
Bloomberg Foundation, 154
Blue Ribbon Committee for Affordable Housing (Los Angeles), 100, 150–151
Blumenfeld, Jane, 156, 163–164
Bodem, Phil, 158
Booker, Cory, 6

boomers, 12, 53
Boston, Massachusetts, 24, 63, 136, 236
informal housing, 17
Boston Globe (newspaper), 17
Boyar, Louis, 43
Bradley, Tom, 150. *See also* Los Angeles, California, mayor of
Braude, Marvin, 65. *See also* Los Angeles City Council
Breidenbach, Jan, 171
Broadacre City, 39
Brown, Jerry, 165–166
Brown, Kate, 207
Brown, Martin, 202, 204
Buchanan v. Warley, 45. *See also* racial zoning
Builder Magazine, 158
bungalow courts, 254
Buscaino, Joe, 165. *See also* Los Angeles City Council
Business Week (magazine), 44

California, 11, 15, 17, 30, 67, 73, 103, 124, 150, 168, 174–177, 183, 185, 192, 213, 235–236, 239–240, 247
housing prices, 11, 75–77
poverty, 76
state legislature, 31, 79, 153, 228, 245, 251
statewide zoning intervention, 23, 33–34, 77–78, 143, 150, 175–177, 180, 184, 198, 236, 240, 251–252
California Association of Realtors, 78, 124
California Department of Housing and Community Development (HCD), 165
California Earthquake Authority, 174
California Environmental Quality Act (CEQA), 11, 213
California Housing Partnership Corporation, 74

INDEX

California Rural Legal Assistance Foundation, 78
California State Association of Counties, 79
California State University, Los Angeles, 64
Canada, 25, 32, 179, 215, 226, 237
 single-family living, 37–38, 215–216
 See also Vancouver, Canada
Canadian Dream, 215
Capote, Truman, 131
Carson, Ben, 4
Cascadia region, 215
Case Study House Program, 64
Castro, Julian, 6
ceiling height, 195, 199, 200, 208, 219, 220, 222, 226, 229, 244
Center for Law in the Public Interest, 70
Centers Plan (Los Angeles), 67–72
Chapple, Karen, 21, 164
Cheng, Wendy, 99
Chicago, Illinois, 9, 24, 37, 46, 61, 90, 98, 136, 236
cityLAB (UCLA), 31–32, 83, 155–156, 162–163. *See also* Cuff, Dana
Clark, Clifford Edward, Jr., 8
Clark, Kenneth, 49
class segregation, 6, 47, 50, 181, 194.
 See also racial segregation; segregation
Clean Air Act of 1963, 66
clemency, for informal second units, 94, 150, 173, 197, 199–200, 208, 230
climate change/crisis, 11, 48, 222
coach houses, 46
Coates, Ta-Nehisi, 49
colonias, 14–15, 17, 99, 149. *See also* informal subdivisions
community ADUs, 254
Companion Unit Act (1983, California), 77, 150, 187
construction loans. *See* loans
Costa-Hawkins Rental Housing Act of 1995, 76

Costa Mesa (Orange County), 169–170
COVID-19, 4, 76, 158, 255
Cuff, Dana, 31, 83, 156, 163–164.
 See also cityLAB

Daly City, California, 150
Davidoff, Paul, 57
Davis, Mike, 182
de Arakal, Byron, 170
de Certeau, Michel, 144
deed restrictions (affordable housing), 190, 251
Denver, Colorado, 24, 53, 236
design manuals, 188–190
design standards/requirements, 86–87
De Soto, Hernando, 147
detached ADUs (DADUs), 195–199, 230, 239
development fees, 78, 150, 164, 167.
 See also impact fees
discretionary approval/review (zoning), 77–78, 153–154, 166, 192, 195, 203, 210
displacement, 12, 43, 197–198, 201, 213–214, 216, 252. *See also* gentrification
Doebele, William, 148
Dougherty, Conor, 183
downzoning, 56, 70, 194, 201–202
Duneier, Mitchell, 49
duplexes, 7, 23–25, 28, 46, 63, 177, 198, 200, 202, 207, 209, 214–216, 222, 225, 236
duplex-zoned lots, 179, 210–211
Durning, Alan, 194
Durst, Noah, 99. *See also* Ward, Peter
Dwelling Act of 1934 (Washington, DC), 46

Eames, Charles, 64
Eames, Ray, 64
Eden in Jeopardy (Lillard), 65
Elder Cottage Housing Opportunity, 22

Ellison, Jeremiah, 209, 214
Elwood, Craig, 64
Estrada, Leobardo, 136, 238
evaluation of projects/zoning changes, 193, 195, 229, 246
exclusionary zoning, 181, 183

Fair Housing Act of 1968, 6, 46, 66. *See also* Affirmatively Furthering Fair Housing
Fan, Stephen, 99
Federal Highway Act of 1956, 43. *See also* highways
Federal Housing Administration (FHA), 41–42, 43, 47, 63, 72, 90
  housing construction, influence on, 42, 46
  lending standards, 42, 44–45 (*see also* redlining)
federalism, 183
Ferman, Louis, 96
Ferman, Patricia, 96
Fine, Barbara, 72. *See also* Hillside Federation
fire
  districts, 62
  in garages, 17, 129, 141, 151, 175
  passageway requirement, 154–156, 164
  safety checks, 226, 230, 244
  smoke alarms, 17, 118, 127–128, 174, 222, 226, 230, 244
  sprinklers, 127, 166, 187–188, 220
Fishman, Robert, 63
Flint, Barbara, 37
Fogelson, Robert, 64
Fortune (magazine), 44
Foster, David, 187, 190
fourplexes, 7, 25, 177, 200, 207, 213, 228
Framework Element of the General Plan (Los Angeles), 70–72
Frey, Jacob, 213

Friedman, Laura, 251
Friends of Santa Monica Mountains, 65
Fuentes, Felipe, 156. *See also* Los Angeles City Council
Fulton, William, 141

Ganong, Peter, 52
garage housing, 93, 141–142, 150, 175. *See also* garage conversions
garage conversions, 6, 15–16, 25, 93–94, 99–101, 103, 106–120, 124, 127–129, 132, 141–142, 153–155, 162, 164, 171, 176, 188, 189, 195, 203, 208, 237–238, 242, 252–253. *See also* garage housing
garage fires, 17, 129, 141, 151, 175
Garage Housing Task Force (Los Angeles), 141–142, 151–152, 173, 175, 244
Garcetti, Eric, 153–154, 165. *See also* Los Angeles, California, mayor of
Genesis LA Economic Growth Corporation (Genesis LA), 156, 162, 172, 177
gentrification, 148, 201, 216, 252. *See also* displacement
Ghost Ship fire (Oakland), 17
GI Bill (Servicemen's Readjustment Act of 1944), 42
Glaeser, Edward, 182
Global North, 14–15, 18, 20, 25, 28, 94–95, 98, 100, 131–133, 143–144, 149, 240–242, 244
Global South, 13–15, 18, 20, 43, 79, 94–98, 100, 118, 145–146, 148–149, 171–176, 240, 242
Good Housekeeping (magazine), 44
Granny Bill (1981, California), 77
granny flats, 6, 80, 82, 118, 123, 153, 165. *See also* second units
Great Depression, 41, 99
Great Recession, 82, 156, 204
growth boundary, 186
Growth Machine, 182–183, 186, 245

Habitat for Humanity, 187
Hall, Carlyle, 70, 162–164, 166
Hamilton, Calvin, 67, 70
Hare, Bradley, 158
Hare, Patrick, 21
Harris, Cheryl, 48
Harris, John, 96
Harris, Richard, 98–99
Hart, Keith, 95–97
Hayden, Dolores, 5, 10, 50–51, 249
height limits (zoning), 23, 65, 180
highways, 43, 62, 66, 72, 90
Hillside Federation (Los Angeles and Ventura counties), 65, 70, 72, 153, 166, 176, 182
Hodges, Betsy, 210
homebuilders, 35, 43, 46, 63, 156–161, 168, 171, 207, 249
homelessness, 10, 12–13, 76
homeowner education, 188
homeowner grants, 18, 173–174, 177, 251–252
homeownership, 3, 21, 239, 251
  and the American Dream, 7, 38–40, 40
  anticommunism strategy, 40
  citizenship, 39
  generational wealth, 48, 75
  policy, 7–9, 39–41, 43–44
  single-family housing, 7–9, 35, 40–41, 43
Homeowners Loan Corporation (HOLC), 41–42
  redlining, 10, 44, 49
homeowners/neighborhood associations, 33, 65, 67, 70, 152, 170, 177, 203, 207, 209
Hondagneu-Sotelo, Pierrette, 145
Hoover, Herbert, 39
House Bill 2011 (2019, Oregon), 207
household overcrowding, 33, 76–77, 129
housing
  affordability, 5–6, 10–13, 51–52, 75–77, 207, 216, 228, 249–252

  cost burden, 11, 74–77
  supply and costs, 11, 72–76, 85, 186, 238
Housing Affordability and Livability Agenda (HALA) (Seattle), 198–200
Housing and Urban Development, Department of, 2. *See also* Fair Housing Act of 1968
housing finance
  lack of access to, 13, 36, 48–49, 126, 143, 147–148, 155, 171–173, 176–177, 226, 253
  loans (*see* loans)
  mortgage lending, 41 (*see also* mortgages)
  racism in, 48–49
  for second units, 156, 162, 171–173, 226, 251
housing policy (US), 8–13, 41–43
Hsieh, Chang-Tai, 52
Hurricane Ida, 17

impact fees, 167, 170, 198. *See also* development fees
inclusionary housing/zoning, 199, 207, 213
incremental development, 13–15, 18, 43, 99, 117–118, 121, 126, 146
Informal American City, The (Mukhija and Loukaitou-Sideris), 18
informal economy, 95–100, 143–145, 240–244
informal housing
  conditions, 17, 124–131, 241, 242–244
  dangerous conditions, 17–18, 101, 127–129, 141, 174–175, 243
  formalization, 21, 30, 34, 141–142, 147–153, 156, 180, 192–193, 199–200, 208, 214–215, 225–227
  in the Global South, 13–15, 146–149
  in the Global North, 13, 98–100, 149–150, 240–244 (*see also* Garage Housing Task Force)

informal housing (cont.)
  legalization, 20–21, 34–35, 142–145, 147–153, 164, 171, 176, 185, 199–200, 208, 220, 226, 230
  ownership agreements, 240
  upgrading, 18, 28, 34–35, 142–143, 145, 147–152, 173–177, 180, 192, 200, 208, 215, 226, 230–231, 244
  See also informal second units
informal second units
  enforcement, 18, 20–21, 25, 88, 107, 110–115, 121, 124, 127–133, 141–144, 146, 149–152, 174–175, 186, 192–193, 199–200, 208, 214, 218, 220, 225–226, 236, 240–244, 247
  formalization of, 168, 173–175, 192, 195, 225–227
  prevalence of, 20, 88, 93–115, 186, 194, 201, 209, 214, 215, 226
informal settlements, 13–15, 17, 97, 132, 145, 147
informal subdivisions, 14–15. See also *colonias*
infrastructure, 14–15, 18, 28, 36, 48, 57, 65, 79, 84, 99, 132, 148–149, 164, 171, 198, 200, 204, 230–231, 253–254. *See also* social infrastructure
infrastructure-poor subdivisions, 149
in-law apartments, 6, 123. *See also* second Units
Innovation Team (Los Angeles), 154–156, 162
International Labour Organization, 97
Irvine, California, 158–161

Jackson, Kenneth, 8, 41
Jefferson, Thomas, 7, 39
Johnson, Marilynn, 99
Jun, Kyu-Nahm, 83
junior accessory dwelling units (JADUs), 23, 164, 170, 177, 236–237, 239–240

Kaplan, Sam, 70
Kaye, Ron, 80
Keats, John, 5
Kennedy, Scott, 187
Klinenberg, Eric, 53–54
Koenig, Pierre, 64
Koretz, Paul, 153. *See also* Los Angeles City Council
Kotek, Tina, 207
Kotkin, Joel, 79–80
Kurtz, Stanley, 4

Ladies' Home Journal (magazine), 44
Lakewood (Los Angeles County) 43, 64, 118
LA Más, 31, 155–156, 162–163, 168, 171–172, 177, 252, 254. *See also* Los Angeles, second unit pilot project
Land
  prices, 50, 238
  titles, 18, 145, 147–149, 171
Land Conservation and Development Commission (LCDC) (Oregon), 201, 202, 207
land use planning, 14, 23, 184, 201, 245
laneway housing (Vancouver), 25–26, 179, 222, 224, 228, 237, 239
LA Weekly (newspaper), 80, 82
League of California Cities, 78–79, 165, 185
Leavitt, Jacqueline, 249–250
Lefebvre, Henri, 144
Lens, Michael, 50
Lerup, Lars, 5
Levitt & Sons, 43
Levittown, New York, 43, 64
Lewis, W. Arthur, 95
Lillard, Richard G., 64–65. *See also* Hillside Federation
Lima, Peru, 146, 243
loans, 13–14, 42–44, 63, 148, 156, 173, 176, 190, 226, 231, 251–253
  construction, 126, 155, 171, 190

home equity, 155, 171
home improvement, 147
  upgrading, 18, 150
  See also mortgages
local knowledge, 28, 184, 247
Logan, John, 182
Long Beach (Los Angeles County), 64
Los Angeles, California
  housing affordability, 63, 72–74, 150–151
  informal housing, 15–18, 20, 34, 88, 93–94, 100–133, 135, 141–143, 149–152, 156, 175, 237–238, 241–243
  mayor of, 31 (*see also* Tom Bradley; Eric Garcetti; Richard Riordan; Antonio Villaraigosa)
  second units, 22–23, 30, 77–82, 152–155, 164–168, 171–173, 177, 251–252
  second unit pilot project, 23, 31, 155–157 (*see also* LA Más)
  single-family housing, 5, 9, 31, 34–35, 37, 63–67, 79, 90–91
  zoning, 17, 37, 44, 62–63, 65, 88, 141, 154–155
Los Angeles City Council, 141, 151, 165
Los Angeles County, California, 5, 20, 23, 32, 34, 63–64, 67, 72–74, 77, 93, 100–102, 104, 106, 115, 131, 133–135, 149, 165, 170, 175, 238, 241, 251, 255
Los Angeles Daily News, 80
Los Angeles Department of Building and Safety, 32, 110–115, 141, 241
Los Angeles Department of City Planning, 67–72, 80–81, 151, 153, 166, 175
Los Angeles Neighborhood Councils, 32, 83–88, 241
Los Angeles Neighbors in Action, 162–163. *See also* Carlyle Hall
Los Angeles Times, 70, 79, 93–94, 100–101, 106, 111, 129, 132, 150–151, 156, 165, 175, 212, 238

Louisville, Kentucky, 45
Loukaitou-Sideris, Anastasia, 144

Making Room (Vancouver), 215, 222, 225, 228
Mangin, William, 146
Mansionization, 197, 207
Martinez, Nury, 165. *See also* Los Angeles City Council
Massachusetts, 184
McCall, Tom, 201
McCone Commission, 66
medium-density housing, 25, 46, 67. *See also* missing middle
middle class, disappearance of, 51
Milwaukee, Wisconsin, 99
minimum lot size (zoning), 22–23, 50, 65, 78–79, 107, 154, 170, 180, 193, 196–198, 211
Minneapolis, Minnesota, 23–25, 29, 35, 179–180, 208–215, 228–230, 235–236, 246, 255
missing middle, 46, 237. *See also* medium-density housing
mixed land uses, 8, 180, 214, 254
modernism, 146
Mollenkopf, John, 245
Molotch, Harvey, 182
Monkkonen, Paavo, 50
moratorium, 18, 149, 200, 218, 230
Moretti, Enrico, 52
Morrow, Greg, 70
mortgage interest deduction (MID), 42
mortgages, 13–14, 42. 172, 190, 226, 253
  brokers, 31
  discrimination, 48–49, 253
  insurance, 33, 42, 44–45, 63, 72, 177, 253
  lenders, 31, 41, 42
  underwriting requirements, 46
  See also loans
MPLS 2040 (Minneapolis), 212–214, 228

multigenerational households, 54–55, 156–157, 249
Mumbai, India, 13, 17
municipal fragmentation, 64
Murray, Ed, 198–199

National Association of Homebuilders, 43
National Association of Real Estate Boards, 39
National Association of Realtors, 39
National Home Week, 43
National Housing Act of 1934, 41
neighborhood character, 22, 38, 50, 56, 61–62, 72, 80, 86–87, 163, 182, 238–239, 253
neighborhood defenders, 183. *See also* Not in My Back Yard
Nelson, Arthur, 41
neoliberal/neoliberalism, 98, 143, 145, 147, 268
Neutra, Richard, 64
New Jersey, 184
Newsom, Gavin, 236
New Urbanism, 10
New York City, 9, 52–53, 63, 87, 136, 183
  basement apartments, 17
  informal housing, 17, 20, 150
  zoning, 44, 183
New York Times, 37, 40, 56–57, 100, 180, 204, 212, 235
Nickels, Greg, 195
Nicolaides, Becky, 98
nonconforming uses (zoning), 107, 194, 201, 209
Not in My Back Yard (NIMBY), 11–12, 65, 90, 182–183, 213, 245 *See also* zoning, opposition to reform
nuclear families, 8, 10, 52–53, 237, 248, 253

Oakland, California, 17, 99, 236
Obama, Barack, 1

O'Brien, Mike, 197, 199
1000 Friends of Oregon, 201, 207
opportunity hoarding, 52
Orange County, California, 61, 77, 137, 158, 169
owner-occupancy requirements, 22, 167, 170, 179, 188, 193, 196–200, 203, 211, 214, 219, 228
Own Your Own Home campaign, 39

Pacoima (Los Angeles), 17, 80, 156–157, 162, 173, 252
Pacoima Beautiful, 156–157, 162, 173
parking, 11, 53, 70, 84–86, 91, 94, 107, 110–111, 115, 120–121, 124, 132, 150, 152, 197, 202, 222, 227
  bicycle, 198, 200
  requirements (zoning), 22–23, 65, 78–79, 123, 150, 155, 164, 166, 179–180, 184, 187–188, 192, 195–196, 198–200, 202–203, 208, 211, 219, 220, 222, 224, 226, 228
Pasadena (Los Angeles County), 78–80, 170
passageway requirement (zoning), 154–156, 164
Peterson, Kol, 202, 204–205
Phoenix, Arizona, 5, 9, 11
Pico Rivera (Los Angeles County), 170
pilot programs/projects, 23–25, 31, 155, 162, 168, 173, 176, 179, 193, 195, 219, 222, 228–229, 246
polancos, 15, 17
Porter, Ed, 187
Portes, Alejandro, 147
Portland, Oregon, 23–25, 29–31, 35, 123, 126, 179–180, 200–208, 210, 215, 228–229, 235, 246, 253, 255
postwar housing construction boom, 46–47, 63, 90
preapproved designs/plans, 188–190, 198
predatory lending, 10. *See also* racism in US housing policy

Primack, Mark, 187, 192
property rights, 33, 45, 49, 62, 77–78, 142, 145, 147–148, 240, 250, 252–253
property values, 28, 102, 152, 182, 220, 229, 238, 247
Proposition 13 (California), 76
public engagement/outreach, 67, 80–82, 179, 182, 184, 193, 208, 211, 214, 219, 222, 228, 246–247
public housing, 12–13, 146. *See also* social housing
public transit/transportation, 25, 66–67, 70, 79, 86, 164, 192, 196, 199, 203, 207, 214
public workshops, 80–82, 88, 153, 180, 188, 200, 202, 207, 210–211, 229, 246, 255

racially restrictive covenants. *See* restrictive covenants
racial segregation, 6, 10, 44–45, 47, 49, 181, 194. *See also* class segregation; segregation
racial zoning, 45–46
racism in US housing policy, 9–10, 48–49, 75, 183
Ramirez, Hernan, 145
real estate listings, 28–29, 32, 34, 101–104, 106–107, 109–112, 115–116, 123, 133–134, 155, 238, 241
recode: LA (Los Angeles), 155
Redfin (website), 101–102
redlining, 10, 44, 49. *See also* racism in US housing policy
Redondo Beach (Los Angeles County), 149
regional governance (planning), 28, 67, 69, 91–92, 177, 181, 201, 209, 231, 247
Regional Housing Needs Assessment (California), 247

rent burden, 74–77
rent stabilization, 76, 148, 151, 176, 187, 244, 251
Residential Infill Project (RIP) (Portland), 207
Residents of Beverly Glen (Los Angeles), 64
restrictive covenants, 10, 45–46, 49, 66
Ridley-Thomas, Mark, 141. *See also* Los Angeles City Council
Riordan, Richard, 152. *See also* Los Angeles, California, mayor of
Rojas, James, 118
Rondini, Niki, 202
Roosevelt, Franklin D., 41–42
Rosendahl, Bill, 153. *See also* Los Angeles City Council
Roy, Ananya, 144

Saarinen, Eero, 64
Sacramento, California, 79, 163, 168, 170, 236
San Antonio, Texas, 5, 9
San Fernando Valley (Los Angeles County), 65, 118, 120, 128, 141, 155–156
San Francisco, California, 19–21, 52–53, 62, 150, 168, 183, 186, 212
 informal housing, 19–20, 103–104
San Gabriel Valley (Los Angeles County), 99
San Jose, California, 9, 52, 168, 186
Santa Cruz, California, 23–24, 29, 31, 35, 78, 179–180, 185–193, 196, 200, 202, 208, 210, 228, 235, 246, 251
Santa Monica Mountains National Recreation Area (Los Angeles and Ventura counties), 65
Sassen, Saskia, 98
Sauls, Matt, 158
Scally, Corianne, 183
Schwarzenegger, Arnold, 79

Seattle, Washington, 23–25, 29–31, 35, 53, 123, 179–180, 193–200, 208, 210, 215, 228–231, 235, 239, 246, 255
Seattle Department of Construction and Inspections, 197
secondary suites (Vancouver), 25, 215–222, 225–230, 237, 239, 241, 244, 247
second units
  benefits of, 21–22, 55
  California state reforms, 33, 77–79, 163–165
  effect on home values, 28, 85, 101–103, 238–240
  housing affordability, 21–22, 132
  opposition to, 28, 34, 37, 55, 78–80, 83–85, 87–88, 152–153, 162–163, 169–170
  perception of, 83–88, 101–115
  uses of, 22, 47, 55, 85
  See also Accessory Dwelling Units (ADUs); Los Angeles, California, second units in
segregation, 6, 10, 44–45, 47, 49–50, 181, 194. *See also* class segregation; racial segregation
Senate Bill 9 (2021, California), 240, 252
Senate Bill 13 (2019, California), 173–174, 176, 193
Senate Bill 100 (1973, Oregon), 201
Senate Bill 1069 (2016, California), 163–166, 169, 192
Senate Bill 1160 (1981, California), 77
Senate Bill 1534 (1983, California), 77, 150, 187
separate conveyance, of second units, 239–240, 251–252
Servicemen's Readjustment Act of 1944 (GI Bill), 42
setback requirements (zoning), 22–23, 155, 163–164, 170, 180, 188, 193, 195, 199, 203, 208, 211–212, 230, 252

Shaw, Randy, 183
Shelley v Kramer, 66
Shoag, Daniel, 51
Shulman, Julias, 64
Sierra Club, 65
Sightline Institute, 194
Silent Spring (Carson), 65
single-family housing
  and the American Dream, 1, 8, 40, 236
  and contemporary needs, 10, 22, 52–55, 209–210, 237
  dominance, 9. 13, 38, 46–47, 70, 90, 186, 200–201, 218
  and the environment, 10, 48, 66, 182
  feminist criticism of, 50–51
  promotion of, 43–44
  size of houses, 52–53
  urbanism, 5, 37, 46, 61, 64, 67, 88, 90–91, 236
single-family zoning
  racial legacy, 6, 12, 213
  reforms, 23–24, 28, 47, 175, 180, 185, 200, 208, 212, 227–228, 236–237, 239, 245–246, 253, 255
  state government intervention, 77, 91, 170, 176–177, 200, 231
  unconstitutional, 51
single-person households, 53–55
Slate (magazine), 212
slum, 65, 80, 87, 93, 101, 142, 146–148, 151, 174
Smith, Mei-Ling, 210
smoke alarms, 17, 118, 127–128, 174, 222, 226, 230, 244
social housing, 182, 216, 255. *See also* public housing
social infrastructure, 28, 36, 53, 230, 255
Soriano, Raphael, 64
Southern California, 61, 64, 66, 72, 90–91, 94, 132, 149, 158, 164, 175

South Gate (Los Angeles County), 149
Spevak, Eli, 201, 204
sprawl, 10–11, 42, 47–48, 63, 72, 90–91, 186, 201, 231. *See also* suburbanization
Springdale, Connecticut, 37, 56
sprinklers, 127, 166, 187–188, 200
square footage limits (zoning), 170, 180, 197, 198, 199, 203, 204, 211, 212, 215, 222
Stein, Clarence, 254
Steinberg, Darrell, 79
St. Louis, Missouri, 37, 72, 194
suburbanization, 5, 8–10
  federal support, 8, 41–43
  See also suburbs
suburbs, 3–5, 28, 37, 44, 46–47, 57, 63–64, 79, 90, 98–99, 118, 150, 181, 235, 238, 248
  criticism of, 10, 22
  inner suburbs, 28, 238, 246
  streetcar suburbs, 46
Supreme Court, 45, 49–50, 66
Sylmar (Los Angeles), 127

tactical urbanism, 100
Taper, Mark, 43
Taylor, Mike, 158
Temin, Peter, 51
tenant protections, 129–130, 148, 151, 174, 177, 180, 226, 231, 252
Tenants Resource and Advisory Centre (TRAC) (Vancouver), 220, 227
Third World, 80, 91, 141. *See also* Global South
Thurmond, Tony, 164. *See also* Assembly Bill 2406
Tighe, Rosie, 183
Time (magazine), 44
Todaro, Michael, 96
Toronto, Canada, 99
traffic, 62, 65–66, 70, 90, 152, 229

trailer parks, 15. *See also polancos*
transportation, 8, 42–43, 48, 57, 66–67, 79, 90, 197, 204
triplexes, 7, 25, 177, 180, 198, 200, 207, 212–213, 225
Trulia (website), 4
Trump, Donald, 3–4, 235
Trutanich, Carmen, 80, 153
Tucson, Arizona, 24, 236
Turner, John, 146
Twitter, 3
two-family houses, 46. *See also* duplexes

United States Supreme Court, 45, 49–50, 66
University of California, Berkeley, 164, 210
University of California, Los Angeles, 16, 30, 86–87, 127–128, 238, 249
  Luskin School of Public Affairs, 30
  See also cityLAB
University of California, Santa Cruz, 186
unpermitted housing. *See* informal housing
upgrading informal housing, 147–150, 152, 168, 173–177, 180, 185, 192, 200, 208, 215, 226, 230–231, 244

Vancity, 226
Vancouver, Canada, 23, 25, 29, 31, 35, 179–180, 210, 215–230, 235, 237, 239, 244, 246–247
  housing prices, 25, 216, 225
  informal housing, 25, 35, 215–230, 241, 244, 247
  secondary suites, 25, 215–222, 225–230, 237, 239, 241, 244, 247
Veterans Administration, 42
Village of Euclid v. Ambler Realty Company, 49–50
Villaraigosa, Antonio, 79. *See also* Los Angeles, California, mayor of

Wall Street Journal, 4, 25, 212
Ward, Peter, 99, 149
Warren, Elizabeth, 6
Washington, DC, 7, 24, 46, 54, 236
   Dwelling Act of 1934, 46
Watts (Los Angeles), 66, 141. *See also* McCone Commission
Wegmann, Jake, 99, 136
Weingart, Ben, 43
Westenhaver, Judge David, 50
Wieckowski, Robert (Bob), 31, 163–164, 173. *See also* Senate Bill 13; Senate Bill 1069
Women's Home Companion (magazine), 44
World War II, 5, 37, 39, 42–43, 61, 66, 72, 90, 98, 202, 218, 225
Wright, Frank Lloyd, 39
Wright, Roderick, 78. *See also* Assembly Bill 1866

Yes in My Back Yard (YIMBY), 12, 214, 225
Yiftachel, Orin, 144

zoning
   enforcement (*see* informal second units, enforcement)
   opposition to reform, 11, 23, 37, 57, 70, 72, 77, 83, 91, 143, 152–153, 156, 165, 182–183, 197, 203, 214, 220, 239, 245
   police power, 49 (see also *Village of Euclid v. Ambler Realty Company*)
   racial segregation, 44–46, 49, 194, 213
   state government intervention/preemption, 23–24, 34, 77–78, 91, 143, 163–165, 168, 170, 176–177, 180–185, 198, 200, 228, 231, 245–246
   See also single-family zoning

Urban and Industrial Environments

Series editor: Robert Gottlieb, Henry R. Luce Professor of Urban and Environmental Policy, Occidental College

Maureen Smith, *The U.S. Paper Industry and Sustainable Production: An Argument for Restructuring*

Keith Pezzoli, *Human Settlements and Planning for Ecological Sustainability: The Case of Mexico City*

Sarah Hammond Creighton, *Greening the Ivory Tower: Improving the Environmental Track Record of Universities, Colleges, and Other Institutions*

Jan Mazurek, *Making Microchips: Policy, Globalization, and Economic Restructuring in the Semiconductor Industry*

William A. Shutkin, *The Land That Could Be: Environmentalism and Democracy in the Twenty-First Century*

Richard Hofrichter, ed., *Reclaiming the Environmental Debate: The Politics of Health in a Toxic Culture*

Robert Gottlieb, *Environmentalism Unbound: Exploring New Pathways for Change*

Kenneth Geiser, *Materials Matter: Toward a Sustainable Materials Policy*

Thomas D. Beamish, *Silent Spill: The Organization of an Industrial Crisis*

Matthew Gandy, *Concrete and Clay: Reworking Nature in New York City*

David Naguib Pellow, *Garbage Wars: The Struggle for Environmental Justice in Chicago*

Julian Agyeman, Robert D. Bullard, and Bob Evans, eds., *Just Sustainabilities: Development in an Unequal World*

Barbara L. Allen, *Uneasy Alchemy: Citizens and Experts in Louisiana's Chemical Corridor Disputes*

Dara O'Rourke, *Community-Driven Regulation: Balancing Development and the Environment in Vietnam*

Brian K. Obach, *Labor and the Environmental Movement: The Quest for Common Ground*

Peggy F. Barlett and Geoffrey W. Chase, eds., *Sustainability on Campus: Stories and Strategies for Change*

Steve Lerner, *Diamond: A Struggle for Environmental Justice in Louisiana's Chemical Corridor*

Jason Corburn, *Street Science: Community Knowledge and Environmental Health Justice*

Peggy F. Barlett, ed., *Urban Place: Reconnecting with the Natural World*

David Naguib Pellow and Robert J. Brulle, eds., *Power, Justice, and the Environment: A Critical Appraisal of the Environmental Justice Movement*

Eran Ben-Joseph, *The Code of the City: Standards and the Hidden Language of Place Making*

Nancy J. Myers and Carolyn Raffensperger, eds., *Precautionary Tools for Reshaping Environmental Policy*

Kelly Sims Gallagher, *China Shifts Gears: Automakers, Oil, Pollution, and Development*

Kerry H. Whiteside, *Precautionary Politics: Principle and Practice in Confronting Environmental Risk*

Ronald Sandler and Phaedra C. Pezzullo, eds., *Environmental Justice and Environmentalism: The Social Justice Challenge to the Environmental Movement*

Julie Sze, *Noxious New York: The Racial Politics of Urban Health and Environmental Justice*

Robert D. Bullard, ed., *Growing Smarter: Achieving Livable Communities, Environmental Justice, and Regional Equity*

Ann Rappaport and Sarah Hammond Creighton, *Degrees That Matter: Climate Change and the University*

Michael Egan, *Barry Commoner and the Science of Survival: The Remaking of American Environmentalism*

David J. Hess, *Alternative Pathways in Science and Industry: Activism, Innovation, and the Environment in an Era of Globalization*

Peter F. Cannavò, *The Working Landscape: Founding, Preservation, and the Politics of Place*

Paul Stanton Kibel, ed., *Rivertown: Rethinking Urban Rivers*

Kevin P. Gallagher and Lyuba Zarsky, *The Enclave Economy: Foreign Investment and Sustainable Development in Mexico's Silicon Valley*

David N. Pellow, *Resisting Global Toxics: Transnational Movements for Environmental Justice*

Robert Gottlieb, *Reinventing Los Angeles: Nature and Community in the Global City*

David V. Carruthers, ed., *Environmental Justice in Latin America: Problems, Promise, and Practice*

Tom Angotti, *New York for Sale: Community Planning Confronts Global Real Estate*

Paloma Pavel, ed., *Breakthrough Communities: Sustainability and Justice in the Next American Metropolis*

Anastasia Loukaitou-Sideris and Renia Ehrenfeucht, *Sidewalks: Conflict and Negotiation over Public Space*

David J. Hess, *Localist Movements in a Global Economy: Sustainability, Justice, and Urban Development in the United States*

Julian Agyeman and Yelena Ogneva-Himmelberger, eds., *Environmental Justice and Sustainability in the Former Soviet Union*

Jason Corburn, *Toward the Healthy City: People, Places, and the Politics of Urban Planning*

JoAnn Carmin and Julian Agyeman, eds., *Environmental Inequalities beyond Borders: Local Perspectives on Global Injustices*

Louise Mozingo, *Pastoral Capitalism: A History of Suburban Corporate Landscapes*

Gwen Ottinger and Benjamin Cohen, eds., *Technoscience and Environmental Justice: Expert Cultures in a Grassroots Movement*

Samantha MacBride, *Recycling Reconsidered: The Present Failure and Future Promise of Environmental Action in the United States*

Andrew Karvonen, *Politics of Urban Runoff: Nature, Technology, and the Sustainable City*

Daniel Schneider, *Hybrid Nature: Sewage Treatment and the Contradictions of the Industrial Ecosystem*

Catherine Tumber, *Small, Gritty, and Green: The Promise of America's Smaller Industrial Cities in a Low-Carbon World*

Sam Bass Warner and Andrew H. Whittemore, *American Urban Form: A Representative History*

John Pucher and Ralph Buehler, eds., *City Cycling*

Stephanie Foote and Elizabeth Mazzolini, eds., *Histories of the Dustheap: Waste, Material Cultures, Social Justice*

David J. Hess, *Good Green Jobs in a Global Economy: Making and Keeping New Industries in the United States*

Joseph F. C. DiMento and Clifford Ellis, *Changing Lanes: Visions and Histories of Urban Freeways*

Joanna Robinson, *Contested Water: The Struggle against Water Privatization in the United States and Canada*

William B. Meyer, *The Environmental Advantages of Cities: Countering Commonsense Antiurbanism*

Rebecca L. Henn and Andrew J. Hoffman, eds., *Constructing Green: The Social Structures of Sustainability*

Peggy F. Barlett and Geoffrey W. Chase, eds., *Sustainability in Higher Education: Stories and Strategies for Transformation*

Isabelle Anguelovski, *Neighborhood as Refuge: Community Reconstruction, Place Remaking, and Environmental Justice in the City*

Kelly Sims Gallagher, *The Globalization of Clean Energy Technology: Lessons from China*

Vinit Mukhija and Anastasia Loukaitou-Sideris, eds., *The Informal American City: Beyond Taco Trucks and Day Labor*

Roxanne Warren, *Rail and the City: Shrinking Our Carbon Footprint While Reimagining Urban Space*

Marianne E. Krasny and Keith G. Tidball, *Civic Ecology: Adaptation and Transformation from the Ground Up*

Erik Swyngedouw, *Liquid Power: Contested Hydro-modernities in Twentieth-Century Spain*

Ken Geiser, *Chemicals without Harm: Policies for a Sustainable World*

Duncan McLaren and Julian Agyeman, *Sharing Cities: A Case for Truly Smart and Sustainable Cities*

Jessica Smartt Gullion, *Fracking the Neighborhood: Reluctant Activists and Natural Gas Drilling*

Nicholas A. Phelps, *Sequel to Suburbia: Glimpses of America's Post-suburban Future*

Shannon Elizabeth Bell, *Fighting King Coal: The Challenges to Micromobilization in Central Appalachia*

Theresa Enright, *The Making of Grand Paris: Metropolitan Urbanism in the Twenty-First Century*

Robert Gottlieb and Simon Ng, *Global Cities: Urban Environments in Los Angeles, Hong Kong, and China*

Anna Lora-Wainwright, *Resigned Activism: Living with Pollution in Rural China*

Scott L. Cummings, *Blue and Green: The Drive for Justice at America's Port*

David Bissell, *Transit Life: Cities, Commuting, and the Politics of Everyday Mobilities*

Javiera Barandiarán, *From Empire to Umpire: Science and Environmental Conflict in Neoliberal Chile*

Benjamin Pauli, *Flint Fights Back: Environmental Justice and Democracy in the Flint Water Crisis*

Karen Chapple and Anastasia Loukaitou-Sideris, *Transit-Oriented Displacement or Community Dividends? Understanding the Effects of Smarter Growth on Communities*

Henrik Ernstson and Sverker Sörlin, eds., *Grounding Urban Natures: Histories and Futures of Urban Ecologies*

Katrina Smith Korfmacher, *Bridging the Silos: Collaborating for Environment, Health, and Justice in Urban Communities*

Jill Lindsey Harrison, *From the Inside Out: The Fight for Environmental Justice within Government Agencies*

Anastasia Loukaitou-Sideris, Dana Cuff, Todd Presner, Maite Zubiaurre, and Jonathan Jae-an Crisman, *Urban Humanities: New Practices for Reimagining the City*

Govind Gopakumar, *Installing Automobility: Emerging Politics of Mobility and Streets in Indian Cities*

Amelia Thorpe, *Everyday Ownership: PARK(ing) Day and the Practice of Property*

Tridib Banerjee, *In the Images of Development: City Design in the Global South*

Ralph Buehler and John Pucher, eds., *Cycling for Sustainable Cities*

Casey J. Dawkins, *Just Housing: The Moral Foundations of American Housing Policy*

Kian Goh, *Form and Flow: The Spatial Politics of Urban Resilience and Climate Justice*

Kian Goh, Anastasia Loukaitou-Sideris, and Vinit Mukhija, eds., *Just Urban Design: The Struggle for a Public City*

Sheila R. Foster and Christian Iaione, *Co-cities: Innovative Transitions toward Just and Self-Sustaining Communities*

Vinit Mukhija, *Remaking the American Dream: The Informal and Formal Transformation of Single-Family Housing Cities*